Learning and Teaching

Learning and Teaching

Prof. S.K. Mangal
M.A., M.Sc., M.Ed., Ph.D. (Education)

Prof. (Mrs.) Shubhra Mangal
M.Sc., M.Ed., M.Phil, Ph.D. (Education)

SHIPRA

(2020, First Published 2017)

Rs. 1600; US$ 56

ISBN: 978-93-86262-42-4

2024 Impression

Learning and Teaching

Published by:
SHIPRA PUBLICATIONS
LG 18-19, Pankaj Central Market,
I.P. Ext., Patparganj, Delhi 110092
Ph. 91 11 22235152/ 6152; 9650028065
info@shiprapublication.com
www.shiprapublication.com

Preface

Learning in the form of acquisition of experiences holds a quite key position in the development of the children right from their very birth. They learn so many things from their own initiatives, observations and experiences in their own environment. The deliberate attempts of organizing desirable learning experiences are later on made on the parts of parents, elders and teachers in the shape of teaching and training in one way or the other for helping them in the realization of their potential. In this connection much responsibility lies on the shoulders of the teachers. They must be well acquainted and properly equipped for carrying out the task of teaching aimed to help the children in acquiring needed learning experiences for their development. On this account they must know what type of development is needed for their students; how should they be helped in acquiring desirable learning experiences for the realization of their developmental goals; what should be their role in one or the other teaching-learning contexts and how should the students be helped in the construction of knowledge for their desired cognitive and overall personality development? But now the question arises when and where a teacher should get opportunity of equipping them with all such essentials about learning and teaching. The best earlier opportunity for this purpose lies in providing teachers all during their pre-service teacher education program. NCTE has taken initiative by issuing the necessary directives to make provision for such essentials by switching over to two years B.Ed. program and drafting new course contents for its implementation. As a result, Guru Govind Singh Indraprastha University, New Delhi has introduced a compulsory paper named as "Learning and Teaching" in its B.Ed. Course. The present text has been written to fulfill the needs and requirements of this course.

Although here this text has been mainly focused on the requirements of GGS Indraprastha University B.Ed. syllabus, however on account of its wide coverage, it may prove equally beneficial to meet the requirements of the similar courses of other universities.

How far it will prove its worth, the judgement will surely lie with its readers. However, as authors, we have the obligations to specify some of its basic features as below.

- It has been strictly written according to the needs of the contents and topics included in the syllabus.
- The style as well as language adopted for presentation is simple and easy to grasp by the average readers.

- The study questions have been given at the end of the text for helping the students in the task of proper comprehension, revision and self-evaluation in the soft cover student edition.
- Upto date references and suggestions for further study in the matter related to each and every chapter have been given at the very end of the text for serving the desired needs of students as well as teacher educators.

Hoped that the text in its present form would be able to serve the interests of those for whom it is being written. We express our gratitude to all those who, in one way or the other, have helped us in this venture. Our special thanks are due to those writers and publishers whose work have been utilized by us in the presentation of this text. The references given side by side and also at the end of the text, would certainly help those students and teacher educators who intend to go deep in the subject.

Any suggestions for bringing improvement in the text will be highly appreciated and thankfully acknowledged.

With good wishes to its readers,

May 15, 2017

S.K. Mangal
Shubhra Mangal

Contents

Preface v

1. Learning and Teaching — Nature and Relationship **1**

Concept of Teaching 1
- Meaning and Definitions of the Term Teaching 1
- Nature and Characteristics of Teaching 4
- Relation of Teaching with other Similar or Related Concepts 5
- Analytical Concept of Teaching 8
- Variables of Teaching 10
- Functions of Teaching Variables 10

Concept of Learning 12
- Meaning and Definitions of the Term Learning 12
- Nature and Characteristics of Learning 16

Relationship between Teaching and Learning 20

2. Nature (Heredity) and Nurture (Environment) **22**

What is Heredity or Nature? 22
The Twins and Heredity 24
What is Environment or Nurture? 25
Relative Role and Importance of Nature and Nurture in Development 26

3. Maturation: Concept and Educational Implications **32**

Concept of Maturation 32
- Meaning of the Term Maturation 32
- Effect of Maturation on Growth and Development 33

Educational Implications of Maturation 36

4. Development: Concept, Influencing Factors and Relationship with Learning **40**

Introduction 40
Human Development: Meaning and Concept 40
Factors Influencing Development 43
Relationship between Development and Learning 48

5. Dimensions of Individual Development **55**

Introduction 55
Physical Development 55
Intellectual or Mental Development 61
Emotional Development 67
Social Development 77
Language Development 85
Moral or Character Development 95
Interrelationship among different dimensions of development 103

6. Theories of Development 106

Introduction 106
Piaget's Theory of Cognitive Development 106
Erickson's Theory of Psycho-Social Development 119
Kohlberg's Theory of Moral Development 125

7. Developmental Tasks and their Implications 138

Meaning of the Term Developmental Tasks 138
Identifying and Naming of the Development Tasks 139
Sources Contributing towards the Upsurge of Developmental Tasks 140
Critical Ages and Developmental Tasks 140
Purposes and Goals of Developmental Tasks 141
Role of Cultural and Social Patterns in Developmental Tasks 142
Developmental Tasks of the Various Stages of Development 143
– Infancy (upto two years) 143
– Early Childhood (from 3 to 5 years) 144
– Later Childhood (from 6 to 12 years) 144
– Adolescence (from 13 to 18 years) 144
Implication of Developmental Tasks 145

8. Behaviourism Perspective 147

What is Behaviourism? 147
Historical Evolution and Development of Behaviourism 147
The Main Characteristics and Features of Behaviourism 149
Evaluation of the Behaviouristic Perspective 150
– Criticism 150
– Merits and Contribution of Behaviourism to Education 151
Behaviourism and Behaviouristic Learning 152
– Thorndike's Trial and Error or S.R. Theory of Learning 152
– Watson's and Pavlov's Classical Conditioning 157
– Skinner's Operant Conditioning 160
– Guthrie's Contiguous Conditioning 168

9. Cognitivism Perspective and Learning 177

What is Cognitivism? 177
Historical Evolution and Development of Cognitivism 177
Main Characteristics and Features of Cognitivism 178
Cognitivism and Theories of Learning 179
– Gestalt Theory of Insightful Learning 180
– Information Processing View Point 183

10. Humanism Perspective and Learning 190

What is Humanism and Humanistic Perspective in Education? 190
Basic Characteristics and Features of Humanism and Humanistic Learning 190
Rogers' Theory of Experiential Learning 191
Bandura's Social Learning Theory 194

11. Constructivism Perspective and Constructivist Learning **196**
Introduction 196
Historical Evolution of Constructivism and its Types 196
Jean Piaget's Individual Constructivism 197
Vygotsky's Social Constructivism 199
Learning in Constructivist perspective or Constructivist Learning 203
– Constructivist Learning Defined 203
Assumptions and Characteristics of Constructivist Learning 203
Educational Implications of the Theory of Constructivist Learning 205

12. Learning as Construction of Knowledge **208**
Introduction 208
Learning as Construction of Knowledge vs. Learning as Transmission and Reception of Knowledge 208
Processes Facilitating 'Construction of Knowledge' 215
– Experiential Learning and Reflection 215
– Social Mediation 220
– Cognitive Negotiability 222
– Situated Learning and Cognitive Apprenticeship 223
– Meta Cognition 231

13. Cognition and Learning **237**
Meaning of Cognition 237
Role of Cognition Learning 238
Socio-cultural Factors Affecting Cognition and Learning 239
– Role of Home and Family 241
– Role of School 242
– Role of Society or Community 244
– Role of Mass Media 246
– Role of Different Cultures 248
– Role of Religion 250

14. Role of Teacher in a Teaching-learning Context **252**
Introduction 252
Role of Teacher as Transmitter of Knowledge 252
Role of Teacher as a Model 253
Role of Teacher as Facilitator 254
Role of Teacher as Negotiator 256
Role of Teacher as a Co-learner 256

15. Intelligence: Concept, Theories and Measurement **259**
Introduction 259
Concept of Intelligence 259
Theories of Intelligence 262
– Unitary Theory 262
– Anarchic Theory or Multi Factor Theory 262
– Spearman's Two Factor Theory 263
– Thurstone's Group Factor Theory 264
– Guilford's Theory Involving a Model of Intellect 264

- Cattell and Horn's Theory of Intelligence 267
- Sternberg's Information Processing Theory of Intelligence 268
- Howard Gardner's Theory of Multiple Intelligence 270

Measurement of Intelligence 277
- Individual Verbal Tests 278
- Individual Performance Tests 279
- The Group Vertical Intelligence Tests 280
- The Group Non-Verbal Intelligence Tests 281
- Individual v/s Group Tests 282

Can Intelligence be Measured like a Piece of Cloth? 284
Concept of Mental Age and Intelligence Quotient 285
Classification of I.Q. 285
The Constancy of I.Q. 286
Uses and Limitations of Intelligence Tests 287

16. Motivation **290**

Motivation — Nature and Meaning 290
The Motivational Cycle 292
Types of Motivation 293
Need of Motivation for the Learners and Teachers 294
The Concept of Needs, Drives and Incentives 294
Strategies or Techniques for Motivating the Students 299
Teacher's role in Motivating, Strengthening and Sustaining Motivation Learners 302

17. Personality — Meaning, Nature and Theories **304**

The Meaning and Nature of Personality 304
Theories of Personality 308
- Type Approach 309
- Trait Approach 311
- Trait cum Type Approach 315
- Psycho-analytic Approach 316
- Humanistic Approach 320
- Learning Approach 323

18. Adjustment — Meaning, Nature and Methods **324**

Meaning and Definitions of Adjustment 324
Nature of Adjustment—In the Context of Teaching and Learning 325
Adjustment as Achievement or Process 326
Areas or Spheres of Adjustment 327
- Personal Adjustment 327
- Social Adjustment 329
- Occupational Adjustment 330

Characteristics of a Well Adjusted Person 332
Methods of Adjustment 333
- Direct Methods 334
- Indirect Methods

References and Suggested Readings 337

1

Learning and Teaching — Nature and Relationship

CONCEPT OF TEACHING

The general notion, popular opinion and the image which we form about an object, people or idea is termed as our concept about them. It is the result of our experiences direct and indirect which we happen to gain about objects, people or ideas. The same is true also for the concept of teaching. By the term concept of teaching we mean all that which we know or ought to know about teaching in terms of its meaning, nature, and characteristics and all that which can distinguish it from the other similar concepts and activities. Looking in this way, if we intend to know thoroughly about the concept of teaching we have to look it from the various angles like below:

- Understanding its meaning and defining it.
- Knowing about the nature and characteristics of teaching.
- Comparing teaching with other similar concepts.
- Knowing about the relationship of teaching and learning.
- Discussing about the analytical concept of teaching.
- Understanding teaching in term of its variables.

Meaning and Definitions of the Term Teaching

Teaching in its simple meaning is referred to either as occupation or profession of a community known as teacher or an activity or activities of a group undertaken to help an individual to learn or acquire some knowledge, skills, attitudes or interests, etc.

However, the meaning and concept of teaching is not so simple as interpreted above. It is a quite complex social, cultural and ethical process designed in a social or cultural context.

By all means and in any shape, it is always designed in a social context and therefore related with the social structures, cultural environment, values and ideals of the people, society and the government. All these factors always stand for dynamicity and therefore, the meaning and definitions of teaching have always been in a state of change depending upon the need of time, place and society. It has resulted into various definitions of the term teaching. Some of such definitions are reproduced below.

H.C. Morrison (1934). *"Teaching is an intimate contact between a more mature personality and a less mature one which is designed to further the education of the latter."*

John Brubacher (1939). *"Teaching is an arrangement and manipulation of a situation in which there are gaps and obstructions which an individual will seek to overcome and from which he will learn in the course of doing so."*

B.O. Smith (1960). *"Teaching is a system of actions intended to produce learning."*

N.L. Gage (1963). *"Teaching is a form of inter-personal influence aimed at changing the behaviour potential of another person."*

B.O. Smith (1963). *"Teaching is a system of actions involving an agent, an end in view, and a situation including two sets of factors — those over which the agent has no control (class size, size of classroom, physical characteristics of pupils, etc.) and those that he can modify (way of asking questions about instruction and ways of structuring information or ideas gleaned.)"*

Edmund Amidon (1967). *"Teaching is defined as an interactive process, primarily involving classroom talk which takes place between teacher and pupil and occurs during certain definable activities."*

Clarke (1970). *"Teaching refers to activities that are designed and performed to produce change in student (pupil) behaviour."*

Thomas F. Green (1971). *"Teaching is the task of teacher which is performed for the development of a child,"*

Let us try to analyse these definitions.

The definition given by Morrison (1934) takes teaching to a disciplined social process in which a teacher by virtue of his ideal position, status, knowledge and experiences influences the behaviour of the less experienced pupil and helps him to develop according to the needs and ideals of the society or government. In this type of teaching the student has to learn and develop according to the ideals set before him by the teacher. The teaching is reduced to what the teacher teaches. The students are there to copy down the model presented by the teacher. There is no interaction but the flow of instructions from the teachers. As a result, the pupils are bound to become the passive listeners and blind imitators.

The definition given by Brubacher (1939) takes teaching to that position where the pupils are required to play the central role and the teacher's task is limited to arrange and create situations for the learning. Here the student themselves have to decide what they want to do and how they will do it. This type of teaching may lead the pupil for independent learning and problem solving.

The third definition given by Smith (I960) terms teaching as an organised system of specific activities that are aimed to help the learner to learn something. Teaching may be carried out in the absence of a teacher A book, nature, teaching machine, tape recorder, etc. may play a role of teacher. The important thing is the role of a system of actions or activities. If it results in some or other types of learning then this system may be termed as teaching. The weakest point of the above definition lies in the fact that it does not mention all the elements of the teaching process, namely, the teacher, taught and the subject matter.

To do away with the above weakness. Smith tried to elaborate his earlier definition, in 1963, by considering teaching as a tripolar process involving:

(i) an agent (the source, human or material that tries to produce learning),
(ii) a goal or target that is to be achieved through the process of teaching, and
(iii) the intervening variable consisting of learning or teaching situation or environment. It may involve physical or human material, conditions and instructional methods.

The definition given by Gage (1962) takes teaching as a process establishing interpersonal relationship between the teacher and the taught as a result of which the behaviour of the latter is modified. Here the relationship plays the key role. In this age of sophistication this type of approach is unable to explain the role of hardwares, programmed instructions and teaching machines where the bond of interpersonal relationship is somewhat missing.

The next definition given by Amidon (1967) considers teaching as a process of interaction between the teacher and the taught. It considers teaching as a co-operative enterprise, a two way traffic and a commonly shared phenomenon. It results in the improvement and development of both the participants *i.e.,* teacher and the taught. It considers teaching as a set of properly planned and clearly defined activities that are undertaken for the achievement of certain objectives. This definition too is limited in the sense that it confines teaching within the interaction of the teacher and taught and that too primarily in the form of class-room talk or a few special activities.

Clarke (1970) in his definition has tried to broaden the base/scope of teaching by taking it as a set of all those organised activities that may result in bringing some change in the behaviour of the pupil or learner.

A year later Green (1971) in his definition tried to delimit the boundary and scope of teaching task. He has defined teaching as a profession or occupation by stating that teaching is what a teacher does for the development of a child.

Actually this is a very narrower and misnomer concept of the term teaching. Neither teaching can be restricted to a profession or occupation of a people or community like teacher nor it can be always relied for bringing desirable improvement or development in the behaviour or functions of the students. It may end in both the ways—desirable or undesirable, hence it cannot be assumed to play a developmental role in all situations.

The above attempt for the analytic description of the definitions may reveal that some of these definitions represent a very limited view of the functions and scope of the teaching act while others elaborate it to the extent of unbridled freedom and undefined tasks of purposeless outcomes. A good definition of teaching, must accomplish the following objectives.

1. It should tell whether teaching is a process or product.
2. It should clearly indicate its constitutional elements or factors.
3. It should reveal its objective.
4. It should say something about its organisational or structural aspect.

If we try to evaluate the definitions quoted so far on the criterion cited above, none of the definitions is said to be a comprehensive and functional definition of the term teaching. There is nothing wrong in the acceptance of truth that it is a quite uphill task to narrate an ideal universal definition of the term teaching. However for the purpose of this text, a somewhat comprehensive and functional definition can be adapted as below:

Teaching is a triadic relation — tripolar process — involving the source of teaching (human or material), student and a set of activities designed and manipulated primarily to bring changes in the behaviour of the student

Nature and Characteristics of Teaching

The widespread notions about these things can be summarized as below:

1. *Teaching is a complex social process:* Teaching is a complex social phenomenon. It is greatly influenced by the social factors. The social and human factors are dynamic and not static and therefore teaching is not a fundamental concept.
2. *Teaching is both art as well as science:* Teaching is both art as well as science as Silverman (1966) expresses it in the following words.

   "To be sure teaching-like the practice of medicine — is very much an art which is to say, it calls for exercise of talent and creativity. But like medicine, it is also a science, for it involves a repertoire of techniques, procedures and skills that can be systematically studied and described and improved. A good teacher, like a great doctor, is one who adds creativity and inspiration to the basic repertoires."
3. *Teaching is a professional activity:* Teaching is a professional activity involving the teacher and the student and result in the development of the student.
4. *Teaching is the output emanating from the teacher:* Teaching is what a teacher does with his student for causing the latter to learn something and it is thus purely an outcome of the teacher's efforts.
5. *Teaching in an organised system of varied action:* Teaching is a system of actions which are varied in form and are related to

content and pupil behaviour in context with prevailing physical and social conditions.

6. *Teaching is amenable to scientific observation and analysis:* What is going in a teaching can be observed, analysed and assessed through teacher behaviour, pupil-teacher interaction and the changes brought in the behaviour of the pupils. Such analysis and assessment may provide essential feedback for bringing desirable improvement in this process.
7. *Teaching is highly dominated by the communication skill:* The flow of communication within the teaching elements like teacher or sources of teaching, student and the teaching activities make teaching a reality and a success.
8. *Teaching is an interactive process:* Teaching is an interactive process carried out of the attainment for some specific purpose and objectives.
9. *Teaching may be carried out in various forms and styles:* Teaching may have various forms like formal and informal, formational or informational, directional or instructional, training, conditioning or indoctrination, telling, showing or doing descriptive or remedial, etc.
10. *Teaching is a specialized task comprising of different teaching skills:* Teaching is a specialized task and may be taken as a set of component skills for the realization of a specified set of instructional objectives (Jangira and Ajit Singh, 1982).

Relation of Teaching with other Similar or Related Concepts

The terms like conditioning, training, instruction and indoctrination are used to denote some or the other kinds of teaching. Sometimes they are mistaken as synonymous with teaching. Let us try to evaluate their relationships.

In fact each of these terms denotes one or the other types of teaching. These are various modes of teaching each of which contribute towards teaching. Teaching is a larger concept and each of these terms is a part or aspect of this large concept.

Teaching, as a whole, is aimed to bring changes in the behaviour of pupils These changes may occur through (i) teaching them how to do or perform a task or act to a situation or stimuli, and (ii) teaching them those things that may contribute towards enriching their knowledge and formation of a system of beliefs. While the former type of teaching (better described through the terms conditioning or training) may result into the shaping of behaviour and conduct, the latter (described through instruction or indoctrination) works as a potent agent for the acquisition of knowledge and formation of beliefs.

The Fig. 1.1 clearly reveals that teaching activities, primarily divided as high or low orders, are distributable along a continue from conditioning to indoctrination.

Conditioning in this way is the lowest level or mode of teaching. As a result a dog may be conditioned (taught) to lift his paw when it hears a bell. Similarly, many of the animals and human beings may be taught to respond

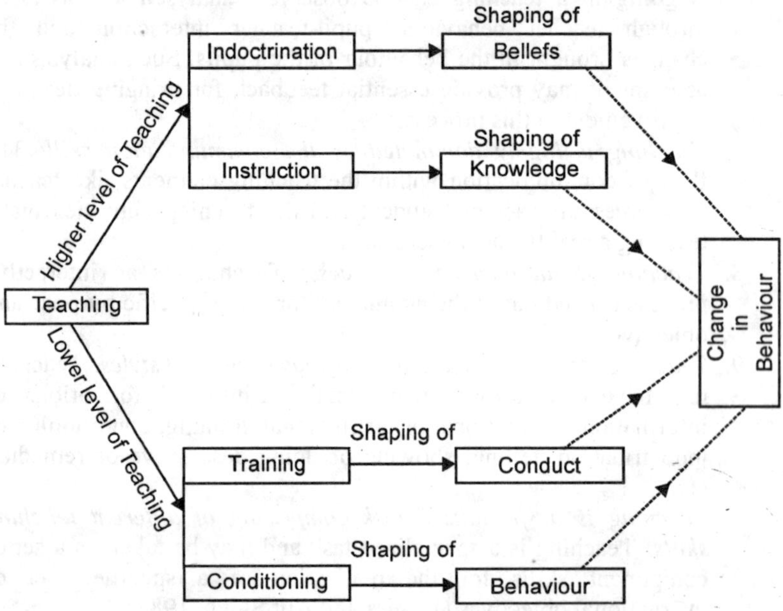

Fig. 1.1: Relationship of the Term Teaching with other Related Concepts

to signals, alarms, signs and warnings through conditioning. Most of our desirable or undesirable behaviours and habits are the creation of the process of conditioning.

Training is concerned with a little more raised level of teaching than conditioning. It helps in shaping conduct and teaching various skills. A worker may be trained to perform certain tasks requiring very specific skills. He may do a number of jobs on some machine skillfully without knowing its basic structure and operation, the utility of his output and similar other questions. Similarly, a variety of animals may be trained to perform highly specific tasks for the circus shows. Here the worker and a circus animal, as far as their teaching is concerned, stand on the same footing. Both are taught through a particular mode of teaching known as training. We can't say that they are being educated. In the case of animals, while starting from conditioning, we seldom cross the stage of training, but for human beings we can move much farther. Here in the case of the worker, we can give him desired knowledge of the machine, its operation and mechanism. He may be acquainted with his work, his contribution towards the economy of the country and similar other things which may shape his behaviour. Which behaviour is the product of training or which is the outcome of teaching may be properly distinguished on the basis of the amount of the degree of intelligence used or demonstrated through such behaviour. While less intelligent or simple behaviour may be produced through training, the complicated behaviour requiring more intelligence need a higher mode of teaching.

Therefore, the distinction between the terms training and teaching may be satisfactorily made through the evaluation of the degree of intelligent behaviour produced by them. If a training results into a demonstrable intelligent and complex behaviour, it may be equated with teaching but if it produces only the simple behaviour requiring no or comparatively less intelligence it is to be termed as training.

Instruction and indoctrination both work on a higher footing than conditioning and training as far as the involvement of intellectual powers and mode of teaching are concerned. But that does not mean that they may be equated with the term 'teaching'.

Instruction, in brief, is mainly concerned with the development of knowledge and understanding in an individual about a thing, system or process. Imparting of knowledge and understanding merely represents one of the many objectives which we want to achieve through the process of teaching. Teaching is much more than the act of acquiring some knowledge and understanding. The conative and affective domains of one's behaviour are badly neglected in instruction. While teaching is aimed towards shaping a total man, the instruction cares only for the development of intellect and affects the cognitive domain of one's behaviour.

Let us also see the distinction between teaching and instruction from another angle which lies in their processes. The face to face interaction of the teacher and taught found in teaching is not so much essential in the process of instruction. Here teacher can be replaced by the programmed material, computer, teaching machine, radio, television video and tape recorder. A teacher may also use these aids and devices in his teaching and hence instruction may be considered a part of teaching.

In short, instruction is always a part or one of the several modes of teaching. Where instruction itself can never be called as teaching, the term teaching may include or cover instruction.

Indoctrination (transmission of doctrine, firm faith or system of beliefs) on the rather end of the continum of the modes of teaching represents a fairly high level of teaching which adds to the establishment or shaping of beliefs and ideals. It requires higher order of intelligence and results in bringing quite stable changes in the cognitive and affective domains of one's behaviour. Like other modes of teaching, indoctrination represents one of the several modes of teaching. When we say indoctrination it also means teaching but the reverse is not true. We may teach without adopting indoctrination as the mode of teaching.

The different modes of teaching — conditioning, training, instruction, indoctrination describéd above — though distinguishable, can not be termed as quite unrelated. Sometimes they may overlap in their processes and outcomes.

Analytical Concept of Teaching

Analysis concerns with the process of breaking or separating out the elements or constituent of a substance. Therefore, a description of the analytical concept of teaching would demand the separation and naming of different elements or components of the task or process of teaching in relation to its various aspects like below: (i) Activities undertaken in the teaching task, and (ii) Educational objectives to be achieved through these activities.

Accordingly attempts have been made to analyse teaching in several ways with a view to understanding it, designing teaching materials and methods for realising the specific objectives, perform the task of teaching effectively evaluate and then modify it (on the basis of feedback for acquiring teaching competency and proficiency). Let us mention some of such attempts:

1. Komisan (1966) has tried to analyse teaching into various specific activities like introducing, demonstrating, contrasting, explaining, proving, justifying, explicating, defining, rating, appraising, amplifying, vindicating, interpreting, questioning, elaborating, identifying, designating, conjecturing, confirming, etc.
2. Gage (1968) tried to analyse teaching in terms of technical skills. According to him: "*Teaching skills are specific instructional techniques and procedures that a teacher may use in the classroom. They represent an analysis of the teaching process into relatively discrete components that can be used in different combination in the continuous flow of the teacher's performance.*"
3. Clarke (1970), while endorsing the viewpoint of Komisar and Gage and suggesting a definition of teaching, has tried to analyse teaching in terms of some specific activities that are designed and performed to produce change in student's behaviour. These activities may have a cognitive, affective or conative nature and belong to different levels as expressed in Bloom's Taxonomy, (Bloom, et all, 1956).
4. Brown (1975) has tried to analyse teaching by considering it as a many sided activity which includes a host of activities like questioning, giving information, listening and such others.
5. B.K. Passi (1976), has concluded that teaching constitutes a number of verbal and non-verbal teaching acts, like questioning, accepting pupil responses, rewarding, smiling, nodding to pupil response, movements, gestures, etc. These acts in particular combination facilitate the achievement of objectives in terms of pupil of pupil growth.

6. N.K. Jangira and Ajit Singh (1982) have presented the analysis of teaching as below:

   "Teaching can be analysed in terms of teacher behaviour at least at three levels, viz., component teaching skills, component teaching behaviours comprising the component skill and atomistic teaching behaviours. Diagrammatically this analysis can be presented as given ahead."

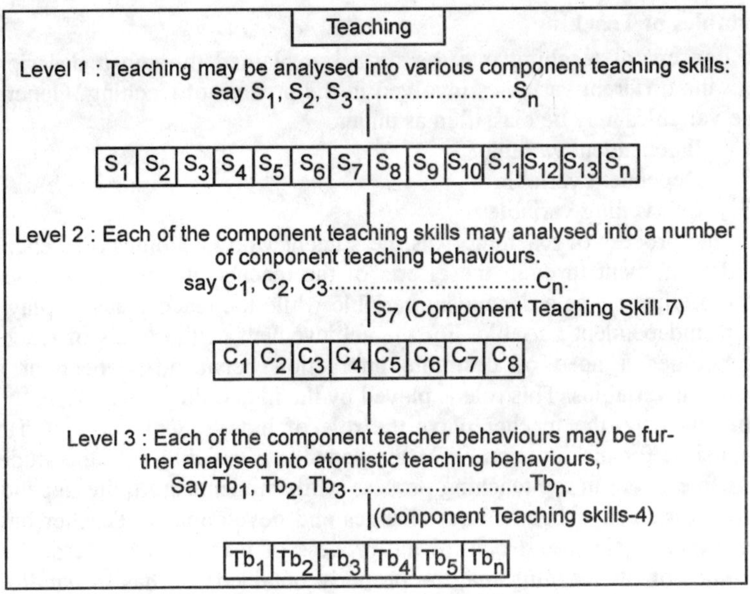

Fig. 1.2: Analysis of Teaching

Based on the above analysis it can be easily concluded that the complex task of teaching may be safely analysed into limited but well defined components called 'Teaching Skills' or 'Technical Skills' of teaching.

The Asian Institute for Teacher Educators (1972) have considered these skills as specifically those activities of teaching that are especially effective in bringing about desired changes in pupils.

In this way, teaching may be viewed as a group of skills known as teaching skills. *A teaching skill is defined as a group of teaching acts or behaviours intended to bring desirable, changes in the pupils behaviour.*

This approach of analysing teaching into some specific component teaching skills and related teaching acts or behaviours has been under severe criticism. As a result, it has now been realized that teaching can not be regarded just a sum total of certain teaching skills. Although it can not be denied that acquisition of teaching skills is very much essential for a teacher for becoming a good teacher yet, in any way, this is not all what is needed. He needs much more and therefore teaching consists of something more than the teaching skills.

Teaching involves interaction. The personality, attitude, interest and way of exercising desirable influence are some of the factors that definitely counts towards effective teaching. A teacher cannot be taken simply as a skilled worker who knows his job by acquiring certain specific skills but one who has the proper guts to act from some superior level knowing how to take appropriate decisions and exercise necessary influence for bringing desirable change in the behaviour of his pupils,

Variables of Teaching

The concept of teaching may be further explained through a description about the different variables involved in the process of teaching. Generally these variables may be classified as under:

1. Independent variable
2. Dependent variable
3. Intervening variables.

In the process of teaching, it is the student who is subjected to changes and development through the efforts of the teacher and teaching process. Therefore he acts as a dependent variable while the teacher has to play the role in independent variable. For the achievement of the goals of teaching there comes a need of desirable interaction between independent and dependent variables. This role is played by the intervening variables.

In this way, the teacher plays the role of independent variable. He is responsible for the functioning of the dependent variable, *i.e.,* the students He is free to act in the teaching process while students are quite dependent on him for seeking behavioural changes and development. Teacher has to plan, organise, lead and control the process of teaching so that desirable outcomes of his teaching may be properly obtained. He has to handle his teaching activities and all the intervening variables in such a way that the desired movability and functionality can be created among his students for achieving the teaching objectives.

The intervening variables as it sounds do not exist for creating some interference or obstacle in the functioning of independent or dependent variable. Rather they help in the smooth functioning of these variables for the realization of teaching objectives. The contents of teaching, methods and techniques of teaching, tactics and strategies of teaching, management of instructional material and teaching environment, etc., are all known as intervening variables. These variables are responsible for bringing desirable interaction between the teacher and the taught by producing proper teaching environment, teaching material and facilities and creating appropriate learning conditions or situations.

Functions of Teaching Variables

In teaching process the active or functional part is played by the independent and dependent variables. Mainly following three types of functions are performed by these variables: (i) Diagnostic functions,

(ii) Prescriptive functions, and (iii) Evaluative functions.

Diagnostic Functions: The goal is to bring desirable changes in the behaviour of students. The initial task needs a proper diagnosis for the prescription of appropriate treatment, (the actual attempts) for bringing desirable behavioural changes in the students. Accordingly, a teacher has to perform the following diagnostic functions.

1. He has to diagnose the entering behaviour of the pupil. His initial potential in terms of cognitive, conative and affective abilities should be properly diagnosed with the help of some diagnostic tests.
2. He has to diagnose and formulate specific educational objectives, the type and amount of behavioural changes he wants to introduce in the student in the light of the entering behaviour and environmental conditions.
3. He has to analyse the content, instructional material and environmental facilities available for carrying out his task,
4. He has to diagnose his own potential and capabilities and bring desirable improvement in his own behaviour for the success of his own mission.

Although the teacher as independent variable is more active in exercising diagnostic functions, yet the role of the student as a dependent variable can not be underestimated. He has also to perform certain important diagnostic functions on the basis of his perception for his abilities and responses like below:

(i) He has to diagnose the strength and weakness of his entering behaviours.

(ii) He has to assess himself in terms of the tools of learning like language and comprehension, power of expression, ability to think and analyse, psychomotor skill and emotional behaviour.

(iii) He has to make efforts for knowing about the behaviour of the teacher, the types of teaching strategies, the nature of the content ahd instructional material for the purpose of initiation and response on his part,

Prescriptive Functions: On the basis of diagnosis the teacher takes decision about the needed prescription for achieving the stipulated objectives. Accomplishment of objectives needs an appropriate interaction between the teacher and the student which in turn needs proper management of the intervening variables by the teacher. Accordingly he has to perform the functions like:

(i) Selecting appropriate contents and organising them into proper sequence.

(ii) Selecting proper teaching techniques, strategies and feedback devices in view of the individual differences among the students.

(iii) Seeking essential co-operation from the student for a purposeful interaction.

In the performance of prescriptive functions also, the teacher is likely to be more active than the students. The prescription is made for the student as to bring desirable changes in his behaviour. He has to work for the purposeful interaction and give his sincere co-operation for the teacher in exercising the various prescriptive functions.

Evaluative Functions: Evaluative functions concern with the tasks of evaluating the progress and outcomes of the prescriptive functions which may be decided in the form of realization of the stipulated objectives. The failure in the realization of the objectives is essentially a failure in the prescriptive functions either due to improper diagnosis or some serious mistakes in prescribing or earning out the treatment (actual teaching) task.

The various evaluation devices in the form of tests, observations, interviews, rating scales, inventories and unstructured projective techniques help in exercising evaluative functions. In contrast to diagnostic or prescriptive functions, the student remains more active in the evaluative functions. He has to respond and evaluate his own progress in terms of the abilities acquired and behaviour changes occurred. He has been taught and helped by the teacher in bringing improvement in his behaviour on the basis of his entry behaviour and his potentialities. Now it is his turn to see how far the treatment prescribed or done by the teacher is helpful for him. If the prescription suits him he can go ahead with it. If, does not, he must give his full co-operation to the teacher (just like a patient who has to consult his doctor and seek his advice) for the further diagnosis and subsequent prescription in order to get maximum advantage for bringing desirable improvement in his behaviour.

CONCEPT OF LEARNING

Learning occupies a quite significant role in one's life and is essentially a focal point of a teaching-learning process. What is learning? What is its nature and characteristics? For throwing light on such issues related with the concept of leaning let us discuss them in brief.

Meaning and Definitions of the Term Learning

Learning situations are most natural and common in life and every one of us is learning one thing or the other although he may not necessarily be aware of it. An individual starts learning immediately after his birth. While approaching a burning matchstick, the child is burnt and he withdraws. Another time, when he faces a burning matchstick, he takes no time to withdraw himself away He learns to avoid not only the burning matchstick but also all burning-things. When this happens we say that the child has learned that if he touches a flame, he will be burnt.

In this way, the behaviour of an individual is changed through direct or indirect experiences. This change in behaviour brought about by experience is commonly known as learning. This is a very simple explanation of the term learning. But a complete understanding of the term needs more clarification and exact definition. Some well-known definitions of the term 'learning' are given below:

Gardner Murphy: *"The term learning covers every modification in behaviour to meet environmental requirements." (1968, p. 205)*

Henry P. Smith: *"Learning is the acquisition of new behaviour or the strengthening or weakening of old behaviour as the result of experience." (1962, p. 260)*

Woodworth: *"Any activity can be called learning so far as it develops the individual - (in any respect, good or bad) and makes him alter behaviour and experiences different from what that would otherwise have been." (1945, p. 288)*

Kingsley and Garry: *"Learning is the process by which behaviour (in the broader sense) is organized or changes through practice or training." (1957, p. 12)*

Pressey, Robinson and Horrocks: *"Learning is an episode in which a motivated individual attempts to adapt his behaviour so as to succeed in a situation which he perceives as requiring action to attain a goal." (1967, p. 232)*

Crow and Crow: *"Learning is the acquisition of habits, knowledge and attitudes, It involves new ways of doing things and it operates on an individual's attempts to overcome obstacles or to adjust to new situation. It represents progressive changes in behaviour. It enables him to satisfy interests to attain a goal." (1973, p. 225)*

Hilgard: *"Learning is the process by which an activity originates or is changed through reacting to an encountered situation, provided that the characteristics of the changes in activity cannot be explained on the basis of native response, tendencies, maturation or temporary states of the organism (e.g. fatigue or drugs, etc.)," (1958, p. 3)*

An overview of these above definitions may clearly reveal that learning may be turned as a process or its outcome in which necessary changes in the behaviour of the learner are brought through experienced-direct or indirect. Here it has been also emphasized that although changes in behaviour are also brought out by the factors other than experience yet all such changes in behaviour are not associated with the process and product of learning. In this connection special mention can be made about the Hilgard's definition. Let us reconsider this definition now.

On the basis of Hilgard's definition of learning the factors or forces responsible for bringing changes in our behaviour can be divided into following three main categories:

1. The factors or forces that bring permanent or enduring changes in our behaviour e.g. maturation.
2. The factors or forces that bring temporary changes in our behaviour like mental or physical fatigue, illness, drugs or intoxicating objects, medicines, sleeplessness, emotions like anger, fear, etc.

3. The factors or forces that bring relatively enduring or permanent changes (the charges lying between the temporary and permanent status-neither too temporary nor too permanent) in our behaviour e.g. training, practice and experiences, etc.

Let us now analyse the type of changes brought out by these three category of factors or forces in our behaviour. First let us consider the effect of maturation.

1. *Learning and Maturation*: These two phenomena are so interrelated that sometimes it becomes difficult to say, definitely, as to which of the behavioural changes are the results of learning and which are the consequences of maturation. For the clear differentiation let us try to make distinction between these two terms.

Maturation, in fact, is a natural process. It is the growth which takes place within the individual. The maturational changes are the results of unfolding and ripening of inherited traits and are relatively independent of activity, practice or experience. Biggie and Hunt clarify these ideas in the following words:

> "Maturation is a developmental process within which a person, from time to time manifests different traits, the 'blue prints' for which have been carried in his cells from the time of his conception." *(Biggie and Hunt, 1968)*

In this way maturation involves changes that are associated with normal growth.

Learning, on the other hand, is a change in a living individual which is not heralded by his genetic inheritance. It is a process which takes place as a result of stimuli from without. The changes in the behaviour, in the process of learning, are always produced through some activity, training or experiences.

Maturation is learning's chief competitor as a modifier of behaviour. The distinction can be made on the following grounds:

If a behaviour sequence matures (develops) through regular stages, irrespective of intervening practices or training, the behaviour is said to be developed through maturation and not through learning. If training procedures do not speed up or modify the behaviour, such procedures are not casually important and the changes do not classify as learning.

On this ground the relatively pure cases like the swimming of tadpoles and the flying of birds can be attributed, primarily, to maturation. But in most of the activities of human beings, it is difficult to decide whether these activities result from maturation or learning. The simplest example is the language development of the child. The child does not learn to talk until he reaches a certain stage or age in maturation, but it is also equally true that he does not learn the language just because he attains that stage. The language is taught to him. The language, which he learns, is that which he hears.

Therefore, the two processes — maturation and learning are closely related to each other. Maturation helps in the process of learning. Learning can only take place if the stage for that type of learning has been achieved through a process of maturation. If the teacher understands the complexity of the changes that are going on as the result of both processes and the interaction between the two, he is not apt to go far astray in his teaching. The reverse will be harmful. For example, forcing a child to attempt to learn certain speech patterns, before a certain maturation has occurred, can disrupt the normal development of speech in the child and do damage. On the other hand, failure, at an appropriate time, to provide specific training in speech may be a cardinal educational error.

2. *Factors Associated with temporary changes in behaviour:* Let us now think over the second category of factors responsible for bringing temporary changes in behaviour. Fatigue, illness, medicine and intoxicating objects, fear, anger, etc. cause serious and quite effective changes in one's behaviour. The person who happened to be quite right when leaving home to his office in the morning may be seen to be quite fussy and irritable after returning home in the evening. This change in his behaviour is the consequence of his getting mentally and physically fatigued. However, the change is quite temporary as the behaviour may turn again into a normal behaviour after taking some rest or refreshment. The same is true with the behavioural changes introduced on account of taking drugs, alcohol and other intoxicating objects. The behaviour becomes normal as soon as one gets rid of the intoxication influences. Similarly, under emotional current one may be drifted away from his normal behaviour but as soon as one comes to his senses after being cooled down, one realises his out-burst and irrational behaviour and begins to behave as usual. In this way, the changes introduced in our behaviour on account of the factors falling in the second category are quite transitory and temporary. The changes in behaviour automatically vanish as soon as the impact of the factors or forces responsible for introducing such changes come to an end. You may very well equate these changes in behaviour to the type of changes called physical changes known to you as a student of physical sciences like change of ice into water, lightening of an electric bulb, etc. On the other hand, the changes brought about by maturation are quite permanent like chemical changes, e.g. burning of the piece of a paper, conversion of milk into curd, etc.

3. *Relatively permanent changes through experience and training:* The third category of changes in behaviour are neither too temporary (as brought out by the factors like fatigue, illness, alcohol, etc.) nor too permanent (as brought out by maturation). They somewhat lie between these two and are therefore may be termed as relatively permanent or enduring changes in one's behaviour. The factors or forces responsible for bringing such changes are named as experiences-direct or indirect, involving training, practice, and formal as well as informal education attempts. Only such type of relatively permanent changes in our behaviour brought out through experience may be associated with the process and product of learning.

Their characteristics of being neither too permanent nor too temporary is a boon to the system of education. Imagine if the results of our learning *i.e.* changes in behaviour might have been too temporary, then the strenuous efforts for making the students learn, remember and utilise the results of learning would have been too futile. Being temporary and transitory changes, all what was learnt by a child could have vanished in no time. Similarly, the introduction of too permanent changes in one's behaviour through learning would have been a quite unpleasant experience as a student's learning to pronounce PUT as pat might become a life long mistake. The done could not be made undone and thus picking up of the bad habits on account of any learning might have ruined the future of ill-fated learners. In this way, it is quite a welcome sign that changes introduced only through experience are termed as learning.

In this way, if we attempt to analyse the nature of changes introduced in our behaviour in reference to the factors responsible for such changes a proper definition of the term learning may be evolved in the following words.

Learning is a process of bringing relatively enduring or permanent changes in behaviour through experience or training.

Nature and Characteristics of Learning

The changes brought out in our behaviour through learning by all means are accounted as an acquired phenomenon. Learning in this way can't be attributed to some or the other hereditary influences. It is earned and acquired by us like other attributes of our personality and that is why learning of all types is given a common name *i.e* acquired behaviour. It has its special nature and characteristics, a glimpse of which you may find through the following description:

1. *Learning is the change in behaviour:* Learning in its any form or shape is always associated with some or the other changes in learner's behaviour. That in why learning is always directed or aimed for bringing changes in learner's behaviour. However, these changes in learner's behaviour should always be desirable ones as the undesirable changes, if these are allowed to happen, prove detrimental to the welfare of the learner as well as to the society.

2. *Change in behaviour caused by learning is relatively enduring or permanent:* Change in behaviour caused by learning is neither too permanent (as caused through maturation) nor too temporary (as caused by the factors like fatigue, illness, etc.). They lie between these two states and are usually referred to as relatively permanent changes implying that although frequent or unwanted changes in the learned behaviour can't take place, yet the needed changes can be introduced in the manner such as getting rid of the bad habits or unlearning a wrong method of doing things etc.

3. *Learning is a continuous life long process:* Learning is, although not inherited, yet its beginning can be very well made right from the conception of the child. The environment available in the womb of the mother may work as facilitator for such learning. We have Abhimanyu before us as an example who was able to learn the art of 'Chakravueh Bhedan' from his father 'Arjuna' in the womb of his mother 'Subhadra'. After birth the process of learning picks up a greater speed with the constant interaction and stimulation received from the physical, social and cultural environmental forces and it does not stop till one's death. Regarding its continuity we have enough evidences that one activity leads to another and the individual engages himself to learn more and more. Every day new problems are faced, new situation are created and the individual has to face these situations and bring essential changes in his behaviour. Thus, it is a never changing process and it is why we refer that it goes from womb to tomb.

4. *Learning is a Universal Process:* We all the living creatures on this earth have the abilities and capacities for learning irrespective of the nature of our species, caste, colour, sex, geographical location or some other such individual differences. Therefore the myths like that members of the upper castes especially Brahmins have more capacity of learning than the members belonging to the lower castes and untouchables, women have inferior learning capacity than men or the blacks possess sub normal capacities for learning in comparison to whites, etc. have no substantial ground. On the contrary, the truth remains that every living being on the earth has been favoured by the nature to possess the capacity to learn according to the species specific characteristics and environment as well as opportunities available for learning.

5. *Learning is purposive and goal directed:* All learning is goal-directed. It is the definiteness of the aim and clear understanding of the purpose which makes an individual learn immediately the techniques of performing a particular task. It is the purpose or goal which determines what he sees in the learning situations and how he acts there in. Therefore, the purpose or goal is the pivot, around which the entire system of learning revolves. In case where there is no purpose, definitely there would hardly be any learning.

6. *Learning involves reconstruction of experiences:* We learn something at a particular stage and it is stored in our learning experiences store in the shape of previous experience or learning for the learning of a future task. However, what has been learnt by us at a particular occasion, always remains in the state of modification in the light of the new or richer experiences gained by us in this respect. As a result the old learning is replaced by the new learning and our previous experiences are restructured and reorganised for giving birth to a new structure composed of the reconstructed experiences. It is therefore education *i.e.* the process of

learning is often referred to as the process of continuous reconstruction of experiences.

LEARNING IS THE CHANGE IN BEHAVIOUR

- Change in behaviour caused by learning is relatively enduring and permanent
- Learning is a continuous life long process
- Learning is a universal process
- Learning is purposive and goal directed
- Learning involves reconstruction of experiences
- Learning is the product of activity and environment
- Learning is transferable from one situation to another
- Learning does not necessarily imply improvement
- Learning does not necessarily imply development in the right direction
- Learning helps in bringing desirable changes in behaviour
- Learning helps in attainment of teaching-learning objectives
- Learning helps in proper growth and development
- Learning helps in balanced development of personality
- Learnign helps in proper realization of goals of life
- Learning helps in proper adjustment
- Learning is a comprehensive process, possessing a wide scope

Fig. 1.3: Nature and Characteristics of Learning

7. *Learning is the product of activity and environment:* The basic condition of the emergence of any learning essentially lies in one's responding actively to the stimuli belonging to one's environment. In case the child is not willing to respond to the stimuli present in his learning environment, he can't be persuaded to proceed on the path of his learning journey. More the learner will respond actively to the stimuli present in his learning environment the more progress he will be able to make in terms of his learning outcomes. Therefore, the key of a successful learning in any

teaching learning-process always lies in the active responding of the learner to the stimuli present or the activities going on in the teaching-learning environment.

8. *Learning is transferable from one situation to another:* Learning has a special characteristic of being transferred from one learning situation to another having positive as well as negative effect. In its positive transfer the learning in one situation helps the learning in another situation but in the case of negative transfer we may observe the adverse effect when learning in one situation hinders or obstructs the path of learning in another situation.

9. *Learning does not necessarily imply improvement:* Learning is often considered as a process of improvement with practise or training. This means that all types of learning helps the child in the path of his progress towards desired ends or results. But this is not always true. The child learns so many things in the class room that do not at all help him to achieve his goal. Habits of idleness, disrespect towards authority, truancy, developing poor hand writing and defective pronunciation and exposition, etc. are among these. Therefore, it should be known clearly that learning does not necessarily imply improvement (with respect to the achievement of an end).

10. *Learning does not necessarily imply the development in right direction:* In a similar way, while defining learning as a process of development, the word development should never be confined to mean 'progress in right direction to achieve certain ends or results'. Hence, as Woodworth clarifies in his definition (see definition no. 4 given earlier), as a result of learning, the pattern of development is free to move to either direction — positive or negative. It is no guarantee that the individual will always pick up good knowledge, desirable habits, interest and attitudes. He has equal chances to be drifted to the debit side of the human personality.

11. *Learning helps in bringing desirable changes in behaviour:* Learning is the process of bringing changes in behaviour. It can help in introducing desired changes in the behaviour of the learner in all its three domains i.e. cognitive, conative and affective.

12. *Learning helps in the attainment of teaching-learning objectives*: The teaching-learning objectives and teaching-learning situation can be effectively reached through the help of learning and consequently the children can be made to acquire essential knowledge, skills, applications, attitude and interests, etc.

13. *Learning helps in the proper growth and development:* Learning helps in reaching to one's maximum in terms of the growth and development under various aspects of growth and development dimensions, namely physical, mental (cognitive), emotional, social, moral, aesthetic and language.

14. *Learning helps in the balanced development of personality:* Our educational efforts are directed to bring an all-round development in the personality of the child. The process of learning results in bringing such an all-round development of the personality.

15. *Learning helps in proper adjustment:* Adjustment is the key of success in life. Learning helps the individual to seek adjustment with his self and environment.

16. *Learning helps in the realization of the goals of life:* Every man has his own philosophy and style of life and he strives to achieve the goals of his life. Learning process helps the individual to realise the goals of his life.

17. *Learning is a very comprehensive process, possessing a quite wide scope:* The world of learning is considered to limit itself to the narrow walls of the activities concerning with intellectual and motor efficiency. It is often thought of as the acquisition of some knowledge and skills memorization certain facts and principles, development of reasoning and thinking power, etc. These are some of the learning activities which formally go on inside the classroom or in any arranged learning situation. But learning is not only limited to these activities. It is a very comprehensive process which covers nearly all the aspects of the human personality. Its scope touches aspects like the formation of habits, development of interests, attitudes a sense of appreciation and critical observation, acquisition of beliefs, perfection of values and ideals and setting of the goals and purposes.

Therefore, learning, as a whole, is not confined to the formal classroom learning activities. Life presents enormous opportunities to learn and learning activities are so numerous that it is difficult to limit them in any specific categories. How one eats, drinks, dresses, what are his specific hobbies, interests, attitudes, beliefs and aspirations, how he strives and what ideals and values he aims at, what is his concept of himself, etc., all are examples of learned and acquired behaviour. And the scope of learning, definitely, embraces all of these aspects into its domain.

RELATIONSHIP BETWEEN TEACHING AND LEARNING

For having insight into the concept of teaching it is also important to know about the concept of a closely related term learning and also to think about its relationship with teaching.

Learning may be properly defined as a relatively permanent change in behaviour (excluding the influence of growth, maturity or lesion). Teaching task or process is also related to realize the same objective as may be clear from the definition of teaching given by Clarke (1970) i.e., "activities that are designed and performed to produce change in student behaviour." It leads us to conclude that teaching consists of all those activities or system of actions that are intended to produce learning.

The question arises whether it is essential for all types of teaching to be ended in some or the other types of learning. Similarly it is essential for a learning that it should be initiated or handled by some or the other type of teaching. Truly speaking such type of cause and effect relationship does not exist between teaching and learning. It is not essential for a teaching to be ended with same or other types of learning. Similarly, learning may also take place without involving the formalities of a teaching process.

It is true that whenever a teacher teaches something to his class, his teaching intends to produce learning or brings relatively permanent changes in the behaviour of the students of his class. But there is no guarantee that what he intends will be fully realized. It is just the same as the doctor gives a treatment to cure the patient but every patient is not cured by the treatment. Therefore, it may be possible that the learning outcomes for the whole class or some particular students may be absolutely nil. It is also possible that while he tries to provide equal opportunities and learning situations through his teaching, the variance in the learning achievement of his students may be quite significant.

Similarly if one decides to learn something, it is not essential for him to wait for a teacher or teaching formalities. He may learn through experience. Self-study or self-learning may also help him in achieving his target. Where teaching is an interactive process involving interaction between teacher and taught, learning may be purely one sided activity needing no interaction.

Therefore in the words of B.O. Smith (1961) it may be safely concluded that *"Learning does not necessarily issue from teaching, that teaching is one thing and learning is quite another."* It is wrong to suggest and accept and learning is directly proportion to teaching or vice versa. Both of these concepts may exist and function independently.

This is one side of the story. It is true that teaching and learning may go quite independently but for the good things to come there is a need of a good friendship between the two. They are to join hands, come near and have a synthesis known as teaching-learning process.

Whatever may be the way or means, both teaching and learning aim the one and same thing, i.e., bring changes in the behaviour of the learner. So it is useless to keep them apart. A good teaching must always be so designed and performed as to result in maximum learning. One should learn economy and avoid wastage of resources. A learner may also be highly benefited through a well organised system of actions (known as teaching) for achieving his learning objectives. Therefore, as Gage (1963) considers, "The process of teaching and learning must he adapted to each other so as to make whatever combination of procedures pay off best."

In any case, as Stones and Morris (1972) put it, we need not consider learning to be an immutable, fixed, given process to which teaching must be adapted. Instead we should concern of a teaching-learning process, both of whose parts (teaching activities as well as learning process) can be changed to make learning more effective. It means that where teaching must make a central concern of the process of education or scheme of pedagogy, the learning, in turn, should be made a central theme and goal for every teaching.

2

Nature (Heredity) and Nurture (Environment)

WHAT IS HEREDITY OR NATURE?

A cat gives birth to a kitten, a cow to a calf and human being to a baby. The members of one species resemble each other and possess characteristics that are common to their species. Now the question arises what is that which is responsible for a particular type of body, shape and other likewise characteristics in the members of one species. Going further we find that there are individual differences even in the members of the same species. A child resembles his sisters, brothers, parents, grand parents, and other members of the family more than the people unrelated to him at all. What is that which causes such similarities and dissimilarities? The answer usually referred to is heredity which means that an offspring inherits most of the personality traits of his parents and forefathers which makes him resemble them. It is in this sense that Douglas and Holland defined heredity in the following words:

> "One's heredity consists of all the structures, physical characteristics, functions or capacities derived from parents, other ancestry or species." (1947, p. 51)

When does a child inherit such personality characteristics from his parents or forefathers and how this process in inheritance is performed? What helps in such inheritance? These are some of the basic questions which need some clarification at this stage. For the answers let us try to understand "how life begins".

How life begins. Life in actual sense begins with the conception, approximately, nine months before birth. The mechanism of conception is explained below:

The male and female reproductive organs produce germ cells. In the males, their testes produce the male germ cells, the spermatozoa, while in the females, their ovaries produce the female germ cells, the ova. Life is the result of the union of these male and female cells.

As a result of coitus at the time of mating, the male germ cells, numerous in number, try to come in contact with female germ cells. The male germ cells are deposited at the mouth of the uterus and try to make contact with the single ovum. (Normally only one ovum is produced in each menstrual cycle). Out of so many spermatozoa only one sperm establishes contact with the ovum and makes it fertilized. The fertilized ovum is the beginning of the life which starts the process of the child's development in the mother's womb.

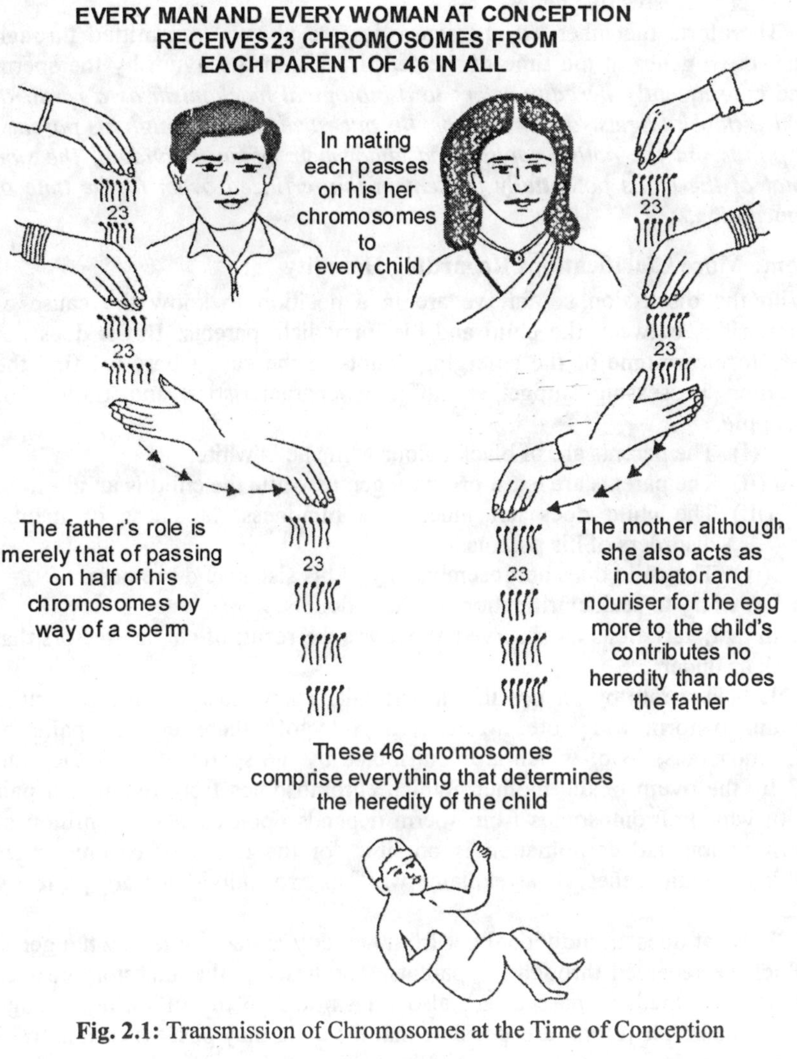

Fig. 2.1: Transmission of Chromosomes at the Time of Conception

The fertilized ovum consists of a semi-fluid mass called cytoplasm and within the cytoplasm there is the nucleus which contains the chromosomes. The chromosomes exist in pairs. In the fertilized ovum (zygote) there are 23 pairs of chromosomes, 23 of which are contributed by the father and 23 by the mother. Each chromosome consists of a number of minute particles called genes. The genes are the physical substances passed on from parent to offspring and thus, are the real carriers and determiners of heredity traits. What we get out of the heredity is the net result of the traits and characteristics of the parents and forefathers transmitted to the zygote through the respective genes.

Therefore, the inherited characteristics are always transmitted through respective genes at the time of the fertilization of the ovum by the sperm and consequently *heredity refers to a biological mechanism as a result of which the child gets something from his ancestral stock through his parents. It points out the native capital and endowment of an individual, the sum total of the traits potentially present in the fertilized ovum at the time of conception.*

Some More Clarifications Regarding Heredity

With the discussion so far we are in a position to know the cause of similarities between the child and his immediate parents. But it does not care to clear some of the emerging doubts in the case where we find the children possessing altogether different characteristics and traits. For example:

(i) The parents are of black colour while he is white.
(ii) The parents are extra-ordinary genius while the child is an idiot.
(iii) The child does not inherit the blindness, lameness or mental disorders of his parents.
(iv) The child does not resemble any of his sisters and brothers.

Let us try to seek clarification for these doubts.

In tact, variations as observed above are the result of chance factors that work as under:

1. It is purely by chance that a particular sperm fuses with a particular ovum to form a zygote. Moreover, in zygote there are 23 pairs of chromosomes, 23 of which are contributed by the sperm of the father and 23 by the ovum of the mother. Which chromosomes from ovum will pair with which chromosomes from sperm depends upon chance. A million of permutation and combination is possible for the union of chromosomes which contain genes. That explains why no two individuals are perfectly identical.

2. What does an individual get from heredity is determined by the genes which he received through his parents. The traits of the ancestors besides those of immediate parents are also transmitted to the offspring through these genes. Therefore, it is possible that the child may possess certain traits that are traceable to one or more of the ancestors, even though they may not be found in either of the parents.

THE TWINS AND HEREDITY

Normally at the time of fertilization, a single ovum is fertilized by a sperm of the male. It results in the birth of a single offspring at one time. But sometimes this normal function is disturbed and there are cases of multiple births — the birth of two or more offspring at a time. The birth of twins is one of such cases where two individuals are born at the same time. There are two distinctly different types of twins namely Identical twins and Fraternal twins.

Identical twins. Usually the fertilization of one ovum by one sperm produces the offspring. Sometimes, however, it so happens that when the ovum splits, as a result of fertilization the two parts fail to unite together. The result is that each part develops into a complete individual. The twins formed thus are called Identical because they, exactly, carry the same genes. They possess almost the same characteristics and are definitely of the same sex.

Fraternal twins. Normally in the ovary of the human female during each menstrual period, only one ovum is matured but it may happen that two or more ova may mature simultaneously and be fertilized at the same time by two different sperms. The result is that two different zygotes are produced. The individuals thus produced are known as the Fraternal twins or Non-identical twins. They have different combination of chromosomes and genes as both ova are fertilized by different sperms. Fraternal twins, therefore, are sure to differ in many traits. Like the identical twins, they need not belong to the same sex. They may belong to the same or opposite sex.

WHAT IS ENVIRONMENT OR NURTURE?

From the above discussion it is clear that the child inherits the traits and characteristics of his parents and forefathers through genes at the time of conception. Therefore, what he possesses at the time of conception is all due to heredity. It is the native capital given to him for starting his life. After conception, how he develops, is the outcome of the interaction between his hereditary characteristics and environment. The forces of environment begin to play their part and influence the growth and development of an individual right from the time of the fertilization of the ovum by sperm. Therefore, from the environmental point of view, not only, what happens after birth is important but what goes inside the womb of the mother after conception has equal significance, also.

The above point of view has given birth to so many meanings and definitions of environment in the following way:

1. "The environment is everything that affects the individual except his genes." (Boring, Langfield and Weld, 1961, p. 422)
2. "Environment covers all the outside factors that have acted on the individual since he began life." (Woodworth and Marquis 1-948, p. 156)

The views expressed by the above writers lead us to conclude that the environment consists of the external forces, which influence the growth and developed of an individual right from his conception. Before birth, the mother's womb is the place where these forces play their part. The nutrition is received by the embryo through the blood stream of the mother. The physiological and psychological states of the mother during pregnancy, her habits and interests, etc. all influence the development. After birth the child is exposed to the numerous environmental forces that are purely external in nature. These can be divided into two parts, physical forces and social or cultural forces. The food, water, climate, physical atmosphere of the home, school, village or city, the physical facilities available are included in the physical forces while the parents, members of the family, friends and class mates, neighbours, teachers, the members of the community and the society, the means of mass communication and recreation, religious places, cubs, libraries etc. are included in the social forces.

These different environmental forces have a desirable impact upon the physical, social emotional, intellectual, moral and aesthetic development of an individual. Their influence is a continuous one, which begins with the emergence of life and goes till death.

RELATIVE ROLE AND IMPORTANCE OF NATURE AND NURTURE IN DEVELOPMENT

Arguments in favour of heredity and environment, showing the relative importance of one or the other, have given birth to an intangible controversy. On the one end, are the hereditarians who claim that heredity is all in all. It decides and sets everything about the personality of an individual. No amount of education or training can change the individual from what he is or has been in his ancestral beings. Education to them is futile. The function of education or environment in the making of the personality, according to them, can be compared to the polishing or painting of the wooden furniture.

Any polish or paint can not change the basic qualities of the wood used in the furniture. It only improves its appearance and increases its life a little.

The environmentalists on the other hand are of the opinion the heredity does not, in any way, affect the growth and development of an individual. Man is the product of his environment. He is what his environment has made him. There is nothing like definite hereditary characteristics or inherited qualities. What a man has done another man can also do if he gets favourable opportunities. Watson, one of the prominent environmentalist went much ahead. He declared *"Give me any child, I will make him what you desire"*. Thus, according to the environmentalists environment is all in all. The growth and development of an individual is the net result of his environment.

Both Hereditarians and Environmentalists have engaged themselves in the psychological experimentations since time immemorial. They put forward their experiments in support of their viewpoints. Some of the mentionable experiments are given below:

Experiments Performed by Hereditarians

1. F.N. Freeman reports an experiment based on the calculation of coefficients of correlation and their comparison. The summary is given below:

Coefficient of correlation of the intelligence test scores of

Identical twins	=	.90
Fraternal twins	=	.60
Siblings (brothers or sisters)	=	.50
Cousins	=	.25

The study shows the increased similarity in intelligence test scores with the increase in the amount of blood relationship. Mathematically, it concludes that Blood relationship is directly proportional to similarity in Intelligence. According to hereditarians, this experiment gives sufficient evidence in favour of the theory or royal blood.

2. The other types of experiments are based on the study of family histories. Two of these famous studies are given below:

(i) *Kallikak family study:* H.H. Goddard studied Kallikak family. Kallikak was a solider who married two women. First was a feeble-minded girl and the other was a normal one. The family line established by the feeble-minded woman contained 480 direct descendents among which only 46 normal individuals were found, the others were criminals, drunkards, feeble-minded, patients, sexually perverted and illegitimate, etc. whereas among 496 direct descendents of line established by the normal woman, all were normal with the exception of five.

(ii) *Juke family study:* This study was conducted by Dugdale Juke was a corrupt fisherman. His wife was also corrupt. About 1200 descendents of the family line established by them were studied. It was found that most of these descendants were paupers and prostitutes. Only a few of them were found normal.

3. *Gallon Fancis, in 1869*, prepared a list of 977 genius and well-to-do persons and investigated about their relatives. They were found to have 536 eminent relatives. For comparison he prepared another list of 977 average men and similarly investigated about their relatives. These 977 average men had but four relatives who were eminent. By this data he concluded that intelligence and all other likewise personality characteristics are transmitted through blood.

4. Various studies on identical twins have also been conducted. G.C. Schwesinger made one of such studies.

He took ten pairs of identical twins for his study. The individuals in each pair were brought up separately in the different environments. After attaining maturity, both the counterparts in a pair were compared. In six pairs, no difference in test intelligence quotient was noted and the remainder differed by fifteen or seventeen points. With this data he concluded that heredity is the important factor in determining the intelligence and other likewise characteristics of personality.

Experiments Performed by Environmentalists

1. Newman, Freeman and Holzinger in 1937, reported a case study of nineteen pairs of identical twins. They found that whereas the I.Q. difference of the identical twins reared together was 5.9 point, it was 8.2 for the twins reared apart. In this study he tried to compare the impact of different environments on the pattern of development by making constant the heredity factor with the help of identical twins. He found that environment plays a decisive role in bringing individual differences.

2. Kodak's analysis based on his experiment also emphasizes the importance of environment. He studied the foster children. The true mothers of these children were tested on some mental test. The average I.Q. of this group of 80 mothers was 87.7. The majority of the mothers fell "below average", 53.8 percent had IQs below 90, 16.3 per cent were borderline and 13.8 were feeble-minded. Yet the average IQs their children was 116. If the heredity determines the future course that these foster children could not have gained much in term of I.Q. This study shows clearly the influence of environment on the growth and development of personality characteristics.

3. The case history of some children reared in the forest by Wolves also throws light on the role of environment in the personality development.

One of such children was Ramu known as the wolf boy. When he was quite young, he is was picked up by a wolf. He remained among the wolves for a pretty long time and became wolf in food habits, speech and other traits. He could only crawl instead of walking and could utter sounds like a wolf.

Similar was the case with two sisters, Amla and Kamla, aged 2 and 9 years. They were found in the forest of Bengal in 1920 from the den of a wolf. They used to talk, walk and act like wolves. Amla died in the hospital after some time, but Kamla was subjected to further study. By providing suitable environment and training, she was made to walk on foot and speak like a human child.

There are so many other studies which support the role of environment in the personality development. Notable among them are studies done by IOWA School of American Educational Psychologists and the Chicago Sociologists. These studies have concluded that environment plays a decisive role in moulding the patterns of one's life. Experiments with twins, siblings and foster children all seem to indicate that children getting privileged environment have all the chances to go ahead in comparison to the children getting less privileged environment.

Now in this way we see that both hereditarians and environmentalists have gone with the different experiments to support their viewpoints. Dr. Prem Pasricha has given beautiful concluding remarks about these experiments. She writes, *"It is quite customary for the Psychologists wedded to either side viz. heredity and environment, to perform experiments and quote finding in favour of either of the factors. It has also been found that the findings of these experiments can be interpreted either way and can be easily made to support the opposite view. When analyzed in an objective manner, it indicates clearly that the two are so closely interwoven that it is difficult to separate the effect of one from that of the other."* (1936, p. 18)

Let us see why it is difficult to have actual experiments for the study of the impact of pure heredity or environment on the growth and development of an individual.

To study the impact of environment we have to take individuals with same heredity. After keeping them in different environments, the comparison can be made. In a similar way for studying the impact of heredity, environmental factors should be made constant. The individuals belonging to different hereditary stock and brought up in exactly the same environments can be compared for this purpose.

There are so many difficulties which are faced while conducting these studies. These are listed below:

(i) In the first place, it is impossible to get individuals having the same heredity. Even the identical twins are not supposed to have exactly the same genes and therefore the same hereditary characteristics.

(ii) If we, for the time being, assume that identical twins at the time of conception, approximately belong to similar hereditary stock, then the question arises — is it possible to experiment upon them right from the time of conception? Right from the time of fertilization and division of ovum, can these twins be subjected to different types of environments for studying the impact of environmental differences? The answer is 'No'. It is only after their birth-approximately nine months after their conception — that the pair is available for experimentation. We can not rule out the environmental effects inside the womb of the mother. Nor can these effects be ruled out as common influence upon the pair. It may happen that one of the twins can get a major share of nourishment and be favoured with the inner environment in one way or the other while the other is neglected to some extent. Therefore, it is difficult to get even the identical twins with exactly the same heredity.

(iii) The environmental influence also can not be controlled. It is very difficult to provide exactly the same environment for different individuals. Even the mother cannot show equal amount of love and affection to her own children. There are individual differences and as a result one individual is likely to be favoured in comparison to others. In the same foster home or orphanage the various individuals may be subjected to different strata of environmental conditions depending upon their own nature as well as the attitude of the keepers and officials. Therefore, the uniformity with regard to the provision of same environment is hard to be maintained.

The main reason for the failure in controlling either the heredity or environmental factor lies in the plain truth that the influence of these factors on the growth and development of the individual is inseparable. Right from the time of conception onwards, the two factors are so intermingled and interwoven that it is hard to say whether a particular characteristics is due to the gene or the environmental influences.

Conclusions Regarding the Relative Importance of Nature and Nurture

1. The supposition, that some particular trait in the individual is exclusively the product of his heredity or environment does not hold any ground. The individual's personality is the product of both heredity and environment. In this connection McIver and Page have said very correctly that *"Every phenomenon of life is the product of both. Each is as necessary to the result as the other. Neither can ever be eliminated and neither can ever be isolated.* " (1949, p. 95).

Whatever character or trait we may consider, it requires both heredity and environment for its development.

2. The controversial arguments regarding the relative importance of heredity and environment are quite useless. The question whether heredity is more important than environment or view versa is of the similar nature as to ask whether the seed or the soil is more important for the proper development of a plant. The seed and the soil do not work independently, but are mutually dependent. The seed has the power to grow into a certain kind of plant but how well it will grow depends on what soil it gets. The plant cannot grow without either the seed or the soil. It needs both. We cannot do away with either of them. It is also useless to say that one of them contributes more in the proper development of the plant.

In the similar way, it is hard to make any statement in favour of either heredity or environment in the process of development of an organism. Both are equally important and indispensable. Also it is wrong to assume that they are opposed to each other. They are complementary and support each other. The remark made by Garrett is worth quoting. *"Nothing is more certain than that heredity and environment are coaching influences and that both are essential to achievement."* (1968, p. 34).

3. In judging the relationship between heredity and environment now it can be said that it is absurd to make statement like heredity or environment. The 'either' and 'or' relationship between these two terms does not exist. It is always heredity and environment. But now the question arises whether the relationship between them is simply of an additive nature or not. The personality of an individual is not just the sum total of his heredity and environment. In this connection Woodworth and Marquis write:

> "The relation of heredity and environment is not like addition, but more like multiplication. The individual does not equal heredity + environment, but does equal heredity + environment." (1948, p. 158).

They further declare that the individual is a joint product of his heredity and environment just in the same way as the area of rectangle is the joint product of its length and breadth.

In this way, like the base, of rectangle, heredity provides us the structure, on which with the help of favourable environment, desired construction can be held. The native powers and energies of the individual, like the seed, lie in the heredity but is up to the environment to extract these energies and to make them able to reach their maximum limits.

4. Let us also study the relationship between heredity and environment from another different angle. As a gift from heredity, we get our working capital but it is the environment which gives us opportunity to invest it. The capital as well as the opportunities for its proper development are essential for the proper success in the business. There are instances where individuals starting from a very meagre amount have been able to earn in millions. Therefore, the extreme view of hereditarianism like Galton, '*Thus far shall thou go and no further*' is not correct. However, if we take it for granted, then even 'thus far' can we go without the cooperation of environment.

If the environment can not help us in growing beyond the limits determined by heredity, at least it gives us enormous assistance within that limits. How far as a rubber band can be stretched depends upon the nature of the raw material used in it. It can be stretched to the maximum limit but stretching even up to this limit, will depend upon the strength of the individual who pulls it and the favourable or unfavourable circumstances at the time of pulling.

Therefore, it is the duty of the teachers and parents to see that every child should get maximum opportunity for his development. It is true, that nothing entirely foreign to one's nature can be acquired. If a tree of cactus is grown, mangoes cannot be had. But to have fine mangoes out of the seed, which heredity has provided, we must be careful like a wise gardener who provides proper manure and water to his plants and cares for their well being and safety as he can. Like him we teachers cannot arrange for the selected seeds and plantation. Heredity factor is out of our control. But environmental influences can be controlled to a great extent. With a proper environment the native powers which may be dormant are awakened and stimulated to activity. Every child is able to get his maximum only when he is provided with the appropriate opportunities for his growth and development.

3

Maturation: Concept and Educational Implications

CONCEPT OF MATURATION

Maturation is a quite known term in the field of developmental psychology and constitutes a quite significant factor in the process of growth and development from the very conception of the child in the womb of his mother. What is generally conveyed through the term maturation can be known properly by paying attention to some important issues related with its concept like: (i) Meaning of the term maturation, (ii) Effect of maturation on growth and development.

Let us think over these issues one by one.

Meaning of the Term Maturation

Maturation, is known for its uniqueness and specificity as a natural process for the growth that takes place within an individual. It was A. Gesell, who used the term maturation in the field of child development in 1919. The changes brought out by maturation are said to be the result of unfolding and ripening of inherited traits and are relatively independent of activity, practice or experience. We can take the help of some well known definitions of the term maturation for knowing and understanding well about its meaning and nature. Let us reproduce a few of them for this purpose.

Mc Geoch (1942): Maturation includes any change with age in the conditions of learning which depends primarily upon organic growth factors rather than upon prior practice or experience.

Thompson (1979): "Maturation" is a name for the growth process during which a structure or function is more and more becoming adult, that is "mature".

A. Gesell (1929): Maturation is the maturity and firmness of the nerves and muscles brought out by the internal mechanism of the body quite independent of the impact of the environmental factors external to the organism.

H.J. Eysenck et al. (1972): Maturation is an autonomous process of somatic, psychological and mental differentiation and integration spread over developmental stages and phases which condition and build on one another in the course of time; as a result of this process the individual growth is completed and consolidated somatically, maturely and spiritually as well as socially and he can thus adapt to life.

A.T. Jersild et al. (1975): Maturation is the process by which underlying potential capacities of the organism reach a stage of functional readiness. This process involves both the changes in structure that come with growth and the progressive exercise of structures that provide ground work for later performances.

Biggie and Hunt (1968): "Maturation is a developmental process within which a person, from time to time manifests different traits, the blue prints for which have been carried in his cells from the time of his conception."

The definitions cited above may help us in drawing following conclusions about the meaning and nature of maturation,

- Maturation in its purest sense is the result of the mechanism of heredity. Heredity contributions decide the course of the changes (behavioural and developmental) observed in the children since their conception in the womb of the mother.
- The effect of the process of maturation continues throughout the developmental period i.e. upto the end of the period of adolescence.
- Maturation helps the children to get matured in terms of their growth and development in all the various aspects — physical, motor, mental, social, moral and spiritual for playing the role of a matured adult in their lives.
- As a natural phenomenon of growth and development, maturation helps in the development of inner potential of the human organisms making them ready and capable of reaching the heights or attaining possible milestones of their personality.
- Maturation is essentially linked with one's organically internal growth processes that are primarily or momentarily, independent of environmental factors external to the organism.

In this way, *maturation as a term and concept stands for a natural and spontaneous process of growth and development guided through the genetically controlled internal mechanism of an organism (quite independent of the impact of training or experience) responsible for bringing changes (behavioural and developmental) with the passage of the time during the developmental age.*

Effect of Maturation on Growth and Development

1. As one grows in age, he or she is naturally bound to be accompanied with some changes in his body, mind and behaviour purely because of the phenomenon of maturation. This is more clear and revealing in the case of lower species like birds and animals. Let us have a look at examples from our environment around us. A bird conceives and as a result lay eggs in its

nest. If we observe, we find that after a few days, there are signs of life in those eggs. A little later young chicks come out from the eggs, jumping here and there, being fed by the parent birds but still unable to fly. However one day, we find that they have grown enough and developed the capacity to fly like the other grown-up birds.

2. Similarly, we observe in the case of tadpoles that as a result of maturation, *i.e.* natural process of growth and development, there is definitely a major change in their behaviour. They are able to swim and after sometime they begin to jump like an adult frog. What is observed in terms of their growth and development here can be purely attributed to the process of maturation. It is also true in the case of the young ones of animals. No training or experience is received by them in the beginning for growing and developing their abilities to walk and run like their adult parents. A baby deer is able to run quite fast just after its birth. How does it manage to eat grass and drink water, is just the result of the process of maturation as there is no such attempt of providing any formal experience or training to it by the parents or the other members of the species for the performance of such behaviour.

In this way, we can have enough evidence from the surrounding nature that explains the role of maturation in bringing desired growth and development in the behaviour and functioning of the small babies of insects, birds and animals.

3. In the case of human beings also, we may observe and notice the impact of maturation on the growth and development of the youngsters from their very birth in almost all the aspects and dimensions of their personality as illustrated below:

- With the passage of the time they grow and develop physically in their height, weight and body proportions and functioning of the internal and external organs. The process of maturation must help them in acquiring physical maturity and thus they turn into fully physically mature adults at the expiry of the period of adolescence,
- Same is true with the other dimensions of their personality as well. They grow and develop as mentally, socially, emotionally, morally and aesthetically mature personality at the time of acquiring adulthood. The process of maturation, *i.e.* an act of the natural growth and development helps them well in this task. However, the question here may arise as to whether the growth and development acquired in the case of human babies for turning them into a fully matured personality in terms of the mental, social, emotional, moral and ethical standards is purely a function of the process of maturation or environmental influences, including training, or a combination of both.
- Definitely here the last one is the appropriate answer and as such it may be easily concluded that growth and development in the case of

human beings for gaining maturity is a combined function of the process of maturation and learning. How does it become a combined function may be well illustrated through a number of instances described as follows:

(i) A child is not able to speak or utter words correctly until he reaches a certain stage or age in maturation. We can't expect a baby of 6 months to speak and utter words correctly even if he belongs to a very high hereditary stock (like the parents are too rich and scholars in the linguistic capacity, say Ph.D. in language) or is being constantly inspired and formally trained in speech. He has to grow and develop in the linguistic capacity in accordance with the maturation level he needs for doing so. In the natural process, he will learn to utter with the maturation of his vocal chords and other similar physical and mental functioning required for learning correct language. At the same time, it is also true that here we can't rule out the impact of favourable or unfavourable environmental influences, including schooling, formal or informal training, for acquiring proper and excellent linguistic ability.

A child at any stage of his schooling or life does not learn the language or develop his language ability just because he attains that stage. Definitely, the language is taught to him. The language which he learns is the one he hears and more specifically the one he gets through specific training. As a result, what a child acquires in terms of his language development at any stage of his life is a joint product of the natural process of growth and development, *i.e.* maturation and the environment influences including training.

(ii) What is true for language development is also true for the development of other mental functioning. The development of mental facilities like thinking, reasoning, problem solving, decision making, analyzing, synthesizing, discriminating, drawing inferences all need maturation as well as planned experiences and training on the part of the youngsters. Normally, we can't expect a child of tender age to be too logical, consistent, methodological in his approach and systematic in thinking and abstraction. He has to wait before he acquires the ability of abstraction, *i.e.* a certain stage of maturation, for developing his mental faculties enabling him to perform mental tasks requiring power of abstraction, creative, imagination, innovation and novelty.

(iii) In case of emotional development also, we can observe a similar phenomenon. A child develops in terms of emotional maturity on account of the process of maturation helped and influenced by the environmental influences. It is true that a child has to be a child in terms of his emotional behaviour. We can't expect him to behave like a grown-up adult. There is definitely an age characteristic emotional behaviour. That is why we can observe a definite pattern of emotional behaviour at each stage of maturation, *i.e.* infancy, childhood, pre-adolescence, adolescence, adulthood and old age. However, how one behaves and why one behaves under the influence of a particular emotion depends heavily on the impact of the environmental influences or feedback one gets from his formal or informal surroundings. The same is true for social, moral, religious or aesthetic standards and aesthetic sense from the individuals belonging to different stages of their maturation.

(iv) Surely age is a great factor. One learns and picks up so many things related to these aspects as he or she grows in age. Take the case of sexual development, a distinctly visible area showing the impact of maturation. As one grows in age, he or she is sure to pick up many things and practices related to sexual activities even without any prior experiences of formal training. Attraction towards opposite sex, to feel the necessity of the satisfaction of sexual urge are thus the peculiar developments that are bound to emerge as and when a child reaches the adolescence stage. However, his attitude and practices towards sex may now be coloured or influenced side by side by the exposures, experiences or formal/informal training he receives for doing so.

Thus from the above discussion, it may be clear that growth and development in the various aspects and dimensions of the personality of an individual is very much helped and influenced by the process of maturation. As one grows in one's age he is helped by the process of maturation for being grown and developed into a full-fledged matured personality. However, how much maturity in the deeds and kinds is shown by an individual again depends upon the quality of experiences, environmental influences, formal or informal training, education, etc. received by an individual for this purpose.

EDUCATIONAL IMPLICATIONS OF MATURATION

The knowledge of the nature and process of maturation contributing towards the growth and development of the children and its valuable inter-relationship and interaction with the process of learning may prove quite beneficial to the parents, teachers and counsellors for planning and providing care, education and guidance to the children in the way described as below:

1. Maturation is a natural process of growth and development. It is guided through hereditary potential and genetic factors. There are many functions and the phenomenon of growth that are entirely governed through the process of maturation and are thus quite automatic and spontaneous among the living organisms including human beings. No prior experience, learning or training is needed for such development and behavioural functioning. In this connection McGraw provides the example of psychogenetic functions (functions common to the race) such as creeping, sitting, standing, stair climbing, etc. Piaget provides the example of cognitive shemas like readings, grasping, sucking, looking, etc. that are purely the functions of maturation; exercise or training is of little advantage in the development and execution of these functioning. In this way many of the gross motor skills and general intellectual functioning can be developed naturally in the growing children. The parents and the caretakers should wait patiently for the outcome of such natural growth. They should not unnecessarily worried or become enthusiastic to bring early development or changes in the behaviour of their infants or children. However, in the case of ontogenetic functions (functions specific to the individual) such as swimming, roller-skating, tricycle riding categorized as fine motor skills or the development of language and other higher cognitive abilities, experiences and training is necessary. Therefore, teachers parents and counsellors should make themselves quite conscious to recognize what functions are purely guided through maturation (not requiring any training) and what are to be supported through training. It can help them in planning the education and guidance on their part.

2. Maturation as a close associate of learning or training in fact provides a solid base for any programme or scheme of effective learning or training. Here, it serves its function in two ways:

(i) Setting stage of learning by providing necessary readiness to learn.
(ii) Acquainting about the limits of development reached through learning or training.

Let us discuss these two aspects of maturation, the knowledge of which carries a lot of valuable educational implications.

(i) Maturation, helps the children to grow and develop physically and mentally for becoming essentially mature and ready for acquiring their age-linked learning experiences and training. The knowledge about the role played by maturity in this respect will surely help us in planning education for the child. We can certainly know that at what age what type of education and training should begin and in what sequence it should occur. We are adequately warned through such knowledge that:

- If the child is not old enough or mature enough to profit by the teaching or training, it has almost no value for him and can be regarded as a mere wastage of time, energy and resources on the part of teachers or trainers. For example, forcing a child to speak, walk or use language before reaching critical age of maturity will prove futile and many times harmful for the well being and proper development of the child.
- When the child acquired necessary developmental readiness through maturation, then no time should be wasted for providing him desirable learning experience and training for the acquisition of his age linked developmental abilities and skills. To miss the train at this time will be a great cardinal educational error. Pointing towards such error Hurlock (1956, p. 8) writes:

  "Should the child not be permitted to learn, even though ready, his interest is likely to wane. Later, when he is expected to learn, his interest may have reached such a low ebb that he will be unwilling to put forth the efforts needed for successful learning."

In this way, knowledge of the outcome of maturation, critical development periods and acquired developmental readiness through maturity, brings into lime light the so called valuable teaching moments in the words of Havighurst (1953). It is these moments when the task of development or behaviour modification should be performed by the teachers and parents for having better results in the welfare of the children.

(ii) Maturation is governed through the forces of heredity mechanism and genetics that are known to put the limits and boundaries on the extent of growth and development of a child during various ages and periods of life span commenting on this aspect Hurlock (1956, p. 7) writes:

> "Maturation, which depends upon the hereditary endowment of the individual sets limits beyond which development cannot go even when learning is encouraged.''

Therefore, we should always keep in mind the limits of one's educability and developmental progress drawn by the genetic structure of the child available for us in the form of his maturation level. We can consider here the cases of severe mentally retarded children whose neural maturation or natural development of the brain has been arrested at a quite low level. For such children, it may be observed that no amount of learning, training or environmental stimulation is sufficient to help them in bringing their behaviour and development into the normal range.

Therefore, it should be clearly recognized by us in planning individual or group education to the children that educational efforts should always be in tune with the limits imposed by the maturation level of the individual child. In this connection, we must always listen to the warning issued by Gesell (1949) in the following words.

> "All educability is dependent upon innate capacities for growth. This intrinsic growth (observed in the shape of maturation level) is a gift of nature. It can be guided, but it cannot be created; nor can it be transcended by an educational agency,"

3. Knowledge of the nature and mechanism of maturation can help us to know about the mile stones to be attained by the children at the various ages of their developmental period. It has been observed and verified through a number of research studies that the majority of children of the same chronological age or critical periods of their development are more similar than dissimilar in the rates of their physical and mental maturation. This similarity has been responsible for helping the educators to create and develop a common programme of training and education to the children of a particular age and maturation level in the classrooms with similar techniques and teaching equipments. It has also helped the parents, caretakers and counsellors to make use of the generated principles and approaches for the brought up and guidance of their children.

4. Maturation stimulated by customary environmental experiences is said to help the children to reach certain milestones in terms of physical, motor and cognitive development and acquire specific behavioural patterns quite normal to their age and developmental period. Such criteria may prove quite helpful in the diagnosis of exceptionalities and abnormalities in the development and behaviour of the grown up children. It can happen in the way given below:

(i) A child may be observed to remain quite ahead and advanced in comparison to the milestones fixed for his age and developmental period. It can help us to plan for his special education by identifying and labelling him as creative or gifted.

(ii) Through comparison with the milestones settled through maturation at a particular age, a child may be observed to leg behind or we may find that his behaviour is more infantile and less complex that would otherwise possible. It may help us to identify and level him slow learner, backward mentally retarded, learning disabled or deprived by diving deep into the causes of his deficient behaviour. Consequently, when a child is observed too slow or too inferior in terms of his growth and development and behaviour patterns quite normal for his age and developmental periods, we must seriously think about the deficiencies remained in his process of maturation or deprivation of customary environmental experiences including educational practices employed in his rearing and schooling.

In this way knowledge of the nature, functioning and outcomes of maturation, and active part played by the joint contribution of maturation and learning may prove quite helpful to the parents, teachers, counsellors and others interested in the welfare of the youngsters, to plan for the practices of better rearing and education to them.

4

Development: Concept, Influencing Factors and Relationship with Learning

INTRODUCTION

The sole aim of education is to bring an all round development in the personality of educand. Educational Psychology, being a science and technology of education, should help in the realization of this aim. As we know, human life starts from a single fertilized cell. The constant interaction with the environment results in the development of the innate capacities, abilities and potentialities of the child. The task of formal as well as informal education is to help the child in his path of development. Therefore, it is imperative that the individuals, supposed to be connected with the task of helping the child to develop satisfactorily, must be acquainted with his nature of the child's development.

It is only with a knowledge of the development of the learner at each stage of his life that it is possible for the teachers to render proper guidance, arrange the learning situations and plan the instructional programmes for bringing desirable harmonious development in their personalities. In the chapter, we would like to know necessary things regarding the meaning, concept and principles of child's development along with its relationship with child's learning.

HUMAN DEVELOPMENT: MEANING AND CONCEPT

For knowing about the meaning and concept of the term development we would like to throw light on the following aspects —

A. Distinguishing the term development from the term growth
B. Stages of Development
C. Various aspects or Dimensions of Development

A. Distinguishing the Term Development from the Term Growth

Mostly the terms growth and development are used interchangeably and taken as synonymous terms.

Both relate to the measurement of changes which occur in the individual after conception in the womb of the mother. Change is the law of nature. An individual starting from a fertilized egg, turns into a full-fledged human adult. In this turn-over process he undergoes a cycle of changes brought about by the process of growth and development in various dimensions — physical, mental, social, emotional, etc. Therefore, in the wider sense, both the terms growth and development can be used for any change brought about by maturation and learning (formal as well as informal education), and essentially is the product of both heredity and environment.

In the strict sense of terminology, these two terms have different meanings that can be put in the way given below:

Growth	*Development*
1. The term growth is used in purely physical sense. It generally refers to an increase in size, length, height and weight. Changes in the quantitative aspects come into the domain of growth.	1. Development implies overall changes in shape, form or structure resulting in improved working or functioning. It indicates the changes in the quality or character rather than in quantitative aspects.
2. Growth is one of the part of developmental process. In strict sense, development in its quantitative aspect is termed as growth.	2. Development is a wider and comprehensive term. It refers to overall changes in the individual. Growth is one of its parts.
3. Growth may be referred to describe the changes which take place in particular aspects of the body and behaviour of an organism.	3. Development describes the changes in the organism as a whole and does not list the changes in parts.
4. Growth does not continue throughout life. It stops when maturity has been attained.	4. Development is a continuous process. It goes from womb to tomb. It does not end with the attainment of maturity. The changes, however small they may be, continue throughout the life span of an individual.
5. The changes produced by growth are the subject of measurement. They may be quantified and are observable in nature.	5. Development, as said earlier, implies improvement in functioning and behaviour and hence brings qualitative changes which are difficult to be measured directly. They are assessed through keen observation in behavioural situations.
6. Growth may or may not bring development. A child may grow (in terms of weight) by becoming fat but this growth may not bring any functional improvement (qualitative change) or development.	6. Development is also possible without growth as we see in the cases of some children that they do not gain in terms of height, weight or size but they do experience functional improvement or development in physical, social, emotional or intellectual aspects.

Hence observed in minute details, both growth and development show differentiation. But in wider and practical sense both terms are used to denote the changes in the organism's physical as well as functional behaviour. These changes which cover physical, emotional, intellectual and social aspects of a human life are roughly divided into four major classes by Mrs. Hurlock (1956, p. 2-3)

(i) Changes in size (ii) Changes in proportion
(iii) Disappearance of old features (iv) Acquisition of new features.

All these types of changes have qualitative as well as quantitative aspects and hence generally, growth and development go hand in hand. And it is in this sense, that the two terms are to be used collectively. Both, taken together, explain the total changes — functional as well as constitutional changes — in the body and behaviour of the individual with the lapse of time after the conception. In this text, in the following pages, these terms will be used in synonymous sense for convenience.

B. Stages of Development

For human organism life starts from a fertilized ovum in the womb of the mother. Not only before birth, but also after birth for many years the child is a helpless organism until or unless he is helped by the continuous process of growth and development and attains maturity. When one attains maturity, one ceases to be called an adolescent and is labelled as an adult member of the society. He is supposed to play a responsible role in the society. Before being called an adolescent, he is named as a child or an infant etc. All of these names — infant, child, adolescent and adult, etc. are linked with various stages of development through which the child passes from birth to death.

There are certain common development or practical characteristics belonging to each stage. The human organism shows peculiar quantitative and qualitative changes in his body and behaviour with the help of which we can say at what particular age an individual belongs to which definite stage of his life.

If we also include the pre-birth period, the life span of a human organism can be divided, conveniently, into the following stages:

Nature of the Stage	*Period and approximate age*
1. Pre-natal (Pre-birth) stage	From conception to birth.
2. Stage of Infancy	From birth to two years.
3. Childhood stage	From 3rd to 12 years or in strict sense up to the on-set of puberty.
4. Adolescent stage	From the on-set of puberty to the age of maturity (generally from 13 to 19 years).
5. Adulthood	From 20 years and beyond or in strict sense from the age of attaining maturity till death.

We do not claim the absolute rigidity in the above classification in terms of either the division of life span into above mentioned stages or the duration of period mentioned against them. There are certainly great individual differences and so we should not imagine that every child will necessarily have each stage according to the period indicated above.

C. Various Aspects or Dimensions of Development

The major aspects, areas or dimensions in which a human child goes ahead for his complete holistic development, can be named as follows:

(a) Physical development
(b) Intellectual or Mental development
(c) Emotional development
(d) Moral or Character development
(e) Social development
(f) Language development

Let us see what we understand by these different aspects of development.

(a) Physical development: The physical development of the individual includes the development of his internal as well as external organs.

(b) Intellectual or Mental development: It includes the development of intellectual powers like the powers of reasoning and thinking, imagination, concentration, creativity, sensation, perception, memory, association, discrimination and generalization, etc.

(c) Emotional development: Under this aspect, starting with the basic instinct, the evolution of various emotions takes place and also the emotional behaviour is developed to the point of emotional maturity.

(d) Moral or Character development: Moral or character development includes the evolution of moral sense and development of character. The individual develops his ethical and moral codes.

(e) Social development: Initially the child is selfish and antisocial. Gradually he is developed into a social being by learning to behave according to the rules and norms of his society and makes adjustment to it.

(f) Language development: It includes the learning of the language for communication and the development of various skills and abilities for the effective use of language.

FACTORS INFLUENCING DEVELOPMENT

Right from the conception, the beginning of life in the womb of the mother, the growth and development of the human beings is influenced by a variety of factors categorized broadly as internal and external. Let us try to throw light on these factors designated as internal and external.

Internal Factors

All those factors which lie within the individual are designated as internal factors. They may include the following.

1. Heredity Factors
2. Biological or Constitutional Factors

3. Intelligence
4. Emotional Factors
5. Social Nature.

Let us discuss the influence of these internal factors on the growth and development of the children.

1. *Heredity Factors:* Heredity factors play their part at the time of the conception of the child in the womb of the mother. What is transferred to the offspring from the immediate parents in the form of genes and chromosomes at this time constitutes the hereditary contribution. This contribution is the real starting point and base of all the growth and development that take place later in the life of the child. It is like a starting capital for one's later earning from the environmental opportunities or a base for the structure of one's total personality. The height, weight, colour of the eyes, colour of the skin, the characteristics of the hair, etc. are just decided by these hereditary influences. The physical structure, nervous system and other things related with one's constitutional make-up, body chemistry and physical development are to a great extent, decided by the hereditary factors. Hereditary factors infact as emphasized earlier, lay the foundation and it is the quality of this foundation which is helpful in the future growth and development. If hereditary contributions are satisfactory then with meagre efforts of the environment forces, we can expect the satisfactory results. However in case hereditary contribution is quite meager then we have to make tremendent efforts for achieving the desired success in terms of the children's satisfactory growth and development.

2. *Biological or Constitutional Factors:* What one possesses in terms of his constitutional make up, somatic structure, physique and body chemistry influence his growth and development throughout one's life. Let us describe the impact of these factors in brief.

(i) The children who are physically weak or have internal disturbances within their physical organs can't be expected to achieve satisfactory result in terms of their normal physical growth and development. They usually suffer with illness and diseases which do not only hamper their progress in physical dimensions but also affect their growth and development in other dimensions-mental, social and emotional, etc.

(ii) The Nervous system which he inherits or gets along with him at any stage of his growth and development, affects his further growth and development in the cognitive dimension.

(iii) The endocrine or Ductless glands are the potent factors for affecting the growth and development of the individual from the very early age. The chemistry of the body is governed by these glands. Each of these glands secrete their own chemicals known as hormones. These hormones, directly poured into the blood stream, are circulated throughout the body. They influence all those tissues on which function of the body system, emotional actions and even thoughts depend and therefore, the functioning of the ductless glands exercise a great influence on various aspects — physical, social, mental, emotional and moral — of one's growth and development. For a balanced growth and development, the normal functioning of these glands is quite essential. In case, there is over activity or under activity on the parts of these glands, then it may yield to serious abnormality in one's growth and development. For example, pituitary gland imbalances may lead to quite abnormal increase in height.

(iv) Biological weak or defective constitutional make up like ugly face, short stature, deformities of the body, etc. may give birth to feelings of inferiority in the child. Moreover, he may face the adjustment problems in the social environment and consequently he may lag behind in the race of growth and development pertaining to various aspects of his personality make up.

3. *Intelligence:* Intelligence, as the ability to learn, adjust and take the right decision at the right time has a significant correlation with the overall growth and development of the children. It affects their social behaviour, moral judgement and emotional make up. An intelligent person is said to exercise reasonable control over his emotions, and is found to carry on well with his personal and social adjustment. In this way, physical, social, emotional, moral and language development of the child is greatly influenced and controlled by the level of his intelligence. Besides this, the course of higher cognitive development is also travelled with the type of intelligence one possess initially with him for this purpose. We can't expect problem solving behaviour, creative, imaginative and inventive venture from a child having sub-normal intelligence.

4. *Emotional Factors:* Emotional factors like emotional adjustability and maturity play a big role in influencing one's overall growth and development. The children who are found to be overwhelmed with negative emotions like fear, anger, jealousy, etc. are adversely affected in terms of their normal physical, mental, social, moral and language development. If one can't exercise a reasonable control over his emotions, he is sure to suffer in terms of his growth and development. He will have to face difficulty in his social adjustment. He may find himself failure in doing some serious mental activity. He may spoil his physical and mental health on account of his bad temperament and abnormal emotional outburst.

5. *Social Nature.* One's socialization helps him in achieving adjustment and advancement in other aspects of his growth and development. He may learn from his environment more on account of his social nature and it may prove a boon to him for his proper growth and development.

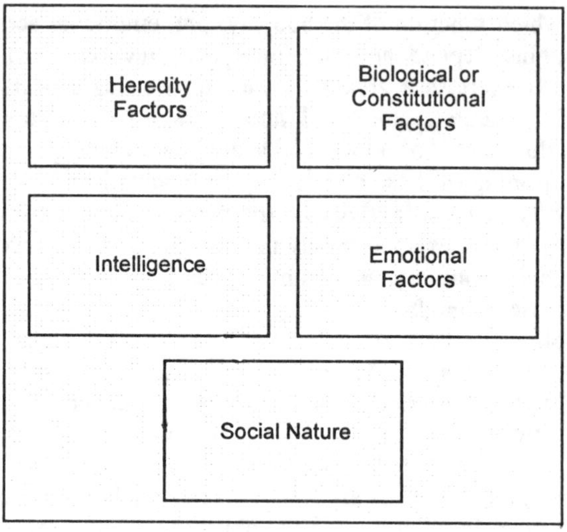

Fig. 4.1: Internal Factors Influencing Development

External Factors

The factors lying outside the individual in his environment are said to be the external factors for influencing his growth and development. They begin their role of influencing one's growth and development just after one's conception in the womb of his mother. They may include the following:

A. Environment available in the womb of the mother: What is available to the child for his care and nourishment in the womb of the mother from the time of the conception till birth is quite important from the angle of one's growth and development. A few mentionable things or factors associated with this period may be cited as below:

- The physical and mental health of the mother during pregnancy.
- Single child or multiple children getting nourishment in the womb.
- The quality and quantity of nutrition received by the embryo within the womb of the mother.
- Whether or not the embryo has been subjected to harmful radiation or rays etc.
- Normal or abnormal delivery.
- Any damage or accident to the child in the womb.

B. Environment available after birth: What one gets from the different conditions and forces of one's environment after his birth influence his growth and development in so many ways. These conditions and environmental forces may be described as below:

1. *Accidents and incidents of life:* The growth and development of an individual is greatly influenced by the good and bad incidents and accidents which one happens to meet in his life time. Sometimes a small injury or incident may change the entire development course of the individual. For

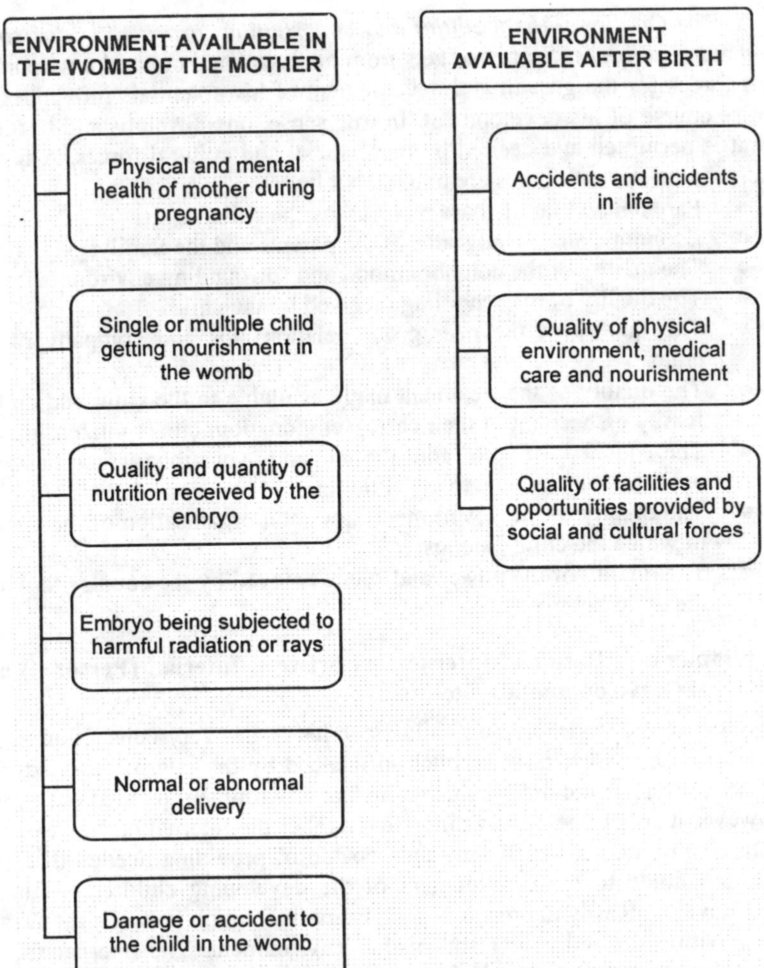

Fig. 4.2: External Factors Influencing Development

example, if nervous system gets a set back it will affect the mental development of the child and in turn it will affect his development in other dimensions — social, emotional, moral and physical.

2. *The Quality of physical environment, medical care and nourishment.* One's growth and development is greatly influenced by the quality of physical environment, medical care and nourishment available to him for his living and working. It may demand open space, balanced diet, good living and working conditions, proper timely medical care, etc. One will achieve the heights of his growth and development to the tune of the proper availability of these things.

3. *The Quality of the facilities and opportunities provided by the social and cultural forces:* What one gets from his social and cultural environment and forces for the growth and development of his potentials influences the entire course of his development. In true sense, one develops and becomes what is permitted and desired by these social and cultural forces. A few of such conditions and forces are pointed out below:

- Parental and family care received by the child.
- Economic and social status of the parents and the family.
- The quality of the neighbourhood and surrounding environment.
- The quality of the schooling received by the child.
- The quality of the peer group relationships and company of the child.
- The quality of the treatment made available to the child and child's family on account of their caste, religion, domicile or citizenship.
- The quality of the educational and vocational facilities and opportunity available to the children.
- The quality of the government, laws and organisation of the society to which the child belongs.
- The quality of the power and status enjoyed by the country to which the child belongs.

Development a Result of Interactions between Internal (Personal) and External (Environmental) Factors

Development of a developing child since his or her very conception in the womb of the mother is very much influenced by the internal and external factors present in the individual and his/her environment pointed out above. However it should be clearly noted that neither the internal nor the external factors can alone are sufficient and capable of providing needed direction and magnitude to the development of the developing children. Actually, their development is the result of a constant interaction between the factors lying within the individual and his/her environment. The internal factors belonging to the individual child provides him a solid base for getting benefitted from what is available for him in the internal environment available in the womb of the mother just after his conception. After birth the external environment available for him in the care and nourishment, physical, social and cultural environment, provides the child opportunities, direction and magnitude for taking his or her development — physical, mental, social, emotional, moral and language to the maximum height. One progresses and develops to the extent of the results or outcomes reached through the constant interaction of the factors lying in him and his environment.

RELATIONSHIP BETWEEN DEVELOPMENT AND LEARNING

Both development and learning co-exist and influence each other in the following ways:

A. Learning and Development

Learning may prove quite helpful in bringing desired development in the various aspects and dimensions of the personality of the growing children. As definition we term learning as a process of bringing desired modification or changes in the behaviour of a learner through experience or training. As a result of learning thus desired changes in the behaviour (cognitive, conative and affective) may take place at one time or the other among the learners and it may result in bringing desired development in the physical, mental, emotional, social linguistic and moral aspects or dimensions of their personality. Let us try to elaborate this assertion.

1. *Learning helps in child's physical and motor development:* Learning in the form of acquiring formal and informal experiences helps a child in his adequate physical and motor development by equipping him with necessary knowledge, skills, habits, interest and attitudes helpful in

(i) maintaining good physical health

(ii) acquiring necessary motor skills and practices for his physical movement, exercising and body fitness.

(iii) taking necessary preventive and curative measures for the protection from the diseases and environmental abnormalities.

(iv) acquiring healthy food and living habits contributing towards proper physical and motor development.

2. *Learning helps in proper mental and cognitive development:* One's mental and cognitive development includes the development of one's mental or cognitive abilities and capacities in a proper functional way. These abilities or capacities may be named as thinking and reasoning power, power of imagination and memorization, ability to analyse, synthesise and conclude ability to discriminate and critically examine or evaluate, ability of taking decision and judgement, power of argumentation and reaching on consent or agreement etc. These are not inherited but are acquired through the deliberate formal experiences or informal experiences (called learning) by an individual in his life.

3. *Learning helps in proper social development:* A child as we know is quite self-centered and unsocial in the beginning of his life but as he acquires and gathers various learning experiences he becomes necessarily mature in terms of his social development. The learning experiences received by him at his home, neighbourhood, school and various other encounters in social situations make him to acquire necessary social virtues, habits, interests and attitudes helpful in his proper social development.

4. *Learning helps in proper emotional development:* Emotional development of an individual asks for attaining a reasonable level of emotional maturity on his part. One must be able to express his or her emotions in a proper amount in a proper way at the proper period and place. Decidedly the acquisition of this ability is not an inherited phenomenon, it is acquired and developed properly through a number of formal and informal experiences called learning in one's life time.

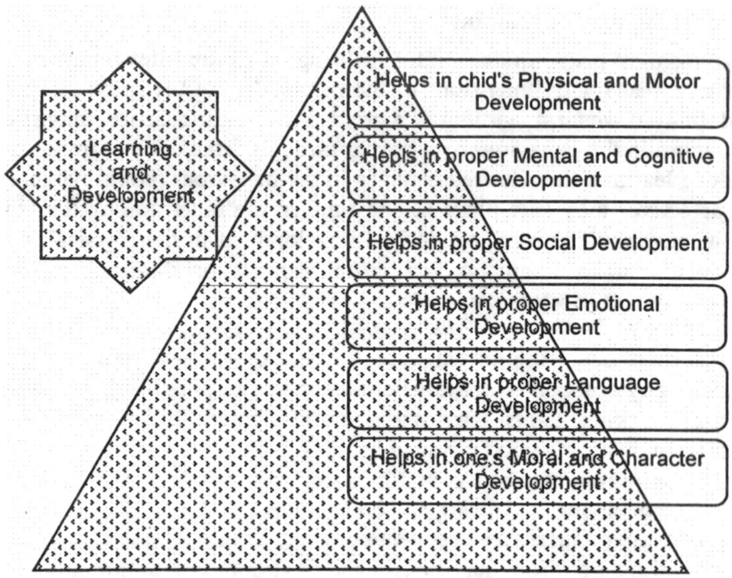

Fig. 4.3: Relationship between Learning and Development

5. *Learning helps in one's proper language development:* The language we speak, or use in our communication in a variety of ways is mainly acquired through a number of informal and formal experiences called learning. We get skilled and competent in the use of one or the other languages to the extent of expertise acquired us by our efforts in learning and using that language. So what a child at a particular age has with him in terms of his language skill is an entire product of his learning or acquired behaviour, rather than a function of his hereditary characteristics.

6. *Learning helps in one's moral or character development:* Morality or character as we know is fashioned or shaped as a result of various experiences or encounters, an individual receives in his life time. No genes and chromosomes are responsible for the character formation in a good or bad way. It is an entirely environmental phenomenon and thus necessarily a product of the formal or informal experiences called learning. By providing desirable learning experiences, we can certainly help a child in the development of morality or character in a desirable ways.

In this way, whatever may be the direction and dimension of one's development, the learning experiences in a formal or informal way essentially help him in reaching the desired maturity level of his development.

B. Development and Learning

One's learning is equally influenced and affected through his level of development in one or the other aspects or dimensions — physical, motor, mental, social, emotional, linguistic and moral of his development. Let us try to examine the nature of these influences in relation to various developmental dimensions.

(*i*) *Physical-Motor development and Learning:* Learning of many physical and motor skills is very much dependent upon the level of maturity earned in terms of one's physical and motor development. One can't learn or practice many of the physical games and can't participate in sports activities unless he or she has attained the desired level of one's physical and motor development. Similarly, learning many of the tasks needing physical and manual labour can't be undertaken properly by an individual unless he enjoys a good level of physical health, motor coordination and physical development.

(*ii*) *Mental or cognitive development and Learning:* Learning and acquisition of knowledge and skills related to various areas or aspects of school curriculum as well as tasks and activities related to living one's life in a desired way depends very much on the level of maturity and development possessed by an individual in his life. While studying the pattern of cognitive development of the children in their development period Piaget well concluded that children belonging to sensori motor, pre-operational, concrete operational and formal operation stages are capable only to learn and acquire well the knowledge and skills fitting properly in their level of cognitive development. As a result, we can't expect from the little children to grasp the abstract concept and learn difficult cognitive skills and definitely have to wait for their desired level of mental maturity for teaching the abstract concept and complex cognitive skills.

(*iii*) *Social Development and Learning:* Learning of a child is very much facilitated and helped through a desired level of social development attained by the developing child. According to Albert Bandura, much of the children's learning is very much carried out through the mechanism of social learning. Many of the behaviours involving one or the other knowledge area, skills and interests are learned by the children through observation, initiation and practice of the observed behaviour. Social company and social interaction, in view of the social constructivists like Vygotsky and Bruner helps much the children in learning so many things by constructing the knowledge in the company and guidance of their elders, knowledgeable peers and teachers. It can only happen well when a child is able to attain a desired level of his social maturity and development and that is why social development of a child is said to be very much iinked with the tasks and responsibilities of his learning.

(*iv*) *Emotional Development and Learning:* A child's emotional development is very much linked with the tasks of his learning. One can learn well when he is found well in tune with his emotional adjustment and emotional development. We can't expect any good learning on the part of a student who is passing under the current of intensive anger, fear, jealousy, envy, hate, joy and excitement. He must be able to exercise proper control

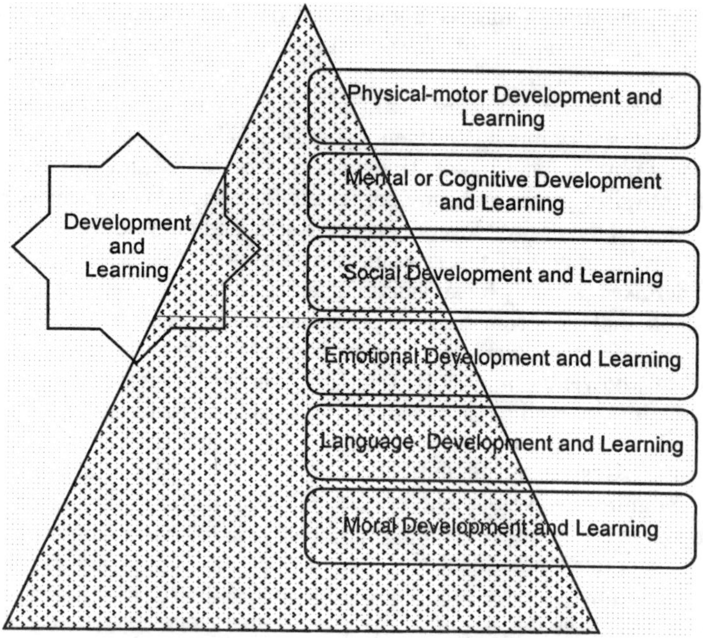

Fig. 4.4: Relationship between Development and Learning

over the aroused emotions not only at the time of his learning and practising but also at the time of the evaluation of his achievements and performances. Decidedly it can happen well only after imbibing a proper level of emotional maturity and emotional development.

(*v*) *Moral Development and Learning:* The processes and products of learning are very much affected and influenced through one's level of character or moral development. The sincerity, punctuality, duty boundness, honesty, truthfulness, respect for other's opinion, faith in cooperation and collaboration, team spirit, etc. the qualities and virtues that are the part and parcel of a man of character prove quite effective as well as instrumentalism carrying out a learning process on a proper line. The students who are morally deviant or ill conceived are found to resort to foul means in carrying out their processes of learning. They play truancy and resort to excuses at the time of learning and cheat at the time of examination and hence fail to learn or acquire well for their proper development and progress. On the other hand morally sound and mature students may be seen to demonstrate a desired level of progress in their learning and progress.

(*vi*) *Language Development and Learning:* Art of communication is the key of learning. One who can grasp and understand well what to be learned, and can communicate or use the outcomes of his learning in a proper way is always adjudged as a good learner and productive citizen. This can only be possible if one's task of learning is properly matched with the level of the communication language used in the process of one's teaching and learning. The students who lags behind in terms of their proper language development (especially in the language to be employed for their learning and classroom teaching) are found to experience difficulties and lag behind in their studies.

In this way, we can see that a child's development in relation to his various developmental dimensions is very much responsible for influencing and affecting his task of learning or acquiring one or the other types of knowledge, skills, interests, values or attitudes. He needs a harmonious, all round holistic development of his personality in relation to various aspects or dimensions of his development for his adequate progress in the task of learning and going ahead well in the journey of his life. Here the question may arise how the task of helping the child is seeking his holistic development may be carried out by a teacher? Let us think in this direction.

Facilitating Holistic Development (for Self and Society)

Holistic Development is characterized with such a development of a developing child in which development is carried out in a well balanced manner in the aspects or dimensions of his development aiming for the proper welfare of his self and the society. It needs to adopt a holistic approach for arranging suitable teaching-learning experiences and plan for the holistic education of the developing children. The things like below may prove quite helpful in arranging such education to the children.

1. *Setting Holistic Aims:* The aims and objectives of the teaching-learning process and programs of school education should be set in such a manner as to cater the need of facilitating holistic development. All the aspects or dimensions of child's development should be equally emphasized leaving no scope of neglecting or promoting one aspect at the cost of others.

2. *Developing a holistic curriculum and programs of school education:* For realizing the aims of a holistic education, the school curriculum involving scholastic and non-scholastic programs should be so chalked out as to provide maximum help for the development of the children in a desired holistic way. Subjects and activities, programs and projects etc. should be so chosen as to facilitate proper holistic development of the children.

3. *Adopting holistic approach in the implementation of the Curriculum and School Programs:* All the necessary means and ways in an holistic way should be called for the proper implementation of the holistic curriculum and programs of school education by taking care of the needed men-material resources. There should be enough variety in the adoption of teaching-learning methods, strategies and individualized or collaborative approaches for providing adequate learning experiences to the developing children for their wholesome and holistic development. Co-curricular activities and non-scholastic programs helpful in the proper holistic

development of the children should be given enough weightage along with the curricular or scholastic activities going on in the school. The children should be provided all initiation and incentives for the realization of their self, construction of the knowledge and expression to their creative and inventive talents. Attempts should also be properly made for imbibing among them the necessary social virtues and urge to contribute significantly towards the welfare of the society. Their holistic development then should necessarily involve the urge to think about the welfare of other and the society in addition to the development and welfare of their self.

4. *Adopting holistic approach towards evaluation:* Evaluation is said to be a controlling key for all what is done in the name of teaching-learning and programs in the school education. Decidedly therefore, earnest attempts should be made to adopt holistic approach in evaluating the outcomes of a holistic education planned for the holistic development of the children. The learning and behavioural outcomes springing in all the developmental dimensions (physical, mental, social, emotional, moral, linguistic and aesthetic) and behavioural domains (conative, affective and cognitive) should be properly assessed and evaluated by taking into consideration a variety of suitable evaluation measures, tools and techniques.

The task of facilitating holistic development of the developing children then needs the active involvement and cooperation of all the stake holders. The educational authorities, school administration, teachers, students and parents should join their hands in planning and implementing the necessary measures for holistic development of the new generation. Teachers have to orient and develop themselves in the capacity to cater to the needs of holistic education and learners have to take all initiative and efforts for doing all what is needed for their wholesome and holistic development by realizing well the importance of holistic development for the welfare of their self and the society.

5

Dimensions of Individual Development

INTRODUCTION

As we know our life starts right from our conception about nine months before our birth in the womb of our mothers. The process of development thus actually starts in the human beings in the womb of the mother. The development taking place in the womb of the mother for nearly nine months is termed as pre-natal development and after birth it is named as post-natal development. It occurs in all the aspects or dimensions of one's personality — physical, intellectual or mental, emotional, social and spiritual or moral at all the stages — pre-natal, infancy, childhood, adolescence, adulthood, old age etc. However, from the educational point of view, we are here in this text are least concerned with the developmental processes going on in the human beings at the pre-natal, adulthood and old age. Therefore, in the chapter we would like to take note of the general pattern of development in human beings at the stages of infancy, childhood and adolescence. Let us begin with the development taking place in the physical dimensions of one's personality.

PHYSICAL DEVELOPMENT

Meaning of the Term Physical Development

Physical growth and development refers to a process which brings bodily and physiological changes — internal as well as external — in an organism from the conception till his death. Generally these changes take place in the following dimensions:

(*i*) *In his gross physical structure or physique.* It involves changes in terms of height, weight, body proportions and general physical appearance.

(*ii*) *In his internal organs.* It involves changes in the functioning of glands, nervous system and other body systems — circulatory, respiratory, digestive, muscular, lymphatic and reproductive.

The process of physical development plays a significant role in the proper adjustment and progress of an organism. In the beginning the infant is quite helpless. He depends upon his parents and other members of the family for the satisfaction of his bodily needs. As a result of the changes brought by physical growth and development, his body organs become adaptable to his increasing body needs and gradually he is developed into a mature responsible adult.

The General Pattern of the Physical Growth in Human Beings

Although there are wide individual differences among the human beings and therefore, it is not possible to describe a perfect general pattern of the growth and development, yet physical growth and development seems to follow, to some extent, a general pattern which can help us to think about some definite structural changes in the case of normal children at each stage of their growth and development.

Below we try to summarize this general pattern of growth and development along with definite structural changes.

(1) *Increase in Height and Weight:* On the average, at birth a baby is about 19 or 20 inches in height and between 7 and 8 pounds in weight, boys being slightly taller and heavier. During the first two years, there is rapid increase in both height and weight. There is a steady and slower growth from the third year till the on-set of puberty. By five years the height of the child, approximately, becomes almost doubled and he acquires almost five times his birth weight. During the period of adolescence we again find a sudden increase in both height and weight. Girls reach puberty about a year or two earlier than boys do. Therefore, between the age of 12 to 14 they are found slightly taller and heavier than boys. But they are again surpassed by the boys. By the end of adolescence, the young men are generally higher and heavier than the young women. Generally both men and women get their maximum height and weight upto the end of adolescence. But there are very much variations in weight as it is more susceptible to environmental influences. Therefore, it is no surprise to note the sudden increase or decrease in weight in later years after attaining maturity.

Weight of the brain increases rapidly in the early years of life. By the time the child completes the age of four his brain gains almost 80 per cent of its final weight, another 10 per cent being added by the time he completes his eight years. By the 20th year, the brain gains almost all its weight.

Age	*Height (in cms)*		*Average Weight (in kgms)*	
	Girls	*Boys*	*Girls*	*Boys*
Below 3 months	55.0	56.2	4.2	4.5
3 months	60.9	62.7	5.6	6.7
6 months	64.4	64.9	6.2	6.9
9 months	66.7	69.5	6.6	7.4
1 year	72.5	73.9	7.8	8.4
2 years	80.1	81.6	9.6	10.1
3 years	87.2	88.8	11.2	11.8
4 years	94.5	96.0	12.9	13.5

Age	*Height (in cms)*		*Average Weight (in kgms)*	
	Girls	*Boys*	*Girls*	*Boys*
5 years	101.4	102.1	14.5	14.8
6 years	107.4	108.5	16.0	16.3
7 years	112.8	113.9	17.6	18.0
8 years	118.2	119.8	19.4	19.7
9 years	122.9	123.7	21.3	21.5
10 years	128.4	124.4	23.6	23.5
11 years	133.6	133.4	26.4	25.9
12 years	139.6	138.3	29.8	28.5
13 years	143.9	144.6	33.3	32.1
14 years	147.5	150.1	36.8	35.7
15 years	149.6	155.5	38.8	39.6
16 years	151.0	159.5	41.4	43.2
17 years	151.5	161.4	42.4	45.7
18 years	151.7	163.1	42.4	47.4
19 years	151.7	163.4	42.4	48.1

Source: Growth and Development of Indian infants and children, Technical Report series No. 18, Indian Council of Medical Research, 1972.

(2) *Changes in body proportions:* The child does not only grow in size but also shows a marked change in the proportion of the different parts of the body. For example, the head constitutes about one-fourth the height of the body at birth, its size is relatively much larger than the arms and legs. As the child grows older, the proportion of the head decreases and by the end of adolescence it becomes one eighth of the body. In addition to head, the other body parts, legs, arms, torso, etc. also show change in proportions as the child requires them more and more in his adaptation to coming life.

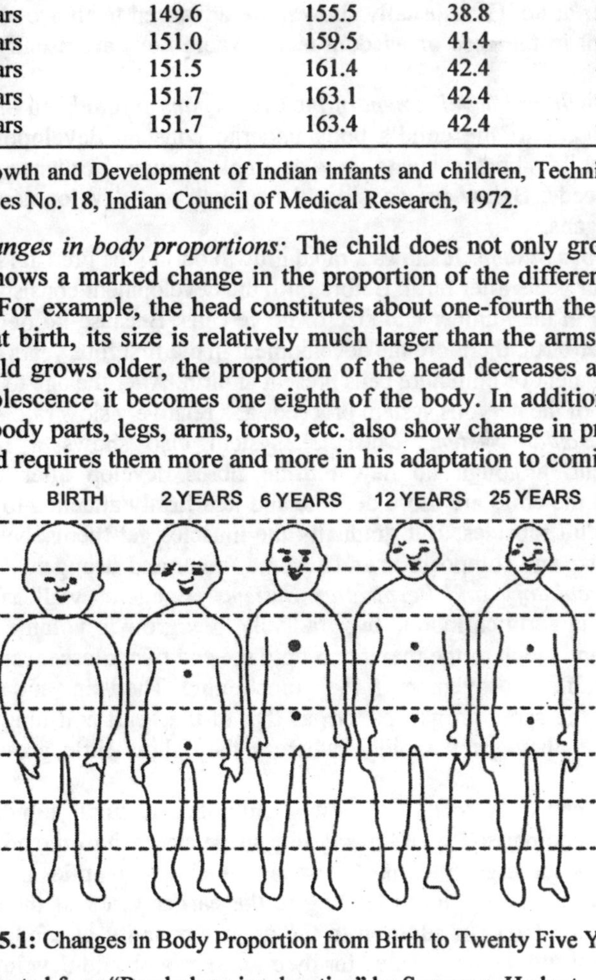

Fig. 5.1: Changes in Body Proportion from Birth to Twenty Five Years

Source: Adapted from "Psychology in education" by Sorenson, Herbert.

(3) *Anatomical growth and development:* The bones of a child are not smaller in size than the bones of an adult, but they differ also in composition. The child's bones contain, relatively, a great amount of water and smaller quantity of mineral matter than do those of the adult. They are more soft and more blood flows through them than through the bones of an adult. This accounts for their greater flexibility. But it also increases the chances of bones deformities and infection.

As regards the eruption of teeth, it has been found that most of the children acquire their milk teeth by the time they are two years of age. Near the end of the fifth year, the permanent teeth begin to appear the growth of which acquires a long time. The last four of the permanent teeth, the wisdom teeth, erupt between the age of seventeen and twenty five years, if they appear at all. Girls usually show more advanced teeth growth than the boys except in the case of wisdom teeth, where boys are usually ahead of the girls.

(4) *Growth and development of internal organs:* From birth onward, the internal organs of the child's body undergo constant development. As a result the child's body systems show desirable change in order to satisfy the growing needs. Below we consider the growth and development of these internal organs.

(*i*) *Nervous System:* It shows a rapid growth during the prenatal period and the first four years after birth. Before birth the development consists primarily of increase in the number and size of nerve cells. Because no new cells are formed after birth, therefore the development in the first four years consists of the development of immature cells present at birth. After the age of four years the growth of the nervous system proceeds at a relatively slow rate.

(*ii*) *Muscular System:* Muscular system also shows a remarkable development, although no new muscle fibres develop after birth. The muscles of the child are more delicate and less firmly attached to the bones than are adult muscles. But gradually the muscles get themselves changed in shape, size and composition and become firmer and stronger.

(*iii*) *Circulatory and Respiratory Systems:* Lungs as well as heart are very small in early childhood but gradually they grow in volume as well as in weight and reach to the maximum upto the end of adolescence. They also show desirable improvement in their functioning. The veins and arteries do not follow the same growth pattern as that of the heart and lungs. Prior to adolescence, they grow rapidly, whereas they show little growth during adolescence.

(*iv*) *Digestive System:* The young child has a small tubular shaped stomach in comparison with the bag like shape stomach of the adults which not only holds a large amount of food but which also empties more slowly. Therefore they require more feeding in the earlier years of their life than they will need later. In addition to the greater quantity of food, they need food with essential energy value for their rapid growth and development.

(*v*) *Lymphatic System:* It is involved in the elimination of waste and the destruction of bacteria in the body. From birth onward this system shows the sign of rapid development until it reaches to its maximum between the age of 11 and 12 years, when the death rate is about the lowest. After 12 years it decreases rapidly.

(*vi*) *Reproductive System:* The development of sex organs shows a peculiar trend in contrast with the overall growth and developmental pattern. Their rate of development is very slow during early childhood but picks up its speed as the child advances towards adolescence and becomes almost developed upto the end of adolescence.

The minute observation of the above mentioned pattern can reveal the following important facts regarding the general trend of physical growth and development:

1. It is very rapid from birth to the age of two or three years.
2. Then, it continues at a diminished rate till the beginning of adolescence.
3. The first three years of adolescence are marked as the years of rapid growth and development.
4. This is followed by a period of slow growth and development to the time of maturity.

Factors Affecting Physical Development of Human Beings

The physical growth and development of an individual is conditioned by both heredity and environment. Some of the important hereditary and environmental factors which influence the process of physical growth and development are:

1. The traits and characteristics inherited at the time of conception.
2. Single birth or multiple births.
3. The physical as well as mental health of the mother during pregnancy.
4. Nutrition received by the embryo within the womb of the mother.
5. Normal or abnormal delivery.
6. Conditions and care at the time of delivery.
7. Look after of the baby and its mother.
8. Nutrition received by the child after birth.
9. Presence or absence of physical defects.
10. The living conditions — physical, social and cultural.
11. The opportunities of recreation, self expression, play and exercise.
12. Presence or absence of illness and diseases.
13. Emotional and social adjustment of the child.
14. Adequate or inadequate rest and sleep.
15. Proper or improper medical care.

Importance of Physical Development and its Educational Significance

All the developmental aspects — physical, intellectual, emotional, social, moral, etc. are closely interlinked. The development of any one of these aspects affects the development of the other. Physical growth and development is not an exception. Certainly, it influences the development in other directions. For example, development of the nervous system influences the development of intellectual powers. Emotional and social adjustment is also linked with physical development. While the children having normal physical development are accepted by their age group, the physical deviates — who are very small, very large, too fat or too thin, etc. — remain isolated. They are often nicknamed, ridiculed and denied participation in the play and recreational activities enjoyed by their age associates. It brings serious maladjustment and personality problems. The young child is intelligent enough to become aware of the fact that he differs in appearance and physical abilities from other children. His attitude towards self is injured and self confidence is shaken. In this case either he becomes shy and timid or becomes aggressive in order to compensate for his inferiority feelings.

Moreover upon the balanced development of the internal as well or external organs depends the balanced functioning of the body systems. The functioning of the body systems decides the interest, attitude and the total behaviour of an individual. For example, glands and their functioning affect his emotional behaviour to a great extent. Similarly his anatomical development, the development of circulatory, respiratory systems, etc. give the person the required abilities for participating in various motor activities.

In this way physical development influences the total make-up of an individual and thus needs a very careful attention. It can help the teachers to achieve one of the most important aims of the educational process — to bring an all round balanced development in the personality of the child. Therefore the knowledge of the process of physical growth and development is very essential for a teacher. Specifically it can serve him in the following ways:

1. He can be aware of the physical deviates, their psychology and problem of adjustment. Consequently he can help them in their social and emotional adjustment as well as in school learning.

2. The children are the back bone of a nation's strength. Their health and proper physical development is an asset to the progress of the country. Our schools have to play decisive role in the task of physical welfare of children. The teacher with the knowledge of physical developmental process can render valuable help in this direction.

3. Needs, desires, interests, attitudes and in a way the over all behaviour of an individual is controlled, to a great extent, by his physical development. Therefore at a particular age level what would be the expected behaviour of the child of that age group can be estimated through the

physical growth and developmental pattern. For example, with the study of the trend of the physical development in adolescence, one can be aware of their growing physical, emotional and social needs. Accordingly, adolescents can be helped by the teacher in the adjustment to their rapid development and changes»

4. Study of the pattern of physical development helps us in knowing what can be expected normally from the children at a particular age level. In turn it can help us to arrange school programmes like curricular and co-curricular experiences, methods and techniques of teaching, time-table, text-books, aid material, seating arrangement and learning environment, etc.

In this way we can see that the knowledge of the process of the physical development helps the teacher in the realization of his objectives. By its knowledge, he does not only become equipped for setting his programmes according to the needed requirements of his students but can also help them in improving their health and attaining proper physical strength and abilities.

INTELLECTUAL OR MENTAL DEVELOPMENT

In the previous discussion we have seen how the mechanism of physical growth and development brings desirable changes in the internal as well as external body organs of an individual in order to increase his physical skill and strength. Due to this development he becomes able to do physical work and to play games he could not, when younger. Similarly, the child at the time of his birth or in early childhood cannot be expected to perform such tasks that require high mental abilities. As he advances in his age, his mental abilities and capacities gradually get developed and he becomes able to solve the problems he could not when younger. *The growth and development of the mental abilities and capacities which helps an individual to adjust his behaviour to the ever changing environmental conditions or to enable him to accomplish a task that needs complex cognitive abilities is referred to as mental or intellectual development.*

Actually, the process of the mental growth and development is responsible for the development of an individual's all cognitive, mental or intellectual abilities like sensation, perception, imagination, memory, reasoning, understanding, intelligence, generalization, interpretation, language ability, conceptual ability, problem solving ability and decision making ability, etc. These abilities are interrelated and never develop in isolation. Therefore, mental development of an individual at any stage of his development, includes the overall development of these abilities.

Growth and Development in Various Areas or Aspects of Mental Development

As said above, mental or intellectual development takes into consideration, the development of various mental abilities and capacities. How these abilities grow and develop from birth onwards is an interesting as well as useful thing to know. Though the development in the areas of various abilities proceeds simultaneously and is continuous yet the studies have revealed possibility of the differences in the rate of overall mental development at various ages. Similarly, it has been also noted that there is a possibility of greater growth and development in one aspect or area of mental activity than in other at one or the other stage of life.

As far as the general characteristics or trend of mental growth and development at various stages is concerned we will be discussing it in Chapter 6 and 7 of this text. However, in the following pages we will try to discuss the changes and development in some of the important mental abilities or aspects of mental power of a small child as he grows older and older.

(1) *Sensation and perception:* Both sensation and perception are considered important aspects of one's mental development. Sensations are elementary impressions gathered by sense organs. When these impressions are interpreted and some definite meanings are attached to them, they take the form of perception.

In the beginning, the child lacks in sensation as well as in perception. His sense organs are not developed. As a result, he cannot discriminate between things and understand their meanings. Focussing of the eye towards the lamp, bright coloured objects, etc. can be said a beginning of an infant's perceptual growth. Later on, he distinguishes people from objects and then familiar people from strangers and in this way his environment, gradually becomes differentiated into perceived objects. These perceived objects become later on associated with a verbal sound that he can recognize when heard.

When he becomes able to use his sense organs, he becomes increasingly conscious of the things around him and begins, to ask a series of questions such as why, what and who. At this time he has a poor perception of space, time, form, movement and distance. For example, due to lack of perception of the size of distant objects, the train, when viewed from a distance, may appear to him as a toy train.

But gradually, his ability of perception gets developed. As the individual passes through the years of his adolescence, the sensory acuity reaches almost to its peak and perceptual pattern become most organized and refined. His perceptions now become more definite, rich and detailed. They are now beginning to be influenced by his beliefs, opinions, ideals, etc., besides his needs, interests and mental sets. They now need not be associated necessarily with concrete objects.

(2) *Concept formation:* Acquisition of concept is another important aspects of the child's mental development. A concept is the generalized meaning that is attached to an object or idea. It is the result of one's perceptual experiences and involves both discrimination and generalization.

Discrimination begins early in life. Sometimes after the child tries to generalise his perceptual experiences and thus begins to acquire concepts. Experience is a great factor in concept formation. In early childhood, the concrete experiences in the form of actual objects help the child in the formation of concepts. He tries to develop various concepts from direct experiences.

In the later period, vicarious experiences offered by reading, movies, lectures, etc., also provide the base for concept formation. In the later years, it is not such that only new concepts are formed, the old concepts may also get a new shape. They may be broadened, developed or the wrong concepts can be altogether abandoned. Normally, in developing, concepts go from concrete to abstract, from vague to clear and from inexact to definite, depending on the type of experiences one receives as one grows older and older.

In this way the concepts of the child in the beginning are characterized by vagueness, indefiniteness and inadequacy. For example, the child has very poor time concepts. As Crow and Crow put it, *"Time as such means little to the young child. He cannot distinguish among 'today', 'tomorrow' and 'next week' except as they represent words rather than actual duration of time." (1968, p. 73)*

Similarly his concepts of spatial relations, distance and depth are very vague and inadequate in the beginning. Gradually, as a result of learning and maturation, they become clear, specific and definite,

(3) *Development of language:* Development of language adds to the mental growth and development of an individual. The growth and development in speech, vocabulary, length of response are some of the important aspects of language development.

At birth the child can utter some crying sounds. By the age of one and little later he may learn to speak a few words. After that speaking vocabulary increases rapidly. Much of the speech pattern, that the child learns, is the result of imitation of others in the environment. During the course of learning to speak it is possible that certain speech disorders like omissions, stuttering, stammering, etc. may develop. Therefore the parents as well as the teachers of small children must remain very cautious about this.

The vocabulary of children in the beginning is too limited. There is continuous increase in the size of one's vocabulary during childhood. Later on as the result of environmental needs and opportunities in learning, the vocabulary goes on developing. Maintenance of the past and addition of the new words in one's vocabulary may continue even upto the period of old age depending upon their reading habits and interests.

In addition to the change in vocabulary and speech, the pattern of giving responses also changes with age. In the early childhood the child's responses are characterized by the one-word response. Also, generally, he uses more nouns than other forms of language. Later on, gradually, he begins to use descriptive words like adjectives and adverbs and his responses include a large variety of words and almost every form of sentence structure.

(4) *Development of memory:* Memory is also an important aspect of mental development. At birth, there is little memory; but gradually with maturation and experiences memory increases. The developmental schedule as discussed by Hurlock and Schwartz indicates that *"memory of an impressionistic kind appears in the first half of the year and instances of true remembrance appear by the end of the first year. During the first year memory is only aroused by sensory stimuli. With the learning of speech the child is able to remember ideationally by the end of the second year. During the first and second years, the memory is stronger for persons and objects than for situation. During early childhood, from 3 to 6 years, situations become significant factors in the child's memory. Also the emotional quality of the impressions influence memory. By 3 years the child can recount the story heard a few days ago and he can also give information about past experiences"* (1964, p. 98)

Therefore the child shows signs of memory from the early childhood. The memory which the child possesses in his young age, is generally a rote memory. He enjoys repetition and seldom uses logic and insight in memorizing a thing. During later childhood and adolescence the memory tends to function more logically and a selection process of remembering and forgetting begins to operate. In the later years of childhood memory tends to decrease. But from which age the downfall begins, it is difficult to say with certainty. It varies from individual to individual and generally besides the age and health, the situation and stimuli which are associated with a particular kind of memory affects significantly, its remembrance or forgetting.

(5) *Development of problem-solving ability:* Problem-solving ability is an important constituent of mental development. An individual needs this type of ability in discovering the solution of the problems faced by him. Both thinking and reasoning power are used in problem-solving. Therefore problem-solving ability depends upon the development of thinking and reasoning. Thinking and reasoning powers begin to grow as early as two and one half or three years. However reasoning at this stage is confined to concrete and personal things from the child's immediate environment. The younger child deals more easily with the concrete than with the abstract. We cannot expect from him to solve complicated problems which require abstract thinking and more developed reasoning. But, gradually, he shows an increase in the ability to deal with abstract as he grows in age. He begins to compare and evaluate the ideas and solve the problems through the utilization of verbal symbols and imaginary concepts.

It follows from this discussion that in the beginning children should be provided with the simple realistic problems depending on concrete situation and related to their own experiences and environment so that they can solve them with insight and understanding. With the increase in the age the more complicated problems requiring abstract thinking and widened experiences may be given to them. In this way, gradually, the children should be made to increase their problem-solving ability.

In addition to these aspects, the other aspects of mental growth and development include attention, imagination, decision making and ability of interpretation, etc. Like other aspects they also change, grow and mature with the increase in age due to maturation and learning.

Factors Affecting Mental Growth and Development

Mental growth and development is controlled by both the hereditary and environmental factors. An individual's mental abilities, at any age of his life, are the products of his heredity and environment. For the child what he gets from his ancestral stock through his immediate parents at the time of conception in terms of mental traits or characteristics and mental apparatus is in fact a valuable asset to his future mental growth and development. But the environment which he gets afterwards for the development of these innate mental abilities is no less significant. The social and cultural experiences, learning opportunities and education which he avails for the developmental process as he advances in age, contribute significantly towards his mental growth and development,

In fact, maturation and learning are responsible for controlling the process of mental growth and development. Maturation helps in achieving physical growth and development which in turn affects the process of mental growth and development. Brain and the nervous system play a significant role in this direction. At birth the brain and the nerves that lead to it, are not fully developed. They grow and develop rapidly after birth and get matured in due course. As the nervous system advances toward maturity, the mental powers of the child also go on developing. Therefore, organic growth of the nervous system is the basic factor in mental development.

Learning in the form of experiences and education helps the developmental process and in fact intensifies it to reach to its optimum level. It is said to play the same part as exercises play in developing physical skills and power as Sorenson puts *it — "A child's legs, arms and body are made stronger by healthful play. We can deduce that the mind with its organic counter-part, the nervous system, improves and becomes better equipped because of use and exercise in the form of reading, calculating, memorizing, speaking imagining and other mental activities."* (1948, p. 32)

Cessation of Mental Growth

At what age does the increase in mental growth cease is a controversial question. Mental growth is a complex process. There is no universal pattern of mental growth for all individuals. Neither is the pattern same for all mental functions or abilities. Therefore it is difficult to tell the age at which mental growth, with all its aspects, will cease to grow. Actually, the age of cessation of mental growth varies with different individuals and with different mental functions or abilities.

Psychologists have tried to give various ages ranging from thirteen to the early twenties or even much later as the age after which there is no further mental growth. The variation in the results is due to the fact that they have worked on the different groups and used different tests of mental ability. Despite such differences in opinion, Sorenson has tried to arrive on some conclusion regarding the age of cessation of mental growth. He writes:

> "It is probably safe to conclude that a person reaches his maximum mental level at about the age of twenty or perhaps a little before or a little after twenty —. It is true that on the average there is only a little mental growth during the late teens — nevertheless this small amount may be very important." (1948, p. 44)

Therefore the age of cessation of mental growth can be estimated as twenty or little before or a little after twenty. But now the question again arises: Does the development of mental capacity or power also cease with the cessation of mental growth at the age of about twenty?

In this connection latest researches have shown that the development in mental power and capacity does not necessarily stop with the cessation of mental growth. In most of the cases the mental power or capacity reaches its maximum in the mid of their thirties. But whatever changes after the natural mental growth occur in the mental abilities of capacities, are definitely the result of learning, experience and education. After attaining their maximum height, mental capacity declines gradually but can be maintained effectively even in the old age by those who keep their minds alert and active.

Mental Development and Education

The knowledge of the trend of mental growth and the subsequent changes in the various mental abilities is of great use for the teacher. Briefly, we can summarise this utility in the following way:

1. It can help him in the selection of curricular and co-curricular experiences at various age levels.
2. It can also help him to arrange learning situations, decide methods and techniques of teaching and the nature of the aid material for the illustration of his teaching.
3. It can also help him to bring appropriate books suiting to the intellectual growth and development of children at different age levels.
4. It makes him conscious that a particular type of work or activity which needs some or the other developed mental abilities, needs to be introduced when the age of acquiring that approaches. We must not be too hasty to give him a particular piece of knowledge of to train him in a particular act if the

mental abilities required for that knowledge or act have not yet been acquired by the child. Definitely, in such cases, we should wait for the ripe stage.

5. If he understands the pattern of mental growth, he can lead his students to acquire their maximum mental capacity and power. He can impart training in problem solving and creative expression. Also he can develop their logical understanding and take them to intelligent learning in place of mechanical fumbling and parrot-like cramming. Their ability of using language, perception and ability to interpret and generalization can also be developed through the natural course of their mental growth and development pattern.

In this way a teacher can lead his students to acquire their maximum mental capacities and powers and help them to use them intelligently and judiciously for the welfare of their own as well as of the society.

EMOTIONAL DEVELOPMENT

Emotional development is one of the major aspects of the human development. Emotions like love, anger, fear, etc. play a great role in the development of a child's personality. Not only his physical development is linked with his emotional makeup but his intellectual, social, moral and aesthetic development are also controlled by his emotional behaviour and experiences. The overall importance of emotional experiences in the life of a human being makes it quite essential to know about the emotions. What are these? What is their origin? How do they develop and influence the personality of the organism? What are the factors which are responsible for their proper or improper development and how can they be made more serviceable to the individuals and society? Let us try to think about these problems.

What are Emotions (Meaning of Emotion)

Etymologically the word 'emotion' is derived from the Latin word 'Emovere' which means 'to stir up', 'to agitate' or 'to excite'. Woodworth by making use of this explanation has defined emotion in the following way:

> "Emotion is a 'moved' or 'stirred-up' state of an organism. It is a stirred-up state of feeling that is the way it appears to the individual himself. It is a disturbed muscular and glandular activity — that is the way it appears to an external observer" (1945, p.410)

Crow and Crow have defined emotion in the following way:

> An emotion "is an effective experience that accompanies generalized inner adjustment and mental and psychological stirred-up states in the individual, and that shows itself in his overt behaviour". (1973, p. 83)

Mc Dougall considering instincts as an innate tendency maintains that all the specific human emotions are derived from instincts. According to him an instinctive behaviour has three aspects:

(i) Cognition (knowing)
(ii) Affection (feeling or experiencing an emotion)
(iii) Conation (doing or striving)

When a child sees a bull coming towards him, he experiences an instinctive behaviour and undergoes the above three processes. Firstly, he perceives the bull, secondly he experiences an emotion of fear and thirdly he tries to run away. Therefore he concludes that an emotion is an affective experience that one undergoes during an instinctive excitement. He discovered 14 basic instincts. Each and every emotion, whatever it may be is the product of some instinctive behaviour. These instincts with their associated emotions can be listed as:

Sl. No.	*Instinct*	*Emotion accompanying it*
1.	Flight or Escape	Fear
2.	Pugnacity or combat	Anger
3.	Repulsion	Disgust
4.	Curiosity	Wonder
5.	Parental	Tender emotion, Love
6.	Appeal	Distress
7.	Construction	Feeling of creativeness
8.	Acquisition	Feeling of ownership
9.	Gregariousness	Feeling of loneliness
10.	Sex, Mating	Lust
11.	Self-assertion	Positive self-feeling or Elation
12.	Food-seeking	Appetite
13.	Laughter	Amusement

From the above definitions and derivation of emotion we can conclude the following important information about emotion:

(1) *The emotional experiences are associated with some instincts or biological drives.* When the basic need is satisfied or challenged (the satisfaction is in danger), the emotions play their part.

(2) *In general, emotions are the product of perception:* The perception of a proper stimulus (object or situation) is needed to start an emotional experience. The organic changes within the body (favourable or unfavourable) may intensify the emotional experiences.

(3) *The core of an emotion is feeling,* which is essentially linked with some sort of impulsive act or urge to do. For the classification let us try to differentiate between feelings and emotions.

Actually every emotional experience, whatever it may be, involves feelings — things of the heart. Feelings and emotions both are affective experiences. There is only the difference of degrees. After perceiving a thing or situation, feelings like pleasure or displeasure can be aroused.

There may be some intensity or degree of strength in these feelings. When the feelings are so strong as enable to disturb the mind and can excite an individual to act immediately — they are turned into emotions. Therefore the urge to do or act (conative aspect) is the most important emotional experience.

(4) *Every emotional experience involves many physical and physiological changes in the organism:* Some of the changes which express themselves in overt behaviour are easily observable. Examples of such changes are the bulge of the eyes, the flush of the face, the flow of tears, the pulse rate, the beating of the heart, the choke in the voice, the fleeing from the situation or the attack on the emotion arousing stimulus. In addition to these easily observable changes there are internal physiological changes.

Examples of such changes are changes in the circulation of blood, the impact on digestive system and the changes in the functioning of some glands like adrenal glands etc.

These changes become so specific and distinguishable in the human being that a simple glimpse can enable us to detect a particular emotional experience in an individual and we can see whether he is in anger or suffers from fear etc.

In addition to the above characteristics the emotions have some more specific things to be told about. These are:

(i) Emotions are prevalent in every living organism,

(ii) They are present at all stages of development and can be aroused in young as well as in old.

(iii) Emotions are the most individual and they differ from person to person.

(iv) Same emotion can be aroused by a number of different stimuli — objects or situations.

(v) Emotions rise abruptly but die slowly. An emotion once aroused tends to persist and leaves behind emotional mood.

(vi) Emotions have the quality of displacement. The anger aroused on account of one stimulus gets transferred to other situation. The anger on account of the rebuking by boss is transferred in beating the children at home.

(vii) One emotion can give birth to a number of like-wise emotions.

(viii) There is a negative correlation between the upsurge of emotions and intelligence. Reasoning and sharp intellect provides a careful check on the sudden upsurge or emotions and on the other hand under emotional experiences the reasoning and thinking powers are decreased.

Kinds of Emotions

If we try to analyse the impact of various emotional experiences upon the well-being of an individual, we can come to the conclusion that the emotions have both positive as well as negative effects. Whether an emotion will prove to be helpful or harmful to an individual depends upon the following factors:

(i) the frequency and intensity of emotional experience.
(ii) the situation, occasion and the nature of stimulus which arouses the emotion.
(iii) kind of emotional experience or emotions.

The last factor — the kind of emotional experience — counts much in this direction. Emotions, in general, can be categorized into two kinds — Positive emotions and Negative emotions.

Unpleasant emotions like fear, anger, jealousy which are harmful to the individual's development are termed as negative emotions while the pleasant emotions like affection (love), amusement, curiosity, joy and happiness which are very helpful and essential to the normal development are termed as positive emotions.

By their nature of positiveness and negativeness it should not be assumed that all the positive emotions are always good and the negative emotions are bad. While weighing their impact, the other factors like the frequency and intensity, situations and the nature of stimuli should also be considered. Excess of everything is bad. Emotions with too much intensity and frequency, whether positive or negative bring harmful effects. On the other hand the so-called negative emotions are very essential for the human welfare. The emotion of fear prepares and individual to face the danger ahead. The child who has no emotion of fear is sure to get injured because he has not learnt to save himself against a possible danger.

Emotional Development during Different Stages of Development

Development, in general, applies to the changes brought about with the passage of time. Emotional development in this respect reflects the following changes:

(i) There is a gradual birth of different emotions in an individual since his birth.
(ii) There are changes in the conditions or nature of stimuli that arouse the child's emotions.
(iii) There are changes in the manner in which the child expresses his emotions.

In the light of these changes we will try to discuss the process of emotional development during different developmental stages.

Emotional Development during Infancy

1. From his very birth, the infant cries and his bodily movements seems to give evidence of the presence of emotional element in him. What are the specific emotions, if any, which he experiences at this stage is a difficult question to be answered.

2. Truely speaking, as Mrs. Hurlock puts it, *"At birth and shortly afterwards the first sign of emotional behaviour is general excitement to strong stimulation. There are no indications of clear cut, definite emotional patterns that can be recognized and identified as specific emotional states.* (1959, p. 216)

Thus, it is the stage of an undifferentiated excitement to any stimulus.

3. The stage of undifferentiated excitement is over in a very short time, when the general excitement becomes differentiated into simple responses that suggest pleasure and displeasure. The stimuli like sudden loud noise, wet, cold or hot objects applied to the baby's skin, feeling hungry and uncomfortable etc. bring unpleasant responses. The stimuli like sucking, patting, and warmth etc. bring pleasant responses.

4. The differentiation of general excitement into pleasant and unpleasant responses takes the following pattern according to Spitz:

> "During the first two months pleasure and displeasure come in response to 'physical' stimulation. By the third month, pleasure is aroused by 'psychological' stimulation as shown in the baby's smile in response to human face. Slightly later displeasure can be aroused by psychological as well as physical stimuli as may be seen in the baby's reaction to being left alone." (Hurlock, E.B., 1959, p. 217)

5. As said above, before the age of six months the emotional behaviour is expressed through pleasant and unpleasant responses, that is, there are only two emotions (distress and delight) up to this stage. When the infant completes his six months, the negative emotions take the lead and gradually in the coming months, fear, disgust, anger, jealousy all are distinguishable. Between the 10th and 12th months the positive emotions like elation, love, sympathy, enjoyment all enter in the field. Up to two years, as the study of Bridges conducted in 1931 shows almost all the emotions, positive as well as negative, take their shape and become quite distinguishable.

6. There is continuous variation in the manifestation of emotions during infancy. In the earlier months it is very difficulty to have distinction on the basis of facial expression and bodily positions. Only the mothers can determine the causes of her child's crying and yelling. Later on gradually they become distinguishable. Moreover in the earlier months of infancy the child reacts more violently to emotionally disturbing situations, but as the infant approaches childhood, his crying, yelling and the vigorous movements of the body parts become less and less violent. Gradually with increasing age there is an increase in linguistic responses and a decrease in motor responses.

Emotional Development during Childhood

As said above, almost all the emotions make themselves distinguishable up to the beginning of childhood. Therefore emotional development after the stage of infancy, concerns itself, only, to the changes in the nature of situations or stimuli arousing emotions and the changes in the expression of emotional experiences. We find the following changes in the child during childhood:

1. In infancy the child is only concerned with his own well-being. Therefore, the emotions are generally aroused by the conditions which are related with his immediate well-being. But as he grows, his world grows larger and he has to respond to a variety of stimuli. During childhood peer group relationship and school atmosphere and other environmental factors influence his emotional behaviour. His emotions get linked with the new experiences and interests and his emotional behaviour gets linked with the new stimuli. At the same time he does not react to various old stimuli. For example, he does not show anger at being dressed, or bathed, neither does he show any fear of strangers.

2. There is a remarkable change in the expression of emotional behaviour in infancy, this behaviour is usually dominated by too much intensity and is usually expressed through motor responses like crying, yelling etc. But in childhood and specially in later childhood, the child tries to express his behaviour through reasonable means and is the result of many factors. In childhood the child is in a position to express his feelings through language. Secondly, he becomes social and realises that it may not be desirable or proper for him to show his emotions at all times. Thirdly, his intellect begins to play a proper role in exercising check over emotional outbursts.

In this way the child advances towards emotional stability and control and during the later period of his childhood, demonstrates on appreciable degree of control over his emotions.

Emotional Development during Adolescence

The emotional balance is once again disturbed in adolescence. The individual once again experiences the violent and intensive current of emotional experiences. With regard to emotional experiences, this is the period of intensive storm and stress. At no stage this emotional energy is so strong and dangerous as in adolescence. It is very difficult for an adolescent to exercise control over his emotions. The sudden functioning of sexual glands and tremendous increase in physical energy makes him restless. Moreover adolescents are not consistent in their emotions. Emotions during this stage fluctuate very frequently and quickly. It makes them moody. Sometimes they are very happy and at other time they are extremely sad and all this happens in a very short time. So there is too much uncertainty in the nature of their emotional states.

At this stage there is strong need of the training of emotions and proper channelization of emotional energy. The Hadow report has emphasized this need in the following words:

> "There is a tide which begins to rise in the veins of youth at the age of eleven or twelve. It is called by the name of adolescence. If that tide can be taken at the flood, and a new voyage begun in the

strength and along the flow of its current, we think that it will move on to fortune." *(Ross J.S., 1951, p. 153)*

Emotional Development in Adulthood

Emotional development reaches its maximum in adulthood. During this stage, generally, all individuals attain emotional maturity. Let us try to understand what is meant by emotional maturity.

Meaning of emotional maturity. In brief a person can be called emotionally mature if he is able to display his emotions in an appropriate degree with reasonable control. An emotionally mature person will possess the following characteristics:

1. Almost all the emotions can be distinctly seen in him and their pattern of expression can be easily recognised.
2. Manifestation of emotions is very much refined. Usually he expresses his emotions in a socially desirable way.
3. He is able to exercise control over his emotions. Sudden inappropriate emotional outbursts are rarely found in him. He is able to hide his feelings and check his emotional tide.
4. The person no more hangs in mere idealism, but he actually perceives the things in their real perspective. He is not a day-dreamer and does not possess the desire to run away from realities.
5. The intellectual powers like thinking, reasoning etc. are properly exercised by him in making any decision. He is more guided by his intellect than his emotions.
6. He does not possess the habit of rationalization *i.e.* he never gives arguments in defence of his undesirable or improper conduct. Also he never puts the responsibility of his own mistakes on others. He is always honest in his behaviour.
7. He possesses an adequate self-concept and self respect. He never likes to do the things or to show such behaviour as can injure his self respect and is adverse to his self-concept.
8. He is not confined to himself. He thinks for others and is keen to maintain social relationships. He never engages himself in such a behaviour which is antisocial and can result in the social conflicts and blockage of social relationships.
9. He has the guts to exercise his emotions at a proper time in a proper place. If there is a danger to his self prestige or if an innocent person is attacked he can rise to the occasion by exercising his emotion of anger. But on the other hand if he commits a mistake and is rebuked by his boss he is equally able to check his emotion of anger. Mature emotional behaviour is characterised by greater stability. Person having such maturity shows no sudden shift from one emotion to another.

As a conclusion regarding the meaning of emotional maturity. I would like to quote Arthur T. Jersild. He is of the opinion that emotional maturity should not involve only simple restriction and control. According to him it is a very narrow view of emotional maturity. He writes, "*An adequate description of emotional maturity must take account of the full scope of the individual's capacity and powers, and of his ability to use and enjoy them. In its broadest sense emotional maturity means the degree to which the person has realized his potential for richness of living and has developed his capacity to enjoy things, to relate himself to others, to love and to laugh: his capacity for whole-hearted sorrow when an occasion for grief arises . . . and his capacity to show fear when there is occasion to be frightened, without feeling a need to use a false mask of courage.*" (Skinner C.E. 1968, p. 281)

The Comparison between the Emotionality of Childhood and Adulthood

The emotional experiences during childhood differ markedly from those of the adulthood. This difference can be easily seen through some of the following distinguished characteristics:

1. *Intensity of emotions:* Children's emotions are characterized by too much intensity. There are sudden outbursts of emotions among children. If a child weeps, he weeps bitterly. In anger, he loses control over himself. But the child's emotional experiences are not so intensive. Volcano-like sudden emotional outbursts are seldom observed in adults.

2. *Briefness of the emotions:* Children's emotional experiences are very brief. Their emotions last for a short time and these end all of a sudden. Whereas in adults the emotions play their part for a quite long time and in the last make their existence drawn over a period of time in the form of 'mood'.

3. *Transitoriness of the emotions:* Children's emotions are transitory in character which means there is a rapid shift from one emotion to another. We find a child weeping and shedding tears, a piece of chocolate is enough to shift his emotion of distress to delight. Similarly, we find a rapid shift from anger to smile, from laughter to tears, or from jealousy to affection. Contrary to this, emotions of adults do not shift so rapidly. They are marked by greater degree of stability.

4. *Frequency of emotions:* On the average, the number of emotional experiences experienced by a child during a day is significantly greater than those experienced by a normal adult. The child passes under different currents of emotional streams during a period of time. Sometimes a specific emotion is repeated so many times. But as the child grows older, he learns to make adjustment and tries to meet situation by reactions other than emotional ones. The result is gradual decrease in the frequency of emotional responses.

5. *Detection of emotionality:* The emotional state of the child is easily detectable. He is very innocent and does not know the art of hiding his feelings and emotions. The behavioural symptoms like speech difficulties,

frequent crying, restlessness, nail-biting and thumb sucking etc. give indications of his emotionality. The adults, on the other hand are generally, able to hide their feelings and emotions. Therefore, in their case, it is difficult for others to know how they feel and detect their emotionality.

5. *The differences in the emotional expression:* An infant in quite unable to exercise control over his violent emotional outbursts. Emotions at this stage are expressed through motor responses. As the child grows, the way of emotional expression gets modified. This modification goes on till the attainment of maturity in adulthood. A mature adult seldom engages himself in the motor activity during emotional stress. He learns to exercise control over his emotions and expresses them in a refined and socially approved way. The emotional expression either in the form of motor responses or in socially unacceptable way is labelled as 'childish'. The emotional response of an adult is always guided by his intellect while in the child, the intensity of feelings rules over the reasoning and thinking power. The adults are able to keep their emotions reserved for a future expression but in childhood it is a difficult task.

Factors Influencing Emotional Development

The emotional development of the child rests on so many factors. The important ones are given below:

1. *Health and physical development:* Physical development and health has a positive correlation with emotional development. Any deficiency in physical side — internal or external — creates emotional problems. The children, weak in somatic structure or suffering from illness, are more emotionally upset and unstable than are children whose health is better. The normal functioning of the glands is very important for the balanced emotional development. Any abnormal increase or decrease in their power of secretion creates obstacles in the proper emotional development.

2. *Intelligence:* Intelligence, as the ability to make adaptation, has a significant correlation with the emotional adjustment and suitability of the child. Meltzer (1937) concluded that —

> "There is less emotional control, on the average, among those of the lower intellectual levels than among children of the same age who are bright." (Hurlock, E.B., 1959, p. 254)

An intelligent person, with his reasoning and thinking powers, exercises control according to the situation and make proper use of his emotions. At every stage the child's intellectual power guides and controls the emotional development of the child.

3. *Family atmosphere and relationships:* Emotional development is very much influenced by the family atmosphere and relationships. The emotional behaviour of the parents and elder members of the cordial atmosphere prevailed at home develops positive emotions among the children, while the conflicts, fights and tensions in family relationships give birth to negative

emotions. Also the treatment, given to a child by the parents and the members of the family, influences his emotional development. The order of birth (whether the first or the youngest child), the size of the family, the socio-economic status of the family, the parental attitude (neglected, pampered and over protected child) — all are the decisive factors in emotional bringing up of the child.

4. *School atmosphere and teachers:* The school life plays an important role in the emotional development of children. The healthy conducive atmosphere of the school always results in the balanced emotional development of children. All such things like the physical facilities provided in the school, the methods of teaching, the organisation of co-curricular activities and social life of the school, the relationship among the staff members and the head of the institution, the attitude of the teachers towards students and the self-example of the teacher's emotional behaviour, influence the emotional development of children.

5. *Social development and peer-group relationship:* Social development of children is closely linked to their emotional development. The more social is the child, the more emotionally adjustable he will prove. Socially rejected or maladjusted children always face difficult emotional problems. The maintenance of proper social relationships and acquisition of social virtues are the effective means for bringing essential modification in the emotional behaviour of the child. The proper social development can only bring the desirable and socially approved emotional development in children.

6. *Neighbourhood the community and the society:* The other social agencies like neighbourhood, the community and society, of which an individual is the member, also exerts significant influence upon his emotional set-up. He picks up so many traits of his emotional behaviour from these surroundings. The brave community is sure to produce fearless and courageous children. The society where the elder members of the society unnecessarily exhibit emotional outburst of anger leads the youngers to such negative development. Similarly so many good or bad things related to emotional behaviour of an individual can be acquired through the impact of neighbourhood and the society.

In this way the factors influencing the emotional development of an individual can be labelled into two categories. In the first category there are personal factors like his physical, physiological, mental and social development. In the second category there are social factors like parents, family, school, neighbourhood, community and the society. Both of these factors exert a significant influence upon the emotional development of the child. While taking care of the proper emotional development of the child, the parents as well as the teachers should keep in view all the factors belonging to both categories.

SOCIAL DEVELOPMENT

What is Social Development?

Human beings possess a unique characteristic which separates them from animal beings. Their behaviour is social. Society is as essential as food to them. They believe in the maintenance of social relationships and try to adjust with others. But this does not mean that the child is born with such social behaviour and social qualities. Like other aspects of growth and development, he develops the necessary social characteristics in him. *The process of the development of such qualities which brings desirable changes in his social behaviour is referred to as social development or socialization of the child.* Social development occupies very important place in the overall process of growth and development. We cannot even describe an individual a person if he has not passed through the process of social development or socialization.

Let us try to think over further. What does this term social development (also described as socialization) mean? Various thinkers have tried to define it. Some of the definitions are given below:

1. *Sorenson: "By social growth and development we mean increasing ability to get along well with oneself and others."* (1948, p. 50)

In this way Sorenson explains that during the process of social development there is a progress in the social abilities or skills of an individual. With these increasing abilities he tries to bring improvement in the maintenance of social relationships. He tries to mould his behaviour and seek adjustment and harmony with others.

2. *Freeman and Showel: "Social development is the process of learning to conform to group standards, mores and traditions and becoming imbued with a sense of oneness, inter-communication and co-operation."* (Hurlock, E.B., 1959, p. 257)

This definition lays stress on the following:

(i) Social development refers to the process by which a person acquires the necessary knowledge, skills and disposition that makes him an acceptable member of his own group.

(ii) It develops group loyalty and encourages mutual dependence, co-operation and cohesiveness.

(iii) It is the process which helps on individual to behave in accordance with social traditions and mores and thus makes him able to adjust in his social environment.

3. *Mrs. Hurlock: "Social development means the attaining of maturity in social relationships."* (1959, p. 257)

This brief definition carries a wide meaning. It asserts that as in the case of emotional development, the goal is to attain emotional maturity, similarly there in the case of social development, the goal should be the attainment of social maturity. An individual should have all the opportunities to modify or improve his social behaviour so that he may be able to maintain proper social relationships and can adjust himself to his social environment.

4. *Garrett: "Socialization or social development is the process whereby the biological individual is converted into a human person.*" (1968 p. 555)

This definition is based upon the distinction between the term 'individual' and 'person'. We cannot name each and everybody as person. The person always possesses some personality. The personality is the product of social interaction between him and his social environment. Socialization and social development — the process of social interaction — helps the individuals to attain essential personality characteristics.

In the light of all these views we can come to the conclusion that social development or the socialization is a process.

(i) which begins with the infant's first contact with other people and continues throughout life,

(ii) it is the net result of his constant interaction with his social environment,

(iii) it helps in learning and acquiring various social qualities and characteristics, and

(iv) with the result of such learning the individual becomes adjusted to his social environment and can maintain proper social relationships.

Development of Social Behaviour during Different Stages of Development

A. Social Development in Infancy

The behaviour of the human infant is not social at birth. He is too much self-centred. He is only concerned with the satisfaction of his physical need. He does not even distinguish between people and inanimate objects.

Social behaviour is said to be taking its birth when the infant first distinguishes between persons and objects. He is dependent upon the adults for the satisfaction of his needs, therefore, normally the baby's first social contacts are with an adult. Mrs. Hurlock in her book 'Child Psychology' has beautifully explained the process of social development during the first two years as a result of the contact with adults. Below we give the summary of her findings.

Duration of Age	*Pattern of Social Behaviour*
During first Month	Cannot differentiate between the human voices and other noises.
Second Month	Recognises the sounds of human beings and gives smiles to the person.
Third Month	Recognises its mother and feels unhappy on separation.
Fourth Month	Shows selective attention to the human face and feels happy in company.
Fifth Month	Reacts differently to smiling and scolding and

Duration of Age	*Pattern of Social Behaviour*
	distinguishes between friendly and angry voices.
Sixth Month	Recognizes familiar persons with a smile and shows definite expressions of fear of strangers.
Eighth and Ninth Month	Attempts to imitate the speech, simple acts and gestures observed in others.
Between the tenth and twelve Month	Plays with his image and even kisses it as if it were another person.
At twelve Month	Can refrain from doing things in response to 'no-no' or some other form of request.
At two Years	Can cooperate with adults in a number of routine activities and becomes an active member of the family.

Social development of infants as a result of contact with other infants and children: With regard to an infant's social reactions to another infant or child it has been observed that his early behaviour is egocentric and selfish. He cannot share his toys with others. He wants to have all things for himself and does not tolerate any external interference. From the thirteenth to the eighteenth month the young child's interest shifts from play materials to the playmates. There is a decrease in fighting for toys and increase in cooperative use of them. Up to 3 years he learns to divide and share his possession with others and to cooperate with them. They are now in a position to engage themselves in the cooperative and organised plays activities. Up to 7 years or so the children seek companionship regardless of sex of the other children. Usually the boys and girls play together at this stage.

Like emotions the early stage of social behaviour during infancy is characterized by negative social characteristics, Imitation, timidity, shyness, rivalry and desire for possession dominate the first two years of development. Between 2 to 6 years both negative and positive aspects of social behaviour are seen. Negativism, rivalry, quarrelling, teasing and bullying, cooperation, sympathy and social approval are some of the new social behaviours which are learned at this stage.

B. Social Development during Childhood

As we have seen that during the period 2 to 6 years a child progresses from being relatively unsocial to distinctly socialized individual. He learns to share, to cooperate and to do things with others. But the circle of his social contacts is limited at this stage. Therefore, we cannot expect much from him regarding his social development.

With the entrance in childhood most of the children begin to go to school. The area of their social contacts is now widened. We note the following changes in the social behaviour of a child:

1. This period is marked by greater degree of social awareness. There is a great expansion of child's social world. Most of the important types of

social behaviour, necessary to adjustment with others, begin to develop at this stage.

2. He tries to seek independence from his parents and other elders and spends less time with them. In actual sense he now drives no enjoyment from them. Thus interest in playmates of his own age gets increased.

3. He becomes an active member of a 'peer groups' and this group gradually replaces the family group in its influence over his behaviour and attitudes. The members of such a group are almost of the same age. They believe in group loyalty and thus try to conform to the rules and the values maintained by their group.

4. We find a sort of segregation among boys and girls of this age. They form their group among members of their own sex because of a definite and clear differentiation between their habits, interest and attitudes etc,

5. The interests and values of the peer group often have a clash with the interests of values of the teachers and parents. The child at this age is caught between the two. On the one hand he aspires for the social values of his own group; on the other hand, he is equally anxious to win the love and affection of his parents as well as of teachers. There a proper balance between these two influencing forces — peer group, parents and teachers — is essential. Being neglected by either side he may develop himself into a maladjusted and antisocial personality.

6. Up to the end of the stage of childhood, *i.e.* 11th or 12th year the child enters the peak of "gang age" with increasing loyalities towards his own gang and conflicts with other gangs, parents and teachers. The gang life develops so many good and bad social qualities in the child.

C. Social Development during Adolescence

Adolescence is a period of rapid change and adjustments. In the social sphere also it holds a greater significance. The social development of this age is marked by the following characteristics:

1. Adolescence is marked with too much sex consciousness, sexual development and the accompanying attraction for opposite sex. Boys and girls of this age try to attract and hold the attraction of each other through their style of dress, manner of talking and other forms of social behaviour. They also try to seek friendship and even sexual relationships. In this way the social behaviour pattern of the adolescence is almost dominated by sexual needs and desires.

2. During this stage group loyalty becomes very much pronounced. Like childhood, it does not confine itself to the gang only but extends to the school, the community, the province and to the nation martyrs and patriots are the product of this age. Cooperation reaches its peak during this period and the individuals are in a mood to sacrifice their own interest for the greater cause of the group, society and nation.

3. Adolescence is also marked with the increase in friendly relationships. The nature of friendship maintained at this stage differs much from that of

childhood. While in the childhood the friends are generally chosen from the neighbourhood or class, in adolescence there is no such bar of distance. The adolescents tend to choose friends of their own age, mental level and from the same socio-economic group to which their own family belongs. Their friendships are based on their common interests, hobbies and skills or the satisfaction of their mutual needs and subsequently tend to last longer than the friendships made in early childhood. It sometimes ties them in life long relationships.

4. Adolescence is a period of intense emotions. Emotional behaviour dominates the social characteristics and qualities of adolescents. An adolescent is highly sensitive, idealist and social reformer by nature. He feels strongly for the weak and sufferers. He is always ready to do some sort of social and community service. From time to time he exhibits his desire for bringing reforms in the social set-up and is highly critical of social evils and injustice.

5. There area of specific interests and social contacts gets widened during adolescence. Besides individual characteristics the culture, socio-economic status of the family, sex education—all effect their social interest and contacts. We find too much diversity in the adolescents regarding their interests and sociability. While some are highly extrovert and sociable the others like to remain aloof and shirk from social contacts and participations.

In the end we can say that adolescence is a period of maximum social awareness, increasing social relationships and intimate friendships. During this age the individual is provided with wide area of interests and opportunities for making social adjustment and learning so many social qualities. During this age an individual prepares himself to play a role of adult in his social life. Up to the end of this stage, the social behaviour of the child becomes almost matured.

Social Maturity

As we have seen earlier, the aim of social development is to gain social maturity. The child while passing through various stages from his very birth strives to attain it. Let us see what does this term social maturity indicate or what are the *characteristics* which are supposed to be present in a socially mature individual?

1. A socially mature individual likes to mix up with people. He is capable of making and keeping friendships.
2. He is not self-centred. He is always ready to sacrifice his interests for the greater cause of groups, society and nation. While demanding and asserting for his rights, he always cares for the social obligations.
3. He possesses the ability for sharing and shouldering the social responsibilities. He is prepared to play the role of a leader or of a staunch follower as the situation demands from him,

4. He is able to make proper decision and take suitable action at the time of any social crisis, problem or situation in which his help is needed.
5. He is very much cooperative. He believes in maintaining relationships and working with others. He does not do anything which hurts the feeling of others. He possesses the social virtues like the feeling of sympathy and kindness, courtesy and cheerfulness. He believes injustice, equality and fraternity and never does anything which disrupts cohesiveness and unity of the social structure.

   Actually speaking he is imbued with all the important social qualities like patience, respect for other's opinions, kindness and sympathy, cooperation, courtesy and politeness, cheerfulness, self-confidence, self-control, sentiment of self-regard, respect for fair sex, religions and culture, etc.
6. The area of his social interests and participation is very wide. He possesses refined tastes and adequate social etiquettes.
7. His social behaviour conforms to the norms, mores, social codes and ethics. He never engages himself in any sort of activities or behaviour which is anti-social and looked down upon by the society.
8. He possesses a strong desire to serve the cause of the society. He feels for evils and malpractices in the society and tries to bring desirable reforms.
9. He possesses a greater degree of adaptability and adjustability. He can make himself adjusted easily to the varying needs of the society and social circumstances.

Factors Affecting Social Development

How to help the child in the task of his social development is a relevant question at this stage. In this task, the individual in addition to his own physical, mental and emotional development is helped by various social agencies. All these factors — personal and environmental — work together in influencing the social development of the child. What are these factors and how they influence the pattern of social development can be seen through the following discussion:

A. Personal Factors

1. *Bodily structure and health:* Development of social behaviour is influenced by the physique and health which one possesses. A healthy child with a normal physique develops self-confidence and a sense of self-respect. He has the strength and ability to make himself adjusted in the challenging social situations. He is always cheerful and cooperative. He is able to mix with the people and maintains proper social relationships. The child suffering from illness or having poor health or any physical deformities and defects develops the feeling of inferiority and feels difficulty in social adjustment. Therefore proper care should be taken for the balanced physical development of the children.

2. *Intelligence:* Intelligence is defined as the ability to make and take the right decision at a right time and the ability to adapt or adjust to new situations. These qualities are very essential for effective social behaviour. The more intelligent a person is, the more adjustable and social he will prove.

3. *Emotional development.* Emotional development of the child bears a positive correlation with the social development. Emotional adjustability and maturity is one of the very important elements of social maturity. The persons who can express their emotions in a proper degree at a proper time are found to possess a healthy social personality. Emotionally maladjusted personalities possess poor social qualities. Therefore due care should be taken for the training of the emotions of the child so that he may not feel any obstacles in the path of his social development.

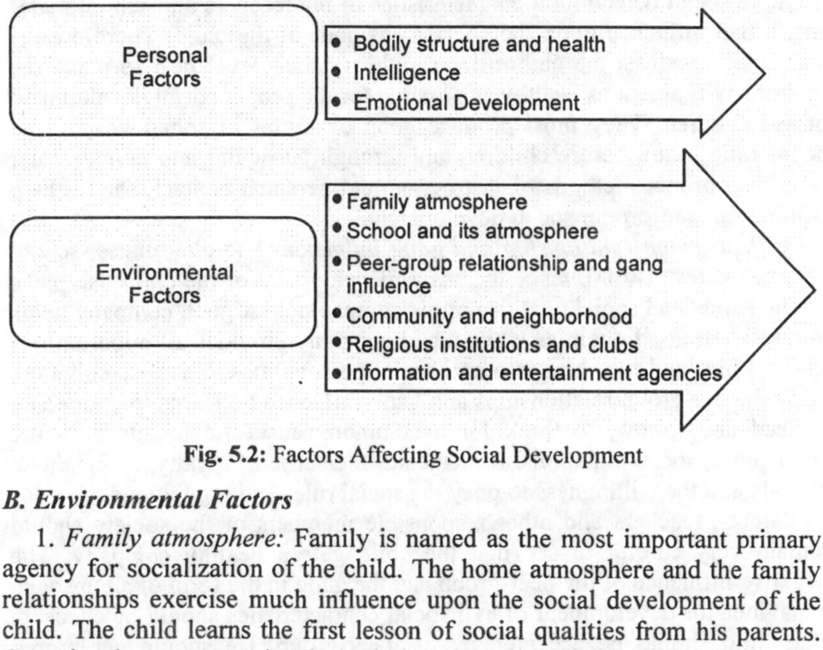

Fig. 5.2: Factors Affecting Social Development

B. Environmental Factors

1. *Family atmosphere:* Family is named as the most important primary agency for socialization of the child. The home atmosphere and the family relationships exercise much influence upon the social development of the child. The child learns the first lesson of social qualities from his parents. Consciously or unconsciously he imitates the behaviour of his parents and members of the family and thus picks up so many good or bad social characteristics which go with him even up to the end of his life. The size of the family, the relationships within the family, attitude of the parents and family members socio-economic status and position of the family in the society, the traditions, culture, values and the ideals of the family — all influence the social development of the child.

The family which provides healthy social atmosphere and where basic needs of children are satisfied produces socially balanced personalities whereas in the homes when the family relationships are under strain and the elders possess negative social characteristics, the child is not brought up properly and consequently the socially undesirable and negative behaviour is produced among children. Therefore it is essential to seek the active cooperation of the parents in providing suitable atmosphere at home for the proper social development of children.

2. *The School and its atmosphere:* Social development in children is greatly influenced by the social environment and functioning of the schools. The human relationships maintained by the school, the kinds of programmes and activities performed, its traditions, values and principles, the social qualities and behaviour of the teachers and school mates — all influence the social development of the child. The school, having a healthy social and democratic atmosphere inculcates so many social virtues among the students while a poor and unhealthy atmosphere of the school and the negative social behavioural characteristics of the teachers and school mates cast a bad influence upon the social behaviour of the child. Therefore the teachers as well as the authorities should try their level best to make the school environment as healthy as possible for the proper social development of the children. They must produce good examples of social virtues and democratic living before children and through curricular and co-curricular activities, proper methods of instruction and personal contact, should help children in their proper social development.

3. *Peer-group relationship and gang influence:* The play mates, school or class mates also influence the social development of the child. He picks up the habits and social qualities of his companions. A good company helps him to learn good qualities while a bad company provides all opportunities to spoil him and turn him into anti social personalities. On the credit side, through peer-group relationships and gang influence he learns to cooperate, to lead and follow, to think for a common cause and to adjust in the challenging social situations. It inculcates the sense of loyalty, sympathetic attitude and the willingness to obey the social rules and regulations.

Parents, teachers and other responsible members of the society should remain very careful to see that the child gets a healthy company. The negative influence of the peer-group and the gang in the form of an unsocial behaviour for development of evil social characteristics should be checked. The child should be accepted by his peer-group. He should get proper environment and opportunities to mix with his peers.

4. *Community and Neighbourhood:* As the child grows older he comes in contact with the social circle of his neighbourhood and the community to which he belongs. The social interests; habits and characteristics of the neighbours unconsciously and consciously, influence the social behaviour of the child. Every community and the society is characterized by its unique cultural pattern, social mores, traditions and social characteristics. The child as a member of the community and the society picks up these things which go on shaping his social behaviour and influence his social development.

5. *Religious institutions and clubs:* The social agencies like temple, church, social clubs, etc. also influence the social development of the child. These places serve as a meeting ground for the members of the society and help in developing social contacts and relationships. The social behaviour of an individual is greatly influenced by the traditions, values, ideals and social characteristics maintained by these institutions.

6. *Information and Entertainment agencies:* Agencies like News papers, Magazines, Radio, Cinema, Television, etc. also exercise their influence upon the social development of children. Sources of information constantly inform the readers, listeners and others about the changes in the social structure, customs, traditions and values and thus bring desirable changes in the social behaviour of individuals. The mass entertainment agencies like radio, cinema, television, etc. play a vital role in moulding and shaping the behaviour of the members of the society. The impact of these agencies in social life can very well be recognized. What a hero or heroine does on the screen is at once imitated. The values of the life, the style of living, the traditions and cultural pattern of the society all undergo a drastic change by the impact of these modern mass agencies.

These agencies should not be allowed to functions unchecked. Society or Government should exercise a desirable control and check upon the functioning of these agencies so that no undesirable and anti social influence is left over the masses. Directly or indirectly these agencies should be made an important means for the assimilation of the social and democratic virtues among the citizens.

LANGUAGE DEVELOPMENT

Language is learned and acquired like other skills. The process of such learning or acquisition just starts with the birth of the child. The things and factors like observation and imitation, interaction with the environment and the demands raised for the realization of the physiological and socio-psychological needs play a significant role in the proper development of language among the children. The developmental process of learning goes on in a quite steady and slower pace as explained here in detail.

The Stage Prior to Actual Language Development

In this initial or starting stage of language development the child seems to get ready or prepare himself for comprehending and utilizing the form of language expressed through symbols or signs. Such readiness on his part may be visible through the actions and activities like below:

(i) In the initial step just after the birth, the child may be seen to get engaged in the activities like weeping and crying.

(ii) Along with weeping and crying actions and sounds, the child gradually may be able to produce other sounds well accompanied with the actions or activities like yawning, and fast breathing.

These actions or activities are absolutely natural automatic and innate and no willful attempts are made for their learning and execution.

(iii) Subsequently, children may be seen to get engaged in the actions and activities involving babbling as a sign of the initial emergence of language development among children. The children are able to demonstrate such early language behaviour at the earlier age of two to three months. Such babbling on the part of infants provide them opportunities for the drill and practice of the vowels and consonant sounds. They may be found to repeat the utterance of others as heared and grasped by them in their own ways. In doing so, they may be seen to produce the sound of vowels earlier than the consonants. They try to utter vowels and consonants in a repeated way and it is this utterance that in termed as babbling on the part of a children. Their babbling although has no parallel in encyclopedia yet it carries a specific purpose and meaning grasped only by those (i.e., parents and family members) who are close to them in understanding their needs and actions.

(iv) Along with their sound producing and babbling behaviour, the children begin to express or communicate their thoughts and feelings with the help of gestures, symbols and signals. In this connection, every child has his own sign or signal system that can only be grasped and understood by his parents and intimate ones. Accordingly, they may be seen to make use of different signs, symbols or signals for conveying that they are hungry, their stomach is now full, they want you to be with them, etc. In this way, during this period or stage of language development a child is not able to use words or sentences in his utterance. He can only communicate his thoughts and feeling either with the use of his own invented signs, symbols and signals or by uttering a few vowels and consonants graspable only by his parents or intimates.

The Stage Related to Actual Language Development

After the initial stage of readiness or preparation, the actual stage of language development among the children usually begins to emerge at the age of 10 and 11 months. In the course of language development, here the task starts with the acquisition of the skill or ability related to oral expression. A child thus first learns to speak and grasp the meaning of certain specific words, sentences and the language composed of these words and sentences. His oral vocabulary gets increased and the abilities and skills related to oral expression get improved. In the subsequent years after getting access to school education and receiving training in using writing skills, he begins to demonstrate efficiency in the using language in its writing form. In this way, now he may be seen to progress gradually on the path of acquiring and using both the forms of language-oral and written for his communication, development and progress. He can develop his language abilities and skills to the extent of utilizing them not only for the purpose of communication but also for the learning of other curricular subjects and seeking his wholesome all round development in different aspects or dimensions of his personality. How does a child's language development proceed during the different ages or stages of his developmental period? Let us try to seek the answer by classifying/categorizing a child's language development under the following aspects or dimensions.

A. Development of oral vocabulary
B. Development of oral expression or speech power
C. Development of reading ability or expression
D. Development of writing ability or written expression

A. Development of Oral Vocabulary

The words related to a language and their vocabulary carry a wide significance in the language development of the children. In the oral vocabulary the children first try to pick up the words. These words later on take the form of sentences and the formation of sentences give birth to a capable form of applied language that can be successfully used for the exchange on communication of their thoughts and feelings. The development of the oral vocabulary takes place in the child gradually at a slow pace. After birth as soon as he begins to utter sounds along with their inherent meanings he becomes capable of grasping the words along with their pronunciation. Every new word grasped or pronounced by him becomes a solid means or instrument of fulfilling one of his needs or purpose and in turn it becomes a appropriate source of reinforcing his language learning behaviour. As a result, he may be seen trying for the grasping, understanding and pronouncing of many new words helpful in the appropriate development of his oral vocabulary.

How the oral vocabulary of children gets gradually developed, the issue has been studied by a number of psychologist and language scholars. Here below we are producing the conclusions derived on the basis of research attempts carried out by the renowned psychologist Smith (1950), Thompson (1962) and Lipsit (1966).

Age of Children	*Vocabulary of Children*
From birth to 8 months	O
From 9 months to 12 months	Three or four words
One and a half years age	Ten to Twelve words
Two years age	272 words
Two and a half years age	450 words
Three years age	One thousand words
Three and a half years age	1250 words

Age of Children	*Vocabulary of Children*
Four years age	1600 words
Five years age	2100 words
Eleven years age	50000 words
Fourteen years age	80000 words
Sixteen years age	More than one Lakh

In this we may see that as soon as the child enters the school going age after getting five years old his oral vocabulary get increased with a good speed. Infact the developed of vocabulary is very much dependant on the subsequent growth and development in the intellectual abilities and social skills as well as the appropriate environment and opportunities available for learning and progress. The oral vocabulary of the children thus gets increased in the proportion of the facilities and opportunities available to him for its adequate development.

The development of oral vocabulary may exhibit many other characteristics and uniqueness besides a mere increase in the acquisition of new words in the manner given below:

1. Generally there are two types of words available in the oral vocabulary of the children one of which are those that are actively used by them for serving their purposes. They understand and grasp their meaning well. The others belongs to the category that are not made into use by the children themselves but they can understand their meaning well if spoken or uttered by someone else.

2. In taking into consideration the value or significance of the utilized words the children's oral vocabulary may be classified into two main categories — General vocabulary and Specific vocabulary. In the first category, we may include the words that are used by the children generally in all situation. In the second category, we may include or put those words that are used by the children in particular situations for serving specific purposes. In the development of general vocabulary among children, the words signifying nouns appear in the vocabulary of the children first, then the words signifying adjectives, pronouns, verbs, adverbs, etc. The development in the area of specific vocabulary goes on with the increase in age. In addition, the development in specific vocabulary is also guided and directed through the type of interactions children make with their environment, and the nature and quality of education and upbringing they receive at the hands of teachers and parents. In general, the specific vocabulary of children may be found to provide space for the words like below:

(i) The words related to colour sense.
(ii) The words related to time sense such as yes for day, today, tomorrow, morning, evening, day, night, winter, rainy or summer, etc.

(iii) The names of animals, birds, vegetables and fruits.
(iv) The body parts such as eyes, ears, nose, hand, feet, legs, stomach, etc.
(v) The words related to currency and money counting.
(vi) The words used in measurement.
(vii) The improper, uncultured and abusive words.
(viii) The words used for showing courtesy and respectful such as thanks, sir, your honour, excuse me, etc.
(ix) The words related to the use of transport and entertainment means like television, cinema, mobile and computer appliances.
(x) The secrete coded language used by the children for interacting with their peers.

3. In the children's oral vocabulary, first we may witness the presence of the words related to the satisfaction of their physical or physiological needs and then the words associated with the satisfaction of their socio-psychological needs. In relation to the development of the vocabulary concerning the satisfaction of their socio-psychological needs, the scope is initially limited to the parents, siblings and other family members. However, as the child grows and develops the area and scope of his social contacts and interaction gets widened and accordingly he gets matured in terms of his increased vocabulary concerning social behaviour and environmental surroundings.

B. Development of Oral Expression or Speech Power

In the task of developing oral expression or speech power among children, the things like pronunciation and understanding of the sounds, words and sentences carry an immense importance. The attempts in this direction get initiated just after the birth. The task of oral expression and speech power development actually begins with the attempts made on the part of the children with their babbling (meaningless and vague pronunciation of sounds). At this stage, they may also try to grasp the meaning conveyed through the sounds and words pronounced by others. Such ability acquired on the part of the children is named as their comprehension ability. Development of this ability actually helps a lot in the oral expression or speech power of the children. Its development takes place in the children before they pick up the ability to speak. When they hear the words like take water, bring milk to the baby, where is the toy, etc. it makes them quite alert and attentive signifying that they are comprehending the meaning of these words and sentences uttered by others. In this way, development of comprehension ability of the spoken words may be termed as a first solid step in the direction of developing oral expression or speech power among children.

The second major step in this direction is concerned with the development of appropriate vocabulary along with its desirable pronunciation. However, a child in the beginning is not able to pronounce the sounds and words used in his language expression. At this stage, generally children may be seen to have incorrect pronunciation of the words and sentences.

In the initial stage children feel pleasure in pronouncing speedily all the words that are present in their vocabulary. However, gradually they learn to speak a particular word that is relevant at a time in a particular situation. Moreover, the speaking of a words precedes the speaking of a full sentence. For example, instead of saying that "I am thirsty and want to take water," the child utters the word 'water' or 'mum', gradually instead of using a single word for conveying his purpose he may begin to use two or more words in combination and thus gradually by the end of two years he learns to speak words sentences like: 'Give me milk', 'I want toy', 'come near me', etc. Later on as he grows in age he begin to make use of simple sentences with a developed vocabulary with him according to his age. Initially the sentences spoken by him are quite small and incomplete. However, upto the age of five years there is sufficient improvement and as a result before entering the school he may be capable of using compound sentences in his language expression.

After entering the school, there is a significant development in his oral and speech power. It happens because he gets wide opportunities of enough exposure, interaction and communication with the peers and teachers. Language is specifically taught as the subject of school, curriculum and he makes its use as a medium of learning and understanding others subjects of the school curriculum. As a result, these happens a great increase in the expressive and speech power of the children.

C. Development of Reading Ability

By the term reading ability we here mean the language ability of a child helping him to identify or recognize the written and printed language symbols, words and sentences in a proper way along with their needed comprehension and understanding on his part. It helps him well in receiving the message, idea or feelings inherent in a written piece of statement. The stages of the development of reading ability among the children may be summarized as under.

(i) The task of the development of reading ability ámong children starts just after they become capable of utilizing their sense organs for getting information or knowledge. Their ability to identity and classifying the objects may help them in identifying or recognizing the letters alphabets. The acquisition of the ability to identify and name the letters may be regarded as the first step taken towards developing reading ability among children. Usually a child of three years may exhibit such ability. When a child is shown an apple in the chart he may first identify it as a picture of an apple and than can associate it with the letter 'A'. This visual experience can lead the child to know and learn the alphabet 'A' for apple.

(ii) Acquaintance and understanding of the letters of alphabet is followed by the knowledge and comprehension of the words. The children who get early mastery over the alphabets may be able to pick up word comprehension also at a quite earlier stage. The starting in this process is made with the learning to read the words composed of a quite few letters.

(iii) It is followed by learning to read a full sentence. Initially they try to read simple and short sentences and then the more difficult and complex ones. Here, the silent as well loud reading can play an important role in helping the children to develop appropriate ability of reading the paragraphs of the texts.

D. Development of Writing Ability or Written Expression

By the term writing ability or expression we mean a language ability of a child helpful for him in expressing his thoughts and feelings in a written form. With the acquisition of such ability the child can now acquire the power of expressing his ideas and feelings through the visual form of the symbolic language, alphabets, words and sentences instead of merely expressing them in an oral form.

It must be clearly noted that the task of developing writing ability is carried out well only after the acquisition of proper reading comprehension and ability on the part of children. A required level of physical and mental maturity is also needed for initiating the acquisition of writing skill on the part of children. It is essential because writing on their part requires proper development of the coordinated muscles of the fingers as well as the development of proper cognitive focusing and attention for copying the alphabets in their appropriate form. It is why, we can't think of developing the writing ability among children during the period of infancy. The things like below usually may help much in developing appropriate writing ability or skill among children.

(i) Attempts should be made to create the state of readiness and motivation among the children for the acquisition of writing skill by paying attention over the proper identification of the structure and formation of the letters, words and sentences.

(ii) We should wait for the necessary acquisition of the level of physical and mental maturity on the part of the developing child in order to becoming necessary fit and capable of doing writing work.

(iii) The initial attempts for the development of writing skill among the children may be made to assist the child manually (by holding their hands desirably at the time of their writing) till then he becomes capable of holding the writing material by himself in an independent way.

(iv) The teachers or parents may draw the letter figures on the sand with their fingers or on papers with the pencil or writing pen. They may then ask the child to copy or imitate it with their fingers or pencils. With sufficient practice they can thus learn gradually writing of all the alphabets.

(v) After learning to write single letters the children should be made to learn writing of the simple words and sentences.

(vi) The help of transcription and dictation may be properly taken for the development of proper writing ability among the children. For this purpose, the children may be given the home task or drill work of copying the passages of a text and they may also be told to write in their notebooks whatever is dictated by the teacher in the class.

(vii) Next step in the development of the writing ability among the children is concerned with providing them desired freedom and opportunity for expressing their thoughts and feelings in the writing form. The writing of essays, letters, short stories, episodes, poem, dramas, critical analysis, etc. falls under the domain of such creative writing. At this stage, they should also be given appropriate knowledge and understanding of the grammar of a specific language and also should be encouraged to demonstrate the required creativity and constructivity in their written expression.

Factors Influencing Language Development

As discussed earlier, the development of language among children takes place only after their birth. As a result, heredity may be said not to play any mentionable role in the development of language. In practice also it actually happens. Language is not inherited, it is acquired, no genes and chromosomes are responsible for getting the linguistic abilities transferred from one generation to another. However, it is not also appropriate to deny any role for the children's heredity in the development of their language. The children inherit a number of things in the form of their physical and mental capacities that may actually work as a potent deciding factor for the learning, acquisition and functioning of language skills among children. For example, in a case where a child is born with deformity and defects in his vocal apparatus-lungs, lips, tongue, teeth, throat or he suffers from acute physical or mental disability then decidedly it may cast a quite damaging and negative effect on the development of proper linguistic ability in him. However, no control can be exercised over such happenings. It is a natural process and accordingly we should not expect from the sufferers to have a normal level of their language development. In this direction, appropriate steps for their adequate adjustment and needed emotional development can only be taken.

By leaving aside the factors associated with inheritance if we try to think over the other things responsible for the development of language among the children then we can talk about them in the manner discussed below:

1. *Physical Health:* Language development of a child is greatly influenced by the nature and quality of the physical health and development of the children. A physically strong and healthy child may be found to put

up necessary energy in the task of acquiring language but the children having health and suffering from ailments may remain deprived of the opportunities to learn language. A physically healthy and fit child enjoys the priviledge of having his physical organs or components in a quite healthy and workable fashion. He knows that the fitness and adequate health of the physical organs like: vocal apparatus, lips, tongue, teeth, lungs, brain and nervous system play a quite significant role in the proper development of language among the children and it can be only possible through the acquisition of a good physical health and normal development on the part of the children.

2. *Mental Health:* An adequate mental health is quite essential for the proper language development of a child. Children who enjoy good mental health may be found to proceed on their language learning path in a satisfactory way. On the contrary, the children passing through anxiety, stress and conflicts may face a lot of difficulty in the task of acquiring desirable language skills. Mentally unhealthy and disturbed children may be found to fall victims of speech disorders and writing mistakes.

3. *Maturation:* The children's language development is very much affected and influenced with the natural growth in their age and maturity level. For the development and functioning of the language skills like speaking, reading, comprehending and writing. Children require a desired level of physical and mental maturity. Attainment of a desired level of such maturity on their part can help them well in the task of the development of language. It is why, it is quite useless to try for the development of speech power among the children unless they acquire necessary maturity for this purpose. Similarly, it is not fruitful to try for the acquisition of writing skill on the part of children unless they acquire necessary physical (proper coordination capability and holding power of their fingers) and mental maturity.

4. *Intelligence and Mental Development:* There is a quite intimate relationship between the acquisition of language and development of the intellectual and mental capacities. The inadequacy and deficiency arising in the development of mental and intellectual capacities may create a great hurdle in the proper development of language among children. Contrarily, the adequate development of mental and intellectual capacities among the children may help them well in their efforts of gaining useful language skills. It is why, the gifted and genious may be found to be imbibed with necessary developed language skills.

5. *Social Development*: Language is learned properly by children through their social interaction and contacts with the elders and peers. Such interactions and contacts can be made by children after gaining desired sociability and social traits and it can be possible only through their adequate social development. Consequently, when the children having adequate social development are found to get ahead on the path of language

development, the child suffering from the inadequacy of their social development may be affected quite adversely in terms of their language development.

6. *Emotional Development:* One's emotions are intimately related with the expression of his thoughts and feelings. Language also serves the function of helping children in the adequate expression of their thoughts and feelings. Accordingly language and emotional developments both may be found to have a quite intimate relationship. The children who are found to be adequately developed and adjusted in respect to the expression of their feelings and emotions may also be seen quite developed in terms of the acquisition of language skills. Contrarily the children facing emotional maladjustment may be found to fall victim of a number of language disorders and deficiencies.

7. *Family Development*: The language is learned through the observation and imitation of the language behaviour of the elders and peers. In this connection, mother is his first teacher. The other members of the family also prove him models for his language acquisition task. He pick up the language spoken in his family. The goodness and limitations shown on the part of family members in terms of the use of language are automatically transferred to the developing children and affects their language development in a quite positive or negative way. Besides this the congenial or uncongenial environment prevailed at home, the economic and socio-cultural status and conditions available in the family may be found to influence the physical, mental, social, emotional and educational development and adjustment of the children which in turn may be found to influence the children's language development in a favourable or adverse way.

8. *Peer Group and Friend Circle:* In the task of acquiring language through the observation and imitation of the behaviour of others the peer group and friend circle of the child also play a quite decisive role. The child spent most of the time outside his family in the company of his peers and friends. Accordingly, the child acquires the language spoken and used by them. Sometimes, the parents and his family members may be astonished to see that the small child is speaking a language other than language spoken by the family members. However, it is very natural for a child of Punjabi family to speak in Haryanavi tone or make use of Haryanavi words, on account of having so many Haryanavi friends and peers. The elders in spite of living in Haryana for so many years may not be able to make use of Haryanavi, but the child inspite of having Hindi as a media of instruction is capable of speaking and using Haryanavi dialect merely on account of the effect and influence of his peers and friends.

9. *Society and Community*: In the acquisition of language society and community to which a child belongs may also play a quite important role. A child is motivated and gets interested in the learning of the language that is

spoken and used by the members of his community and society. As a result, a child belonging to Anglo-Indian society may naturally develops a tendency to use so many English words and accents in his speech and writing of the language. Similarly, we can usually visualise the effect of local dialect and regional languages such as Bihari, Rajasthani, Haryanavi, Punjabi on the dialects used and language spoken and written by the children belonging to the communities who make use of these local or regional languages.

10. *School Education and Environment*: The school environment and education available to the children for their language development may also affect the language development of the children in a quite substantial way. The quality of teachers available in the school, the methods and techniques used for language teaching, the media of instruction employed in the school, the types of experiences provided to the students for the development of language and its use through the organisation of curricular activities, the interaction and communication carried out among the students and teachers, etc. may be cited as a sizable factors contributing towards the proper development of language among children.

11. *Learning Potential and Factors associated with Learning:* The language is the subject of learning. It is learned and acquired like so many skills and traits of one's personality. Its acquisition is therefore very much depends on the quality and level of the learner's learning potential. The children who have potential to learn better in a short time may also pick up better speed and learn language skills in a better way in comparison to those who have little interest or enthusiasm and are relatively slow in learning. Moreover, as we know one's learning is also influenced and affected through a number of other related factors like level of aspiration, achievement motivation, interest and attitude, opportunities for healthy competition and cooperation, rewards and incentives, learning environment, methods and techniques used for learning, time devoted and energy spent for learning, the environmental situation prevailed at the time of learning. The suitability and unsuitability of these factors may positively or adversely affect the language development of the children. In addition the availability of appropriate direction, guidance, timely assistance, provision of appropriate evaluation and feedback also may prove a potent contributing factor for the proper development of language ability and skills among the children.

MORAL OR CHARACTER DEVELOPMENT

Development of morality or character formation is regarded as one of the important and essential aim for a system of education and the pattern of bringing up the children in almost all the societies and communities of the world. The fundamental principles and practices of all the different religions and sects also propagate and emphasize on the development of morality and character formation among their followers. Universally, thus it is almost believed by the societies and communities of the world that the welfare of the human beings as individual and the group as a whole depends upon the proper development of morality and character formation among all the members of the group or community and for this purpose efforts should be made right from the early upbringing and education of the children. Question arise what is this morality? Is it inherited or learned? What is the nature or pattern of its development among the human beings? Can it be explained on the basis of stage specific developmental theories discussed in the preceding chapters? How can we help our youngesters to have proper development in their morality or character? Let us think over these issues in the present chapter.

What is Morality?

Etymologically, the term morality, has been derived from the Latin word 'mores', meaning manners, customs, or traditions. Societies and communities from their very birth throughout world have tried to establish essential ways, manners and norms for helping them to co-exist and progress properly in the form of certain moral or ethical codes for being followed by every member of their group. Such observance of the moral codes on the part of the members of the group has been referred to as conduct or morality on their part. In this way, morality is nothing but a pure conformity to the moral or ethical code of a society on the part of its members. Emphasizing further on such meaning of the term morality Hurlock (1956: 404) writes:

> "To act in a moral way means, thus to act in conformity or group standards of conduct. Immorality is failure to conform or behaviour directed against the interest and welfare of the group."

Therefore what is moral or immoral, totally rests on the decision of the right or wrong of a conduct as prescribed in the moral or ethical code of a society. It is natural that such moral codes or standards may be found to vary from group to group or society to society and it is therefore an accepted fact that there cannot be any uniform and generalized criteria of judging morality or immorality. However, as a concept, one's morality may be taken or regarded as an equivalence to his character that has been defined as *"sum of all the tendencies which an individual possesses"*. (Dumville, 1938, p. 311).

The definition provided by Dumville is somewhat capable of providing a comprehensive view as it tries to suggest that character or morality possessed by an individual is the sum total of all his tendencies — innate as well as acquired. As a whole it takes into consideration the following:

(i) In the first place there are instincts which are inborn and innate. They provide the native mental capital for a person at the time of birth in order to start his life.

(ii) With increasing age and experience instinctive behaviour is replaced by habit formation. At this stage habits mechanise the behaviour of an individual. But as they are mechanical in nature they have no power to control or manipulate the behaviour pattern,

(iii) Instincts give birth to emotions and these emotions play an important part in the personality or character development. The various emotions centred round an object or idea often combine themselves to form a composite group or organisation. When this organism or structure takes a permanent structure in the mind of an individual he develops a sentiment regarding that particular object or idea.

(iv) In the last stage the various sentiments are combined so as to form a system or organisation. The equilibrium of this system is maintained by the intellect and the master sentiment.

This system of properly organised sentiments, which is known as morality or character of an individual, is completely an acquired disposition. In actual sense the moral development or character formation of an individual can be compared with a building which possesses the foundation in the form of (refined) instincts. The emotions can be taken as the bricks for building the walls and roofs of the sentiments. The sentiment of self-regard is the cement or the adhesive material. In this way, morality or character like building consists of the foundation material and the other constructive material and thus defined as the sum total of what an individual possesses.

In this way, as a general sense, as it may appear most of the time "the domains of morality or character" in the words of Ormond (2003) *"may include such traits (acquired-tendencies) as honesty, fairness, dependability, concern for the rights and welfare of others, and other pro-social behaviour helping, sharing and comforting, and so on. The term immoral behaviour typically refers to actions that are unfair, cause physical or emotional harm, or violate the rights of others"*. (p. 86).

In conclusion we can repeat the saying of Ross that "morality or character is just the organised self". (1951, p. 129) Instincts, emotions, habits, temperament, will and sentiments — all are the constituents of one's morality or character. The organisation of these constituents into one whole in the form of a permanent mental structure is taken as a morality or character of an individual. Therefore the study of one's morality or character need complete understanding of one's habits, motivation, will, sentiments, intellect, self image and many other factors affecting this total personality. The person's behaviour in the social situation is governed by his moral sense. Therefore, morality or character in its essence can be defined as an organised and stable mental structure of an individual existing in the form of one's moral sense or reasoning which determines his social behaviour.

Morality is an cquired or Learned Phenomenon

The traits of good or bad conduct, conformity or non-conformity to the moral code of the social group or capability of behaving by judging an act as right or wrong is not an inherited phenomenon. Its blue prints do not lie in the chromosomes or genes of an individual. Although, the inherited physiological and cognitive structure, to some extent, may be considered to provide some basic foundation to the inclination and preferences for psycho-social behaviour but as far the studies of concept development and patterns of behaviour have revealed, the existence of moral sense and demonstration of moral behaviour on the part of individuals are purely the subject of their environmental influences rather than hereditary contributions. Calling morality as an acquired or learned phenomenon, Hurlock (1956: 405) writes:

> At birth, the child has no conscience and no scale of values. Thus, he is neither moral nor immoral Instead, he is 'non-moral in the sense that his behaviour is not guided by moral standards. Before he can behave in a moral way, he must learn what the group to which he belongs believes to be right or wrong. This he will learn gradually through the childhood years.

Morality, in this way, should be taken as an acquired and learned phenomenon both in terms of acquiring moral sense or reasoning and demonstrating moral or ethical behaviour in conformity to the moral or ethical code set by the society. The ability to Judge one's own conduct and that of others (moral reasoning) in terms of evaluating what is right or wrong comes through actual personal experiences and training received by the child as he passes through the various ages and stages of his developmental period.

Levels of Character or Morality

According to *Cronbach,* there *are five* levels of character or morality which are shown in the Fig. 5.3.

1. *Amoral stage:* This stage lasts from birth to two years. At this stage, the performer does not know or realise that his choice has good or bad effect on others or affects the welfare of others *e.g.* plucking flower from a neighbour's garden. Wants are the sole motivation for a newly born infant who has no concept of good or bad. At this stage he has no control over emotions, cries at the time of every need without bothering whether or not the cry disturbs others.

2. *Self centred stage:* It lasts from 2 to 6 years. At this stage the person gratifies his own needs and wishes without caring for the effects of his own act on others. His action interferes with the happiness of others though he may not desire to violate the rules. The choice in this case is selfish and if fixation takes place, the person may develop miserly and selfish habits,

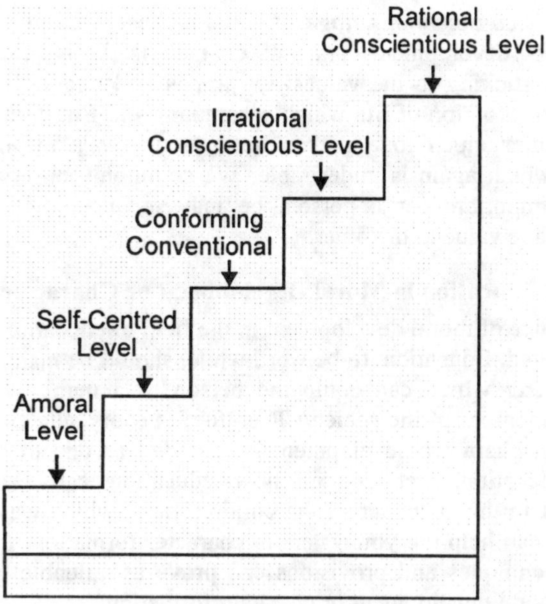

Fig. 5.3: Levels of Character or Morality

source of trouble to himself and others. The selfish choices are gradually reduced by socialisation. Selfish choices may also sometimes be seen in case of man of character.

3. *Conforming-conventional stage:* The child in his early life is at this stage. The person may do as the Romans do even when his behaviour harms others. A person may not copy because of resulting punishment. Many good citizens follow conventional pattern of behaviour to avoid bad consequences by breaking the norms.

4. *Irrational-conscientious stage:* The internal self-criticism which is responsible for making a person dissatisfied with some conduct even though that conduct will satisfy his external goals is called conscience. It can be compared with the concept of Super-ego as given by Sigmund Freud.

When a person acts in the light of the values held emotionally rather than rationally *e.g.* speaks the truth irrationally, he is said to exhibit irrational conscientious behaviour. He will always speak the truth even if he were to be hanged for it.

Some people opine that since we attach topmost importance to value, we should consider it the best form of morality whereas others believe that people not able to tell gracious social lies will find it most difficult — rather impossible to get along with the world. No doubt many irrational conformers have good adjustment with the community in spite of the fact that rigid truthfulness proves an obstacle or hindrance in certain social situations.

5. *Rational conscientious stage:* It is the highest stage of one's morality or character development and it characterised by rationally (not emotionally) sticking to the values *e.g.* war is undesirable because of the undesirable destruction of life which accompanies it. But destruction of life may not matter much to a person because war is a means to prevent oppression which again is undesirable. We commonly observe that if two values are important for a person, he may reconcile both of them or subordinate one value to the other.

The Role of Education in Moral Development or Character Formation

The importance of moral development in the field of education can never be under-estimated. Education, to be worthwhile, should be man making and it is the character which can equip the person as a man — the able and responsible member of the society. Therefore at every stage, in any system of education, character development is regarded as one of the important aims of education. Let us see how education can bring desirable development in the character of the children or in which way schools and the teachers can help the youngsters in character formation. In general, the following techniques and provisions can prove as valuable guide-lines in the task of moral development or character formation:

1. *Proper training of instincts and emotions:* Instincts form the rock-bottom of character. Therefore, the first step in the formation of character is the sublimation and modification of instincts. The emotions, which control the behaviour of an individual, take their energy from different instincts. In fact instincts and emotions give birth to so many elements of one's character. Nature of instinctive and emotional behaviour contributes much to the character development. Therefore, proper care should be taken to modify and sublimate the instinctive impulses and emotions along socially desirable channels. For instance, the crude instinct of combat and emotion of anger after sublimation can be channelised into patriotic and philanthropic deeds and thus they may help in character formation.

2. *Training of will power*: Proper care should be taken for the development of a strong will power among the children. Firm determination and power of taking right decision at a right time are products of will power and these two qualities are very essential for the development of a strong character. There is a perfect correlation between will and the character. There are so many undesirable and negative things which we do and think them bad but due to weakness of our will cannot do away with them. A man of strong will can make himself free from these harmful factors and can remove the obstacles in the path of his character development.

3. *Organisation of good habits:* Habits also form a path of the character. Therefore, due care should be taken to develop healthy habits among the children through proper conditioning. The wrong habits need extinction through de-conditioning and proper understanding.

4. *Development of worthy ideals:* What a person does and how he will behave in a particular situation depends much on his aims of life and the ideals for which he strives. In other words the character of a person can be judged through his values and ideals. Higher the ideals and goals of life, the stronger is the character of a person. Therefore, the children should be made to develop worthy ideals, higher values and noble aims of life so that they can imbibe good virtues in them.

5. *Organisation and Development of proper sentiments:* Character is referred to as the system or organisation of sentiments, therefore, every care should be taken to develop a well organised stable system of healthy sentiments among the children. First of all due consideration should be paid for developing right type of sentiments like sentiments of patriotism, moral sentiment, social sentiment, intellectual sentiment, aesthetic sentiment and self-regarding sentiment. Later on all these positive like wise sentiments should be well organised with the help of the master sentiment *i.e.* self-regarding sentiment. The strength of one's character always depends upon the sentiment of self-regard. Therefore, children must be helped to develop a strong sense of self respect and a sentiment of self-regard. In developing this very important sentiment the following points should be kept in mind:

(i) Due respect must be shown for the individuality of the child.
(ii) The child should be given reasonable freedom in day to day work.
(iii) He must be encouraged to do his work independently and every care should be taken to build his self-confidence.
(iv) He must get proper love and affection coupled with an adequate sense of security.
(v) He must be helped to share and play a role of responsible individual in his school and social life.

6. *The role of suggestion:* Suggestion occupies an important place in the formation and development of character. Children are very sensitive to suggestion. Therefore, help of suggestion should be taken in character formation. But as far as possible, positive suggestion should be given to the children for bringing desirable improvement in their behaviour. This can be achieved through the ideal stories and the life sketches of great men and women. Teachers and parents may provide the living examples. After stepping in for character development, the children should be told that they are making satisfactory progress. Auto-suggestion can also bring very good results at this stage. The feeling, that he is improving day by day and acquiring good habits and characteristics, can immediately help the child to become a man of character.

7. *The role of imitation:* Child is imitative by nature. He imitates what he sees and hears. To him his parents, elders and the teachers are ideals. He imitates them consciously and unconsciously. Hence, it is essential that the teachers, parents and other elder members of the society should place the ideal examples of their own conduct and character. Every care should be

taken by the parents and teachers that nothing undesirable should be imitated by the children. They must be provided with healthy and inspiring atmosphere inside the school and at their homes. They should not be made to fall prey to bad company and unhealthy society.

8. *Role of reward and punishment:* Punishment and reward both occupy an important place in the development of character. In the modern age of democratic values and applied Psychology, the role of punishment in character formation is decried. It is said about it that it creates complexes in the mind of the students and does more harm than good. The main function of punishment is negative as it can only check wrong things, but it certainly cannot develop the desired attitude.

No doubt there is some truth in these observations but we cannot give up the punishment completely in our educational system. Sometimes punishment appears to be the only tool that can curb down the undesirable activities. But as far as possible the punishment should be resorted to only when other measures fail. Most of the time, positive measures like rewards, praise, appreciation and other methods for the due incentive and encouragement should be applied.

9. *Role of moral instructions and religious education:* No one can question the utility of moral and religious education as an instrument for character formation. In one form or the other provision should be made for its inclusion in a sound system of education. Religious education in a secular state like India creates some doubts in the mind. Such type of education need not be based upon some narrow rigid sectarian feelings. In fact it should emphasize the lofty moral and human values and keep itself away from the rituals of the various religions. It should teach the children to pay respect to all the religions and men of character irrespective of caste, colour and creed.

The moral values may be inculcated in the children by suggestions through short stories like the stories from *Panchtantra* and *Hitopdesh*, *Ramayana* and the *Mahabharata*. Biographies and autobiographies of the great men may also serve the purpose. Prayer assembly, talks on morality and other programmes of co-curricular activities can also be made use of for the moral and religious instruction.

10. *Proper socialization of the child:* Social development and character development bear a positive correlation. A socially developed child always behaves according to the norms and values of the society and therefore is more conscious of his character. Therefore every care should be taken for the proper social development of the child. He must be helped in the inculcation of desirable social virtues and maintenance of essential social relations with his peers and other members of the society.

11. *Proper mental development of the child:* Character formation is also linked with the proper mental development of the child. Intellect plays a vital role in the organisation of the elements of character. How a person will

behave in a particular situation and face the realities of life depends much upon his intellectual powers. Therefore proper care should be taken to develop the intellectual powers like reasoning, thinking, imagination, memory and concentration, etc.

12. *The role of the school, family and the society:* Environment plays a vital role in the development of character. From the very birth or right from the time of conception, the environmental forces begin to influence the behaviour of the child. Parents and the family is the first social institution where the foundation stone regarding the character of the child is laid down. Outside the family, the neighbourhood, community and the social forces influence the conduct of the child. When he goes to school, the school atmosphere along with the teachers and school-mates cast its influence upon the character of the child. Therefore, it is essential that all these social forces must join their hands in the task of the children's character formation. The social environment as a whole must be so suggestive and inspiring that the children can pick up the habits and characteristics essential for proper character development.

In fact moral development or character formation is a gigantic task. Without the active cooperation of all the involved persons-children, parents, teachers and all the important social agencies it is hard to achieve some fruitful results in this direction. We have to exploit all the resources at our command and should strive hard by all the methods and techniques in our possession. The observation made by Skinner and Harriman reminds us of the same. In their words:

> "There is no curriculum or method that will produce character (or develop morality) by magic. On the contrary, every experience in the home, at church, on the playground or at school presents an opportunity for character development. " (1937, p. 261)

Character formation, in its true sense, is an all round development and needs an all round effort. Paying attention over all the aspects it is needed that a programme of character formation should be chalked out and it should be implemented with the hearty cooperation of all the involved partners.

INTERRELATIONSHIP AMONG DIFFERENT DIMENSIONS OF DEVELOPMENT

The different dimensions of child's development — physical, mental, social, emotional, language and moral show a high degree of correlation or interrelationship among themselves *i.e.* each one of them has a great potential to affect or influence the development of a child in other dimensions and in turn is influenced by the pattern of development going on in other aspects or dimensions of child's development. Let us have a look at the type of interrelationship existing among different dimensions of child's development.

1. Let us take the case of child's physical development, A normally physically developed child has a normal functioning of his body systems including his glands. He is reasonably satisfied with the physique, structure, functioning and appearance of his body. It helps him to gain sufficient gains in terms of his adequate development, functioning and adjustment in other areas or dimensions of his development. A sound body has a sound mind, more competency and capacity to exercise proper restraint over the expression of emotions, more energy and confidence in having friendship and social relationship with others, more opportunities to learn language from the social company of others and exercise self-restraint for enabling him to avid with the code of conduct and morality. In this way, one's normal and adequate physical development is helpful to him in seeking his proper development and adjustment in the other areas or aspects of his development. However, it is the one side of the story. On the other side, the physical development of the child is also greatly benefitted through the development going into the other aspects of his development. It is properly affected through his mental, social, emotional, language and moral development. Inadequacy and deficiency in one or the other aspects of his development proves quite costly to him in terms of his adequate physical development, health and adjustment. The child lacking in emotional and social development may be deprived with the appropriate opportunities of playing with their peers and team mates, he may not be able to exercise desirable control and restraint over his emotions and thus may suffer from emotional and social maladjustment problems causing one or the other physical and health problems to the affected child. A socially or morally deviant child may pick up undesirable unhealthy habits like smoking, alcoholism, drug addiction and host of others proving too damaging and undesirable for his adequate physical development and normal well being.

2. Similarly, we may find that child's mental or cognitive development has the sufficient strength, power and capability of influencing and affecting one's development in other dimensions in a desired way as well as getting influenced in return in the reciprocal way, Cognitive development and language development may exhibit a strong interrelationship on this account. The language learning may play a key role in the adequate development of children's mental or cognitive development. The children who are intellectually or mentally more developed may be seen to show more speed and efficiency in terms of language learning. The children equipped with adequate mental abilities may also be found to get ahead in terms of their proper emotional and social development and on reciprocal basis the adequate emotional and social development may contribute much towards the proper intellectual or social development of the children.

3. Emotional and social development of the children may be found to play a great role in influencing the development of children in relation to other aspects/dimensions of their development. Children who are

emotionally sound, socially competent and mixing have greater chances of getting ahead in terms of their mental/intellectual development, physical development and well being as well as acquiring the desired language learning abilities. Contrarily, the development in other dimensions may also influence the emotional and social development of the children on an equally reciprocal basis.

4. One's moral development also equally affects and influences his development in other dimensions — physical mental, social, emotional or linguistic. Moral development helps one to learn socially desirable habits, get adjusted well in his socio-cultural environment and acquire sufficient will power, strength and self-confidence for going ahead in his physical, mental, emotional, social and language development. A person defeated on the front of adequate moral development may lose all grounds concerning his adequate development and welfare in almost all various aspects and dimensions of his personality or development. On the other hand, children's moral development may be found to be affected in a great way with the type of development going on in their physical, mental, social, emotional and linguistic development. We can't expect from a socially deviant or emotionally maladjusted child to avid with the accepted norms of the society or code of ethics.

In this way, we may find a close intercorelation existing among the various dimensions of a child's development. It is why, we should always aim to have an all round balanced growth and development in all the aspects or dimensions of a child. A lop sided development in one dimension at the cost of others may bring quite negative results/impacts on the well being of the concerned individual. Therefore, the system of school education should be so geared as to seek harmonious development of the children in respect to the different dimensions of their development.

6

Theories of Development

INTRODUCTION

We all have our origin from a fertilized ovum in the womb of our mother. It is the process of growth and development that has given us our shapes and sizes, abilities and capacities to function in physical, mental, emotional, socio-cultural and moral ways. How this process of development in various aspects or dimensions such as physical, mental or cognitive, emotional, social, moral or linguistic is carried among the developing or growing children? What factors or things contribute or influence the development of children related to one or the assets of his personality? The questions like these have been a serious issue before researchers and scholars in education psychology and sociology. As a solution, they have arrived at their own ideas, principles and developmental theories. We would be discussing a few of these developmental theories in this chapter known as:

A. Piaget's Theory of Cognitive Development
B. Erickson's Theory of Psycho-Social Development
C. Kohlberg's Theory of Moral Development

A. PIAGET'S THEORY OF COGNITIVE DEVELOPMENT

Jean Piaget, a Swiss biologist later on turned into a cognitive and child psychologist is known well for providing a stage theory of cognitive development for explaining the development of thinking in human beings from infancy to adulthood.

So keen was his interest in the study of cognitive and child psychology that he along with his wife (a former student of his at the Rousseau Institute) devoted almost all the precious years of their early married life to studying the cognitive development of their own three children by making them the subjects of their laboratory studies. As a result, today his theory of cognitive development has no parallel in the history of research in the field of developmental, cognitive and child psychology. For understanding this theory concerning the stages of cognitive development, let us first try to understand the major theoretical premises on which the theory stands.

Piaget's Theoretical Notions

Piaget designed a proper framework to understand the structure, functioning and development of the cognitive network of the human mind. He postulated that, like physical organs of the human body, there are two aspects of the human mind: one is referred to as cognitive structure and the other as cognitive functioning.

Cognitive Structure

Unlike other creatures, the human baby is born with a few practical instincts and reflexes such as sucking, looking, reaching and grasping. Therefore, the initial cognitive structure of infants is supposed to incorporate only those cognitive abilities or potentials which help them to do such acts such as look, reach out or grasp. Piaget named these abilities or potentials as *schemas* and termed them as the basic building blocks of our thinking. He defined them as the organized systems of actions or thought that allow us to mentally represent or "think about" the objects and events in our world (Woolfolk, 2004, p.30). Let us try to understand the meaning conveyed by the term 'schema' more clearly by referring to a particular schema like the 'sucking schema'. It refers to one's general cognitive ability or potential to suck objects. This schema is more than a single manifestation of the sucking reflex. It can be thought of as a cognitive structure that makes all acts of sucking possible. However, the description of this act of sucking differs in relation to contents *i.e.,* specific responses to specific stimuli such as the mother's nipple, a spoon, a toy, etc. We thus conclude that a schema represents a unit of one's cognitive structure in the shape of a general potential to perform a particular class of behaviours (like sucking, grasping, calculating, etc.), the content of which is related to the conditions that prevail during any particular manifestation of that general potential.

The various schemas with their contents thus form the basic structure of the human mind. The earlier schemas represent those reflexes and instincts that are biologically inherited. However, as a child grows, with the interaction of physical and social environment, he is able to form different schemas, resulting in changes and modifications in his cognitive structure.

Cognitive Functioning

The structure of an organism is said to play a decisive role in its functioning. Therefore, what is available to an individual in terms of his schemas decides how he is going to respond to the stimuli present in his physical or social environment. On the other hand, the individual has to adapt to his environment for survival as well as proper growth and development. The key to his cognitive development thus lies in his constant interaction with an adaptation to his physical and social environment. The task of such adaptation is carried out through the processes of assimilation and accommodation.

Assimilation refers to a kind of matching between the already existing cognitive structures and the environmental needs as they arise. In a situation where a six-month old infant is given a new toy it is likely to respond by putting the toy in his mouth. This is assimilation, as what the child did was to assimilate, incorporate or fit ideas about the new toy into already existing cognitive structures about old toys. His cognitive structure about old toys revolved around the sucking schema, therefore, he at once responded by performing the act of sucking.

Now, in case the new toy is too big to be picked up and placed in the mouth, it will certainly need a change or modification in the already existing cognitive structure. The child will have to change his old ways of thinking and behaving in order to adapt or adjust to the new situation. Consequently, now instead of sucking, the child may respond by pushing or grasping the toy. This is called *accommodation* as one tries to accommodate or adjust to new ways of thinking and behaving in place of assimilating or behaving in the same old fashion. Thus, whereas in the process of assimilation, one's responses are supposed to bank upon one's past experiences and already compiled stock of information, in the process of accommodation one has to learn new ways of thinking and behaving by making changes or modifications in one's existing cognitive structure. For instance, when the child is offered milk in a tumbler instead of the feeding bottle, first he tries his old way of behaving, *i.e.,* sucking. Afterwards, as a result of accommodation he picks up the new ways and consequently makes the necessary modification in his old cognitive structure.

Parallel to the concept of the processes of assimilation and accommodation linked with the process of the child's cognitive development, Piaget postulated the concept of *equilibration.* He asserted that the process of assimilation or accommodation helps the organism to adjust or maintain a harmonious relationship between himself and his environment. This adjustment mechanism was called equilibration by Piaget. It can be defined as an innate tendency or continuous drive on the part of an organism to organise its experiences (through assimilation or accommodation) for obtaining optimal adaptation to the changing demands of its environment by maintaining a proper balance between its cognitive structure and the changing demands of its environment. In fact, it is the need of seeking optimal adaptation or maintaining balance between himself and his environment that makes an individual feel uncomfortable and start reorganising his cognitive structure for equipping himself with new ways of thinking and behaving.

In this way Piaget highlighted the role of the following factors in one's cognitive make-up and its functioning:

1. The biologically inherited reflexes and mental dispositions as the fundamental cognitive structure.
2. The changes and development brought about in the cognitive structure through maturation (*i.e.,* the process of natural growth).
3. The changes and development in the cognitive structure brought about through experiences (interaction with the physical and social

environment) involving the processes of assimilation, accommodation and equilibration.

Stages of Intellectual Development

As already pointed out, Piaget, on account of his biological background, traced the initiation of human cognitive development in terms of biologically inherited ways of interacting with the environment. He further postulated that the changes and developments in one's cognitive structure are brought about by interaction with one's physical and social environment. This task is carried out through the mechanism of equilibration, resulting in constant organisation of one's cognitive structure by the interplay of accommodation and assimilation. This task of constant organisation of the mental structure is an individual phenomenon; we may, therefore, find wide differences between children in terms of possession of cognitive abilities. However, as Piaget concluded, this organisation of the mental structure in all children always takes place in a particular order involving definite stages of intellectual development. Thus, although children of the same age may differ in terms of possession of mental abilities, the order, in which the abilities evolve, and the pattern of development are quite constant and universal. Let us discuss this pattern of intellectual development in terms of the four developmental stages suggested by Piaget.

Sensori-motor Stage (From birth to about two years)

Piaget called the first stage of intellectual development the sensori-motor stage because (a) it is characterized by the absence of language, and (b) it is limited to direct sensory and motor interactions with the environment. The cognitive development at this stage occurs along the following pattern:

1. At birth the infant exhibits a limited number of uncoordinated reflexes such as sucking, looking, reaching and grasping.

2. During the next four months the uncoordinated reflexes are coordinated into simple schemes providing the child with a general potential to perform certain classes of behaviour. For example, the infant now tries to suck anything which is put into his mouth, stares at whatever he sees, reaches for everything and grasps all that is put into his hands.

3. By the age of eight months the infant is able to react to objects outside himself. He begins to realize that the objects around him are separated from himself and they have their independent and permanent existence. Prior to such development his view of the environmental objects is quite transitory, *i.e.,* what is out of sight is purely out of mind. For example, if the infant is playing with a toy and you pick it up, hide it somewhere while allowing the child to watch your act of hiding the toy, he will at once forget about it. For him the toy placed under a blanket or hidden somewhere has disappeared and is no more. With the passage of time, gradually the concept of object permanence evolves in the cognitive structure of the infant. He begins to

realize that the objects continue to exist even though he cannot see or experience them. Thus he begins to search for the objects that are hidden. For example, if you hide a toy in the blanket the infant will try to lift the blanket and search for the toy. In case you have shifted it somewhere, he will proceed to investigate its whereabouts under the assumption that the object has its permanent identity. When he does so we may infer that the child has been able to see or experience the object in his mind by making its mental image. Now he can proceed to the next stage of intellectual development involving the symbolic world of language by leaving behind the pure sensory or motor exploration.

4. Another significant achievement for the child of sensory motor stage according to Piaget is that by the end of the period of infancy he may step into logical goal-directed actions. Throwing light on this aspect Woolfolk (2004) writes, *"Think of the familiar container toy for babies. It is usually plastic, has a lid, and contains several colourful items that can be dumped out and replaced. A six month old baby is likely to become frustrated trying to get to the toys inside. An older child who has mastered the basics of the sensori-motor stage will probably be able to deal with the toy in an orderly fashion by building a 'container toy' scheme, (1) get the lid off (2) turn the container upside down, (3) shake if the items jam, (4) Watch the items fall. Later on the child is also soon be able to reverse this action by refilling the container."* (p. 32-33).

Pre-operational Stage (about 2 to 7 years)

While stepping into this stage, the child begins to replace direct action in the form of sensory or motor exploration with symbols. The learning of the language provides him with a good tool for thinking. He begins to utter worlds to ask for something rather than just reaching out to get it. In addition to words, his thinking is also characterized by other symbolic representations or images of the things in the environment. This stage can be further sub-divided into: (1) the pre-conceptual phase (approximately two to four years), and (2) the intuitive phase (approximately four to seven years).

1. *Pre-conceptual phase:* This is the period of the rudimentary concept formation and is characterized by the following features:

(a) In the early part of this stage, the children seem to identify objects by their names and put them into certain classes. However, they usually make mistakes in this process of identification and concept formation. For example, they think all men are *'daddy'* all women are *'mummy'* and all dogs are *'montu'*.

(b) Their mode of thinking and reasoning is quite illogical at this stage. It is neither inductive nor deductive but rather transductive in nature. For example, the child at this stage would reason like: as "cows are big animals with four legs and a long tail. This animal is also big and has four legs and a long tail, therefore it is a cow".

(c) Their thinking is sometimes too imaginative and far removed from reality. It may be seen in their play activities when a block of wood is turned into a riding horse or motor cycle and a doll into a baby. Moreover, at this stage they are unable to distinguish between living and non-living objects. For them the doll in their hands is a live baby who can cry, smile and sleep. Similarly, the dreams they have are, for them, real and concrete events.

(d) The other major characteristic of the cognitive structure of the child at this stage is concerned with his egocentric nature. By egocentric Piaget means that the child can see the world only from his own standpoint. He considers that the sun and moon are following him, the rain falls to delight him, and obviously what exists in the external environment is specifically meant for him. He cannot think that people may have different opinions and differ in their modes of thinking and conclusions. He considers himself as the centre of a world of people who are supposed to perceive the things the way he does.

2. *Intuitive phase (approximately four to seven years)*: At this stage the child progresses towards the formation of various concepts at a more advanced level. For example, now he will agree that apples, oranges and bananas are all fruits despite the difference in their shape, colour or taste. But what he thinks or solves at this stage is carried out intuitively, rather than in accordance with any logical rule. Consequently, as Piaget concludes, the child's thinking at this stage in not logical and is full of contradictions. It is clearly reflected in the absence in him of the two main cognitive characteristics namely, reversibility (ability to reverse) and conservation (ability to see an object as permanent even though its arrangement or appearance is changed as long as nothing is added or taken away).

For example when a child realizes that not only has he a brother but his brother also has a brother in him, it can be said that the child has developed the reversible quality in his cognitive operations. However, at the pre-operational stage children are seen not to possess the reversible characteristic in their mental functioning. For them moving from A to B may not carry the same meaning as moving from B to A.

Similarly, the thinking of pre-operational children at the intuitive stage is marked by an inability to conserve in terms of quantity as well as number as may be understood through the following experiments:

Experiment No. 1: A child belonging to the pre-operational age say five years old is shown two identical containers filled with the same quantity of coloured water. The child will agree that both have the same amount. Now the experimenter pours the water from one of the containers into a taller but narrower container and asks the child to compare the amount of water in this taller container with the amount in one of the old containers.

The inability to conserve in terms of quantity makes the child think that there is more water in the taller container even when the child has observed that the same amount of water has been poured into it (see Figure 6.1). The child in this experiment is likely to say that the taller container has more water because the level of the water is higher in this container. According to Piaget this happens because the child at this stage fails to realize that the amount or quantity of a material does not change with the change in the shape or appearance of its container. In other words, the child belonging to the preoperational stage shows a marked inability to conserve continuous quantity.

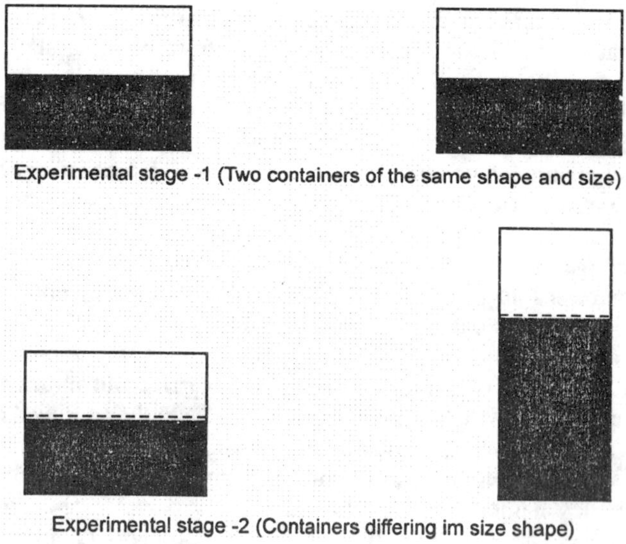

Fig. 6.1: Experiment Demonstrating Inability for Conservation in Terms of Quantity

Experiment No. 2. A child is shown two sets of beads arranged in one-to-one correspondence. The child is asked if the beads in the two rows are equal in number. The child would say that they are. The beads in one row are then spaced further apart (or spaced closer together) and the child is then asked to tell which row has more beads.

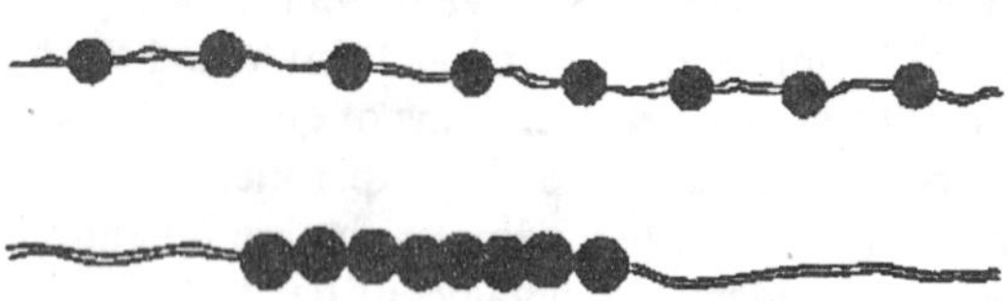

Fig. 6.2: Experiment Demonstrating Inability for Conservation in Terms of Number

Here with reference to Figure 6.2 the child belonging to the pre-operational stage is likely to say that the bottom row has more beads. What leads the child to think in such an illogical manner? The answer according to Piaget lies in the fact that the concept of the conservation of numbers is not yet developed in the child. He is therefore, unable to realize the simple fact that a mere change in appearance or arrangement of some objects cannot increase or decrease their number. As a conclusion it may be said in connection with intellectual development of the child belonging to the pre-operational stage that although the child's cognitive structure or thinking is seen to be operated through symbols instead of motor and sensory actions, yet his thinking at this stage is characterized as illogical and full of contradictions.

Concrete Operational Stage (about seven to eleven years)

This stage shows marked developments in the cognitive functioning of the child.

1. The child now learns to deal with concepts and ideas that exist only in mental terms. He can now think about things and figure out discrepancies and relationships.
2. He begins to think in terms of a set of interrelated principles rather than single bits of knowledge. As a result he can think in terms of systems.
3. His thinking becomes more logical and systematic. He can now make use of inductive and deductive approaches in terms of reasoning and arriving at conclusions.
4. The child now develops the ability to conserve both in terms of quantity and number of objects. He can now very well think that the change in appearance of an object does not alter either its quantity or its number.
5. The thinking of the child is no longer 'rigid' and 'irreversible'. A female child who has a sister now clearly realizes that her sister also has a sister.
6. The child now is no longer ego-centric in his thinking. He does not think of himself as the centre of the external world and does not perceive the world only from his own standpoint. He does not find it difficult to appreciate that other people have experiences, views and ideas that differ from his own.
7. The child now develops the abilities to deal adequately with classes. He can classify objects. He develops the ability of serialisation like arranging things from largest to smallest and vice versa. The number concept is also developed, but it all happens in a very simple concrete form.
8. The child now learns to carry out rather complex operations or tackle problems as long as they are concrete and not abstract. For example, the child now realizes the importance of cardinal numbers and ordinal numbers. He can operate symbolically by combining, reversing and forming associations among different objects.

In this way, the child reaches a satisfactory level in terms of intellectual development by his thinking becoming quite systematic and logical. However, what is done or thought by him at this stage is done purely on a concrete level. His thought processes are limited to real events observed or the actual objects operated by him. He is unable to think in abstract terms.

In this way the concrete operation stage can actually by a pre-preparation for the final stage of formal operations mainly concerned with abstractions.

Formal Operation Stage (about 12 to 15 years)

The intellectual development and functioning takes a very sophisticated shape at this stage as the child learns to deal with abstraction by logical thinking. Actually he learns to utilize the tool of symbolism as effectively as possible in the process of thought and problem solving. The child now gets interested in forms. He begins to construct relationships between concrete operations and between symbols. Generalizations and framing of rules by operating in abstract terms become quite possible at this stage. The child now begins to appreciate that some hypothetical problems can be solved mentally by applying the same rules as would be applied to concrete problems. He begins to look at problems in many ways and explore various solutions but in a very systematic and logical way. For example, if a child of this stage is shown five colourless, odourless liquids in test tubes and is asked to find out what combination of the five will produce a brown liquid, he is likely to discover the possible combination by adopting a systematic approach, *e.g.,* combining the first and second, then first and third, then first and fourth and so on. Thus it is quite distinctive in comparison to the children belonging to earlier stages of cognitive development who will simply resort to trial and error for finding the solution.

Moreover, the child's thinking at this stage does not remain only concrete but becomes hypothetical, with considerations given to the most unusual ideas. Hence the creative aspects in the child are very much visible during this age not only in terms of concrete operations but also in terms of abstraction and pure imagination. For example, previous to this stage, if we were to ask a child to imagine he has three fathers, he might reply that it is no use imaging such a thing as one can only have one father. However, in the formal operational stage such thoughts involving unusual ideas are possible. Here one can imagine figures and shapes and can fly in the air without wings as is often done by children when studying poetry, algebra and geometry.

The other noticeable characteristic of this stage, as Piaget found, was the child's interest in dealing with things that do not exist in reality instead of the things concerning the present which are actually perceived by him.

In fact, Piaget was of the opinion that the thought processes and the intellectual functioning of a child at the formal operational period reflect the beginning of the most advanced stage in the functioning of his cognitive system. It provides a ladder to reach the limits of a person's intellectual development and actualize his potentiality to the maximum in the available circumstances. The higher order of intellectual functioning developed through this stage, according to Piaget, is usually characterized by the presence of the most sophisticated cognitive abilities like the ability to: (a) build up multiple hypotheses and a number of alternate solutions; (b) verify all possible solutions in a systematic and logical way; (c) generalize and arrive at abstract rules that cover many specific situations.

In this way, according to Piaget, after the expiry of the formal operation stage the child may reach full intellectual potential. He may discover the solutions of problems through mental manipulation of symbols by adopting a logical and systematic procedure known as scientific thinking and problem solving rather than a reflexive, motor or sensory manipulation as is done at the sensory motor stage; or by exposing his thinking operationally in more concrete terms as done at the concrete operation stage. It thus represents a stage which helps the child to attain mental maturity with respect to the development of his cognitive abilities.

Critical Evaluation of Piaget's Theory

Piaget's theory on intellectual development has been questioned and challenged on the following grounds:

1. Piaget's views on the pattern of intellectual development are not as uniform and universal as claimed by him. He based his theory on detailed observations of European children as they grew up in 1920s, 1930s and 1940s. The subsequent researches in Europe and outside have demonstrated significant deviations from the chronological ages linked with different stages of intellectual development by Piaget.

2. The Piagetian view that thinking proceeds in distinct stages has also been seriously challenged. It has been found that cognitive performance at particular ages is usually very inconsistent.

3. Piaget's claim that children below the age of concrete operations are incapable of logical thinking and are egocentric has been refuted by a number of research studies. It has been established that children are able to both think logically and show sensitivity and concern for the feelings and viewpoints of others at every early ages.

4. The claim that a child is unable to perform an intellectual task like conservation at ages below those specified by Piaget has also been questioned. A number of studies have shown that it is possible to train children to carry out not only tasks like conservation but also very typical complex formal operations at ages below those specified by Piaget.

5 Piaget has linked biological maturation with the development of cognitive abilities and thus made a certain stage of maturation necessary for learning the cognitive task related to that maturation age. He is thus often blamed for being a pure nativist who gives singular importance to biological maturation for the intellectual development of the child. However, this criticism is one-sided, as Piaget believes that maturation works only as the framework for intellectual development and the necessary material and means are supplied by one's physical and social environment. His stand on this issue may become quite clear through the following assertion of Inhelder and Piaget (1958):

> The maturation of the nervous system can do not more than determine the totality of possibilities and impossibilities at a given stage. A particular social environment remains indispensable for the realization of these possibilities. It follows that their realization can be accelerated or retarded as a function of cultural and educational conditions.

If we examine the nature of the criticism levelled against Piaget's theory we find that most of it is one-sided. For example, as is clear from the above quotation, it is not true that Piaget's theory does not take the environmental experiences into account. Similarly, we can visualize that, while laying down different stages of cognitive development, Piaget does not mean that all children belonging to all cultures essentially pass through these stages in the chronological periods specified by him. As he gives due recognition to the forces of biological inheritance, maturation and environmental experiences in the formation and functioning of one's cognitive structure, the possibility in terms of variation in ages for reaching a particular stage of intellectual development cannot be ruled out. Consequently, the actual age at which certain types of mental abilities appear varies from child to child or from culture to culture. Irrespective of this acknowledgement linked with the individual differences with regard to intellectual development, the contribution of Piaget's theory can never be underrated. Whatever points we may raise against the universality and validity of his theory, it would always be remembered that intellectual development involves stages as specified by Piaget and occurs in the same order irrespective of the individual and environmental differences or geographical and cultural barriers.

Appreciation and Contribution to Education

Piaget, an acknowledged international authority in the field of child psychology and cognitive development, has contributed a great deal to the theory and practice of education. His contributions may be briefly summarized as follows:

1. Piaget interpreted and defined intelligence in a practical way. From birth onwards the individuals has to struggle for survival and seek adjustment with his environment. Intelligence in terms of his cognitive structured and functioning helps him in this task. Therefore, the intelligence of an individual can only be assessed in terms of the nature of adjustment (balance between him and his environment) he is making at a particular time under the prevailing circumstances. This means that one's intelligence is a dynamic function. It really has some purposes or functions and it is these functions that help us to measure the intelligence of a person. Interpreting intelligence in this way has led to intelligence tests being devised with emphasis on the mechanism of adaptation on the one hand, and maintenance of the balance between abilities and environmental demands for the development and welfare of the child on the other.

2. Piaget's theory has highlighted the importance of drives and motivation in the field of learning and development. It has utilized the concept of equilibration for this purpose by defining it as the continuous drive towards equilibrium or balance between the organism and its environment. Piaget's equilibration can be equated with Freud's sex gratification and Jung's self-actualization for activating one's behaviour.

3. Piaget's theory provides valuable information and advice on curriculum planning and structuring the schemes of studies. Since children of a particular region tend to reach a particular stage in their intellectual development at a particular age, what is to be planned in terms of their curriculum or scheme of studies must always be in tune with the expected level of their maturation and mental abilities. In other words, an ideal curriculum should provide the appropriate experiences at the proper time. For example, it is no use teaching world geography to students studying in first or second standard because at that age they have not yet acquired the necessary concepts like country, stage, or even city. Therefore, it is more appropriate to teach them local geography such as their neighbourhood, school, classroom and so on. Similarly, teaching algebra to the students of fourth or fifth standard is pointless as children of this age may not have acquired the ability to deal with abstractions. Piaget's theory may help in this direction by providing a suitable framework of the learning experiences in view of the cognitive development of the children and the needs of society.

4. The knowledge of Piaget's theory may prove quite valuable to teachers and parents for making them aware of the nature of the thought processes of the children at a particular level of maturation or chronological age. They may also get some idea of the changes that take place in the cognitive structure and functioning of their children. This type of knowledge may prove quite beneficial to them in dealing with the children and planning their training and education.

5. The major contribution of Piaget's theory is its analysis and suggestion of the optimal conditions for an individual's learning and development by introducing the concept of assimilation, accommodation and equilibration. According to Piaget, learning and development are the net result of interaction between a person's cognitive structure and his environmental experiences. For optimal learning to take place, the experiences or information presented must be of such a form and nature that it can be assimilated into the present cognitive structures, but at the same time different enough to necessitate a change in those structures calling for accommodation and resulting in new learning. Consequently, if the new information or learning is completely unrelated to previous learning, it will certainly not fit in with the present cognitive structure and so would not be understood. On the other hand, if it is too simple or unchallenging, it will be completely assimilated and hardly any need for further learning will arise. Therefore, according to Piaget's theory, for acquiring learning it is essential that experiences or material presented to

the learner are somewhat new and moderately challenging to initiate the phenomenon of accommodation but at the same time these experiences should be sufficiently linked and related with one's old learning so that they may be reasonably easy for being assimilated and understood by the learner.

6. Since the Piagetian theory considers both physical and social experiences as quite indispensable for one's intellectual development, it has placed a major responsibility on parents, teachers and others directly or indirectly connected with the education and welfare of children to arrange for the most appropriate and stimulating environment for their children.

7. Piaget's theory may be said to have the following implications vis-a-vis the children of nursery and elementary school:

(a) Since the children of this age are able to think only in concrete terms, it is advisable to allow them to experiment with materials in order to accommodate new understanding and to acquire new learning by themselves. For instance, to give the idea of the fractions 1/4, it would be best to cut an apple into four equal parts and then show one piece physically to show that the meaning of the fraction 1/4 is 'one out of four parts'.

(b) The teacher must try to emphasize discovery learning rather than teaching or telling each and every part of information to the students. They should try to set up environments in which the students can have a wide variety of experiences for self or discovery-learning.

8. Piagetian theory conveys that symbolic thinking adopted by children in their thought process after the sensory motor stage is not limited to the use of language only. There may be children who prefer to use images, relationships and other symbols instead of language as a tool for their thinking and may make better progress in terms of further learning and cognitive advancement. Therefore, the teaching-learning process should not be limited to the use of verbal communication, but should involve other symbolic expression and means for the communication of ideas suited to the circumstances and nature of the learner.

9. The last but not the least contribution of Piagetian theory is its emphasis on the individualization of education. It has advocated the need of child-centred education by saying that the educational experiences must be built around the learner's cognitive structure. What is suitable, appropriate and challenging to his cognitive structure must be given for him to acquire new experiences and develop his cognitive abilities. Since cognitive structures are sure to vary from child to child, in providing education, we have to think in terms of tailoring the educational material according to each child's cognitive structure. For this purpose the teacher has to know the level of functioning of each student's cognitive structure and then plan for his further learning and cognitive development accordingly.

B. ERICKSON'S THEORY OF PSYCHO-SOCIAL DEVELOPMENT

Eric Erikson was a native of Germany. He spent his early adult years studying art and travelling around Europe. A meeting with the famous psychoanalyst Sigmund Freud in Vienna led to an invitation from Freud to study psychoanalysis. It was a turning point of his career. He emigrated to America for this purpose and also to escape from the threat of Hitler. In America, he studied Native American traditions of human development and continued his work as a psychoanalyst. In 1950, he brought out his psychosocial theory — a developmental theory of the eight stages of man covering the entire life span rather than childhood and adolescent development like all other theories of development.

Introducing his theory, Erickson postulated that the development of an individual is the result of his interaction with his social environment. Right from his birth, his social development puts him under specific pressures or conflicts (called crises) by making specific demands at different ages or developmental stages of his life. The individual tries to meet these specific demands or resolve the crises by reacting psychologically in his own way, depending upon his circumstances. The complexity of the demands from society or social environment goes on increasing as the child advances on the ladder of growth and development. So, at each stage of his development, the child faces a new crisis, *i.e.* an issue that needs to be resolved at that particular stage of development. The way in which the 'crisis' of each stage is resolved has a major bearing on the development of one's personality which in turn is reflected as the positive and negative aspect of one's behaviour. Erickson discovered eight such issues or crises of life arising at different ages or periods of one's development and linked them with the eight stages of one's psycho-social development covering one's entire life span as outlined in Table 6.1.

Table 6.1: Age span for the stages of psycho-social development

Stage of psycho-social development	*Specific age or period*
Trust vs. Mistrust	Birth to 1½ years
Autonomy vs. Shame and Doubt	114 years to 3 years
Initiative vs. Guilt	3 to 6 years
Industry vs. Inferiority	6 to 12 years
Identity vs. Role Confusion	Adolescence (12 to 20 years)
Intimacy vs. Isolation	Early adulthood (20 to 45 years)
Generativity vs. Stagnation	Middle adulthood (45 to 65 years)
Ego integrity vs. Despair	Later adulthood (65 years onwards)

The above division outlines the types of crises that need to be resolved at particular stages or periods of one's life. It also identifies the different stages of psycho-social development, *i.e.* the personality traits that are likely to develop at a particular stage. For example, one may go on acquiring positive traits like trust, independence, initiative, industry and identity, etc., to develop into a meaningful personality. On the other hand, one can develop into a troublesome, confused and doomed personality by failing to successfully resolve the crisis of one's age and developing negative traits like mistrust, shame, doubt, guilt feeling, inferiority and the like. Since these behaviour traits, modes of adjustment or psychological build-up are acquired through one's active interaction with the social environment, the stages of development are referred to as psycho-social development. These different stages of psycho-social development should not be considered to begin suddenly or end abruptly. In fact, one stage evolves into another through the whole life cycle and the crisis of issues not resolved during one stage is supposed to carry over into the stages that follow in some way or the other as revealed through the following discussion:

Stage I: The period of trust vs. mistrust (Birth to 1½ years): In the first one and a half years of life, the infant is confronted with the crisis termed *trust* vs. *mistrust.* During this period the baby is completely dependent upon its mother or caretaker for the satisfaction of its needs. The way it is nourished, handled, protected and kept safe and comfortable at this stage may provide the baby with a sense of security or insecurity, a feeling of trust or mistrust in the mother or caretaker and ultimately in its surroundings. The sense of trust or mistrust with regard to the environment gained in this way at this stage of development may then be carried over to the stages of development to follow and consequently reflected in the developing personality.

Stage II: The period of autonomy vs. shame and doubt (1½ to 3 years): Having gained a primary sense of trust and security with regard to his environment, in the second and third years of his life, the child now passes through the second stage of psycho-social development. With the newly developed motor or physical skills and language ability, the child now engages in exploring his environment and experimenting with his strengths and limitations for achieving a sense of autonomy and independence. The child now needs proper safety measures against the risks involved in activities like walking, running, pulling, and handling the objects of his environment or in terms of learning undesirable language but this does not mean that he should be denied a reasonable degree of freedom to acquire a sense of independence. Within the bounds of safety, he must be provided adequate opportunities for the acquisition of a sense of autonomy and knowledge about his limitations.

Children who are denied the opportunity to develop a sense of independence by over-protective, harsh or restrictive parents begin to doubt their ability and ultimately begin to feel embarrassed or ashamed in the presence of others. However, the development of the sense of doubt and shame within reasonable limits is not harmful. A healthy sense of doubt helps the child to set his own limits and the development of shame helps him to develop a sense of right and wrong. Therefore, at this stage of psycho-social development, the child needs to be helped in striking a balance between the conflicting needs of his social environment to acquire a sense of autonomy and develop a sense of doubt and shame for the adequate development of his personality.

Stage III: The period of initiative vs. guilt (3 to 6 years): The third stage of psycho-social development between three to six years of age is characterized by the crisis of initiative versus guilt. Equipped with the sense of trust and autonomy the child now begins to take initiative in interacting with his environment. He asks questions about each and everything, explores his environment ceaselessly, and engages in planning and carrying out activities of various kinds. The extent to which the initiative for carrying out physical and mental exploration is encouraged or discouraged by the parents and the available social environment, goes a long way in developing ability in the child to initiate plan and carry out these activities in later life.

In case the child is discouraged from taking the initiative by his parents and guardians not having faith in him, or is pulled down by unhealthy criticism, punishment or rebuke for minor failures, the child is sure to develop a sense of guilt leading to hesitation, indecision and lack of initiative in planning and carrying out his life activities. Although in case of failure he feels a reasonable amount of guilt for having failed to take the initiative at the right time or made mistakes in planning and carrying out his activities, this enables him to learn from his failures. However, to allow this to develop into a guilty conscience is harmful to the development of the child's personality. Therefore, there is a need to resolve the crisis of *initiative* vs. *guilt* at this stage of psycho-social development and it can be properly done if we allow the child to experiment with his initiative by properly supervising and guiding his activities and encouraging him to develop a habit of self-evaluation of the results of his initiative.

Stage IV: Period of industry vs. inferiority (6 to 12 years): Generally, by this age children begin to attend to school where they are made to learn various skills and the teachers as well as the school environment generate pressures on them to work hard in order to perform well. Parents also now begin to make demands upon the children to lend their hand with household duties or in some cases saddle them with occupational responsibilities. They have also to compete with their peers in terms of competence and productivity in school and other social situation. Now, in case the child performs well in school, home or in other social environments or is admired for his intellectual or motor pursuits he will be likely to develop a sense of industry filled with a sense of achievement. Such a child will consequently be motivated to work harder and achieve more in terms of competency and productivity. On the other hand, if his performance remains inferior to that of his peers or he does not satisfy his teachers and parents with his performance, he may begin to look down upon himself and develop a sense of inferiority.

The teachers and the school environment thus play a very significant role in helping the child out of the industry versus inferiority crisis. For the child, the school becomes the place where success and failure are defined. Therefore, it is the duty of the teachers and school authorities to structure their classroom and school environment in such a way as to help the students to maintain a positive attitude and view themselves as capable and valuable individuals.

Stage V: The period of identity vs. role confusion (12 to 19 years): This stage, beginning with the advent of puberty, is marked with the crisis *of identity vs. role* confusion. Equipped with the sense of trust, autonomy, initiative and industry, adolescents begin to search for their own personal identity. The sudden changes in their bodies and mental functioning and the altered demands of society compel them to ask questions of themselves like, who am I? What have I become? Am 1 the same person I used to be? What am I supposed to do and in which manner am I to behave?

Erickson asserts that at this stage, the adolescent's search by questioning and redefining his own socio-psychological identity established during earlier stages is definitely linked with *(a)* his sudden and rapid bodily changes, and *(b)* anxiety and pressures related to the need to make decisions about his future education and career. Consequently, the adolescent tries to search for his new role and identity. He experiments with various sexual, occupational and educational roles to understand who he is and what he can be.

The extent to which an individual is able to develop a sense of identity will depend upon the degree of success he achieves in resolving the crisis related to all the previous stages. Failure in resolving the crises of those periods would be likely, at this stage, to result in role confusion and consequently the individual will not be able to find himself. He may then feel completely bewildered, not knowing what to do and how to behave on his own. He may be unable to make the decision about his educational or professional career or about making friends. The lack of self-identification and role confusion may also lead to over identification with villains and clowns, showing a type of childish and impulsive behaviour or developing conformity in taste and style and intolerance of others. On the other hand, if the psycho-social development of the adolescent results in his achieving a sense of identity, it will result in the individual developing the required confidence in his ability to do things, make him properly balanced in terms of emotional reactions and will place him in harmony with his environment.

Teachers and parents can play a very constructive role in helping adolescents through this identity versus confusion crisis. The adolescents, craving for identity must be fully recognized and it should be clearly understood that adolescents want to be identified as adults and must, therefore, be treated as such and not as children as many teachers and parents tend to do. They should never be belittled or humiliated in front of their peers or anyone else for that matter. They must be assigned responsibilities independently or collectively and be trusted for their promises and conduct.

Stage VI: The period of intimacy vs. isolation (20 to 45 years): This is the sixth stage of psycho-social development, and spans the years of early adulthood. During this stage the individual tends to develop a sense of intimacy or commitment to a close relationship with another person.

Throwing light on this aspect Erickson (1950), writes:

> Thus the young adult, emerging from the search for and the insistence on identity, is eager and willing to fuse his identity with that of others. He is ready for intimacy, that is, the capacity to commit himself to concrete affiliations and partnerships and to develop the ethical strength to abide by such commitments even though they may call for significant sacrifices and compromises.

Thus, during this stage, the individual seeks to form close personal attachments by merging his identity with that of another person. The relationships develop into such a close involvement that he tends to risk even the loss of his ego or image as is evidenced in the harmonious relationships between husband and wife and intimate friends, and in the ideal relationship between a teacher and his pupil. The ultimate sense of intimacy is clearly visible in terms of the mutual identity experienced at the time of simultaneous orgasm in sexual intercourse with a loved partner of the opposite sex. Another form of such intimacy is seen in sacrifices made for one's close friends or for members of one's family.

The opposite of intimacy is isolation. When one fails to develop an adequate sense of intimacy by merging one's identity with that of another person or when relations deteriorate for one reason or another, one tends to develop a sense of isolation — a pulling away from relationships and breaking off of ties. Alternatives have to be developed for intimate relationships. It is essential to maintain equilibrium in such cases as the deviation from or denial of intimate relationships is costly in terms of a normal and happy life. This does not mean, however, that isolation is altogether undesirable or harmful. A certain degree of isolation is crucial to the maintenance of one's individuality and the development of one's personality in the desired direction, but if it exceeds certain limits, it may become a serious handicap to the establishment and maintenance of close ties and may lead to loneliness and self-absorption. The crisis of *intimacy* vs. *isolation* needs to be resolved by striking a balance between the two contradictory needs — the need for intimacy and the need to maintain one's individuality. The degree to which one succeeds in resolving this crisis is said to secure one's adjustment with one's self and the world one lives in.

Stage VII: The period of creativity vs. stagnation (middle adulthood — 45 to 65 years): An individual's life up to this stage is taken up with trying to establish himself in a professional career. Now, he needs to satisfy his need for generality, a concern to establish and guide the next generation. This is realized through nurturing his own children, guiding and directing other young people and by engaging in some kind of creative, productive or fruitful activity that may prove beneficial to society. Instead of caring only for himself or for those in his family or friends who are close to him, he participates in the welfare of the future generation as represented by his own children, pupils, subordinates and young people in general. This is, in fact, an effort at extension of one's self and its merger with self or others in society.

As opposed to the sense of generativity, there is a tendency on the part of the individual to become egoistic and selfish. This leads to stagnation and personal impoverishment. Although it would be quite natural to pause in one's life's work to reflect upon, evaluate and consolidate one's achievements and to regroup one's energies for future productivity, an excess of this habit may result in self-indulgence and psychological invalidism. A balanced adjustment between the extremes of the need for generativity and the need for inactivity is thus required so that in the time of inactivity one may become more energetic and be able to put renewed efforts into rendering service to society and future generation.

Stage VIII: The period of ego-integrity vs. despair (old age, about 65 onwards): This stage of psycho-social development is associated with later adulthood or old age. Although the precise commencement of old age cannot be determined because some people remain physically and mentally active well into their eighties and nineties, others feel, look and act old even in their fifties, yet biologically speaking, old age may be said to begin when people cease to reproduce.

During this last stage of psycho-social development one is confronted with the final crisis of one's life span, termed *ego-integrity* vs. *despair.* Ego-integrity refers to the integration or culmination of the successful resolution of all the seven previous crises in the course of one's life. The successful resolution of the previous crises provides a sense of fulfilment and satisfaction to one's ego. When one reflects on one's past and feels satisfied over what has been done, one is sure to develop a positive outlook about oneself and the world around. A person with a developed sense of ego-integrity is at peace with the life he has lived and has no major regrets over what could have been or for what should have been done differently. On the other hand, persons who have not been able to successfully resolve the previous crises of the developmental stages are sure to feel differently. They look back on their lives with despair and feel dissatisfied with the way they have lived their lives. The thought that they now have no time left for changing the course of their lives and doing what should have been done, makes them feel miserable and, consequently, they are doomed to develop a deep sense of despair. These people can become desperately afraid of death. On the other hand, people who have no regrets for the way their lives have been lived and who have an admiration or love for their ego are easily able to accept the inevitability of their death and live life as fully as they can till their last breath.

At the same time, despair is not the absolute negative aspect of one's personality. To feel satisfied or dissatisfied about one or the other issue is common and natural. One may regret many mistakes and deficiencies of one's life, but this should not be stretched to the point where one develops a sense of disaffection with one's ego and begins to hate oneself and then sink into a state of utter depression. It is, therefore, essential to strike a balance between the conflicting needs of ego-integrity and despair and to successfully resolve the final crisis of one's life resulting in a well-balanced optimistic outlook for oneself and the outside world in order to live the remaining days of one's life as gracefully and productively as possible.

In a summarised form, Erickson's stages of psycho-social development covering entire life span of an individual may be represented in the manner given ahead.

Table 6.2: Erickson's stage of psycho-social development along with the needs and expectations from the individual

Stages of Psycho-Social Development	*The person and Specific age*	*Needs and Expectations*
1. Trust vs. Mistrust	Infant (Birth to 1½ years)	Needs maximum comfort with minimal uncertainty to trust himself / herself, others, and the environment
2. Autonomy vs. Shame and Doubt	Toddler (1½ years to 3 years)	Works to master physical environment while maintaining self-esteem
3. Initiative vs Guilt	Pre-Schooler (3 years to 6 years)	Begins to initiate, not imitate, activities; develops conscience and sexual identity
4. Industry vs Inferiority	School age child (6 years to 12 years)	Tries to develop a sense of self worth by refining skills
5. Identity vs Role confusion	Adolescent (12 to 20 years)	Tries integrating many roles (child, sibling, student, athlete, worker) into a self-image under role model and peer pressure
6. Intimacy vs Isolation	Young Adult (20 years to 45 years)	Learns to make personal commitment to another as spouse, parent or partner
7. Generativity vs Stagnation	Middle Age Adult (45 to 65 years)	Seeks satisfaction through productivity in career, family, and civic interests
8. Integrity vs Despair	Older Adult (65 years onwards)	Reviews life accomplishments, deals with loss and preparation for death

KOHLBERG'S THEORY OF MORAL DEVELOPMENT

Lawrence Kohlberg a psychologist belonging to the University of Harvard, was born in 1927, grew up in Bronxville, New York. In his later student career, he stayed on at Chicago for graduate work in psychology, at first thinking he would become a clinical psychologist. However, he soon became interested in Piaget and began interviewing children and adolescents on moral issues as an extension of the Piaget's work on children's moral reasoning and development. As a result of his study he got success in putting forward a theory of the development of moral judgement. The sample of his study consisted of hundreds of children belonging to different ages of childhood and adolescence from different family set ups, cultures and countries.

In his concept of morality, and moral judgement it may be seen that he differs from the popular view that children imbibe the sense and methods of moral judgement from their parents and elders by way of learning. According to him *as soon as we talk with children about morality, we find that they have many ways of making judgements which are not internalized from the outside, and which do not come in any direct and obvious way from parents, teachers and even peers* (Kohlberg, 1968). Going further he clarified that internal or cognitive processes like thinking and reasoning also play a major role in one's moral development, i.*e.* the way children make moral judgement depends on their level of intellectual development as well as on their upbringing and learning experiences.

For studying the process of moral development in human beings, Kohlberg first defined *moral development as the development of an individual's sense of justice.* For estimating one's sense of justice he concentrated on one's views on morality with the help of a test of moral judgement consisting of a set of moral dilemmas. For instance, should a man who cannot afford the medicine his dying wife needs, steal it? Should a doctor mercy-kill a fatally ill person suffering terrible pain? Is it better to save the life of one important person or a lot of unimportant persons? For the purpose of creating interest among the children he interviewed, he tried to put before them these moral dilemmas in the form of story or narrative descriptions like below.

Heinz Steals the Drug

In Europe, a woman was near death from a special kind of cancer. There was one drug that the doctors thought might save her. It was a form of radium that a druggist in the same town had recently discovered. The drug was expensive to make, but the druggist was charging ten times what the drug cost him to make. He paid $200 for the radium and charged $2,000 for a small dose of the drug. The sick woman's husband, Heinz, went to everyone he knew to borrow the money, but he could only get together about $1,000 which is half of what it cost. He told the druggist that his wife was dying and asked him to sell it cheaper or let him pay later. But the druggist said: "No, I discovered the drug and I'm going to make money from it." So Heinz got desperate and broke into the man's store to steal the drug-for his wife. Should the husband have done that? (Kohlberg, 1963, p. 19)

After putting such dilemma before the subject, he persuaded him to respond. However. Kohlberg was not really interested in whether the subject says "yes" or "no" to this dilemma, he wanted to know the reasoning behind the answer that can reflect his level of moral reasoning needed to assess the subject's level of moral development. For this purpose, he went ahead to put the question like "Why do you think Heinz should or should not have stolen the drug?" For further probing he planned to ask questions like "Do you think that Heinz had a right to steal the drug?" Was he violating the druggist rights? What sentence the judge should give Heinz, once he was caught? In this way, many of such questions were there with Kohlberg for finding out the reasoning behind his subject's answers.

Finally with the help of the analysis of the responses Kohiberg got from his subjects, he came to the conclusion that like the Piagetian stages of cognitive development, there also exist universal stages in the development of moral values, and the movement from one stage to another depends on cognitive abilities rather than the simple acquisition of moral values of one's parents, elders and peers. He then identified three levels of moral development, each containing two stages as shown in Table 6.3.

Table 6.3: Kohlberg's three levels and six stages of moral development

Level I	**Pre-moral or Pre-conventional Morality (Age 4 to 10 years)**
Stage 1:	The state of obedience for avoiding punishment
Stage 2:	The stage of conforming to obtain rewards and favours in return
Level II	**Conventional morality (Age 10 to 13 years)**
Stage 3:	Good interpersonal relationships (The stage of maintaining mutual relations and approval of others)
Stage 4:	Maintaining social order (The stage of obedience for avoiding censure by higher authority or social systems)
Level III	**Conventional Morality involving self accepted moral principles (Age 13 or not until middle or later adulthood or never)**
Stage 5:	Social contract (Stage of conforming to the democratically accepted laws and mores of
Stage 6:	Universe ethical principle (Stage of conforming to the universal ethical principles and the call of one's conscience)

Let us now briefly discuss these levels and stages of morality.

Level I. Pre-moral or Pre-conventional Morality (4-10 years)

At this level, the child begins to make judgements about what is right or wrong, good or bad. However, the standards by which he measures the morality are those of others. He is persuaded to take such judgements either to avoid punishment or to earn rewards. Development of morality at this level usually follows the following two stages:

Stage 1. Obedience and Punishment Orientation

In the beginning, the child's morality is controlled by the fear of punishment. He tries to obey his parents and elders purely to avoid reproof and punishment. Actually the Kohlberg's Stage 1 resembles the Piaget's first stage (Heteronomous stage of morality) of moral reasoning. The child assumes that powerful authorities hand down a fixed set of rules which he or she must unquestioningly obey. To the Heinz dilemma, the child typically says that Heinz was wrong to steal the drug because "It's against the law," or "It's bad to steal," as if this were all there were to it. When asked to elaborate, the child usually responds in terms of the consequences involved, explaining that stealing is bad "because you'll get punished" (Kohlberg, 1958).

Stage 2. Individualism and Exchange

At this stage of the moral development children begin to recognize that there is not just one right view that is handed down by the authorities. Different individuals have different viewpoints. "Heinz," they might point out, "might think it's right to take the drug, the druggist would not." Since everything is *relative,* each person is free to pursue his or her *individual* interests. One boy said that Heinz might steal the drug if he wanted his wife to live, but that he doesn't have to if he wants to marry someone younger and better-looking (Kohlberg, 1963, p. 24).

In this way, the second stage of the premoral or preconventional level, children's moral judgement is based on self-interest and considerations of what others can do for them in exchange or return. Here they value a thing because it has some practical utility for them. They obey the orders of their parents and elders and abide by some rules and regulations, because it serves their interests.

Level II. Conventional Morality (10-13 years)

At this level of moral development also, children's moral judgement is controlled by the likes and dislikes of others — the conventions, rules and regulations and the law and order system maintained within society. Stealing or mercy-killing would thus be judged wrong because it is considered wrong by society at large and by the legal system. In this way, the conventional level of morality may be regarded as the level where the child identifies with authority. It is characterized by the following two stages:

Stage 1. Good Interpersonal Relationships

In the early years of the second level of moral development, the child's moral judgement is based on the desire to obtain approval of others and avoid being disliked by being declared a good boy or a good girl. For this purpose he begins to judge the intentions and likes or dislikes of others and acts accordingly. As concluded by Kohlberg, children of this stage of moral development believe that children should live up to the expectations of the family and community and behave in "good" ways like a good boy or good girl. Accordingly as Kohlberg discovered many of his subjects argued that Heinz was right to steal the drug because "He was a good man for saving the life of his wife simply because no husband would have sit back and watched his wife die." As example, Kohlberg quotes the response given by his subject Don (aged 13 years) as below.

> It was really the druggist's fault, he was unfair, trying to overcharge and letting someone die. Heinz loved his wife and wanted to save her. I think anyone would. I don't think they would put him in jail. The judge would look at all sides, and see that the druggist was charging too much. (Kohlberg, 1963, p. 25).

Kohlberg concluded from such responses of his subjects that by responding in such a way, they were demonstrating the level of their conventional morality because it assumes that the attitude expressed would be shared conventionally by the entire community — "anyone" would be right to do what Heinz did.

In case we try to find similarities and dissimilarities between the Piaget's theory of moral development and Kohlberg's theory of moral development, we can fairly analyze that there lies substantial similarities between Kohlberg's first three stages and Piaget's two stages being covered during the entire period of childhood. In both the developmental theories, we may observe the similar sequence characterized with a shift from unquestioning obedience to a relativistic outlook and to a concern for good intention on the part of wrong doers. The difference lies in the fact where in Kohlberg's theory these shifts occur in three stages rather than two as emphasized in Piaget's theory of moral development.

Stage 2. Maintaining the Social Order

According to Kohlberg, Stage 3 reasoning works best in two-person relationships with family members or close friends, where one can make a real effort to get to know the other's feelings and needs and try to help. At Stage 4, in contrast, the respondent becomes more broadly concerned with *society as a whole.* Now the emphasis is on obeying laws, respecting authority, and performing one's duties so that the social order is maintained. In support of his conclusion Kohlberg again cites the responses of his subjects to the Heinz story. Many of his subjects were found to utter that they understand that Heinz's intention or motive was good but they cannot condon the theft. What would happen if all of us started breaking the laws whenever we felt we had a good reason? The result would be Chaos; society could not function.

In this way the children reaching the moral Stage 4, begin to take moral decisions from the perspective of the society as a whole. At this stage children's moral behaviour and judgements are governed by conventions as well as the laws and mores of the social system. The standards of others are now so established that it becomes a convention to follow them. The children now follow the rules and regulations of society and take decisions about things being right or wrong with a view to avoiding censure by the elders, authorities or the social system.

Level III. Post conventional morality involving self-accepted moral principles (Age 13 and afterwards)

This marks the highest level of attainment of true morality as the controlling force for making judgements now rests with the individual himself. He does not value a thing or conform to an idea merely because of consideration of the views of others, conventions or the law and order system of the society but because it fits onto the framework of his self-accepted moral principles. However, to reach this level is not an ordinary thing. One may be able to attain it in the beginning or middle of his adolescence or it may be postponed for him till the middle or later adulthood or he may never attain it in his life time. This highest level of moral development is also characterized by two separate stages as described below.

Stage 1. Social Contracts and Individual Rights

At Stage 5 as Kohlberg concludes, individuals begin to ask. "What makes for a good society?" They basically believe that a good society is best conceived as a social contract into which people freely enter to work toward the benefit for all. They recognize that all rational people would agree on two points: (i) getting certain basic rights, such as liberty and life, to be protected; and (*ii*) needing some democratic procedures for changing unfair laws and for improving society. In support of his conclusion Kohlberg quotes the responses of his subjects to Heinz dilemma. Many of his respondents make it clear that they do not generally favour the breaking of laws; laws are social contracts that we agree to uphold until we can change them by democratic means. Nevertheless, his wife's right to live is a moral right that must be protected.

In this way, at this stage the individual's moral judgements are internalized in such a form that he responds positively to authority only if he agrees with the principles upon which the demands of authority are based. The individual at this stage begins to think in rational terms, valuing the rights of human beings and the welfare of society. For example, at this stage in reference to the rights of the human being, the decision about mercy-killing may be left to the individual who is suffering, and if so needed, the concerned laws may be amended for the welfare of society at large.

Stage 2. Universal Principles

This stage of moral development is the highest stage or perfection achieved in terms of moral reasoning and development of morality. In propagating his theory of moral development, Kohlberg believes that there must be a higher stage of moral development — as just conceived by him through his stage 6 — which defines the principles by which we get the type of justice as conceived by the great moral leaders like Mahatma Gandhi and Martin Luther King. The principle of justice is universal and requires us to treat the claims of all parties in an impartial way, respecting the dignity of all people as individuals and humans. According to Kohlberg, we can reach this stage in case we begin to look at a situation purely through one another's eyes. Take the case of Heinz dilemma, reaching this stage would essentially require that all parties — the druggist, Heinz, and his wife — try to view the things from other perspectives for seeking justice and fair solution of the problem. As a result, in the end, they would all agree that the life of the wife must be saved by sacrificing the narrow interests related to money or conventional laws.

In this way at the Stage 6 of our moral development the controlling forces for making moral judgements are highly internalized. The decisions of the individual are now based upon his conscience and the belief in universal principles of respect, justice and equality. He does what he, as an individual thinks right regardless of legal restrictions or the opinion of others. Thus, at this stage people act according to the inner voice of their conscience provide evidence of sharing, helping and defending the victims of injustice and lead a life that they can without self-condemnation or feeling of guilt or shame.

From the above discussion of the Kohlberg's stages of moral development, it is clear that although children begin to think about morality in terms of justice or right and wrong at a very early age, yet they have to wait until adolescence or adulthood for the dawning of the stage of true morality. Also, it is not essential that all people pass through the third level of moral development. Most adults are not able to cross the second level and few can reach Stage 5, and among these there are very few who, being intellectually quite sound, can think rationally and base their moral judgement purely on the dictates of their conscience at the risk of life and property.

Evaluation of the Kohlberg's theory of Moral Development Appreciation

Kohlberg's theory of Moral Development is appreciated on the following grounds:

1. Kohlberg is the first psychologist who tried to present a comprehensive stage theory of moral development by stating that the development of moral reasoning is characterized by a series of qualitative distinctive stages. He claimed that an individual progresses through them in order, without skipping any. Each of the Kohlberg's stage builds upon the foundation laid by earlier stages but reflects a more integrated and logical consistent set of moral beliefs than those before it (Ormond, 2003, p. 88).

2. Kohlberg's theory of moral development provided an unique description for explaining the progression to higher stages of our moral reasoning by taking into account Piaget's stage of cognitive thinking or

logical reasoning. Kohlberg proposed that advanced moral reasoning (Post conventional reasoning) requires formal operational thought for abstract understanding of the purpose of the laws and rules to help society run smoothly (Kohlberg, 1976). Hence the post conventional level of morality does not appear until adolescence (the concrete operational stage of their cognitive development). In this way, for the development of his theory of moral reasoning, Kohlberg tried to adopt the base provided through Piaget's stages of cognitive thinking. Consequently, it appears that development of moral reasoning and cognitive thinking travel side by side. However, in his theory of moral development while explaining advanced moral reasoning Kohlberg put up a different view. He asserted that progression to an advanced stage of cognitive development does not guarantee equivalent moral development. One may have a quite develop cognitive structure and functioning, but it is not essential that he must demonstrate the same higher level of his moral reasoning in tune with his higher cognitive development. It was thus a unique feature in the moral development theory of Kohlberg in its assertion that it is quite possible to be logical operational in logical reasoning but preconventional in moral reasoning implying that cognitive development is a necessary but insufficient condition for moral development to occur (Ormond 2003, p. 90).

3. In addition to make use of the Piaget's stage of cognitive thinking or logical reasoning for building his sequential stages of moral reasoning, Kohlberg also tried to make use of Piaget's concept of disequilibrium as an instrument or explanation for the development of advanced moral reasoning among the children. As we know Piaget proposed that when a child is unable to assimilate the new learning, he experiences a state of disequilibrium, which makes him eager to expand his ways of thinking and reasoning to accommodate and learn the new thing. Following the foot step of Piaget, Kohlberg in his theory of moral development advocated that one progresses to a higher stage of moral development only when he faces disequilibrium by realizing that his beliefs about morality are unable to address the events and dilemma he is experiencing at present. In this way, Kohlberg theory of moral development produced a unique way of presenting certain problematic situations or dilemmas before the growing children for letting them experience disequilibrium and gradually restructure their thoughts about morality for moving to the subsequent higher stages of moral development.

4. Kohlberg's theory of moral development provided substantial weightage to the role of experience, modelling and social interaction in the development of morality among children. It emphasized that morality is a learned behaviour and moral reasoning is developed through successive stages with close interaction of child's individuality with his environment — particularly social and cultural.

5. The Kohlberg's theory of moral development has been able to suggest

and expect from the individuals to demonstrate a higher stage of moral reasoning where they no longer accept their own society and existing rules but think reflectively and autonomously for bringing changes to make the society progress and humanity flourish. In this way, his theory may provide enough ground to work its way towards the thinking of the great men like Socrates, Martin Luther King and Mahatma Gandhi and thus inspiring us to proceed toward the challenging vision of our highest moral development.

Criticism

Kohlberg's theory of moral development has been the subject of criticism highlighting its fallacies as below:

1. An important limitation of Kohlberg's theory of moral development lies in the fact that it deals with moral reasoning rather than with moral behaviour. Many individuals at different stages of the moral development may be found to demonstrate similar type of moral behaviour and individuals at the same stages may behave morally in different ways. In practice, there may be a quite weak link, between moral reasoning and moral behaviour. A child may have reached a higher stage of moral reasoning as established by Kohlberg through the analysis of the responses to the presented moral dilemmas but it is not essential that he should also behave and demonstrate morality suitable to this moral stage. Thus children might learn so many things about moral decisions or moral reasoning at various ages, but what they do may be another matter. Therefore, it can be properly said that Kohlberg's theory is not able to provide a proper answer for the simultaneous development of moral reasoning and moral development across the various ages.

2. Kohlberg through his specific stages of moral development has tried to draw a line among the types of moral development reached by the individual at the different ages. In practice, however, the picture regarding such fixed pattern across the varying ages involving different individuals may not be so clear. An individual at one period of his life span may be found to demonstrate more than one type of morality — pre-conventional, conventional or post conventional depending upon the situation he faces for doing so. In this way, contrary to Kohlberg's assumption, moral behaviour is more context or situation oriented than the age specific moral development attained by the individuals.

3. Kohlberg's theory is also criticised on the ground that young children are probably more advanced in their moral reasoning then established by Kohlberg. Even pre-schoolers have some internal standards of right and wrong, regardless of what authority figures might tell them and regardless of what consequences certain behaviours may or may not bring (Smetana, 1981).

4. It is also said that Kohlberg's stages are culturally biased. It is argued that how stage model based on the Western philosophical model can be applied to non-western cultures without considering the extent to which

they have different approaches and outlooks towards morality. It is also doubtful to apply this model to the moral developmental pattern found in the children belonging to traditional village and tribal cultures.

5. Carol Gilligan (1987), believes that Kohlberg; theory is sex biased as it does not adequately describe female moral development. Gilligan observes that Kohlberg's stages were derived exclusively from interviews with males and therefore reflect a decidedly male orientation. She charges that Kohlberg's stages focus on the issues of rights and rules, fairness and justice but omit other aspects of morality especially compassion and caring for those in need that are more characteristic of the moral reasoning and behaviour of females.

6. Kohlberg's concept of the post conventional morality has also been a subject of severe criticism. Kohlberg's has advocated for the morality of consciousness or autonomous thinking on the part of the individuals reaching the post-conventional level. Practically it is nothing but a sort of an open war with the established ethical codes and organized functioning of the society. If everybody acts according to the morality of his own, then certainly there will be a chaos. It is absolutely dangerous for people to place their own principles and ethics above society and the law. Moreover, everybody cannot be so worthwhile and selfless as the great thinkers and reformists like Martin Luther King or Mahatma Gandhi, therefore, it is unwise to preach and advocate for the development of such unbridled level of consciousness and morality among the individuals.

7. Lastly, it can also be said that Kohlberg's theory of moral development is not so comprehensive as claimed to provide answers for all the moral dilemmas and thus is not able to guide our moral reasoning to face all the situations in our life without ambiguity and confusion. It has its weakness and limitations like other theories of development. Although Kohlberg claims that his stage six of moral development is capable of equipping an individual with the decision making tools needed for the toughest moral dilemmas. However, in practice there may lie many issues that the principle of justice arrived at this stage frequently fail to resolve. One such issue may be abortion. Justice for whom and in what ways, is the issue that can hardly be resolved properly at the satisfaction of all the parties involved. The decision have to vary with the situation. In this way, the stages described in Kohlberg's theory are certainly not aimed for providing a ready made answer to the moral dilemmas. These represent particular mode or pattern of moral reasoning at the specific ages and thus can never be thought as universally applicable to provide solution to all types of moral issues raised in varying situations.

However, on the basis of the criticism, laid down above, it should not be assumed that Kohlberg's theory is to be discarded or it has little significance for understanding the mechanism of moral development among human beings. Despite the criticism, there is no doubt that Kohlberg's accomplishment in bringing his theory of moral development is great. His theory offers valuable insights into the nature and development of moral reasoning among children and adolescents. He has not just expanded on Piaget's stages of moral judgement but has done so in a quite convincing and appropriate way by having a beautiful blend of individualistic and socialized trends of constructive approach for the development of moral reasoning on the part of human beings.

Educational Implications of Moral Development Theory

The moral development theory provided by Kohlberg has enough potential to direct and guide the way of teachers and parents for helping the children develop morally by highlighting some of the essential facts like below:

1. The moral development is essentially a learned phenomenon. As Kohlberg (1968) asserts the stages of moral development are not the product of maturation. The sequence related to development of moral reasoning do not simply unfold according to genetic blueprint. It is therefore much needed on the part of we elders that we should never blame heredity for the child's level of moral reasoning and moral development.

2. The child at his early years of development (infancy and early childhood till the age of 4 or 5 years) is neither moral or immoral but is essentially non-moral, in the sense that he has no moral thinking regarding good or bad of an act. He may pick up the things belonging to others without feeling any need of asking or informing them about it simply due to the reason that he feels nothing bad or wrong in doing so. Since no moral sense or reasoning lies with the children of this age, we elders should behave accordingly without blaming them for their act of disobedience, unsocial or antisocial behaviour as these children are quite ignorant about the goodness or wrongness of their behaviour.

3. The children belonging to Kohlberg's first three stage of moral development believes in the eternal nature of the rules and the authority of the elders. They want to obey their orders and rules without questioning their validity. Accordingly we elders must be quite cautious in putting rules and regulations before the children belonging to this age span. The rules once made should not be altered then and there. The children without any discrimination should be made to follow them. It is essential at this stage because children have not attained enough mental maturity for deciding at their own that what is right or wrong for them. It is in the interest of the children, their peers, parents, teachers and community as a whole that they should be made to observe the rules and regulation regarding their appropriate individual and social behaviour,

4. The children prior to their entry into the age of adolescence can only grasp the concrete ideas and form related to morality. At this stage, for them examples are always better then precept. In childhood, therefore, they should be presented with models of appropriate behaviour by the elders for

being observed and imitated. The abstraction regarding moral reasoning or concept is out of reach to the children belonging to the development period of childhood. It is therefore futile to expect from them to talk about soul, the fruits of Karma, rudiments of religion and God

5. With the development of their intellectual abilities, older children belonging to adolescence stage now no longer believes in the eternity or non-changing pattern of the rules. They can't be expected to obey the elders and observe the set rules silently as happens in childhood. They need reason and satisfactory answer to their question "why". Therefore, we should be quite cautious in emphasizing about the rules and moral conduct at this stage. Rather making them follow the rules and ethical norms blindly, they should be told about the significance of such behaviour from the individual as well as social point of views. They should be allowed to ask questions and remove their doubts about the appropriateness and inappropriateness of their behaviour in practising morality at home, schools and other social situations. Discussion and debates on the moral issues should also be encouraged and children need to given opportunities as well as freedom to reason about the prevalent social and ethical norms for their better adoption in their lives.

6. The parents and teachers should also recognize the importance of the principle of reciprocity as believed by the individuals in their period of childhood If you do good to others, others also behave with your nicely. Judging the impact of a bad act or foul saying on one's self may force the children to behave in a proper way. If one thing is pinching them, it will do the same to others. Stimulating and encouraging such thinking and feelings on the part of children may help them imbibe and practice good things.

7. Kohlberg strongly emphasizes that the goal of moral education is to encourage and help the individuals to develop to the next stage of moral reasoning and morality. According to him the most common tool for doing this is to present a "moral dilemma" for making the child confronted with a situation involving his moral reasoning and judgement. The child may adopt view, characterizing his developmental age but may not be able to resolve the moral dilemma, he may then be forced to adopt the moral reasoning belonging to the next stage of moral development. Kohlberg's device of inducing conflict, resembles equilibration model emphasized by Piaget. When a new thing does not fit into the existing cognitive structure through assimilation, one has to go for the due enlargement of his cognitive structure for doing away with the state of disequilibrium. In this way, both the moral development theories (given by Piaget and Kohlberg) urge to adopt a cognitive conflict inducing approach for helping the child to move further on the higher stages of his moral development. In this method, teachers are urged to lead discussion groups in which children have a chance to grapple actively with moral issues. For the proper inducement of cognitive conflict, it is well cared to encourage arguments that belong to

one stage above those of most of the class. Since students do not find sufficient, the level of moral reasoning which they presently have with them for resolving the confronted moral issue, they will be stimulated and interested in the acquisition of the moral reasoning belonging to the higher stage of their moral development and this will definitely help them in their pursuit of higher and higher moral development

8. Kohlberg's theory of moral development inspire and motivates us that it is quite possible to attain the true morality characterized with selfless feelings of doing good to others, adherence to the principles of equity, equality, moral justice and human rights being preached and practised by the great men of the history like Gandhi and Martin Luther King. Students, for this purpose, should be exposed to the lives and works of the great social reformers, freedom fighters, social revolutionaries, philosophers, and religious figures. They should also be given reasonable freedom to express their original ideas and views about the prevalent social structure, laws and ethical norms along with their zeal to replace them with some suitable ones. May be that there may be a quite few to attempt to reach this highest stage of moral reasoning but surely these are the ones who are responsible for leading the society and humanity to a more illuminated path and certainly we should make provision for them in our system of education.

7

Developmental Tasks and their Implications

MEANING OF THE TERM DEVELOPMENTAL TASKS

The term and concept regarding developmental tasks was first introduced by Robert Havinghurst of the University of Chicago, USA by providing a definition as below.

"Developmental task is one which arises at a certain period in the life of the individual successful accomplishment of which leads to his happiness and success with later tasks, while failure leads to unhappiness and difficulty with later task." — Havighurst, R.J., 1972

A close analysis of the above definition may lead us to conclude about the meaning of the term developmental tasks as under:

(i) Development task is essentially linked with the development and developmental period (from birth till the expiry of the adolescence) of an individual.

(ii) Developmental tasks are age specific and essentially linked with the developmental stages of one's life.

(iii) An individual at a particular age span or stage of his growth and development is expected to perform certain tasks (performing certain types of conative, cognitive and affective behaviour) quite specific to his age and stage of development.

(iv) The adjustment with the self and the environment depends upon the extent to which one in capable of performing these age specific and developmental stage related developmental tasks.

(v) In case one is successful in accomplishing the related developmental tasks (specific to his age and developmental period) he feels happy at present and expected to perform future tasks successfully in his later life, the failure on the other hand makes his life miserable at present and puts a question mark on his ability to perform future tasks successfully in his later life.

(vi) Key of happiness and adjustment, in this way lies in the proper identification of developmental task and learning the ways and means of their successful accomplishment during the related developmental periods of one's life.

After having some acquaintance with the meaning and nature of the developmental tasks the questions can now be raised regarding: (i) The identification and naming of the developmental tasks; (ii) The sources contributing towards the upsurge of the developmental tasks at a particular age and development period; (*iii*) Critical ages at which the society expects its members to master the developmental tasks of that age; (*iv*) Purposes and goals of developmental tasks; (*v*) Role of the cultural and social pattern regarding expectation of certain developmental tasks from its growing youngsters; (*vi*) Specific developmental tasks associated with the stages of developmental period.

Let us think over all such issues.

A. IDENTIFYING AND NAMING OF THE DEVELOPMENT TASKS

Developmental tasks are related with the change in behaviour belonging to all the three domains of behaviour namely conative, cognitive and affective. What a developing child is expected to do, think and feel at a particular age or stage of one's developmental period for his adequate adjustment in one's social and cultural environment can then work as a base for the identification and naming of various developmental task at a particular age or stage of one's life. Since there lies a number of activities or tasks belonging to these three behavioural domains that can be expected to be executed by the growing children of developmental period, therefore the list for the identification and naming of the developmental task will naturally be too lengthy and exhaustive. However, for illustration purpose let us try to mention the name of the developmental tasks needed to be performed by the growing children as below:

(*i*) *Conative Developmental Tasks:* Crawling, sitting, standing, walking, riding, jumping, running, throwing, catching, controlling elimination of bodily wastes, combing, dressing, eating, biting, stretching, stopping, drinking, kneeling, holding, leaning, smashing, balancing, identification by touching, seeing, smelling or hearing, writing, handling the instruments, dancing, dining, driving, knitting, playing the musical organ, teasing, posing, handling of the technologically advanced instruments, etc.

(*ii*) *Cognitive Developmental Tasks:* Recognising, recalling, reproducing, selecting, listing, labelling, measuring, counting, reading, underlining, classifying, distinguishing, explaining, justifying, interpreting, choosing, modifying, illustrating, comparing, analysing, synthesizing, concluding, contrasting, arguing, generalizing, associating, criticising, evaluating, summarizing, verifying, reporting, supporting, predicting, using, solving, relation, etc.

(*iii*) *Affective Developmental Tasks:* Accepting, attaining, showing specific interests, attitudes and aptitudes for things, ideas, processes and persons, demonstrating particular or generalised habits of thinking, feeling and actions, demonstrating a particular level of social and emotional maturity, sex behaviour, personal and social adjustment and moral sense, etc.

B. SOURCES CONTRIBUTING TOWARDS THE UPSURGE OF DEVELOPMENTAL TASKS

Development tasks specific to an age and stage of development may be necessitated and brought in existence on account of the following factors:

(i) *Maturation:* As the child matures, i.e. grows in age, he definitely needs certain tasks to be performed by him as to adjust himself according to the changing needs of his growing age. Examples of such tasks are learning to crawl, stand, walk, dress, etc.

(ii) *Adjustment to the physical, social and cultural environment:* Many developmental tasks are necessitated, on account of seeking proper adjustment to one's physical, social and cultural environment. Sometimes physical environment puts pressure on the growing child to learn proper ways and mean of adjusting one's self according to the condition prevailing with one's physical environment. Hilly, desert or coastal areas demand specific activities and ways of living from the growing children as it generates some typical developmental tasks for them. Similar is the case with the needs and pressures put up by one's social and cultural environment for learning the execution of specific developmental task suiting to one's age and developmental stage. One needs to learn the use of a special appliance i.e. telephone, mobile, Internet, or read, write and speak a particular language, learn specific social and cultural behaviour, etc. according to the demands of one's social and cultural environment at a particular age or stage of one's life.

(iii) *Adjustment to One's self:* Many developmental tasks are necessitated on account of seeking harmonious relationships or adjustment to one's self. Sometimes one needs to fulfill the demands of his own desires, basic interests, liking and disliking, philosophy of life, values and aspirations, somatic structure, cognitive and emotional characteristics, etc. The aspiration regarding studying a particular course of instruction and choosing a particular course or profession are examples of such demands needed for the adjustment of one's self. Accordingly, the individual is forced to include the related tasks in the list of developmental tasks suiting to his growing age like trying to get entry into a specific academic and professional course or preparing oneself for the entry into the desired profession and vocation.

In this way, developmental tasks are mostly generated naturally on account of maturation or the pressures put on the individual for getting adjusted to one's self and his environment.

C. CRITICAL AGES AND DEVELOPMENTAL TASKS

As emphasized earlier the developmental tasks are very much age and developmental stage specific. Hence particular type of developmental tasks need to be carried out at a particular age and developmental stage level. The age spans during which the growing children are expected to perform a certain type of developmental tasks in a particular society and cultural group are termed as critical ages and periods of the life. These critical ages and periods of life present a quite ripe stage in terms of maturation and learning experiences gained from one's environment for performing the developmental tasks relevant to the critical ages and periods of life. As a result, we can't expect from a growing child to perform a certain type of developmental task unless he or she has not reached the required stage of maturation and development *i.e.* entered in the period of the relevant critical age. Going further we can't also expect from a more mature child or adult to perform certain developmental tasks after the expiry of the critical age period *i.e.* learning gymnastic skills, etc.

D. PURPOSES AND GOALS OF DEVELOPMENTAL TASKS

It is well in the interest of the growing children, parents and teachers for being acquainted with the nature of the developmental tasks needed to be performed by the children at some specific age and developmental period of the life. The purposes and objectives realized through such knowledge may prove fruitful in the following way:

1. It may provide the norms and normal expectations of a particular society or cultural group from its growing children in terms of the general behaviour pattern (demonstrable through conative, cognitive and affective tasks) during the various ages and developmental periods of life.
2. It may help in setting the minds and attitudes of the children for making desirable attempts to learn the execution of the developmental tasks relevant to different developmental periods of their life.
3. It may provide proper guidelines to the teachers and parents for helping the youngsters in their adequate growth and development by providing richer experiences for the execution of the developmental tasks related to the critical ages and stages of their life.
4. It may help the society or a cultural group to develop its own set of developmental tasks needed to be performed at one or the other stages of development of their growing children in view of the changes or future developmental course of that very society and cultural group.
5. The knowledge of the critical age's specific developmental tasks may help the children, teacher and parents to plan their obligation and duties well in advance in view of the targets lying ahead in terms of the required expected stage of maturity and experiences gained for executing the developmental tasks relevant to different critical periods of life. What is expected at present and what lies ahead in terms of the level of the developmental tasks to be performed by the growing children, the knowledge of such aspects may prove a boon to the planner of education and development, besides a source of self motivator to the youngsters themselves.

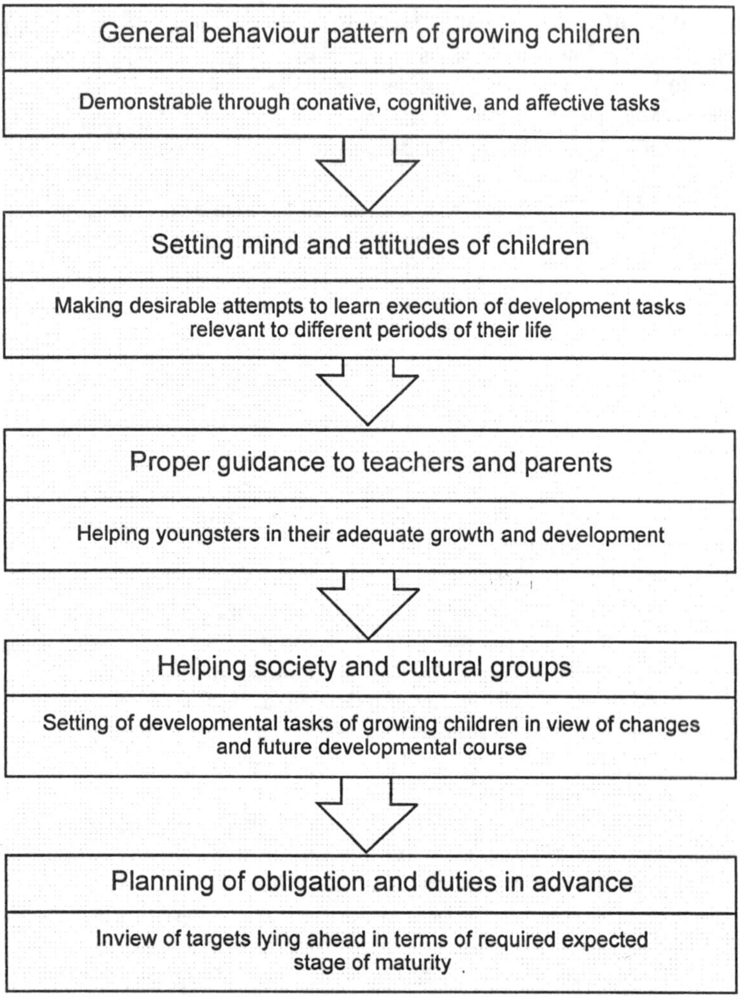

Fig. 7.1: Purposes and Goals of the Knowledge of Developmental Tasks

E. ROLE OF CULTURAL AND SOCIAL PATTERNS IN DEVELOPMENTAL TASKS

The developmental tasks besides being age specific are also said to be influenced by the nature of the life patterns prevailing in a social and cultural group. That is why we can't expect the same type of developmental task performed by our youngster as happens in the case of English, American, Japanese or African children. For example in our social and cultural set up the children acquire puberty at a quite early age in comparison to the children of European nations. It may definitely affect the expectation from them in term of the developmental tasks selected to their sex behaviour, emotional and social maturity etc. Similarly, there may be so many types of social and cultural behaviour, patterns, mental makeup, etc. that may be expected from the children of the quite developed countries and fast moving societies in a sharp contrast to the children belonging to developing and deprived social segments. Such differences may essentially force to adopt a some what different approaches in planning the developmental tasks relevant to the critical periods of the life. In reality it so happens and thereby we may clearly observe that the list of the developmental tasks needed to be performed by the growing children at the specific ages and periods of their life varies from culture to culture and society to society.

E. DEVELOPMENTAL TASKS OF THE VARIOUS STAGES OF DEVELOPMENT

The developmental period as we know in the human being ranges from birth to the attainment of maturity *i.e.* expiry of the adolescence period. The significant stages of development during this period may be named as stage of infancy, stage of childhood and stage of adolescence. Let us try to know about something about the nature of development tasks needed to be performed by the youngsters during the above mentioned three developmental stages of our life.

Infancy (upto two years)

- Learning to crawl, stand, walk, run, climb, jump, throw, etc.
- Learning to drink and to take solid food
- Learning to talk
- Learning to acquire physiological stability
- Learning to control elimination of bodily wastes
- Learning to explore the physical environment surrounding him
- Learning to play with toys
- Learning to accomplish the skill of tricycling
- Learning to pay attention towards the things, persons and events
- Learning to recognize and identify the things and persons
- Forming simple concepts of social and physical reality
- Learning to recite the poems and stories
- Learning to imitate the behaviour and actions of others
- Learning to acquire almost all the positive and negative emotions in his behaviour expression
- Learning to shift his attention from the play material to his playing mates
- Learning to take interest in the company of his age mates and other growing children
- Learning to relate oneself emotionally to parents, sibling and others.

Early Childhood (from 3 to 5 years)

- Learning to acquire competencies in the motor skills like walking, jumping, climbing, sliding, tricycling, hopping, galloping, skipping, throwing, bouncing and catching
- Learning to acquire simple basics in language skills like, speaking, listening, reading and writing
- Learning sex differences and sex modesty
- Learning to distinguish right and wrong and developing a conscience
- Learning to develop right concepts related to social and physical reality
- Learning to remain away from the parental fold and enjoy the companionship of other children
- Learning to give up his "I" feeling and develop the 'We' feeling
- Learning to acquire the ability to sense similarities and dissimilarities and compare and contrast the things
- Learning to control overt expression of emotions.

Later Childhood (from 6 to 12 years)

- Learning motor and physical skills necessary for playing different indoor and outdoor games
- Learning to get along with age-mates
- Learning appropriate sex roles
- Building whole some attitudes towards oneself as a growing organism
- Development of necessary skills in language and communication, computation, sketching and drawing, etc.
- Development of various interest, attitudes, liking and dislikings towards, the things, persons and ideas
- Developing concrete and abstract concepts regarding things, persons, ideas and processes
- Development of conscience, morality and scale of values
- Development of the capacity to reason, think and problem solving
- Development of the loyalty towards the group.

Adolescence (from 13 to 18 years)

- Development of abilities, motor and physical skills for playing difficult complex and hard indoor and outdoor games
- Development of abilities, motor and physical capacities for performing mental tasks and physical labour
- Development of mental and cognitive abilities to perform difficult mental tasks and operations.
- Development of all types of concept — requiring concrete or abstract operation

- Learning to accept one's physique and satisfaction with one's appearance
- Learning to play a masculine or feminine role
- Learning to develop new relations with age mates of both sexes
- Learning to acquire maturity in sex behaviour
- Development of a sense of one's own identity
- Learning to gain the means and ways for economic independence
- Development of sentiments towards things, persons, places and values
- Learning to acquire civic sense, social responsibilities and ways of democratic living
- Learning to build a sense of belongingness to one's social group, culture, community and nation
- Learning to adjust with a sense of self-sacrifice and martyrs like feelings for the cause of society, religion, nation and humanity
- Gaining vocational awareness and get ready for entering into higher academic or professional courses of study
- Gaining competencies and skills for meeting the needs of specific interests and aptitudes
- Striving to gain desired height on the mental, emotional and social maturity scales
- Preparing for playing the roles of a matured adult in future life.

In this way, every society and cultural group has somewhat a list of general and specific developmental task specifically associated with ages and developmental periods of life. It expects from the youngsters belonging to the developmental age for the successful execution of these tasks for their proper adjustment with themselves and their physical, social and cultural environment.

IMPLICATION OF DEVELOPMENTAL TASKS

Developmental tasks as stated earlier are quite age specific and stage specific. The well being, development and progress of the developing children very well depends on the successful executions of these developmental tasks very much expected from them at a particular age or stage of their development. The parents and teachers must be quite careful in providing appropriate opportunities and facilities to their developing children for the performance and execution of these age and stage specific developmental tasks in proper way. It is true for them in caring for the children belonging to the entire period of developmental age i.e. infancy to adolescence. Since, as a secondary school teacher, you are more concerned with the children belonging to adolescence, therefore, here we would like to focus on the implications of developmental tasks mainly associated with the adolescents.

A glimpse on the list of the developmental tasks of adolescence provided earlier in the chapter may make us to conclude that an adolescent is expected

- to attain maximum limit in terms of his physical and cognitive development.
- to gain proper emotional and social maturity in respect to his emotional and social development.
- to get prepared for playing the role of a mature girl/boy in future life
- to earn the necessary civic sense and morality in tune with the demands of his community/society.
- to prepare him for acquiring self sufficiency in economic aspect by getting entry into courses or vocation of his choice
- to have an adequate adjustment to the members of opposite sex and his/her sex instincts and urges.

In view of the developmental tasks of the above nature expected from an adolescent, it is expected from we elders — teachers and parents to do all what can be possible for them in carrying over these developmental tasks in a proper way. What can be done on our part in this concern can be summarised in the way given ahead.

- To provide suitable curricular and cocurricular, formal and informal experiences for the proper cognitive development of the adolescents.
- To provide needed opportunities and help to the adolescents to reach at their maximum in terms of their physical development, strength and stamina.
- To arrange for the needed educational, vocational and personal guidance and counselling to the adolescents for their educational, vocational and personal adjustment and progress in their life.
- To arrange for the needed sex education to the adolescents
- To care for meeting the needs, interests, attitudes and aspiration of the adolescents.
- To provide desired curricular and co-curricular experiences and needed formal and informal opportunities for helping the adolescents to attain the needed emotional, moral and social maturity for playing the role of a mature responsible adult.
- To act as a role model or producing role example to the adolescents for helping them in the proper execution of their development tasks.

8

Behaviourism Perspective

WHAT IS BEHAVIOURISM?

Behaviourism represents a school of psychology or doctrine that lays emphasis on: (i) the study of behaviour for knowing about the individuality of an individual; and (ii) use of the method of conditioning for the acquisition of all types of behaviour — conative, cognitive and affective.

HISTORICAL EVOLUTION AND DEVELOPMENT OF BEHAVIOURISM

American psychologist John B. Watson (1878-1950) is generally known as the father of the doctrine or school of psychology referred to as behaviourism. However, his contemporary Ivan Pavlov (1849-1936), the famous Russian psychologist was infact the pioneer in conducting useful experiments with the idea and views held in behaviourism. Behaviourism as a new doctrine stood boldly against the then prevalent method of introspection or self-observation for studying human behaviour. He argued that a thing like mind or consciousness that can not be observed or tested scientifically should not be made subject of study for knowing about the individuality of an individual. It should be replaced with our observable and measurable behaviour.

Consequently, behaviourism as a method of studying behaviour focused its attention totally on the overt or observable behaviour. For this purpose, it tried to reduce all of man's activity, including his thinking, feeling and volition to the level of that behaviour which could be observed and objectively recorded. Thus, a behaviourist is not interested in the feeling of fear (because it is not measurable) but pays attention to the changes in heart rate and blood pressure which are the effects of fear and can be objectively measured. The theory of behaviourism as propagated by Watson was in fact based on the findings of the Russian psychologist Ivan Pavlov (1849-1936), the propagator of the theory of classical conditioning.

In his classic experiment, Pavlov conditioned a dog to salivate at the sound of a bell by substituting that sound for the sight and smell of meet and concluded that all behaviour is a response to some stimulus in the environment. Watson tried to apply this approach in the field of human behaviour. In the famous experiment with an 11-month old baby named Albert, he conditioned the baby's behaviour to fear a rat by substituting the rat with a sudden loud noise. He concluded that behaviour is merely the response to some environmental stimulus. How we behave and why we behave in a particular way can be successfully demonstrated and explained through habit formation or conditioning. Thus conditioning through environmental influences and not hereditary endowments or innate differences is responsible for shaping the behaviour of a child.

Behaviourism, thus, tried to project human beings as little more than rather complex machines which respond in a particular fashion to a particular kind of stimulus. The behaviour of an individual may, thus, be supposed to be controlled by environmental forces, and not by hereditary endowments or innate differences.

His strong convictions about the stimulus response automatization and environmental influences made Watson assert boldly in 1930.

> Give me a dozen healthy infants, well informed and my own specified world to bring them up in and I will guarantee to take any one at random and train him to become any type of specialist I might select — doctor, lawyer, artist, merchant, chief and yes, even beggar-man and thief, regardless of his talents, penchants, tendencies, abilities, vocations and race of his ancestors.

The doctrine of behaviourism propounded by Watson and his disciples, thus, ushered a new era in the field of psychology by making it somewhat materialistic, mechanistic, deterministic and objective like most of the physical and natural sciences. However, it suffered from a number of drawbacks, limitations and shortcomings. For this reason it has been subjected to criticism and has been modified and refined in a number of ways by contemporary psychologists like Lashley, Tolman, Hull and Skinner. While Lashley devoted himself to neurophysiology and Tolman believed in purposive behaviourism, B.F. Skinner, a leading American behaviourist of the present age, emphasized a system of learning known as *operant conditioning,* quite different from the type of conditioning advocated by Pavlov and Watson. The task of behaviour modification he advocated and the teaching machines he popularized by using the principles of reward, yield significant influence in the field of psychology, education and medicine.

Important Events in the Evolution of Behaviourism

- Pavlov (1897) published the results of an experiment on conditioning after originally studying digestion in dogs.
- Watson (1913) launched the behavioural school of psychology (classical conditioning), publishing an article, "Psychology as the Behaviourist Views It."
- Watson and Rayner (1920) conditioned an orphan called Albert B (Little Albert) to fear a white rat. Watson and assistant Rosalie Rayner conducted the famous "Little Albert" experiment.

- Thorndike (1905) formalised the "Law of Effect".
- Skinner (1936) wrote "The Behaviour of Organisms" and introduced the concepts of operant conditioning and shaping.
- Clark Hull's (1943) *Principles of Behaviour* was published.
- B.F. Skinner (1948) published *Walden Two* in which he described a Utopian society founded upon behaviourist principles.
- Bandura (1963) published a book called the *"Social learning theory and personality development"* which combines both cognitive and behavioural frameworks.
- B.F. Skinner (1971) published his book *Beyond Freedom and Dignity,* where he argues that free will is an illusion.

THE MAIN CHARACTERISTICS AND FEATURES OF BEHAVIOURISM

The main ideas and assumptions associated with the doctrine of behaviourism may be outlined as below:

1. *Nature of the learner:* When born, his/her mind is 'tabula rasa' (a blank state). He has no free will, his environment determines his behaviour. Heredity has no role in shaping the nature of the learner.

2. *Environment is every thing:* One's environment play a quite dominant role in shaping one's behaviour and giving direction and dimensions to his personality development. The individual and his behaviour is the sole product of his interaction with the environment.

3. *Similarity between human and animal learning:* The propagators of behaviourism believed that there is a little difference between the learning that takes place in human and that in other animals or birds. Therefore research can be carried out on animals/birds and findings may be generalized to human beings.

4. *Psychology should be considered as a science:* Behaviourism defined psychology as a science of behaviour. It tried to assert that psychology should be considered as a science because here we can have a scientific study of the behaviour of the animals and human beings, through its systematic and objective observation under controlled condition. Expressing his view on this account. Watson stated that "psychology, as a behaviourist views it, is a purely objective experimental branch of natural science. Its theoretical goal is ... prediction and control". (1913, p. 158)

5. *Focusing on observable behaviour:* Behaviourism focused on the study of one's observable behaviour as opposed to his internal behaviour (what is going inside the mind and consciousness) and internal events like thinking and feeling. For this purpose, it argued that it is only the observable behaviour that can be objectively and scientifically measured, therefore it is the only one that can be made a subject of experimental and scientific study by the psychologist and researchers.

6. *Behaviour as a stimulus-response mechanism*: In view of behaviourism all behaviour, no matter how complex, can be reduced to a

simple stimulus-response mechanism. The whole purpose of the science of psychology is centred around this stimulus-response mechanism mentioned by Watson as:

"To predict, given the stimulus, what reaction will take place; or, given the reaction, state what the situation or stimulus is that has caused the reaction." (1930, p. 11).

EVALUATION OF THE BEHAVIOURISTIC PERSPECTIVE

Behaviourism as a school of psychology and doctrine has been appreciated as well as criticized equally by its supporters and critics.

Criticism

The propagators and believers in other schools of psychology or doctrine have raised their voices against behaviourism by pin pointing the defects and short comings as below:

- Behaviourism is a one-dimensional approach to understanding human behaviour and that behavioural theories do not account for free will and internal influences such as moods, thoughts and feelings.
- Behaviourism does not account for other types of learning, especially learning that occurs without the use of 'enforcement' and 'punishment'.
- People and animals are able to adapt their behaviour when new information is introduced, even if a previous behaviour pattern has been established through reinforcement.
- The critics, especially believing in Humanism, express doubt in the applicability of experimental findings of the behaviourism based on animal research to the human beings. They emphasize on rejecting these findings as they view humans as being unique, not to be compared or equated with animals.
- The behaviour, that is made the subject of study in behaviourism is limited to the observable external behaviour. The other type of behaviour — unconscious, sub-conscious and internal behaviour in the shape of thinking and feeling is almost neglected in such a study. A total picture of an individual can only be portrayed through the study of his behaviour in its total aspect.
- It is improper to say that people are born a blank slate (tabula rasa). They certainly have some inborn instincts, reflexes, tendencies and appetites with them at the time of their birth.
- Man is the product of both the heredity and environment. Heredity provides the base for the growth and development of the personality of an individual. A complete denial of the role of heredity by behaviourists is quite inappropriate as hereditary endowments (the role of genes and chromosomes) also play a decisive role in one's growth and development as well as shaping one's behaviour.

- Cognitive psychologists have also expressed their disagreement with the mechanistic stimulus-response approach of the behaviourists. They argue that the role of cognitive processes such as memory, thinking, problem solving, etc. cannot be ruled out between S-R or R-S mechanism.

Merits and Contribution of Behaviourism to Education

Inspite of its opposition and criticism, behaviourism is credited to bring a new era in understanding the human behaviour and processes of learning. Its advantages and contribution in the field of education may be briefly summarized as below:

1. Behaviourists in the study of behaviour rejected the notions of structuralists for figuring out what people were feeling or seeing or the functionists's notion of how and why they were thinking. Instead, they focused on what was actually being done by the people and observed by the observer or investigator. In this way, they introduced the scientific method for studying behaviour, which is essentially based on the objective observation of the behaviour and the events. Behaviourism thus helped in replacing introspective measures with the scientific and objective measures.

2. Behaviourists, while giving second place to hereditary characteristics, highlighted the role of environment in shaping and modifying the behaviour of children. It helped in revolutionizing all the programmes and methods related to education, training and rehabilitation by emphasizing a greater need to provide the best possible learning situations and environment for better growth and development of the child.

3. The approach to dealing with abnormal and mentally sick persons as well as delinquent, maladjusted, backward and problem children was also drastically changed on account of the experimental findings of the behaviourists. In particular, the techniques of shaping behaviour and the behaviour modification programmes advocated by the behaviourists unshared a new era into this field.

4. Since behaviourists did not believe in entities like the *'mind'* and the mind-body problem, the mental approach to human behaviour was altogether discarded. As a result, all concepts related to the doctrine of mentalism like sensation, emotion, perception were dropped from psychology and education texts, giving way to new concepts like stimulus, response, habits, learning, and conditioning.

5. Behaviourism helped in extending the scope of educational psychology to include the study of animals as a way to learn more about human nature.

6. Behaviourism advocated the use of reinforcement and rewards (in place of punishment and unpleasant experiences) as inducement for the acquisition of desirable behaviour and for giving up the undesirable.

7. Behaviourism highlighted the role of motivation and definition of the aims and purposes in learning and shaping of behaviour.

8. Behaviourism gave rise to new ideas and innovations in the field of learning and instruction like programmed learning and individualized self instructional programmes involving teaching machines and computer-assisted instruction.

BEHAVIOURISM AND BEHAVIOURISTIC LEARNING

Behaviourism as a school of psychology or doctrine is credited to propagate a number of useful learning theories for helping the learners and teachers in carrying out the teaching-learning process in a more satisfactory and productive way. A few of such learning theories propagated by the major thinkers and psychologists belonging to the school of behaviourism have been outlined in the table given below:

Name of the Theory	*Main Propagator*
1. Trial and error theory of learning	E.L. Thorndike (1874-1949)
2. Theory of classical conditioning	Ivan Pavlov (1849-1936)
	J.B. Watson (1878-1958)
3. Theory of operant conditioning	B.F. Skinner (1904-1990)
4. Theory of contiguous conditioning	E.R. Guthrie (1886-1959)
5. Hull's systematic behaviour theory	Clark, L. Hull (1884-1952)

All these above cited learning theories try to propagate and apply the view points emphasized by the doctrine of behaviourism in their own ways. However, for the purpose of illustration we would be discussing only the first four behavioural learning theories, namely trial and error, classical conditioning, operant conditioning and Guthrie's contiguous conditioning, in the coming pages of this chapter.

Thorndike's Trial and Error or S.R. Theory of Learning

Thorndike propagated his theory with the help of the experiments performed on chickens, rats and cats. For this purpose he put them under different learning situations, Pierre Flourens (1794-1857) proposed that conclusions drawn from animal experimentation should be equally applicable to man. This proposition started the chain of experimentation, in the field of learning with animals. Thorndike selected chickens, rats and cats for experimentation. He placed them under different learning situations and studied them carefully. With the help of these experiments, he tried to evolve certain laws and propagated his theory of connectionism or trial and error learning. It is interesting to know the type of experiments he performed with these animals. For illustration, below we narrate one of his experiments.

He put a hungry cat in a puzzle box. There was only one door for exit which could be opened by correctly manipulating a latch. A fish was placed outside the box. The smell of the fish worked as a strong motive for the hungry cat to come out of the box. Consequently, the cat made every possible effort to come out. The situation is described by (1911) himself as "*It tries to squeeze through every opening; it claws and bites at the bars or wires, it thrusts its paws through any opening and claws at everything it reaches.*" In this way, it made a number of random movements. In one of the random movements, by chance, the latch was manipulated. The cat came out and got its reward responses. Now it was able to open the door without any error in other words, learned the way of opening the door.

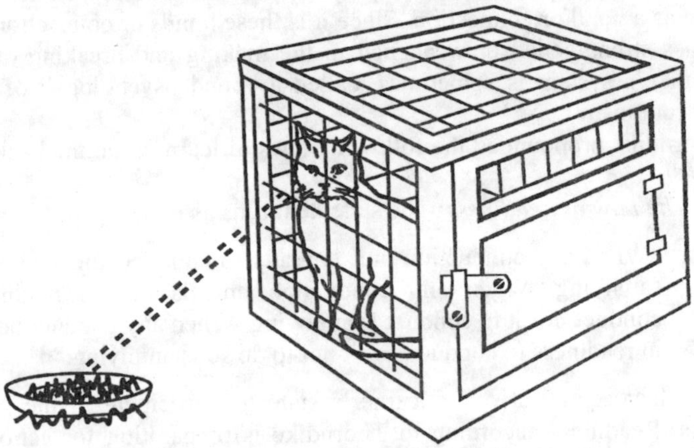

Fig. 8.1: Thorndike's Cat is Trying to Come Out

The experiment sums up the following stages in the process of learning:

1. *Drive*: In the present experiment it was hunger and was intensified with the sight of the food.
2. *Goal*: To get the food by getting out of the box.
3. *Block*: The cat was confined in the box with a closed door.
4. *Random movements*. The cat, persistently, tried to get out of the box.
5. *Chance Success*: As a result of this striving and random movement the cat, by chance, succeeded in opening the door.
6. *Selection (of proper movement):* Gradually, the cat recognized the correct manipulation of latch. It selected the proper way of manipulating the latch out of its random movements.
7. *Fixation*: At last, the cat learned the proper way of opening the door by eliminating all the incorrect responses and fixing the only right responses. Now it was able to open the door without any error or in other words, learned the way of opening the door.

Thorndike named the learning of his experimental cat as "Trial and Error Learning". He maintained that the learning is nothing but the stamping in of the correct responses and stamping out of the incorrect responses though trial and error. In trying for the correct solution the cat made so many vain attempts. It committed errors and errors before getting success. On subsequent trials, it tried to avoid the erroneous ways and repeat the correct way of manipulating the latch. Thorndike called it "Learning by selecting and connecting" as it provides an opportunity for the selection of the proper responses and correct or associate them with adequate stimuli. In this reference, Thorndike has written, "Learning is connecting. The mind is man's connection system." (1931, p. 122)

As a result learning is caused by the formation of connection in the nervous system between stimuli and responses. There is definite association between sense impression and impulses to action. This association can be known as a bond or connection. Since it is these bonds or connection which becomes strengthened or weakened in the making and breaking of habits Thorndike's system is sometimes, called a "bond psychology" of simply "Connectionism".

Thorndike propounded the following laws of learning on the basis of his theory:

(1) *The Law of Readiness:* The statement runs as under:

> "When any conduction unit is ready to conduct, for it to do so is satisfying. When any conduction unit is not in readiness to conduct, for it to conduct is annoying. When any conduction unit is in readiness to conduct, for it not to do so is annoying."

This law is indicative of learner's state to participate in the learning process. Readiness according to Thorndike is preparation for action, it is very essential for learning. If the child is ready to learn he learns more quickly, effectively and with greater satisfaction than if he is not ready to learn. It warns us not to make the child learn till he is ready to learn and also not to miss any opportunity of providing learning experience if the child is, already, prepared to learn. The right movements concerning the learning situation and the learner's state of mind should be very well recognised and maximum use of this knowledge should be made by the teacher. He should also make an attempt to motivate the students by arousing their attention, interest and curiosity.

(2) *The Law of Effect:* In the words of Thorndike, the statement of the law runs as under:

> "When a modifiable connection between situation and response is made and is accompanied or followed by a satisfying state of affairs, that connection's strength is increased. When made and accompanied or followed by an annoying state of affairs, its strength is decreased."

In simple words, it means that the learning takes place properly when it results in satisfaction and the learner derives pleasure out of it. In the situation when the child meets a failure or gets dissatisfaction, the progress on the path of learning is blocked. All the pleasant experiences have a lasting influence and are remembered for a long time, while the unpleasant ones are soon forgotten. Therefore, the satisfaction and dissatisfaction, pleasure or displeasure obtained as a result of some learning ensure the degree of effectiveness of that learning.

In other words, this law emphasizes the role of rewards and punishment in the process of learning. Getting reward as a result of some learning motivates and encourages the child to proceed on the same path with more intensity and enthusiasm while the punishment of any sort discourages him and creates distaste and repulsion towards that learning.

(3) *The Law of Exercise:* This law has two sub-parts — law of use and law of disuse. The statements regarding these sub-parts run as under:

> Law of use: "When a modifiable connection is made between a situation and response that connection's strength is, other things being equal increased."
>
> Law of disuse: "When a modifiable connection is not made between a situation and response, during a length of time, that connection's strength is decreased."

In this way, Law of use refers to the strengthening of connection with practice while the law of disuse to the weakening of connection or forgetting, when the practice is discontinued. In brief, it can be said that Law of Exercise as a whole, emphasizes the need of repetition, practice and drill work in the process of learning.

Changed form of the 2nd and 3rd Laws: In the later years of his life, Thorndike changed his stand on the laws of exercise and effect.

He experimented upon a blindfolded man who was asked to draw a line of three inches in length. Mere repetition did not bring any change or improvement. So, he concluded that practice without rewarding the response was meaningless, which follows that in the process of learning connections get strengthened by being rewarded and not by just occurring.

Regarding the Law of Effect he began to think that rewards and punishment were net equal and opposite in effect. Rewards strengthen the connection considerably whereas punishment does not weaken the connection to the same degree. The intensity and speed of reward in casting influence upon learning is greater than that of punishment. It also brings healthy and desirable improvement in the personality of the child. In this way, he began to give more importance to rewards and praise in place of punishment and blame.

All these three laws — law of readiness, law of effect and law of exercise have a wide field of application in the teaching-learning process. These laws imply the truth of the well known proverbs and maxims like,

"You can lead a horse to water but you cannot make him drink/'

"Nothing succeeds like success."

"Practice makes a man perfect."

Some More Laws of Learning Given by Thorndike

(*i*) *Law of Multiple Response or Varied Reactions:* The law implies that when an individual is confronted with a new situation he responds in a variety of ways before arriving at the correct response.

(*ii*) *Law of Attitude:* Learning is guided by a total attitude or 'set' of the organism. The learner performs the task properly if he has developed a healthy attitude towards the task.

(*iii*) *Law of Analogy:* An individual responds to a new situation on the basis of the responses made by him in similar situations in the past. He makes responses by comparison or analogy.

(*iv*) *Law of Associative Shifting:* The statement of law runs as "We can get any response from the learner of which he is capable, associated with any situation to which he is sensitive". In other words, any response which is possible can be linked with any stimulus. Thorndike clarified his stand through one of his experiments in which he demonstrated how a cat can be trained to stand up at command. He concluded that first of all, a bit of fish is dangled before the cat while you say "Stand up". After enough trials, there will be a stage when you would not need the help of the fish. The oral signal or command will alone evoke the response. The idea put through this law gave birth to a new theory of learning known as Theory of Conditioning.

Educational Implications of Thorndike's Theory and His Various Laws of Learning

Theory of trial and error has enough educational significance. It tries to explain the process of learning, carefully on the basis of actual experiments performed. Not only the animals but human learning also, to a greater extent, follows the path of trial and error. A child while confronted with a Mathematical problem, tries so many possibilities of its solution, before he arrives at a correct one. Even the discoveries and inventions in the various fields of knowledge are the results of trial and error process.

For example, let us take the discovery made by Archimedes in the form of his well-known principle. He was confronted with a problem given by his Emperor. There was a *Drive* that he will be beheaded if he could not get the solution of problem. There was a *Block,* as he could not think of any solution. The problem was difficult. He went on experimenting and made a number of attempts (trials) for the solution of his problem. One day while taking his bath, he got *Chance success* in one of his attempts and this led to the formulation of the law of floating bodies.

But the excessive use of the method, trial and error, without caring for the development of understanding should not be encouraged in any circumstances. We cannot reduce the human learning as mechanical and blind-folded as advocated by this theory. It must be supported by reason, understanding and insight. Trials and practice coupled with insight, will make the process of learning more effective than either of the methods adopted alone.

As far as the Thorndike's laws of learning are concerned, it goes without saying that Thorndike has done a valuable service to the field of learning and teaching by providing these laws. These laws imply the following things in general:

1. In the process of teaching and learning the main task of the teacher is to see what things he likes to be remembered or forgotten by his students. After this, he must try to strengthen the bonds or connections between the stimuli and responses of those things, which are to be remembered, through repetition, drill and reward. For forgetting; the connections should be weakened through disuse and annoying results.

2. The child must be made ready to learn. His interest, attitude and mental preparation is essential for the smooth sailing in the teaching-learning process.

3. It is also emphasized that the past experiences and learning give an adequate base for the new learning. Therefore, the teacher should try to make use of the previous knowledge and experiences of the students. The child must, also, be encouraged to see similarities and dissimilarities between the different kinds of responses to stimuli and with the help of comparison and contrast should try to apply the learning of something in one situation to the other similar situations.

4. The child should be encouraged to do his work independently. He must try the various solutions of the problem before arriving at a correct one. But every care should be taken to see that he may not waste his time and energy. He should not be allowed to repeat his mistakes and proceed blindly without using his reasoning and thinking powers and utilize the past learning experiences.

In short, Thorndike's theory and laws of learning have contributed a lot to educational theory and practice. It has made the learning purposeful and goal-directed and has brought motivation in the forefront. It has also given impetus to the work of practice, drill and repetition and realised the psychological importance of rewards and praise in the process of teaching and learning.

Watson's and Pavlov's Classical Conditioning

After performing various experiments upon the subjects like dogs, rats and cats, Psychologists like Watson and Pavlov gave birth to a new theory of learning known as Conditioned Response Theory or simply as Learning by conditioning. For understanding what is conditioning and what does this theory imply, it is desirable to have an idea of the type of experiments performed by these psychologists.

Experiment by Pavlov. In one of the experiments, Pavlov kept a dog hungry for the night and then tied him on to the experimental table which was fitted with certain mechanically controlled devices. The dog was made comfortable and distractions were excluded as far as it was possible to do so. The observer kept himself hidden from the view of the dog but able to view the experiment by means of a set of mirrors. Arrangement was made to give food to the dog through automatic devices. Every time when the food was presented before the dog, he also arranged for the ringing of a bell. When the food was presented before the dog and the bell was rung, there was automatic secretion of saliva from the mouth of the dog. The activity of presenting the food accompanied with a ringing of the bell was repeated several times and the amount of saliva secreted was measured.

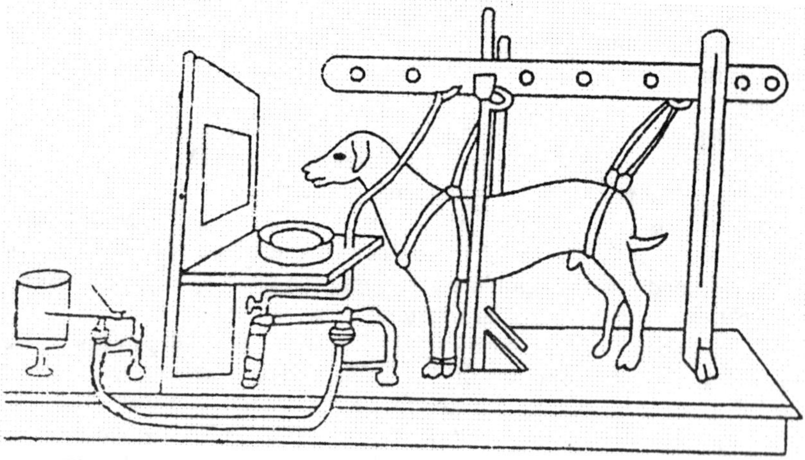

Fig. 8.2: Diagrammatic View of the Experiment Conducted by Pavlov. (Garrett, General Psychology, 1968, p. 254)

After several trials the dog was given no food but the bell was rung. In this case, also the amount of saliva secreted was recorded and measured. It was found that even the absence of food (the natural stimulus), the ringing of the bell (an artificial stimulus) caused the dog to secrete the saliva (natural response).

It considers the learning as a habit formation and is based on the principle of Association and Substitution. It is simply a stimulus-response type of learning where in place of a natural stimulus like food, water, sexual contact, etc. the artificial stimulus like sound of the bell, sight of the light of a definite colour, etc. can evoke a natural response. When both the artificial or neutral stimulus (ringing of the bell) and natural stimulus (food) are brought together, several times, the dog becomes habituated or conditioned to respond to this situation. There becomes perfect association between the types of stimuli presented together. As a result, after some time natural stimulus can be substituted or replaced by an artificial stimulus and this artificial stimulus is able to evoke the natural response.

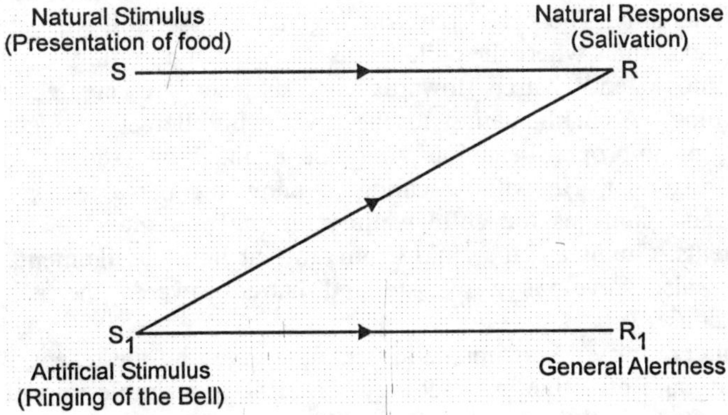

Fig. 8.3: Diagrammatic Presentation of the Experiment

In this experiment, the dog learned to salivate at the sound of the bell. This kind of learning was named as Learning by Conditioning.

Another Experiment: In one of the experiments done by Watson the subject was a human baby of 11 months. The baby was given a rabbit to play. The baby liked it very much and was pleased to touch its fur. He watched carefully the pleasant responses of the baby. After some time in the course of the experiment, a loud noise was produced to frighten the baby. As soon as the baby touched the rabbit. The baby was frightened. Each time when he tried to touch the rabbit, the loud noise was produced and he gave fear response. After some time he began to fear the rabbit, even if no loud noise accompanied it. In this way, he learned to fear the rabbit through conditioning.

From these experiments, Watson and Pavlov etc. concluded that all types of learning can be explained through the process of conditioning. What is this process, can be understood through the following conclusion:

It is a learning process whereby an artificial stimulus is able to behave like a natural stimulus when both natural and artificial stimuli are presented together. In this kind of learning, association plays a great role since the individual responds to an artificial stimulus because he associates it with the natural stimulus.

The conditioning theory of learning put forward by Watson and Pavlov actually involves the conditioning of the Respondent behaviour through a process of stimulus association and substitution. Here the responses of the learner become so much conditioned — behaving in the same way or responding similarly to the similar situation that he does not care for the natural stimuli for evoking the related natural response. As a result the new substituted stimulus behaves like original stimulus and is able to evoke the desired response.

Educational Implications of the Theory of Conditioning

The phenomenon of conditioning does not limit itself to such laboratory experiments only. The day to day learning at home, school, etc. consists of plenty of examples where the child learns through conditioning.

Fear, love and hatred towards the subjects are created through conditioning. A mathematics teacher, with his defective methods of teaching or improper behaviour, may be disliked by students or by a particular student. He without caring to know the basic reason, always rebukes and punishes the child while returning him the checked home-assignments. Gradually, the child begins to fear home assignments of any sort. He also develops a distaste and hatred towards the subject of Mathematics.

On the contrary the sympathetic treatment given by the teacher and his interesting and effective methodology can bring a desirable impact on the students through the process of conditioning. They develop a positive attitude towards the subject and love their teacher as well as the subject taught by him.

The use of audio-visual aids in the teaching-learning process involves the conditioning theory in making the students learn so many things. The child gets an idea of a particular object or phenomenon through this aid. For example, the teacher shows him the picture of a cat, along with the written words 'cat'. The teacher speaks out 'cat' and asks the student to say 'cat' every time when the picture is presented. After some time the picture of the cat is not presented, only the written word 'cat' is shown. But the child responds to it by saying 'cat' He associates the written word 'cat' with the picture of the cat and sound of the word.

In developing desirable habits, interests, attitudes, sense of appreciation in the children etc., the conditioning process may help the teachers and parents a lot. Not only it helps the development of proper behaviour in them, but also is helpful in removing so many bad habits — unhealthy attitudes, superstition, fear and phobias — through reconditioning. A child who fears a particular object can be made to seek pleasure with it. Another child who thinks it a dangerous sign if a cat crosses his way can be made to give up his misbelief. In this way, the conditioning theory throws light on so many aspects of learning and helps the teacher and parents in their task.

Skinner's Operant Conditioning

Although classified and included in the category of conditioning, operant conditioning differs a lot from the classical conditioning advocated by Pavlov and Watson. The most outstanding difference lies in the order related with the initiation and response *i.e.,* stimulus response mechanism. In classical conditioning the organism is passive. It must wait for something to happen for responding. The presence of a stimulus for evoking a response is essential. The behaviour cannot be emitted in the absence of a cause. The child express fear only when he hears a loud noise, the dog waits for food to arrive before salivating. In each of such instances, the subject has no control over the happening. He is made to behave in response to the stimulus situations. Thus, the behaviour is said to be initiated by the environment, the organism simply responds.

Skinner revolted against "no stimulus, no response" mechanism in the evolution of behaviour. He argued that in practical situations in our life we cannot always wait for things to happen in the environment. Man is not a victim of the environment. He may often manipulate the things in the environment with his own initiative. Therefore, it is not always essential that there must be some known stimuli or cause for evoking a response. Quite often, most of our responses could not be attributed to the known stimuli. The organism itself initiates the behaviour. A dog, a child, or an individual "does" something, "behaves" in some manner, it "operates" on the environment and in turn the environment responds to the activity. How the environment responds to the activity, rewarding or not, largely determines whether the behaviour will be repeated, maintained or avoided.

From where Skinner got the cure for such ideas is a question that can arise at this stage. Definitely, it was from the studies and observations of an earlier psychologist named Edward Lee Thorndike. Through his experiments, for propagating his famous trial and error theory of learning. Thorndike concluded that the rewards of a response (like getting food after a chance success through the randomized movements) leads to repetition of an act and the strengthening of S-R associations. These conclusions made Skinner begin a series of experiments to find the consequences of the rewards in repeating and maintaining behaviour. Based on the findings of his experiments, he concluded that *"behaviour is shaped and maintained by its consequences. It is operated by the organism and maintained by its result"*. The occurrence of such behaviour was named as operant behaviour and the process of learning that plays the part in learning such behaviour was named by him as operant conditioning.

For understanding what Skinner propagated through his theory of operant conditioning, let us try to build a base by defining and explaining some of the concepts used by him for bringing out his theory.

Respondent and Operant Behaviour

As we have seen, the earlier theories of learning assumed the existence of a known stimulus as a necessary pre-requisite for evoking a response. Skinner, first time, got the idea that most of the responses could not be attributed to the known stimuli. He defined two types of responses — -the one 'elicited' by known stimuli which he called as "respondent behaviour" and the other "emitted" by the unknown stimuli which he called as "Operant behaviour". Examples of respondent behaviour may include all reflexes such as jerking one's hands when jabbed with a pin and the papillary constriction on account of bright light or salivation in the presence of food.

In the respondent behaviour the stimulus preceding the response is responsible for causing the behaviour. On the other hand, in the operant behaviour the stimulus causing such behaviour is unknown and it is not important to know the cause of the behaviour. Here it is not the stimulus but the consequences of the behaviour which are more important and hence the operant behaviour is controlled by the strength of its consequences instead of stimuli. Examples of such behaviour may include the behaviour like moving one's hand, arms or legs arbitrarily, a child abandoning one toy in favour of the other, eating a meal, writing a letter, standing up and walking about and similar other everyday activities.

Operant: Skinner considers an operant as a set of acts which constitutes an organism's doing something *e.g.*, raising its head, walking about, pushing a lever, etc.

Reinforcer and Reinforcement: The concept of reinforcement is identical to the presentation of a reward. A reinforcer is the stimulus whose presentation or removal increases the probability of a response re-occurring. Skinner thinks of two kinds of reinforce — positive and negative.

A positive reinforcer is any stimulus the introduction or presentation of which increase the likelihood of a particular behaviour. Food, water, sexual contact, etc., are classified as positive reinforcers. A negative reinforcer is any stimulus the removal or withdrawal of which increases the likelihood of a particular behaviour. Electric shock, a loud noise, etc., are said to be negative reinforcers.

The Schedules of Reinforcement: Skinner put forward the idea of planning of Schedules of reinforcement of conditioning the operant behaviour of the organism. The important schedules are as under:

1. *Continuous Reinforcement Schedule:* It is hundred per cent reinforcement schedule where provision is made to reinforce or reward every correct response of the organism during acquisition of a learning. For example, a student may be rewarded for every correct answer he gives to the questions or problems put by his teacher.

2. *Fixed Interval Reinforcement Schedule:* in this schedule the organism is rewarded for a response made only after a set interval of time *e.g.,* every 3 minutes or every 5 minutes. How many times he has given correct response during this fixed interval of time does not matter; it is only on the expiry of the fixed interval, that he is presented with some reinforcement.

3. *Fixed Radio Reinforcement Schedule:* In this schedule the reinforcement is given after a fixed number of response. A rat, for example, might be given a pallet of food after a certain number of level presses. A student may be properly rewarded after answering a fixed number of questions, say 3 or 5. Fixed ratio schedule is used in some factories, and by employers of casual workers or labourer where salary is paid on a piece

work basis, number of garments sewn and number of baskets of fruit packed.

4. *Variable Reinforcement Schedule:* When reinforcement is given at varying intervals of time or after a varying number of responses, it is called a variable reinforcement schedule. In this case reinforcement is intermittent or irregular. The individual does not know when he is going to be rewarded and consequently he remains motivated throughout the learning process in the wait of reinforcement. The most common example of such schedule in human behaviour is the reinforcement operation schedules of gambling devices. Here rewards are unpredictable and keep the players well motivated though occasional returns.

Conclusion about the Various Reinforcement Schedules

Reinforcement and its schedules play a key role in the conditioning of operant behaviour and acquisition of a learning. Where a continuous reinforcement schedule increases the response rate, the discontinuation of reinforcement may result in the extinction of that response or behaviour. Continuous reinforcement schedule thus yields the least resistance to extinction and the lowest response rate during learning. Therefore, learning of a response takes place quickly if every correct response is rewarded, but it is easily forgotten when the reinforcement is stopped. If reinforcement is given after a varying number of correct response or at varying intervals of time the response is remarkably resistant to extinction. However, the fixed interval reinforcement schedules are found to provide the lowest yield in terms of performance as the individual may soon learn to respond correctly only when the time or turn of reinforcement arrives. Similarly, he may lose interest in getting reinforcement after a fixed interval or fixed number of correct responses. Weighing all these properly, Skinner suggests to begin with 100 per cent schedule, practice the fixed interval or fixed ratio schedule and finally arrive at the variable reinforcement schedule for better results in learning or training.

Defining Operant Conditioning

Operant conditioning refers to a kind of learning process whereby a response is made more probable or more frequent by reinforcement. It helps in the learning of operant behaviour, the behaviour that is not necessarily associated with a known stimuli.

Distinction between Classical and Operant Conditioning

Classical or respondent conditioning is based on respondent behaviour. Specifically, it deals with responses that invariably follow a specific stimulus and are thus elicited *e.g.,* blinking at a bright light. Jumbling at an electric shock, salivation to the test of food, and so forth. In this, greater importance is attached to the stimulus for eliciting the desired response. That is why, it is also called S type conditioning.

On the other hand, operant conditioning helps in conditioning or learning of operant behaviour — behaviour that is emitted (rather than elicited). The organism seems to initiate operant behaviour on his own without a single, explicit, preceding stimulus. In this type of learning much emphasis is placed on the response rather than the stimulus causing the response. That is why it is also named as type R conditioning. In type S conditioning, the problem with the trainer or teacher is to select appropriate stimuli for evoking desired response. On the other hand in R type conditioning, out of many responses which an organism is capable of giving the problem with the trainer or teacher is to evoke only the appropriate responses and then fix them properly with the help of suitable reinforcement.

The difference between these two types of conditioning may thus be summarized as under:

Classical Respondent Conditioning	*Operant Conditioning*
1. It helps in the learning of respondent behaviour.	1. It helps in the learning of operant behaviour.
2. It is called type S conditioning to emphasize the importance of the stimulus in eliciting desired response.	2. It is called type R conditioning because of the emphasis on the response.
3. In this type of conditioning beginning is made with the help of specific stimuli that bring certain responses.	3. Here beginning is made with the responses as they occur "naturally" or "unnaturally" shaping them into existence.
4. Here strength of conditioning is usually determined by the magnitude of the conditioned response i.e., the amount of saliva (as in the case of classical experiment of Pavlov with the dog).	4. Here strength of conditioning is shown by the response i.e., the rate with which an operant response occurs as a result of some reinforcement.

Skinner's Experiments Regarding Operant Conditioning

B.F. Skinner conducted a series of experiments with animals. For conducting the experiments with rats, he designed a special apparatus known as Skinner's Box, It was a much modified form of the puzzle box used by Thorndike for his experiments with cats. The darkened sound-proof box mainly consists of a grid floor, a system of light or sound produced at the time of delivering a pallet of food in the food cup, a lever and a food cup. It is arranged so that when a rat (hungry or thirsty) presses the lever, the feeder mechanism is activated, a light or a special sound is produced and a small pallet of food (or small drops of water) is released into the food cup. For recording the observations of the experiments, the lever is connected with a recording system which produces a graphical tracing of the lever pressings against the length of time the rat is in the box.

To begin with, Skinner, in one of his experiments, placed a hungry rat in the above described box. In this experiment pressing of the bar in a desirable way by the rat could result in the production of a click sound and presence of a food pallet. The click-sound acted as a cue or signal indicating to the rat that if it responds by going to the food cup, it will be rewarded. The rat was rewarded for each of his proper attempts for pressing the lever. The lever press response having been rewarded, was repeated and when it occurred, it was again rewarded which further increased the probability of the repetition of the lever press response and so on. In this way, ultimately the rat learned the art of pressing the lever as desired by the experimenter.

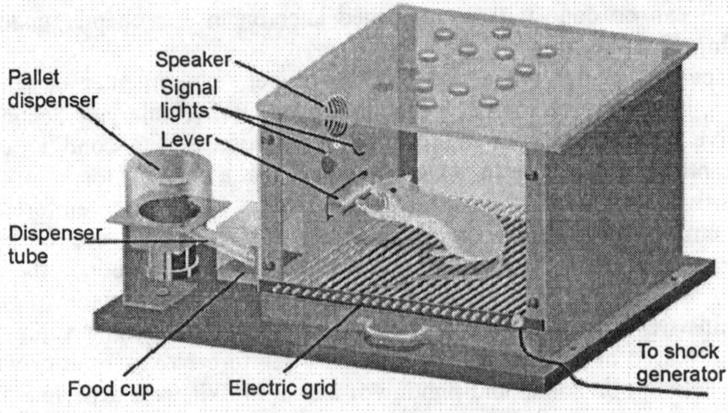

Fig. 8.4: A Rat in a Skinner Box

For doing experiments with pigeons, Skinner made use of another specific apparatus called "pigeon's box". A pigeon in this experiment had to peck at a lighted plastic key mounted on the wall at head high and was consequently rewarded by receiving grain.

Fig. 8.5: A Pigeon in a Pigeon Box

With the help of such experiments, Skinner put forward his theory of operant conditioning for learning not only the simple responses like pressing of the lever but also for learning the most difficult and complex series of responses.

Mechanism of Operant Conditioning

Operant conditioning as emphasized earlier is correlated with operant behaviour. An operant is a set of acts that constitutes an organism's doing something. Hence the process of operant conditioning may start with the responses as they occur "naturally" or "at random". In case they do not occur naturally, then attempts may be made for shaping them into existence. How it can be done will be explained later on in this chapter under the heading "Shaping".

Once a response (as desired by the trainer, experimenter or teacher) occurs, it is reinforced through a suitable reinforcer (Primary or Secondary, positive or negative). In due course this response gets conditioned by constantly reinforcing it. In Skinner's experiment a pallet of food worked as a positive primary reinforcer for the hungry rat. He got the reinforcement after emitting a certain response (pressing of the lever as desired by the experimenter). The Secondary reinforcement may also produce the same results as brought about by the primary reinforcement. It is a sort of neutral stimulus which acquires the reinforcing properties (rewarding value) after getting paired or associated with a primary reinforcer *(e.g.,* food or water). The clicking of a sound and lighting of a bulb in Skinner's experiment may work as secondary reinforcement if they are paired with the appearance of a pallet of food.

The important thing in the mechanism of operant conditioning is the emitting of a desired response and its proper management through suitable reinforcement. Here, the organism is to respond in such a way as to produce the reinforcing stimulus. The subsequent reinforcement gradually conditions the organism to emit the desired response and thus learn the desired act.

Shaping

There are situations especially in case of the acquisition of complex behaviour and learning of difficult skills, etc., where there may arise very remote chances of occurrence. In such cases waiting for an organism to behave in specific way at random (the natural occurrence) may take a life time. For example, the chances for a pigeon to dance in a specific way are extremely remote. The same holds true for a child learning Russian or even table manners. In these situations, where the desired responses do not occur at random (or naturally) efforts are made for eliciting the appropriate responses. It is done by building a chain of responses through a step by step process called "shaping".

In one of his experiments for shaping the behaviour of a pigeon — to teach it to walk in a figure 8.5 — Skinner watched its activity and gave it a small amount of grain (reward) for its every proper movement. At first the pigeon got his reward for simply turning in the right direction, then for taking a step in the right direction, then for making the correct turn, and so on, until it had learned to do a complete figure eight.

Shaping, in this way, may be used as a successful technique for making individuals learn difficult and complex behaviour and also for introducing desirable modifications in the behaviour. Behaviour modification technique and aversive therapy used in treating the problem behaviour and abnormality have come into existence through the use of the shaping of behaviour mechanism.

Implications of the Theory of Operant Conditioning

Theory of operant conditioning has revolutionized the field of training or learning by bringing forward the following practical ideas and implications:

1. A response or behaviour is not necessarily dependent (contingent) upon a specific known stimuli. It is more correct to think that a behaviour or response is dependent upon its consequences. Therefore, for training an organism to learn a particular behaviour or response, he may be initiated to respond in such a way as to produce the reinforcing stimulus. His behaviour should get the reward and in turn he should again act in such a way that he is rewarded and so on. Therefore, the learning or training process and environment must be so designed as to create minimum frustration and maximum satisfaction to a learner to provide him proper reinforcement for the desired training or learning.

2. The principle of operant conditioning may be successfully applied in the task of behaviour modification. We have to find something which is rewarding for the individual whose behaviour we wish to modify, wait until the desired behaviour occurs and immediately reward him when he does. When this is done, the rate with which the desired response occurs goes up. When the behaviour next occurs, it is again rewarded, and the rate of responding goes up even more. Going in the same way, we will be able to make the individual learn the desired behaviour.

3. The task of the development of human personality can be successfully manipulated through operant conditioning. According to Skinner. *"We are what we have been rewarded for being. What we call personality is nothing more than consistent behaviour patterns that summarize our reinforcement history. We learn to speak English, for example, because we have been rewarded for approximating the sounds of the English language in our early home environment. If we happened to be brought up in a Japanese or a Russian home, we would learn to speak Japanese or Russian because when we approximately sound in that language, we would have been attended to or rewarded in some other way."* (Hergenhahn, 1976, p. 87)

4. The theory of operant conditioning does not attribute motivation to internal processes within the organism. It takes for granted the consequences of a behaviour or response as a source of motivation to further occurrence of that behaviour. Food is reinforcing to a rat or pigeon.

Knowledge of correct response is reinforcing to a learner. Secondary reinforcers also prove very important sources of motivation for a learner. Verbal praise, positive facial expressions of the trainer or teacher, feeling of success, scores, grades, prizes, medals and the opportunity to do the work of one's liking, all constitute good motivator. In this way operant conditioning provided an external approach to motivation.

5. Operant conditioning lays stress on the importance of schedules in the process of reinforcement of the behaviour, in trying to train or learn a behaviour, therefore, great care is to be taken for the proper planning of the schedules of reinforcement.

6. This theory advocated the avoidance of punishment for unlearning the undesirable behaviour and for shaping the desirable behaviour. Punishment proves ineffective in the long run. It appears that punishment simply suppresses behaviour and when the threat of punishment is removed, behaviour returns to its original level. Therefore, operant conditioning experiments suggested to perform appropriate behaviour and ignoring the inappropriate behaviour for its gradual extinction.

7. In its most effective application, theory of operant conditioning has contributed a lot towards the development of teaching machines and programmed learning. The theory of operant conditioning had led us to think that learning proceeds most effectively if

(i) The learning material is so designed that it creates less opportunities for facing failure and more opportunities for gaining success,

(ii) The learner is given rapid feed-back concerning the accuracy of his learning, and

(iii) The learner is able to learn at his own pace.

These principles originating from operant conditioning have revolutionized the training and learning programmes. As a result, mechanical learning in the form of teaching machines and computer assisted instructions have replaced usual class room instructions.

Guthrie's Contiguous Conditioning

Edwin Ray Guthrie (1886-1959), an earlier behaviourist, was professor of psychology at the University of Washington. While he was influenced by some of the theoretical findings of his contemporaries like selection, connection and associate shifting advocated by Thorndike and classical conditioning propagated by Watson and Pavlov, he took a quite distinctive stand in propounding his own theory of learning. He devised a new model of learning by synthesizing his idea of temporal contiguity (togetherness of stimulus and response) with the Pavolian model of classical conditioning.

The Guthrie-Horton Experiment

Guthrie tried to propagate his theory on the basis of a number of experiments on cats performed in collaboration with G.P. Horton by using a puzzle box (an apparatus similar to that used by Thorndike in his experiments). The experimental situation consisted of placing a cat in the box with a small pole in the middle of the box as a release mechanism. The cat could escape through a door by touching the pole from any side and in any manner. There was an arrangement of food for the cat outside the cage which it could reach after its release. Guthrie and Horton carefully observed approximately eight hundred escapes by a number of cats from a puzzle box and noted that each cat learned to escape from the puzzle box in its own manner. The specific response learned by a particular cat was the one that the cat had hit upon just before it escaped from the box. For example, if a cat used its paw to press the pole, it learned to use its paw in almost the same way for coming out whenever it was put in the box. They also noted that very often the cats after escaping from the box, would ignore the food that was offered to them. Inspite of their lack of interest in the food, however, they were just as quick in their escape from the box the next time they were placed in it irrespective of the way in which they were placed in it, the manner in which they sought their release was the same as was used by them for their first escape. The cats never tried new ways of release. This was referred to as stereotyped behaviour. On the basis of his experiments, Guthrie reached certain conclusions and laid down basic principles for explaining learning. These conclusions and principles are discussed in detail in the following pages.

1. *Law of Contiguity:* The law of contiguity proposed by Guthrie is the real corner-stone of his unique theory of learning. Guthrie asserted that all rules by which stimuli and responses become associated to give birth to any learning may flow from a single law, the law of contiguity. He gave two explanations for his law:

> A combination of stimuli which has accompanied a movement will on its recurrence tend to be followed by that movement (1952).
>
> What is being noticed becomes a signal for what is being done (1959).

According to these interpretations stimuli acting at the time of response tend to evoke that response on their recurrence and consequently if something has been done by us in a given situation, then in case we are provided again with that situation, we will tend to do the same thing. It happens on account of the formation of a close association between a stimulus or stimuli and the response and this association is formed on account of contiguity, i.e., the coming together of the stimulus (or pattern of stimuli) and a response.

2. *One Trial Learning:* Most behaviourists believe in the law of frequency which implies that learning is proportional to the strength of an association which in turn depends upon the frequency with which it has occurred. This is why Thorndike emphasized repetition and drill for a satisfactory state of affairs. Similarly, Watson and Pavlov also emphasized

the repetition of the association between conditioned and unconditioned stimuli for the conditioning of a required response. In contradiction to these behaviourists, Guthrie (1942) completely rejected the law of frequency by saying:

> A stimulus pattern gains its full associative strength on the association of its first pairing with a response.

In other words, there is no need for repetition of the S-R bond as the association develops its full strength and the learning becomes quite complete after only one pairing between the stimuli and the response. Guthrie thus emphasized one-trial learning in preference to the need for a number of trials for the establishment of an association. In other words, one experience or trial is sufficient to establish an association, i.e., learning.

3. *The Recency Principle:* Guthrie's theory also rests on the principle of recency which states that what was being done in the past in the presence of a set of stimuli will tend to be done next when that stimulus combination occurs.

4. *Movement-produced Stimuli Function:* Learning is the result of contiguity between a pattern of stimulation and a response. The stimuli present in one's environment and the responses one makes to them are, however, separated by a fairly long interval of time and, therefore, cannot be thought of as contiguous. There must definitely be some thing to fill in the gap or interval between the occurrence of an external stimulus and the response finally made to it. Guthrie explained this by inventing the term, movement-produced stimuli.

Movement-produced stimuli are those stimuli (distinctly different from the external stimulation that initially caused the movement) which are produced by the movement of our body and are responsible for conditioning the responses to elicit the desired behaviour. Thus, when a response is being initiated by an external stimulus, the body takes on the responsibility of producing the stimulus for the next response and that response can furnish the stimulus for the next one, in the shape of a chain reaction (chaining) for the movements in a desired direction. To throw light on the mechanism of movement-produced stimuli Guthrie (1935) writes:

> Such a movement as listening or looking is not over like a flash or an explosion. It takes time. The movement, once started, maintains itself by the stimuli it furnishes. When the telephone bell rings we rise and make our way to the instrument. Long before we have reached the telephone the second has ceased to act as a stimulus. We are kept in action by the stimuli from our own movements toward the telephone. One movement starts another, then a third, a fourth, and so on — our movements form series, very often stereotyped in the form of habit. These movements and their movement-produced stimuli make possible a far reaching extension of association or conditioning.

5. *Learning of Acts or Behaviour:* Our behaviour may involve learning of many skills like driving a car, playing badminton, typing a letter, eating a meal, etc. A skill is made up of many acts and acts are made up of many movements which result from muscular contraction and it is these muscular contractions that are directly predicted by the principle of association. Therefore, learning of a skill or performing an act consists of learning thousands of associations between specific stimuli and specific movements.

While the learning of a single movement (requiring association between a specific stimulus and a specific response or movement) requires only one trial and its degree is not dependent on practice. For example, the skill of typing or playing badminton involves an enormously large number of specific S-R bonds each of which is learned in a single trial. Naturally, it will require time and practice for the establishment of all the necessary connections or bonds and we may therefore, conclude that learning of an act or skill needs practice and it is the practice which helps in attaining proficiency in performing an act or skill. The need of such practice can be better emphasized in the words of Guthrie and Horton (1946):

> Learning of an act does take practice. We assume that the reason for this is that the act names an end result that is attained under varied circumstances and by movements varied to suit the circumstances. Learning an act as distinguished from a movement does require practice because it requires that the proper movement has been associated with its own cues. Even so simple an act as grasping a rattle requires different movements according to the distance and direction and position of the object. One successful experience is not sufficient to equip the infant with an act because the one movement acquired on that occasion might never again be successful.

6. *Role of Reinforcement or Reward:* It was noticed by Guthrie in the behaviour of the cats that though they often ignored the food placed outside the box, this did not affect their proficiency in coming out of the box. This observation led him to disagree with Thorndike and re-define the role of reward or reinforcement. Reward or reinforcement according to him, is not an essential condition for the re occurrence of the previous response. In other words, learning is not dependent on reinforcement of behaviour. The law of contiguity, accompanied by the recency principle, is enough to explain the learning behaviour. The animal is likely to repeat the preserved association between being in the puzzle box and moving the pole resulting in its release. Therefore, regardless of the food it gets after its release, the animal would try to repeat the last response which helped it to obtain its release.

Reward or reinforcement like food in this case, according to Guthrie, may simply work as a mechanical arrangement for changing the stimulating conditions and thereby preventing unlearning. In the words of Guthrie (1940):

> The animal learns to escape with its first escape . . . what encountering the food does is not to intensify a previous item of behaviour but to protect that item from being unlearned.

7. *Forgetting and Extinction of Behaviour:* According to Guthrie's conclusion, extinction or forgetting (weakening or disappearance of the association or bond between a stimulating condition and a response) occurs not due to non-reinforcement but due to the phenomenon of interference. He accepts an extreme form of retroactive inhibition (interference in old learning by new learning) to explain extinction and forgetting. According to him, for the extinction and forgetting of a wrong response of undesirable learning one is required to learn something new in such a way that the old learning is completely knocked out. According to Guthrie (1942):

> Forgetting is not a passive fading of stimulus-response associations contingent upon the lapse of time, but requires active unlearning which consists in learning to do something else under the circumstances.

8. *Role of Punishment:* The role played by punishment in learning or forgetting a behaviour was also studied by Guthrie. He accepted the role of punishment in this situation but emphasized that punishment is effective only through its associations resulting in a new response to the same stimuli. In the words of Guthrie (1952):

> It is not the feeling caused by punishment, but the specific action caused by punishment that determines what will be learned. In training a dog to jump through a hoop, the effectiveness of punishment depends on where it is applied, front or rear. It is what the punishment makes the dog do that counts or what it makes a man do, not what it makes him feel.

In this way, punishment works not because it induces certain kinds of painful experiences but because it forces the organism to do something different and thus establishing inhibitory conditioning of unwanted habit resulting in a behaviour incompatible with the punished behaviour. For example, in punishment meted out to a dog which is in the habit of chasing your motorcycle, a slap on the nose or a slap on the rear is equally painful to the dog. However, the slap on the nose in this case would prove more effective because, the slap on the nose will tend to make him stop and jump backward in the presence of the motorcycle, resulting in incompatible behaviour. On the other hand, a slap on the rear will make him continue forward, perhaps with a little more speed and will thus fail in its purpose by eliciting a behaviour not incompatible with the punished behaviour.

Thus, for making punishment effective, we have to arrange things in such a way that stimuli that previously elicited an undesired response, now elicit an unwanted response (incompatible with the punished response) that can make the organism think of changing its ways of behaviour so that it may learn a favourable response, instead of an unfavourable one.

9. *Motives and Drives:* On the basis of his studies, Guthrie concluded that motives and drives occupy an important place in the field of learning as they provide for the maintenance of stimuli for keeping the organism active until a goal is reached. For example, by being hungry or thirsty one is stimulated and this stimulated behaviour is maintained until one gets food or water. Similarly, when one is anxious to achieve a target it stimulates one and the stimulated behaviour is maintained until one gets what one aspires to in terms of money, success or recognition. Drives and motives are, therefore, not only physiological but also socio-psychological and external and in this way any source of stimulation, whether internal or external, capable of maintaining stimuli can be termed as a useful motive or drive for accelerating the movement of the organism to reach a goal.

10. *Transfer of Training:* While rejecting the formal discipline theory outright, Guthrie's theory of learning gives some consideration to Thorndike's identical element theory of transfer. Therefore, according to it similarity between two situations may act as a deciding factor for the probability of a similar response in two situations. Guthrie's theory, however, asserts that transfer in two situations can only take place if the stimulating conditions in both the situations are identical and consequently on account of the variation in the stimulating conditions there is no guarantee that a child who learns something in his study room will be able to reproduce it in the classroom or examination hall.

Summary of Guthrie's Theory of Contiguous Conditioning

Guthrie's theory is based on a single law of learning, that is, the law of contiguity which states that when two events occur together, they are learned. In other words, learning is based on the association or connection between a stimulus and a response and this association occurs simply because of the contiguity, that is, occurrence of the stimulus and response together. For maintaining the chain of contiguity between the external stimuli and the responses finally made by us our body through its movements, tends to produce the stimulus for subsequent responses in a chain-like mechanism. However, as far as learning in the form of establishing a bond between a stimulating situation and a response is concerned, it occurs in a single trial and this association tends to be continued until there is change in the stimulating conditions or a response is prevented from occurring. The association once made, on this bond once established, makes the organism exhibit the same response (usually in the form of the last movement which helped it to reach a goal like a cat hitting the pole in a particular way to escape from the box) in case it is faced with the same stimulating conditions and when this happens we say the organism has learned the way it should behave to attain its goals (Fig. 8.6).

Contribution and Educational implications of Guthrie's Theory of Contiguous Conditioning

Guthrie's theory based on a single law of contiguity has wide implications in the field of education:

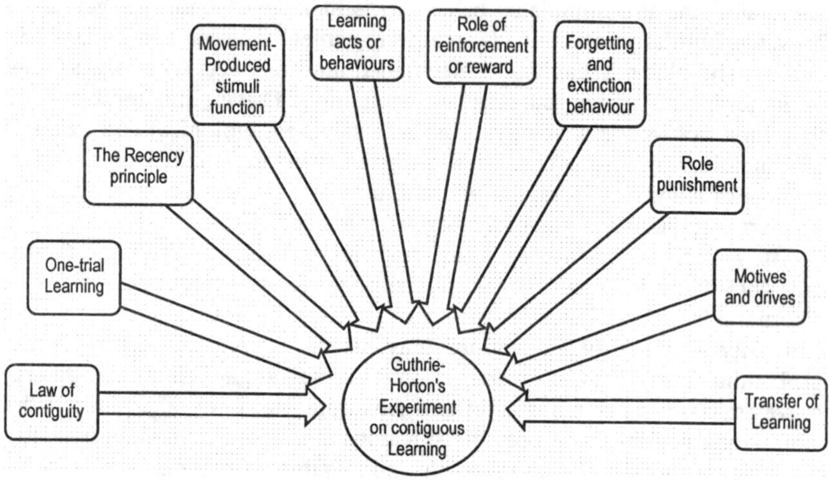

Fig. 8.6: Guthrie's Contiguous Conditioning

1. Guthrie's emphasis that learning is complete after only one pairing between the stimuli and the response makes us take care in the organisation of stimulating conditions for eliciting the desired response.

2. The law of contiguity and the recency principle which emerged from this law require that in case we want to revoke a learned response we have to arrange for the occurrence of stimulating conditions identical to the ones in which the response behaviour has been learned. It makes us exercise caution in learning things in the way in which these are going to be utilized by us in the future. For example, if a student teacher is required to teach in the class after becoming a teacher, he must be trained in the actual classroom set up. Similarly, if a student has to be examined in a classroom laboratory or particular examination set up, he can be expected to do better only if he has been taught in conditions in which he is required to demonstrate his performance later on. It enables us to introduce radical changes in the teaching-learning materials, processes and conditions so that the associations made at the time of learning are utilized to the maximum at the time of utilization of the outcomes of learning. The school programme or the task of formal learning must be made so functionable and natural as to coincide with the real life settings so that what is learned at school may prove useful to the learner in real life.

3. Guthrie's theory lays stress on the need of drill and practice as this generates more and more stimuli for eliciting the desired behaviour. According to Guthrie, since learning is complete in terms of the

establishment of an association between a stimulus and response, every learning in itself is a unique experience and its transfer from one situation to another cannot properly take place until the two situations are identical. As it is very difficult for stimulating conditions to be identical, we must make the child practise a behaviour under different stimulating conditions. For example, for learning addition of numbers like two and two the child should not learn only from the blackboard or in his note-book but must also learn it through making various associations (in the form of two and two equals four) with the help of concrete objects like chalks, books, pens, apples, etc. in the school or outside the school.

4. Guthrie believes in the interference theory and the mechanism of retroactive inhibition to explain the causes of forgetting. We must, therefore, make sure that the interference caused to the past learning by the new learning is avoided. For minimizing forgetting he advocates that what is being learned should be learned properly and the new learning should be so planned and associated that it may cause least interference to the past learning. A thing to be learned properly needs strengthening of the bond or association between stimuli and response when it is learned the first time. This may necessitate the following:

(a) Since any behaviour is a complex of movements in response to a complex of stimuli, for evoking a desired response or making the child learn a particular behaviour we must have the support of as many stimuli as possible. The more the stimuli used for evoking a desired response, the less will be the likelihood of a interfering or distracting behaviour.

(b) In order to evoke a desired response, we must look for all the ways and means for evoking that particular response. All types of drives, motives and means like rewards and punishment must be utilized for evoking and then intensifying the response.

5. Guthrie's theory provided valuable cues and ways for breaking bad habits. For this purpose, Guthrie outlined the following three different techniques:

(*i*) *Threshold Technique:* This technique according to Guthrie (1938) consists of:

> Introducing the stimulus at such weak strength that it will not cause the response and then gradually increasing the intensity of the stimulus, always taking care that it is below the 'threshold' of the response.

For instance, suppose there is a boy who does not like to take a bag full of books, note-books, etc. on his shoulder while going to school. If the mother puts the bag on his shoulder, he throws it down and insists that it should be carried by some servant. Now, the technique consists of first putting some eatables and objects of light-weight toys in the bag and ask him to carry it on his shoulder. If he carries it, then we can gradually increase the weights of these and finally replace these things with books and note-books etc. and so break his habit of not carrying the school bag himself.

(ii) Fatigue Technique: The fatigue method consists in allowing an individual to perform the task concerning the bad habit repeatedly to the point that he becomes too tired to continue further and thus making him allergic to that task. For example, a little boy who is in the habit of tearing paper unnecessarily may be set right by being allowed or rather forced to tear papers to the point where the task is no longer fun. As a result, the paper will become a cue to doing something other than tearing them. As a result, the child will develop an attitude of avoidance.

(iii) Incompatible Response Technique: In this technique, an undesired response elicited by particular stimuli is inhibited by a simultaneous presentation of both types of stimuli, the one causing undesired response and the other a stronger stimulus producing a response which is incompatible with the undesired response. For example, if a child is afraid of a dog then he would be allowed to come close to the dog in the presence of his mother, a dominant stimulus for evoking warm relaxed feelings in the child. The pairing of dog and mother will create a feeling of relaxation in the child. Once such relaxation has been experienced by the child, it will pave the way for the child to face the dog alone (without pairing it with his mother) without showing any sign of fear.

All these three techniques can be safely employed by teachers and parents in the task of breaking bad habits as all of them are based on the following general rules:

(a) first find the cues that are responsible for the undesired responses concerning the bad habit, and then

(b) practice another response in the presence of these discovered cues for getting rid of the undesired response.

9

Cognitivism Perspective and Learning

WHAT IS COGNITIVISM?

This new school of contemporary psychology is the result of the wave of intellectualism demonstrating faith in man's higher cognitive abilities and capacity to adapt to his environment and struggle for perfection. It may be defined as one of the school of psychology or doctrine that lays emphasis on the role of the cognitive structure and cognitive processes like thinking, memory, knowing and problem solving etc. in one's learning or behaving in one way or the other. The underlying concept of cognitivism involve how we think and gain knowledge for our needed adjustment, development and progress in our life.

HISTORICAL EVOLUTION AND DEVELOPMENT OF COGNITIVISM

The roots of cognitivism may be traced back to the early decades of 20th century in the cognitive outlook of the propagates of gestalt psychology, like Max Wortheimer (1880-1943), Kurt Koffka (1886-1941), Wolfgang Kohler (1887-1967) and Kurt Lewin (1890-1947), etc. These Gestaltists vehemently opposed the behaviourism doctrine of stimulus-response conditioning or machine like operation of human behaviour. They advocated an overall mental functioning and insight in place of a molecule and mechanistic approach for the study of human behaviour and explanation of human learning. Gestalt psychologist provided a unique theory of learning known as Theory of Insightful learning, emphasizing the role of insight or intelligence in one's learning and understanding the things in his environment.

Taking clue from the gestaltists, the other contemporary psychologists also tried to evaluate the role of higher cognitive processes in one's learning and behaving. The notable American psychologist, Edward Chace Tolman (1886-1959) provided the lead in this direction by propounding a theory of learning in 1932 with the publication of his work "Purposive Behaviour in Animals and Men". His theory known as Tolman's sign learning stands midway between the behaviouristic S.R. theories and cognitivistic gestalt theories. While advocating his cognitivistic views, he compared the behaviouristic S.R. learning system with the operational activities of a telephone exchange — "incoming calls from sense organs" and "outgoing messages to muscles". However, learning according to his cognitivistic views can't be reduced to so simple mechanism undertaken through simple S.R. connections of a telephone switch-board but involves complex cognitive activities helped by the brain processes. Edward Tolman, thus by his revolutionary cognitivistic views tried to make notable contributions in the field of learning, thinking and creative functioning. While explaining the problem-solving behaviour of the higher organisms, he stated that the organism tries to set up mental hypotheses about the ways to solve problems and then sets out to test these hypotheses through purposeful behaviour.

The cognitivistic ideas of learning behaving and developing were further advanced through the sincere efforts of Jean Piaget and J.S. Bruner who are famous for their theories of cognitive development and cognitive functioning. Equally notable was the work of the Information Processing theorists like George A. Miller (1960), Atkinson and Shiffrin (1968), and Craik and Lokhart (1972) who provided the famous cognitive theories of learning named as (i) Miller's Information processing theory, (ii) Three stage Information Processing Theory and (iii) Levels of Processing Theory respectively.

In its latest trend cognitive psychology is using the metaphor of the mind as computer: information comes in (input), is being processed (process), and leads to certain outcomes (output). It has come up with the idea and application of artificial intelligence for the explanation of human behaviour and development of the new psychological theories.

MAIN CHARACTERISTICS AND FEATURES OF COGNITIVISM

The main idea and assumptions associated with the doctrine of cognitivism may be outlined as below:

1. In sharp contrast to behaviourism, cognitivism does not consider people as "programmed animals" that merely respond to environment stimuli. Rather it considers them as rational beings that require active participation in order to learn, and whose actions are a consequence of thinking.

2. Like behaviourism, cognitivism is also interested in the observations of the changes in behaviour, but only as an indication of what is occurring in the learner's head.

3. Cognitive perspective challenges the limitations of behaviourism in its focus on observable behaviour. It incorporate mental structure and process into their learning theories.

4. Cognitive psychologists share with behaviourists the belief that the study of learning should be objective and that learning theories should be developed from the results of empirical research. However, cognitivists disagree with the behaviourists in one critical aspect. By observing the responses that individuals make to different stimulus conditions, cognitivists believe that they can draw inferences about the nature of the internal cognitive processes that produce those responses.

5. The main theme of this new school is cognitive revolution (sometimes referred to as the 'white-box' theory) which postulates that internal processes are the subject matter of psychology. This contrasts with behaviourism (sometimes called the 'black-box' theory). By referring to it as the black box theory, it is implied that behaviourists are concerned with the output or response (R) of the organism in a certain situation, and to some degree with the input or stimulus (S) but do not consider what transpires between the stimulus and the response. This unexplored element is represented by a 'black box' which intervenes between S and R.

6. Cognitive psychology studies man's thinking, memory, language, development, perception, imagery and other mental processes in order to peep into the higher human mental functions like insight, creativity and problem solving.

7. Cognitive psychologists are totally opposed to the stimulus-response approach of the behaviourists. They maintain that there is more to learning and behaving than just single responses to stimuli. The human mind does not accept an information from its environment in exactly the form and style it is conveyed to him. The conveyed information is compared with the information already stored in the mind, it is then analysed and often enlarged upon and given a quite new form. Finally, it is subjected to interpretation and then used or stored according to the need of the time.

8. Cognitive psychology presents the system's viewpoint to explain the behavioural mechanism. In this system, whatever is conveyed through stimuli in the environment is the 'input'. The cognitive functioning of the human mind is the 'process' and the result of the cognitive functioning is the 'output' or the 'product'.

9. The central issues that interests cognitive psychologists include the internal mechanism of human thought and the processes of knowing. Cognitive psychologists have attempted to find out the answers to mental structures, such as what is stored and how it is stored, and to mental processes concerning how the integration and retrieval of information is operated. The theoretical assumptions in cognitive psychology lend instructional systems a hand in the design of efficient processing strategies for the learners to acquire knowledge, *e.g.*, mnemonic devices to reduce the workload of the short-term memory, rehearsal strategies to maintain information, and the use of metaphors and analogies to relate meaning of the new information to prior knowledge.

COGNITIVISM AND THEORIES OF LEARNING

The various thinkers associated with the school of cognitivism have brought out a number of theories mainly focusing on two different aspects, namely (i) the course of cognitive development of the developing children and (ii) the way in which they learn or acquire one or the other things. On the first issue, we can very well mention the works done by Jean Piaget and

Jerome Bruner in the name of Piaget Theory of Cognitive Development and Bruner's Theory of Cognitive Development. On the second issue, we can here mention the various theories of learning based on cognitivism like Gestalt's theory of Insight, Tolman's sign learning and a host of Information processing theories. All of these developmental and learning theories reflect the views and philosophy of cognitivism in one way or the other, therefore, it is quite relevant to know about them for getting acquainted with the implication of cognitivism to the learner, teacher and teaching-learning process. However, since in this text, we are mainly focusing on the learning among children and adolescents, therefore here we would like to throw light mainly on two cognitive theories named as (i) Insightful learning, and (ii) Information processing theory of learning.

Gestalt Theory of Insightful Learning

The learning theory named as "Learning by Insight" is the contribution of Gestalt Psychologists. Gestalt Psychology began with the work of German psychologists who were studying the nature of perception. Wertheimer is, generally, considered to be the Gestalt Psychology founding father. Wertheimer, Kohler, Koffka and Lewin all four of these men, originally German, eventually settled in America, are the leaders of what is historically known as Gestalt Psychology.

"Gestalt" is a German noun for which there is no English word equivalent, so the term was carried over into English psychological literature. The nearest English translation of Gestalt is 'configuration' or more simply 'an organised whole in contrast to a collection of parts, Gestalt psychologists consider the process of learning as a Gestaltan organised whole. A thing cannot be understood by study of its constituent parts but only by study of it as a totality, is a basic idea behind this theory.

In the practical sense, Gestalt Psychology is primarily concerned with the nature of perception. According to it, an individual perceives the thing as a whole while the Behaviourists and Stimulus Response theorists define perception in such a way as to make it analogous with taking photographs. They think that sensation comes prior to meaning and consider these who acts as separate. But the Gestalt Psychologists do not separate sensation of an object from its meaning. They are of the opinion that unless a person sees some meaning in an object he will pay little or no attention to it. Further more, to a Gestalt Psychologist, the meaning of sensation or perception is always related to the total situation. According to them perception always involves a problem of organisation. A thing is perceived as a relationship within a field which includes the thing, the viewer and a complex background incorporating the viewer's purposes and previous experience.

Gestalt Psychologists tried to interpret learning as a purposive, exploratory and creative enterprise instead of trial and error or simple stimulus-response mechanism. Learner, while learning, always perceives the situation as a whole and after seeing and evaluating the different relationships takes the proper decision in an intelligent way. He always responds to the proper relationship rather than the specific stimuli. Gestalt Psychology used the term 'insight' to describe the perception of the whole situation by the learner and his intelligence in responding to the proper relationships. Kohler, first of all, used this term (insight) to describe the learning of his apes. Kohler conducted many experiments on chimpanzees and brought out a book 'Mentality of Apes' in 1925 which was the result of his experiments, conducted during the period 1913-17 on the Canary Island.

These experiments show learning by insight. Some of them are given below:

(i) In one experiment, Kohler put the chimpanzee, Sultan, inside a cage and a banana was hung from the roof of the cage. A box was placed inside the cage. The chimpanzee tried to reach at the banana by jumping but could not succeed. Suddenly, he got an idea and used the box as a jumping platform by placing it just below the hanging banana.

(ii) In other experiment, Kohler made this problem more difficult. Now it required two or three boxes to reach the banana. Moreover, the placing of

Fig. 9.1: Kohler's Experiment on Chimpanzee

one box over the other required different specific arrangements.

(iii) In a more complicated experiment banana was placed outside the cage of the chimpanzee. Two sticks, one larger than the other, were placed inside the cage. One was hallow at one end so that the other stick could be thrust into it to form a longer stick. The banana was so kept that it could not be picked up by one of the sticks. The chimpanzee first tried these sticks one after the other but failed. Suddenly, he got a bright idea. The animal joined the two sticks together and reached the banana.

In these experiments, Kohler used many different chimpanzee. Sultan, who was the most intelligent of Kohler's chimpanzees, could solve all the problems. Other chimpanzees could solve the problems only when they saw Sultan solving them.

With such experiments, Kohler concluded that in the solution of problems, his apes did not resort to blind, Trial and Error mechanism. They reacted intelligently. Kohler used the term 'Insight' to describe the learning of his apes. Insight involves the following criteria:

(a) The situation as a whole is perceived by the learner.
(b) The learner tries to see and judge the relationship between various factors involved in the situation.
(c) As a result, the learner is helped in the sudden grasping of the solution of the problem.

On the similar line experiments were conducted by the Gestalt Psychologists. All the experiments have shown that at some stage there is a new organisation of the perceptual field resulting in getting a solution all of a sudden. Therefore, the learning according to them is re-structuring the field of perception through insight. As a whole, Insight depends upon the following factors:

(a) *Experience.* Past experiences help in the insightful solution of the problems. A child cannot solve the problem of Modern Mathematics unless he is well acquainted with its symbolic languages.
(b) *Intelligence.* Insightful solution depends upon the basic intelligence of the learner. The more intelligent the individual is, the greater will be his insight.
(c) *Learning situation.* How insightfully the organism will react, depends upon the situation in which he has to act. Some situations are more favourable than the others for insightful solution. As a common observation, insight occurs when the learning situation is so arranged that all the necessary aspects are open for observation.
(d) *Initial efforts.* Insightful learning has to pass through the process of trial and error. But this stage does not last long. These initial efforts, in the form of simple trial and error mechanism, open the way for insightful learning.
(e) *Repetition and Generalization.* After having an insightful solution of a particular type of problem, the organism tries to repeat it in

another situation, demanding similar of solution. The way found in one situation helps him to react insightfully in the other identical situations.

Educational Implication of the Theory of Insightful Learning

This theory brings the following important facts into lime light.

1. The whole is greater than the parts and therefore, the situation should be viewed as a whole.
2. The use of blind fumbling and mechanical trial and error should be minimized. The learner should try to see relevant relationships and act intelligently.
3. The purpose or motive plays the central role in the learning process.

Based on the appeal of this theory, teachers are required to pay attention to the following aspects:

(i) Subject-matter (learning material) should be presented in Gestalt form. While teaching the topic, parts of a flowering plant or flower the initial start should not be made by presenting the different parts. The plant or flower as a whole should be presented before them and later on the parts should be emphasized. The problem of Mathematics requiring solution should be presented as a whole and after grasping it as a whole, it should be tried for the solution.

(ii) In the organisation of the syllabus and planning of the curriculum, the Gestalt principles should be given due consideration. A particular subject should not be treated as the mere collection of isolated facts or topics. It should be closely integrated into a whole. Similarly, the curriculum, comprising of different subjects and activities should reflect unity and cohesiveness.

(iii) This theory had brought 'motivation' in the fore-front by assigning purpose and motive, the central role in learning process. The child should be motivated by arousing his interest and curiosity and he should be acquainted well with the specific aims and purpose of his learning.

(iv) The greater contribution of the Insight theory of learning is that it has made learning an intelligent task requiring mental abilities instead of blind fumbling and automatic responses to specific stimuli. It has called a halt to age old mechanical memorization, drill and practice work which lack in basic understanding and use of thinking, reasoning and creative mental powers.

Information Processing View Point

What is Information Processing?

In its simple meaning information processing stands for an act of processing the information i.e. to analyse, employ or make use of information for gaining some knowledge or experience. In the words of Joyce and Weil

"Information processing refers to the ways people handle stimuli from the environment, organise data, sense problems, generate concepts and solutions to problems, and employ verbal and non-verbal symbols." (1972, p. 9).

In this way information processing deals with the ways and means an information (sensory input or data) is handled by an individual for deriving desired meaning for its further use. Consequently, the handling or processing of the information may help an individual to gain new experiences and insight for the solution of felt problems or modification of his ways of behaving.

Information Processing Theories or View Points about Learning

The way people do process the availed information (resulting in gaining new experiences or bringing modification in their behaviour), may give birth to significant theories of learning. This very assumption has led to the formulation and establishment of some well known learning theories termed as information processing theories of learning. The key question answered by all these information processing theories of learning is "Cognitively, what processes are occurring in a person's brain when they are presented with a learning situation". Consequently they throw light on the mechanism how the human brain senses, processes and recalls information. The working of our brain in terms of information processing, may be easily equated to the working of computers. Like computers, thus the information processing in human brain may find its expression in the mechanism of input, processing and output. The brain receives sensory impulses from the environment and decides to process this input as warranted. Processing depends on the nature and complexity of the data as perceived by the learner. The way, information is received, processed and recalled by the learner then decides the outcomes of his learning.

For gaining some idea about the nature and functioning of Information Processing theories of learning we can here discuss some of the popular theories and models of instruction developed by the eminent psychologists. In their description, we may easily notice a significant trend that all of these Information Processing theorists to approach learning primarily through a study of Memory and that is why we can find due mention of the terms related to the process of memorization like temporary memory, short term memory, long term memory, recall, retrieval, etc. Let us begin with the description of these theories one by one.

Three Stage Information Processing Theory

This theory is the outcome of the ideas propagated by Atkinson and Shiffrin (1968, 1971). According to this theory, learning is the outcome of the processing of the information carried out by human brain at the following three stages.

(i) Sensory registry

(ii) Short term memory and
(iii) Long term memory.

1. The process of learning or memorization, thus starts with the interaction of one's sense organs with one's environment. The sensory information is first picked up by one or more sense organs, then it travels through the nervous system and reaches the brain for its interpretation. The sensory information stays in the nervous system (Just as to register its presence) briefly say about a second or two for giving brain the time for its interpretation. After being registered in the sensory register, it can be responded immediately or may be transferred to the short term memory. Usually it depends upon the nature of sensory information and its interpretation by own brain. The brain may interpret it as useless or of little significance and thus may order for its disappearance from the sensory register or it may be ordered for its monitoring at a low attention level. As an example of such type of information processing at the sensory registry level we can cite the driving of our car while carrying on a conversation, here we can monitor and respond to driving conditions without transferring the information to short term memory.

2 The information not processed or vanished at the level of sensory registry then travels to short term memory (STM) of our brain. It may here automatically stay for upto 20 seconds. However, it can be retained as long as an individual wants it in his short term memory through rehearsal or repetition. Short term memory is equivalent to ones working memory. It is here the information is duly processed by the brain for its proper interpretation, assimilation and responding. There are usually three means that are employed for the information processing or handling of cognitive tasks in STM. These are:

(i) Encoding the information in to chunks.
(ii) Breaking the information into its sub parts and then processing them one at a time.
(iii) Practising skills until they are automatic.

3. The information unprocessed at the short term memory stage, is then transferred to the long term memory (LTM). LTM is thought to have unlimited capacity and duration. It is used for storing and procession sensory information on a permanent basis. The stored as well as organised information in the LTM in the coded form is transferred back to the short term memory where it is decoded and employed for response as desired and ordered by our brain.

Levels of Processing Theory

This theory of information processing has been put up by Craik and Lokhart (1972) as an alternative to the above discussed information processing theory postulating three stages — sensory, working and long term memory for the processing of information. The main ideas lying within this theory may be summarised as below:

- Memory is of only one kind rather than of three types namely, sensory, short term and long term.
- Ability to learn or remember is dependent on how deeply information is processed by us.
- Levels of such processing may range from very shallow to very deep.
- The greater the depth of processing, the better can the material be learned or remembered. For example, information that involves strong visual images or many associations with existing knowledge will be processed at a deeper level. Similarly, information that suits our interests or serve our purposes well will receive more processing than other stimuli events.
- The things that are meaningful to us are processed quite deeply in comparison to the meaningless or less meaningful stimuli and consequently are learnt or remembered well.
- Processing of information at different levels in carried out quite unconsciously and automatically unless we attend to that level. For example, we are usually not aware of the sensory properties of stimuli, or what we have in own working memory, unless we are asked to specifically identify such information. From this it follows that there is hardly any place for the mechanism of attention in the processing of information. It may thus be taken as an interruption in processing of information rather than a cognitive process in its own right.

Sternberg's Information Processing Approach

Sternberg (1977) made use of the information processing approach for the explanation of children's learning and development.

While producing his view points, Sternberg's suggested that development is skills-based and continuous rather than staged and discontinuous as stage theorists such as Piaget believe. His focus has been on the intelligence and cognitive abilities of the learner. This focus on intelligence separates his ideas from stage theorists because it rejects the idea of incremental stages, but rather suggests that development occurs in the same way throughout life differentiated only by the expertise of the learner to process new information. In this way, while providing explanation for the development of the children he deals solely with information processing aspects of development and does not incorporate any facets of biological development into his theory. Moreover, Sternberg's model does not differentiate between child and adult learning. According to him, much depends upon the competency of an individual for processing the information.

The more competent a person is in information processing, the more heights he will touch in terms of his cognitive development and skill of learning. Moreover, in information processing social and cultural context also play a great role. Learning and development does not occur in vacuum, it needs the assistance of social interaction and the children's learning and cognitive development takes place better in the company and guidance of the elders.

Miller's Information Processing Theory

This theory has been put forward by George A. Miller as an extension of the earlier approaches of cognitive psychologists expressing learning primarily in terms of the study of the process of memorization. The main ideas lying behind his theory may be summarized as below:

(i) Information processing helps in acquiring new experiences and learning new ways of behaving.

(ii) Students learn better while they are activity processing, storing and retrieving information.

(iii) Information processing helps the students to build desirable cognitive structures (structuring of the subject matter for its proper comprehension and understanding)

(iv) Successful encoding is essential for the proper processing of the received sensory information or data. Working memory (STM) also processes the information for being transferred to Long Term Memory (LTM) by encoding the information. Therefore, meaningful encoding is a must for the desired task of information processing.

(v) Miller (1956) presented the concept of "Chunking" for the meaningful organisation or encoding of the subject matter at all level of cognitive processing. Classical example of chunks is the ability to remember long sequences of binary numbers because they can be encoded into decimal form. For example the sequence 10100 01001 11001 101 1010 could easily be remembered as 20 9 25 5 10. Of course this would only work for someone who can convert binary to decimal numbers (i.e. the chunks are meaningful).

(vi) We can expand the capacity of a person holding information in his short term memory by utilising the concept of chunking. It can hold 5-9 chunks of information (seven plus or minus two). Therefore information should always to organised in the form of chunks (meaningful units) for its better processing and fruitful learning out.

(vii) The second useful concept regarding that of the information processing (other than chunking) propagated by Miller is concerned with his acceptance of the computer as a model of human learning. Like the computer, the human mind takes in information, performs operations on it to change its forms and content, stores and locates it and generate responses to it. Thus information processing according to Miller involves: (i) gathering and representing information, i.e. encoding, (ii) holding

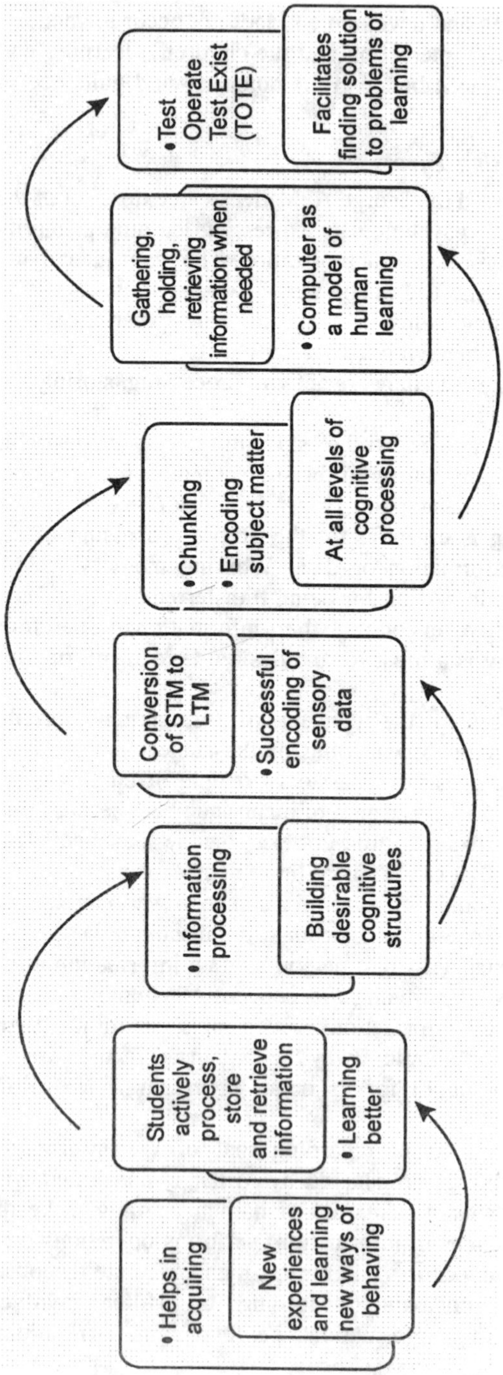

Fig. 9.2: Miller's Information Processing Theory

information i.e. retention, and (iii) getting at the information when needed i.e. retrieval.

(viii) The third useful concept emphasized in Millers information processing theory is known by the term TOTE (Test Operate Test Exist).

By introducing this concept, Miller et. a. (1960) suggested that TOTE should replace the stimulus response mechanism as the basic unit of behaviour. In a TOTE unit, a goal is tested to see if it has been achieved through the mechanism of information processing. If not, an operation is performed to achieve the goal, this cycle of test-operate is repeated until the goal is eventually achieved or abandoned. By adopting this technique, an individual may be capable of finding the solution of his problem or learning the desired way for achieving his goal.

Educational Implication of the Theories of Information Processing

All the theories of Information processing described above in general may be said to have the followings as their educational implications.

1. The information (verbal or nonverbal) should be organised in terms of meaningful units for its better processing and fruitful learning outcomes.
2. Students should be helped in focussing on the most important details and separating less vital information.
3. Students should be helped in making connection between new information and what they already know.
4. As far as it is adequate and possible, students should be provided for repetition and review of information.
5. The learning material experiences (Instruction) should be organised in a clear systematic and organised way.
6. Always we must focus on meaning not memorization of information on the part of students.

10

Humanism Perspective and Learning

WHAT IS HUMANISM AND HUMANISTIC PERSPECTIVE IN EDUCATION?

As a matter of definition humanism has been defined in the free dictionary.com as a system of thought that focuses on human and their values, capacities and worth.

Historically however as a new perspective and paradigm in the field of education and human behaviour, humanism emerged in 1960's with the efforts and view points of the psychologists like Abraham Maslow, Carl Rogers, Gordon Allport and Malcolm Knowles (a proponent of androgogy). Regarding the view point, Humanism as a philosophy or new school of psychology provided more importance and value to the human being by not considering him merely as a sophisticated machine or a victim of the conflict between the Igo and Id as proposed by behaviourists like skinner and psychoanalyst like Freud. Humanists also differed from the cognitivists who consider man merely as an intellectual or creator with no consideration for the voice of the heart, human values and dignity. In contrast to the other prevalent schools of psychology and perspectives in education, this new school and perspective in human behaviour and education may be found to be characterized with features and characteristics discussed ahead.

BASIC CHARACTERISTICS AND FEATURES OF HUMANISM AND HUMANISTIC LEARNING

(i) Here due emphasis is laid over human freedom, values, dignity and potential.

(ii) People do not act as a mere machine or rational being but demonstrate a lot of intentionality and values in their behaviour and learning.

(iii) Human being should be considered as a purposeful being, capable of adapting himself his environment and choosing his own course of action in order to achieve the goals which he has selected for himself. These goals may be as simple as the satisfaction of a common physical need or as lofty as the attainment of self-realization or personal fulfilment.

(iv) We must give due regard and weightage for the existence of freedom of choice, expression and free will among the human beings in organizing learning experiences and providing opportunities to them for their education and development.

(v) It is essential to study the person as a whole for knowing and understanding him as a human being. The study of his goals, motives, interests and attitudes, values and ideals, ways of learning and behaving should be studied well for providing opportunities for him for his living and development.

(vi) Human nature, interests and values should not be sacrificed for the sake of following traditions, establishing cruel discipline and using rigid methods of instruction.

(vii) Humanistic view point or perspective on learning advocates to adopt.

(a) reasonable flexibility in following curriculum, methods of teaching, behaviour modification and assessment of the learning and behavioural outcomes of the learners.
(b) individualization of the teaching-learning of the students in tune with their basic humane nature and individuality.
(c) sympathetic treatment and patient hearing for the needs and problems of the learners for providing humane treatment, care and attention to them for their wholesome development and well being.
(d) child centered approach in place of subject centered and teacher dominated methodologies and approaches.
(e) the policy of laying emphasis on positive reinforcement *(e.g.* rewards and praise) over the negative and aversive means *(e.g.* punishment and blame).
(f) the scheme of continuous and comprehensive evaluation, for helping the children in their wholesome development and purposeful learning.
(g) the policy of laying emphasis over the experiences and activities for helping the learners in their purposeful learning.

Humanistic learning thus provides an all together new perspective quite different from the behaviouristic, cognitive and constructive perspectives for the children's learning by making the task of their learning as humane as possible in terms of adopting humanistic attitude and humane methods of teaching and dealing with the children. As an illustration of the application of humanistic approach or view points in the field of human learning we are hereby producing a brief description of two theories named as Roger's Theory of Experimental Learning and Bandura's Social Learning Theory.

ROGERS' THEORY OF EXPERIENTIAL LEARNING

Carl Rogers in his book freedom to learn for the 80's (1983) presented his full theory of experiential learning. It aims to throw light how the learners are able to learn and construct their own knowledge with the experiences gained in their socio cultural environment through their self-initiated efforts. Let us try to know how Rogers developed and produced his ideas related to his theory of experiential learning.

In his search for the basic nature of learning, Rogers tried to distinguish two types of learning — cognitive and experiential. He termed *cognitive learning* as meaningless in itself unless it is subjected to some use. Such learning is knowledge based and thus may include the learning of vocabulary, multiplication table, mathematical formulae, historical events and geographical facts. The experiential learning, on the other hand, is quite vital to one's progress and welfare. It is associated with the application of the acquired knowledge such as learning about engines in order to repair a car, learning psychological principles and methods in order to help the children get rid of bad habits. The experimental learning is learner-centred. That is to say, it cares for the needs, and wants of the learner. Carl Rogers has tried to enumerate these qualities of experiential learning in the following way:

1. Experiential learning is characterized by *personal involvement* of the learner.
2. It is *self initiated.* The learner willingly takes initiative to engage in such type of learning.
3. It is characterized by *self-evaluation.* The learner himself is interested in evaluating the results and outcomes of such learning by applying it to the realization of learning objectives, *i.e.* he wants to test his knowledge of repairing an electrical gadget by actually doing the repair.
4. It leaves a *pervasive effect* on a learner. Whatever is learned through this method can be made into use when and where he needs,

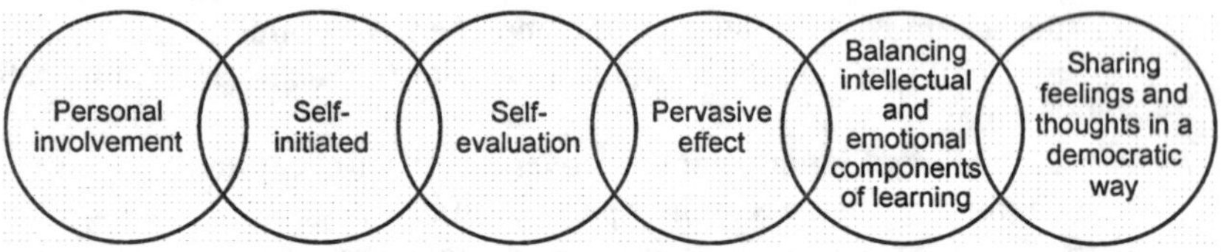

Fig. 10.1: Roger's Theory of Experiential Learning

Rogers, as a humanist, believes in the strength and potentialities of human beings. According to him, all human beings have a natural inclination for learning and a desire to grow and progress. The role of the teacher and the parents is thus to help their children in their inherent desire for personal change and growth. Teacher as well as the parents have to care for and facilitate such learning which helps the children to grow and develop according to their requirements. The attempts of the teachers and the parents in realising the objectives of experiential learning may, thus include the following provisions:

1. Arranging a favourable and positive climate for learning.
2. Helping the learner or learners to have clear-cut objectives and purpose of his/her learning.

3. Organising the learning resources and making them available to the learners.
4. Balancing intellectual and emotional components of learning,
5. Sharing feelings and thoughts with learners in a democratic way.

Thus, the primary responsibility of a teacher lies well in his sincerity as a helper, a guide and a facilitator in the ongoing teaching-learning process. He is not there to provide mere information or demonstrate his skills in any area of information or fact-finding. Through many tools and materials and his own characteristic ways, a teacher, while following the doctrine of experiential learning, has to play the role of a learning facilitator. For realising this objective, as Rogers points out, a learner must at least take care of the basic conditions that facilitate learning. According to him, learning is well facilitated when:

1. *threat* to the self of the learner is minimum;
2. learning resources and climate are in favour of the learner;
3. the learner participates completely in the learning process and has control over its nature and direction;
4. it is primarily based on direct confrontation with practical, social, personal or research areas.
5. self-evaluation is the principal method of assessing progress or success; and
6. the learner realizes the importance of learning and develops an openness as well as willingness to learn.

Thus experiential learning is, in fact, a learner-centred enterprise. Here the learner is the key figure in the ongoing teaching-learning process. The role of a teacher is to facilitate such learning. The primary responsibility of learning and change in the behaviour of the learner for his personal and social development lies with him. However, he is to be properly helped, guided and kept on the proper track by the teacher as and when the need of doing so arises. The main thing is to help the learner realize the importance and significance of the learning task. If we can make him see the profit or gain of the learning task, we can very well realize the objectives of learning. Therefore, according to Rogers, learning must be linked with the motives, goals and ideals of the learner. Accordingly, for a learner who is interested in becoming rich in learning, pertaining to, say, such topics as economics, investment, financing, banking, etc., the concept of learning may be of great importance. Decidedly he will take more genuine interest in the learning of topics and subjects which are helpful in realising his motives and ambitions, as compared to other students of his class who have significantly less interest in money matters.

Summing up, it can be easily concluded that Carl Rogers, through his theory of experiential learning, advocates a humanistic and learner-centred approach to be adopted in class rooms by the teachers, with the sole purposes of making the learning process more humane and suitable to the needs and interest of the learners, and turning it into more significant and purposeful event from the angles of their personal and social growth and development (by emphasizing more on application than on theory alone).

BANDURA'S SOCIAL LEARNING THEORY

Observation of other's behaviour may play a leading role in learning and acquiring various things concerning one's environment. The cognitive psychologists who appreciate the role of observation in learning are termed as social psychologists and the theory of learning they propagate is known as the social learning theory Albert Bandura was a prominent American social learning theorist and the social learning theory is often designated as Bandura's social learning theory.

Introducing his theory Bandura (Lewin, 1978) writes:

> We do not blindly respond to environmental stimuli. Rather, we pick and choose from many environmental options, basing our decisions on our own insights and past experiences. This we do through vicarious or observational learning by incorporating and imitating the behaviour of those around us.

Observational or vicarious learning (learning through indirect experiences) rather than the learning based on direct experiences is thus the base of the social learning theory. The advocates of this theory emphasize that most of what we learn is acquired through simply watching and listening to other people. The children from the very beginning keenly observe the behaviour of others, most commonly of the people nearest to them like parents, members of the family, teachers, the older members of society, etc. In turn, they try to imitate and do what they observe. The power of observational learning can be confirmed through laboratory experiments as well as through observation in our daily life. A child who sees his father throwing utensils around simply because he has not been served food of his taste, learns such behaviour and reproduces it in similar circumstances. He may also incorporate and imitate the behaviour of the characters he reads about in novels, hears about over the radio or sees on TV or in movies. The persons whose behaviour he observes and often imitates are known as models and observational learning is referred to as *modelling.*

Direct experiences no doubt constitute the most effective and powerful sources of one's learning but the role of indirect experiences leading to observational learning can also not be underestimated. In many cases, they prove more desirable, less expensive and more beneficial than the direct experiences. Commenting on this aspect Bandura (1977) writes:

> One does not teach children to swim, adolescents to drive automobiles and novice medical students to perform surgery by having them discover the appropriate behaviour through the consequences of their successes or failures. The more costly and hazardous the possible mistakes, the heavier is the reliance on observational learning from competent examples.

Observational learning can thus provide extra dimensions and opportunities for the learners in addition to their learning through self-experience and direct involvement with environmental consequences. It has certainly reduced the need of an individual going through every experience himself and thus helped him to learn from the examples of others.

How does Learning take place?

According to the social learning theory, one learns through observations by incorporating and imitation the behaviours of others taken as models belonging to one's social environment. According to Bandura (977), the following processes or steps are usually involved in this land of learning.

1. *Attending to and perceiving the behaviour:* In this step the learner is made to observe the behaviour of the person acting as a model. Here the total behaviour or a particular aspect of it may attract attention and become the subject of close attention.

2. *Remembering the behaviour:* In this step, what the learner observes is filed away in his memory in the form of mental images.

3. *Converting the memory into action:* In this step, a behaviour observed and remembered by the learner is analysed in terms if its acceptability to the learner with reference to the demands of his self and his environment. It is transformed into action only afterwards and thus the observed relevant and accepted aspects of the model's behaviour are imitated by the learner.

4. *Reinforcement of the imitated behaviour:* In this final step, the behaviour of the model imitated by the learner is reinforced for proper adoption and further continuance.

Let us see how these steps may work in one's learning. Suppose a young girl happens to watch a T.V. programme concerning the preparation of some new dishes. She takes keen interest and is greatly influenced by the demonstration on the T.V. screen. She tries to keep in her memory all that she has observed on the screen and then enters her kitchen to convert the remembered conservation into action. The new dishes are thus prepared by her in accordance with her observation of the performance on T.V. of the Home Science Specialist. Her Learning of the preparation of the new dishes may then be reinforced by the response she gets from the members of her family who taste the new dishes.

In this way, social learning *i.e.,* learning through observation and modelling proves to be an effective means of learning many things concerning one's behaviour. How one displays love and anger, shows sympathy and prejudices, speaks and writes, dresses and eats, takes initiative or shies away, all depend upon what has been observed, remembered, imitated and reinforced in context of the vicarious or model learning as propagated by the social learning theory.

11

Constructivism Perspective and Constructivist Learning

INTRODUCTION

Constructivism is relatively a modern view point or new philosophy emerged in the field of education and psychology. It has provided an altogether new direction for our understanding to how does a child learn and develop intellectually. The philosophy of constructivism has been responsible for giving birth to the concept of constructivist learning. Actually, what we term as constructivism, may be found to represent a paradigm shift from education based on behaviourism to education based on cognitivism. Behaviourism and behaviouristic theories of learning have been responsible for giving birth to our traditional system of education, instruction and learning. In this system, knowledge or skill is directly poured in the minds of the students through lecturing or demonstration. Students remain most of the time passive listeners or silent spectators. They are, latter on, required the time passive listeners or silent spectators. They are, latter on, required to reproduce or re-represent the reality of the facts communicated to them by the teacher. In this system learner is least bothered from where the communicated knowledge has come, he has to simply receive, revise, practice and then reproduce it in the form and shape communicated to him. Constructivism as a philosophy and ways of learning is totally opposed to the system propagated by behaviourism. It assumes and pleads that the learners should play an active role in the process of learning or cognitive development by constructing their own knowledge on the basis of their past experiences and their present interaction with the environment. The belief that a learner can learn only when he is able to construct the required knowledge by himself individually or socially is thus the main focal point of the philosophy of constructivism.

HISTORICAL EVOLUTION OF CONSTRUCTIVISM AND ITS TYPES

As a basic philosophy underlying human learning the roots of constructivism may be traced to the philosopher Giambattista Vico belonging to 18th century, who emphasized that humans can understand only what they have themselves constructed or learned by themselves. Later on John Dewey, the famous educational practitioner and philosopher emphasized the role of experience in education by asserting that "Education is a process involving continuous reconstruction and reorganization of experiences". The process of such continuous reconstruction and reorganization of experiences needed for the development of a child paved the way, later on, for Jean Piaget (the famous child and cognitive psychologist) to put up his theory of cognitive development and constructivist learning by coining the notions like cognitive structure, assimilation, accommodation and equilibrium, etc. Later on, the psychologists and scholars like Lev Vygotsky (the famous Russian psychologist), Jerome Bruner (the famous American cognitive psychologist), and Ernest Von Glaserfeld (a German psychologist), provided their own view points and explanation for the development of the ideas related to constructivism and constructivist learning. The approaches adopted for propagating their constructivism have given birth to a number of types of constructivism known as below:

1. Individual constructivism propagated by Swiss psychologist Jean Piaget.
2. Social constructivism propagated by Russian psychologist Lev Vygotsky.
3. Radical constructivism propagated by German psychologist Von Glaserfeld.
4. Cognitive constructivism (A blend of individual and social constructivism) propagated by American psychologist Jerome Bruner.

However, in this chapter we would be focussing our discussion only on the first two types of approaches of constructivism.

JEAN PIAGET'S INDIVIDUAL CONSTRUCTIVISM

Before Piaget, a few cognitive psychologists put up their information processing approach for explaining the mechanism of construction of knowledge by the individual minds. They argued that knowledge construction begins with the sensory input of the information or knowledge in the human mind. The human mind as a information processing system converts sensory input into symbol structures (propositions images or schemas), and then processes (rehearses or elaborates) those symbol structures so knowledge can beheld in memory and retrieval. In such a way, according to information processing theorists, individuals try to reconstruct outside reality by building accurate mental representations (within their minds) that usually reflect "the way things really are".

Piaget raised his voice against such non-constructive and non-creative aspect of constructivism by asserting and proving that knowledge is not a mirror of realty but rather an abstraction that grows and develops with cognitive activity. He strongly put up his views on this account in the following words.

> "Knowledge is not a copy of reality. To know an object, to know an event is not simply to look at it and make a mental copy or image of it. To know an object is to act on it. To know is to modify, to transform the object, and to understand the process of transformation, and as a consequence to understand the way the object is constructed." (Piaget, 2003, p. 5).

In this way, Piaget successfully argued that knowledge acquisition occurs through knowledge construction. But knowledge construction is not so simple or automatic process as put up by information processing theorists. It is true that the task of knowledge construction is executed in the minds of the individuals but it is done not by passive reception of transmitted information (sensory input), but by the active interaction with objects and ideas. The nature of this interaction, according to Piaget is an adaptation involving three mental processes, named as assimilation, accommodation and equilibration.

In understanding about a new thing, first the child attempts to know about it through the help of his past experiences (assimilation) but when he fails to do so it creates a stage of disequilibration in his mind. As a result, he tries to learn new ways of understanding and doing this (accommodation). It makes him to seek equilibration or adjustment in terms of knowing the new thing or doing new task by constructing knowledge by himself through the cognitive processes involving, assimilation, accommodation and equilibration.

In this way, according to Piaget learning occurs as a product of the knowledge construction process carried out internally in the minds of individual through dynamic interaction of the individual and the environment by means of the process called self-regulation or equilibration (helped by assimilation and accommodation to bring needed changes in the cognitive structure of the individual).

It may be noted here clearly that Piaget's constructivism is less concerned with "correct" representation and more interested in meaning as individual constructs for himself for his adaptation. It may be more clear to you through the following example taken from Woolfolk (2004, p. 222).

> A young child who has never been to the hospital is in her bed in the paediatric wing. The nurse at the station down the hall calls over the intercom above the bed, "Hi Chelsea, how are you doing? Do you need anything?" The girl looks puzzled and does not answer. The nurse repeats the question with the same result. Finally, the nurse say emphatically, "Chelsea, are you there? Say something!" The little girl responds tentatively, "Hello Wall-I'm here."

In this example, as Woolfolk comments Chelsea, the small girl, encountered a new puzzling situation — a talking wall. She has no prior experience as such and her existing cognitive structure does not permit her to derive the correct representation of the reality. She here tries to construct her own knowledge based upon her prior knowledge and existing cognitive structure. The sound is coming from a particular side, the wall is persistent and she now makes sure that the wall is talking to her. In this way, Chelsea, makes use of what she knows and what the situation permits her for constructing her own knowledge by least caring whether it is the representation of the reality or not.

Accordingly, in Piaget's constructivism, knowledge is constructed by reflecting on and coordinating one's own conditions or thoughts, not from mapping external reality. In addition, the constructivism propagated by Piaget, focuses on individual knowledge, beliefs, self-concept, or identity, that is why it is referred to as individual constructivism. Here the knowledge is constructed by the individual himself quite independently without seeking help from others (like Chelsea in our example) purely based on the self-perception and prior knowledge or experiences. It is also sometimes called as psychological constructivism simply on the basis that construction of knowledge is purely the matter of one's psyche and psychological life. The mental and emotional state as well as the available cognitive structure, helps the individual to construct the knowledge by himself. In addition of naming Piaget's approach to construct knowledge as individual constructivism and psychological constructivism. Some psychologists have also named it as "First were constructivism" or "Solo constructivism" with the due emphasis that Piget was the first to be credited for laying foundation for the constructivism and constructivist views of learning.

VYGOTSKY'S SOCIAL CONSTRUCTIVISM

Lev Vygotsky, (1896-1934), the famous Russian psychologist, brought out a type of constructivism known as social constructivism quite distinctive from the individual constructivism of Piaget. Piaget's constructivism was merely the handy work of individual's independent efforts for constructing knowledge by himself without providing any significance to the social interaction and activities. Vygotsky, on the other hand, in his approach to constructing knowledge, provided immense weightage to social interaction, cultural tools, and activity by accepting them as the main instruments for shaping individual development and learning. On account of relying heavily on social interactions and the cultural contacts to explain learning, Vygotsky constructivism is usually referred to as social constructivism and the viewpoint he emphasized, for such constructivist learning." Let us try to highlight the main ideas and essence propagated by him in his theory.

(i) Learning is a social process and it can be carried out best in a social environment.

(ii) Learning involves knowledge construction and this knowledge construction task should be essentially carried out on a "social plane".

(iii) Knowledge building or acquisition on the part of an individual is helped much if it involves his interaction with two or more people, his elders or peers, by making use of the social interaction tools like language discourse and social context.

(iv) Knowledge construction task may be viewed completely in terms of its two phases — (a) Simple and initial phase, and (b) Complex and later phase.

In its first phase, the experiences a child encounters spontaneously in his day to day life, social interaction and cultural exchanges, help him to construct knowledge involving essential simple spontaneous concepts. The construction of knowledge on his part here is absolutely based on his own reflections on everyday experience. It is thus his own effort for understanding his world.

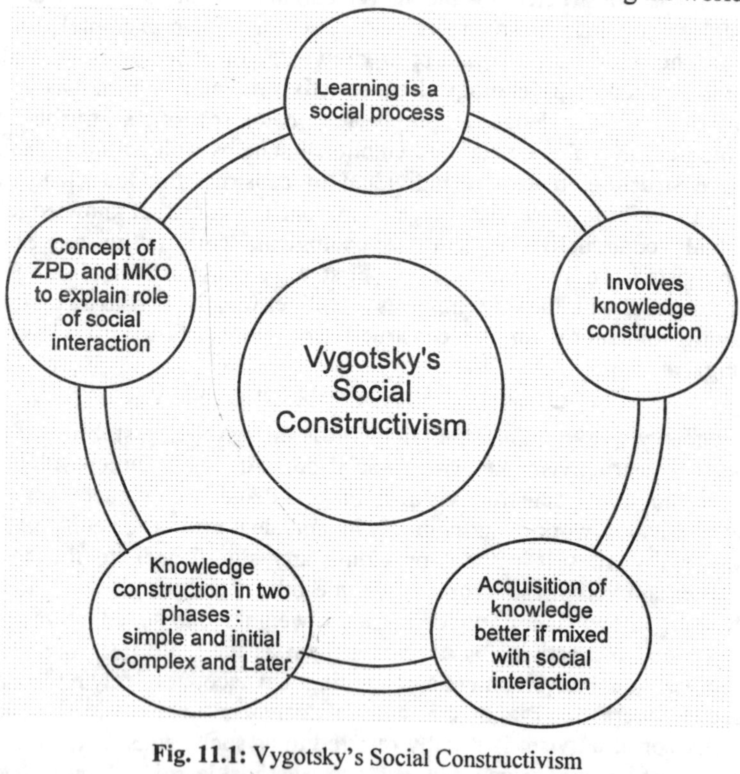

Fig. 11.1: Vygotsky's Social Constructivism

In the second phase, the knowledge construction task is carried out on a relatively higher level. The simple spontaneous concepts developed by the individual can provide him as an essential base in the form of pre-existing conceptions for the acquisition of higher order concepts and knowledge. The task here is not executed independently by the individual but he is helped and guided by an adult or experienced peer to construct knowledge for the development and progress of his self. Vygotsky in this way was not against the struggling on the part of an individual to construct the knowledge independently without expecting any help from his elders or peers. But he was of the opinion that individual constructivism can only help an individual in building some preliminary or simple concepts and the higher concepts needed for his proper development can only be resulted through social constructivism-interaction and guidance from the adults and peers.

(v) For explaining the role of social interaction, culture and guidance of the elders in the construction of knowledge on the part of a child Vygotsky, coined two terms namely ZPD and MKO. Let us try to know what Vygotsky meant by these terms.

More Knowledgeable Other (MKO: The term more knowledgeable other (MKO) is somewhat self-explanatory; it refers to someone who has a better understanding or a higher ability level than the learner, with respect to a particular task, process, or concept. Although the implication is that the MKO is a teacher or an older adult, this is not necessarily the case. Many times, a child's peers or an adult's children may be the individuals with more knowledge or experience. For example, who is more likely to know more about the diversified application of a mobile phone, tablet or recently loaded video game than the child or their parents?

Zone of Proximal Development (ZPD). A second aspect of Vygotsky's theory is the idea that the potential for cognitive development depends upon the "zone of proximal development" (ZPD). This is an important concept that relates to the difference between what a child can achieve independently and what a child can achieve with guidance and encouragement from a skilled or more knowledgeable partner. (See Figure 11.1)

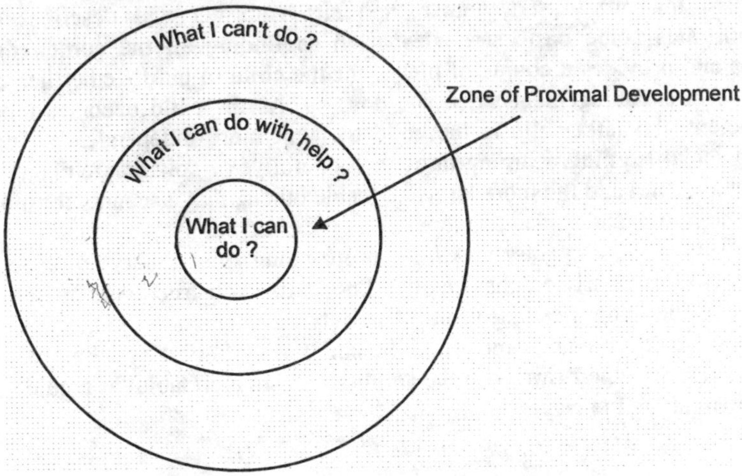

Fig. 11.2: Zone of Proximal Development

In this way, Zone of Proximal Development (ZPD) actually represents that zone or area where a child can solve a problem with the assistance (scaffolding) of a more knowledgeable other (an adult or more able peer). Proximal simply means "Next". It carries two meanings. The one is that for the child in his task of problem solving or behaviour modification, the person lying next to him in knowledge and experience (superior) thus may help a lot. He can learn and develop himself intellectually and socially more in supervision or collaboration with the adults or peers. In its second meaning, the term proximal or next conveys that key to stretching the learner for taking him on the path of cognitive and social development on the part of we adults to know well in advance what lies in that person's ZPD — to what extent he can be helped to go ahead on the path of his cognitive and social development in view of his existing potential. The ZPD of children according to Vygotsky depends on a number of factors, like age, their individuality, the differing nature of the impact of home and family, society and culture in which they are brought up, etc. The circumference of the children get widened as the child advances in their age, gets opportunities for learning and are exposed to wider social and cultural experiences. Taken together, the MKO and the ZPD form the basis of the scaffolding component of the cognitive apprenticeship model of instruction. In this regard, Vygotsky explained that when a student is at the ZPD for a particular task, providing the appropriate assistance (scaffolding) will give the student enough of a 'boost" to achieve the task. Once the student, with the benefit of scaffolding, masters the task, the scaffolding can then be removed and the student will then be able to complete the task again on his own.

In this connection, Shaffer (1996) has provided an illustration of a young girl who is given her first jigsaw. Alone, she performs poorly in attempting to solve the puzzle. The father then sits with her and describes or demonstrates some basic strategies, such as finding all the corner/edge pieces and provides a couple of pieces for the child to put together herself and offers encouragement when she does so. As the child becomes more competent, the father allows the child to work more independently. It is called social learning, learning through cooperative or collaborate dialogue between a child and the more knowledgeable others, that, accounts for most of the cognitive and social development of the children.

In this way, Vygotsky, while propagating his theory of social constructivism clearly emphasized that knowledge construction is an active process of deriving meaning from the variety of experiences lying in one's social and cultural environment and the children learn best by taking sense of something on their own with the adults (or peers more able) as a guide to help them along the way.

LEARNING IN CONSTRUCTIVIST PERSPECTIVE OR CONSTRUCTIVIST LEARNING

In its simple word meaning constructivist learning is the learning based on the philosophy and approach of constructivism. Our traditional methods of learning, specially those dominated with teacher centred and subjected centred approach are based on behaviourism. The learning and training experiences, methods and practices here all are dependent upon the theories of learning such as Thorndike's connectionism, classical conditioning and operant conditioning. The cognitivism as a philosophy and approach opposed the learning methods propagated by behaviourists. It brought the role of one's intellectual functioning and mind in constructing knowledge, understanding the new experience and then assimilate it in its existing cognitive structure. The Gestalt methods of insightful learning, and cognitive learning methods propagated by cognitive psychologists like Piaget and Bruner (discovery learning, concept attainment model and inquiry based investigation, etc.) may be cited as the valid attempts for giving birth to the learning methods and approaches associated with constructivism. Apart from the Gestalt psychologists and other cognitive psychologists, Piaget and Bruner, John Dewey (Staunch believer in the role of experience in the construction of knowledge), Vygotsky and Von Glaserfeld also provided a solid base for the origin of constructivism learning by propagating their own views about constructivism.

Constructivist Learning Defined

Constructivist learning originated from the philosophy of constructivism, is the learning (a step ahead from cognitive learning of cognitive psychologists) that assumes that learners construct their own knowledge on the basis of their prior knowledge and interaction with their environment alone or in a group quite independently or assisted and guided by their teachers, elders and knowledgeable peers for attaining the desired learning outcomes in a teaching-learning situation.

ASSUMPTIONS AND CHARACTERISTICS OF CONSTRUCTIVIST LEARNING

The assumptions and characteristics inherent in constructivist learning may be broadly outlined as below:

1. Set of theories known as constructivist theories of learning differs from the behaviouristic theories of learning in the sense that these do not consider learning as a machine like stimulus-response mechanism or treat the organism as a black box. These are also one step ahead to the cognitive theories of learning. Cognitive theories recognize the importance of the mind in making sense of the material with which it is presented. Nevertheless, it still pre-supposes that the role of the learner is primarily to assimilate whatever the teacher presents. Constructivist learning in its

individualistic as well as social forms strongly asserts that the learner is the key figure and thus needs to be necessarily involved actively in making sense of the material to himself either single handed or in a joint enterprise with the teacher.

2. The term constructivist learning in its broad and comprehensive form includes all types of learning and approaches that help a learner to construct or discover the facts and things related to his knowledge by himself. He can do it all alone by interacting with his environment or making sense of the content material. The knowledge construction task on his part may also be properly executed in social encounters or it may be helped and guided by the teacher, elders and knowledgeable peers. Consequently, the learning termed as discovery learning, learning incorporating inquiry approach, investigation method, problem solving (individualistic learning) as well as learning incorporating discussion method or entering into a dialogue on the part of the teacher with the learner, project or activity centered learning, cooperative learning, etc. all maybe adequately covered in the term constructivist learning.

3. As a characteristic feature constructivist learning may be attributed with the following main epistemological assumptions for guiding its plànning and organisation:

- Knowledge is physically constructed by learners who are involved in active learning.
- Knowledge is symbolically constructed by learners who are making their own representations of action;
- Knowledge is socially constructed by learners who convey their meaning making to others;
- Knowledge is theoretically constructed by learners who try to explain things they don't completely understand.

4. Knowledge construction task guided by a constructivist theory is more or less an individual phenomenon in the sense that it is the individual who has to come forward for constructing his own knowledge or make sense of what is presented or faced by him in his environment or teaching-learning encounters. There lies wide individual differences in relation to making a sense or derive some meaning of the presented material or demonstrated activities to a number of students in a class. For example, in case we ask the students of a class to read about some concept from their text for coming out with their meaning or understanding, it will not be unusual to find out that it may differ from student to student. Here, we can come to the conclusion that what the students read does not produce a single meaning (inspite of the fact that reading material is the same). The meaning derived by each one of them is their own meaning constructed by their individual self-mostly based on their prior knowledge and experience.

5. Constructivist learning theory has a strong belief and conviction, supported by the solid research findings and day to day observations, that

the best way to learn is to allow students construct their own knowledge instead of having someone construct it for them. An example here may prove helpful is proving this underlying belief of the constructivist learning.

> Think of a time when you as a student were taught something by your teacher in a lecture-type classroom situation. Then contrast it against a time when you had to prepare to teach that something to the students of your class as a teacher. I think most of the time you will agree that you learned and understood the material better when you were preparing to teach the material. This is because here in the situation, you have constructed the knowledge and made out a sense of it by yourself.

6. Constructivist learning does not focus on single response or single solution of a problem since such fixation and rigidity may prove a great hindrance on deriving their own meanings and suggesting their own solutions to the faced problems. It therefore advocates for a flexible curriculum, and wide varieties in the teacher-students interactions and ways of learning and doing on the part of students.

7. Constructivist learning theory expects from the teacher to facilitate the knowledge construction process of his students as properly as possible. For this purpose, he first try to access the entry behaviour of his students with regard to thing or skill the student is supposed to acquire. He then wisely assist or lead him to his learning path enabling him to a large extent to build his knowledge by himself for developing needed understanding and application of the learned things.

EDUCATIONAL IMPLICATIONS OF THE THEORY OF CONSTRUCTIVIST LEARNING

Educational implications of the constructivistic theory of learning may be broadly discussed as below:

1. The learner must be given due responsibility of taking charge of his learning. He has to construct or discover knowledge and derive meaning of the obtained information through his own initiative and efforts. This fact should be very clearly told and instilled in his mind.

2. Constructive theory of learning conveys that the task of the teacher is not to pour the ready made material in the minds of the students. Knowledge getting or construction from one's own initiative and efforts is more important than the mere receiving of the knowledge prepared or constructed by others. Therefore, teachers should refrain themselves in providing direct instructions or content material to the students rather than motivating and helping them in their knowledge construction task.

3. Whenever a concept is taught, teacher must search out his students' understanding and prior experiences about the concept for the necessary planning of its learning (by constructing knowledge related to this concept) on the part of the students. First, the students should be made to grasp the

understanding of the concept on the basis of their prior learning or experiences about the concept. After then, the task of its understanding must be put before them as the challenge. They must be provided essential environment for the needed understanding and reflection on the materials and experiences available for their reading or doing. In no case teacher should be in hurry to communicate his understanding or conclusion about the concept. Whether it is an independent effort of the individual learner or cooperative venture in cooperative learning, in all cases, the students should be helped for knowing and discovering the meanings by themselves.

4. For leading the students on the path of the acquisition of new learning, solving difficult and complex problem or discovering the facts related to a concept, it is quite advantageous to put students in situations that might challenge their previous conceptions and creating contradictions to encourage them on discovery path for their individual efforts or engage in discussion with their peers, teacher or elders.

5. While interacting with the students for helping them in the construction of knowledge and deriving the meanings from the presented content material or demonstrated practical activities and experiments, the teacher should have enough patience in dealing with the students. He must try to inspire and motivate them for playing their role in this direction as an active and independent enquirer or discoverer of the knowledge. For this purpose, it is advisable to: (i) wait long enough after posing a question so that the students have time to think about their responses and be able to respond thoughtfully by deriving their own meanings, and (ii) provide enough time for students to discover by their own or to construct their own knowledge and understanding when learning something new.

6. The task of construction or discovery of knowledge and derivation of own meanings on the part of students needs a lot of flexibility in terms of the planning and organization of learning experiences. Therefore, the use of constructivist learning calls for the elimination of a standardized curriculum.

7. Constructivist learning demands from the teachers to focus on making connections between facts and fostering new understanding in students by allowing, inspiring and guiding their students on their learning path. It expects from the teacher to tailor their teaching strategies to students' needs and responses and encourage them for being active partner in the teaching-learning process to carry out the necessary processes of thinking, analysing, interpreting and constructing knowledge. For encouraging reflective thinking, creativity and constructiveness on the part of their students, for being engaged in the knowledge construction process, it is advisable to have a proper democratization of the teaching-learning process. Instead of asking a fixed response question the teacher should rely heavily on the holistic presentation of the content, putting the open ended questions, elaboration of the responses and use of divergent thinking on the part of student causing

multiplicity of responses. Moreover, there must be a proper flow of communication between the teacher and student and among the students for the needed conversation, help and guidance to keep the students always on the track of the required knowledge getting path.

8. Since students have to construct their own meaning and discover the knowledge on their own, constructivist learning outcomes does not fit in the traditional evaluation patterns. It is therefore, necessary to maintain continuity and comprehensiveness in the scheme of evaluating the constructivist learning outcomes. As far as possible care should be taken to combine the needed evaluation programs with high performance standards and make it a subject of encouraging and leading the learners on their learning paths instead of merely measuring their learning output and assigning them grades, etc. In constructivist learning, there is thus emphasis on the elimination of grades and standardized testing. It calls for the flexible, comprehensive and continuous program to the constructive and creative output of the learners for providing timely assessment, motivation and assistance to the learners in getting them engaged in the task of constructing and discovering the knowledge by themselves.

12

Learning as Construction of Knowledge

INTRODUCTION

Learning in constructivist perspective or constructivist learning as discussed in the preceding chapter lays emphasis over the type of learning that is based on the philosophy of constructivism. This type of learning is totally opposed to the traditional system of learning propagated by behaviourism. Here in this type of learning, the needed knowledge is himself acquired by the learner through his own efforts, *i.e.,* the task of knowledge acquisition is carried out by the learner through an active process of knowledge construction. What is this knowledge construction task? How does it add to one's learning or acquisition of one or the other type of knowledge or experience? How the learning as construction of knowledge is different from the learning as transmission and reception of knowledge? What is the exact nature of the knowledge construction process and how is it facilitated by certain known elements such as experienced learning, reflection, social mediation, cognitive negotiability, situated learning, cognitive apprenticeship and meta cognition. In the lines to follow in the chapter we would try to know all about these.

LEARNING AS CONSTRUCTION OF KNOWLEDGE VS. LEARNING AS TRANSMISSION AND RECEPTION OF KNOWLEDGE

The philosophy and view point that holds learning as "Construction of Knowledge" is relatively quite a new and modern one than the age old prevailing notion considering learning as "transmission and reception of knowledge". Therefore, let us start our task of knowing about these two quite opposite and contradictory notions in order of their historical existence.

Learning as Transmission and Reception of Knowledge

In view of the propagators of our age old traditional system of teaching-learning, the child's mind is like a blank slate. We as the elders, parents and teachers through our guidance, teaching and training try to write on this slate and as a result child learns new things, acquires new knowledge and gain new experience through a deliberate process involving transmission of knowledge by the elders and reception of the knowledge on the part of children as learners. Here in this system knowledgeable people-parents, teachers and elders work as a transmitter-transmitting the knowledge to a receiving end. On the receiving end, there lies the children/students in the capacity of the learners. Knowledge getting task, in this way, in a teaching-learning process formally organised in a classroom, is just confined to the transmission and reception of knowledge.

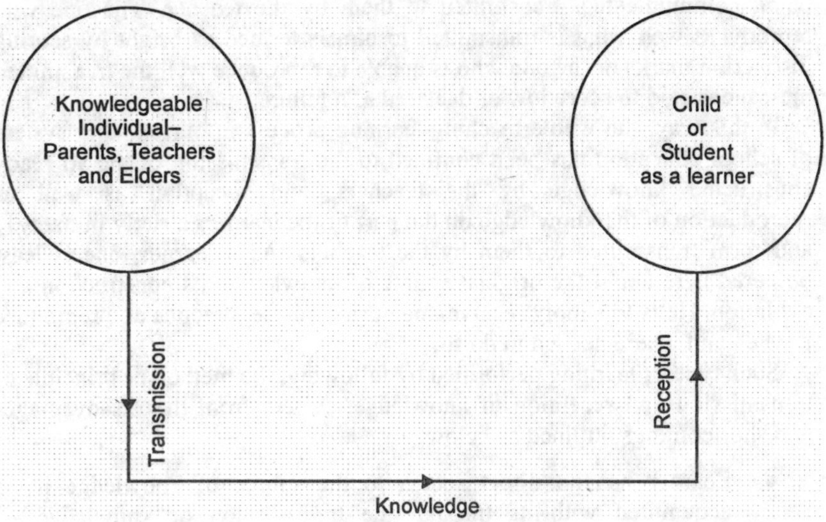

Fig. 12.1: Learning as Transmission and Reception of Knowledge

As a result, in the class room situation, the teacher or trainer who has knowledge and skills (gained through his own day to day experiences, study or professional training) tries to transmit it to the learners present in a particular teaching-learning set up through lecturing or demonstration. They have to remain active for performing their transmission job. While learners have no role to play in the knowledge transmission work. They have to remain most of the time as the passive listeners or silent spectators, their role is merely to remain alert and attentive for grasping or receiving. What is being told or exhibited by their teachers or trainers in the name of imparting knowledge or teaching skills.

The task of transmission and reception of knowledge is thus may be well equated with the task of the transmission of electric or sound energy from the transmitters (transmitting instruments) to the receivers (receiving instruments). The receiving instruments at their ends receive or get the same message (in original) as being transmitted from the transmitting instruments. If the current/signal supplied is low or weak, there will be a quite dim light or inaudible sound to receive and if it is a normal or above, then the intensity of light or sound will be found increasing in the same proportion. Here in class room situation, also the quality of the acquisition of knowledge and skills on average will surely lie on the quality of knowledge and skill transmitted and grasped by the learners. Since learners have no role in creating, constructing or understanding the things to be transmitted to them by their teachers in their own ways, their quality as a learner needs to be acknowledged, ascertained or evaluated through the quality of the reproduction or re-representation of the reality of the facts being communicated/ transmitted to them by the teacher. The one who reproduces well what is transmitted to him is termed as bright by scoring distinction marks or the one who is unable to reproduce well the transmitted message is said to score low or declared as a failure.

In this way, the whole teaching-learning process in our existing system of school education has been confined to the transmission of the all ready constructed knowledge by the teachers, and reception as well as reproduction of the knowledge on the part of the learners strictly in the way and form transmitted to them by the teachers. As a learner, one is least bothered here about the original source of knowledge, its construction and evolution. He is to simply receive, memorize, revise, practice and reproduce it when and where needed to do so.

Such type of learning performed by following, the method or principle of transmission and reception of knowledge, suffers from the disadvantages and shortcomings outlined as below:

- Learner has no direct access to the source of knowledge he is acquainted with its through the transmission of knowledge — parents, teachers and elders.
- The knowledge he gets is constructed and compiled by those who are going to transmit it to him. He has no role in the construction, compiling or pooling the knowledge for his learning. He is completely dependent on others for the acquisition of the desired knowledge and skills and can't ever learn to acquire the same through his independent efforts.
- The teaching-learning process, have becomes a purely one sided affair. Teacher as a knowledgeable person tries to transmit the required information / knowledge / skill to the learners without taking any note of their interests and abilities. The learners here usually remain quite passive and inactive by simply listening and watching the things by the teacher, it may give many learners in the class, time and opportunity for being bored, or getting inattentive the extent of getting drowsy and going to sleep.
- Knowledge is transmitted here by the teacher without caring for being understood or grasped properly on the part of the learners. Moreover, since it is not generated or constructed through their own experiences and not based on their needs and requirement it is neither motivating nor at all comprehensible and graspable to them. It can only be memorized or crammed with least consideration of its

meaning and application. Such meaningless acquisition of knowledge becomes an useless burden, hardly to prove any worthwhile for them in their future life activities.

- Memorization of the received transmitted facts, also itself becomes a problem and nuisance to them. The memorized facts may easily vanish from the memory of the learners and they may feel a great difficulty in recalling them at the time of their use. This usually happens with the learners in writing the answers at the timing their examinations or responding at the time of interviews. In this way the short time gain of reproducing the received knowledge on the part of the learners through the mode of one sided transmission by the teachers may not be at all realized by the learners and hence, the learning through the mode of transmission and reception of knowledge becomes totally redundant to the learners in all its ways and means turning the efforts of teaching-learning process as waste and futile.

In view of the defects and deficiencies pointed out above the learning acquired through the mode of transmission and reception of knowledge, has come under severe attack and criticism. The whole system and philosophy associated with this mode of learning has also been subjected to severe criticism. As an alternative, it has been recommended by the modern psychologists and educationists to replace it with the philosophy of constructivism practising construction of knowledge by the learner himself for the acquisition of that knowledge in a proper way. Let us throw light on the new concept of learning.

Learning as Construction of Knowledge

Constructivism as a philosophy and approach to education believes that any worthwhile learning involving necessary acquisition of a piece of knowledge can properly take place only by getting into the knowledge construction task on the part of a learner. It, therefore, advocates that nothing should be directly told or poured in the minds of the children through mere lecturing or demonstrating one or the other things by a teacher or trainer. Such transmission of the already constructed knowledge on the part of the knowledge gives to the learners who are supposed to remain as passive listeners and silent spectators in the teaching, learning process does not serve any useful purpose in terms of yielding proper learning output. It may only encourage spoon feeding, mechanized rote memorization and misdirected teaching-learning act resulting in loading the minds of the learners with the knowledge that carries no useful meaning and application to them in their real life. It therefore, asserts that in any process of teaching-learning (self or guided) the learner should be allowed to play key role. He is to decide what to learn and how. His interests, motivation, needs and individual worth should be properly taken into account while interacting with him in the classroom or making him engaged in the self or guided discovery task. Therefore the main task before we elders, parents or teachers is to arrange for such learning situations and environmental facilities as to help the children to construct or discover the knowledge they need by their own efforts. They should be allowed to remain continuously busy in such knowledge construction or reconstruction of the previously earned knowledge that is required by them for their gradual step by step development and progress in their life. Such learning based on the construction of the needed knowledge by their own attempts, thus emphasized on learning by doing and experiencing the things and facts of life by themselves. Let us see how?

The early experiences of a child by getting burning sensation from the hot objects like flame of a candle, burner, hot plate, chapati, hot milk, etc. may help him to construct his own knowledge regarding the hot objects and in the light of this knowledge he learns to take precaution while touching and using these hot objects.

In this way, right from the days of infancy, one tries to learn by constructing his knowledge regarding various things and events related to his environment. His first hand experiences may help him much in his knowledge construction task. The subsequent experiences, further in this regard may help him to bring modification / alteration or addition in the type of knowledge or information held by him so far. For example, the knowledge construction arrived at first hand experiences make him fearful about a thing, the subsequent reconstruction of knowledge (through pleasant or unfearful experiences about the thing) may help him to face that thing with no fear or hesitation of any sort.

The task of constructing the knowledge for learning one or the other things for one's needed adjustment to the self and the environment may be adjudged as a quite natural phenomenon for the developing child. It is based on his own reflections and drawing inferences from his personal day to day encounters or first hand experiences. Since these may lie wide variations among the learners in terms of having reflections and drawing inferences from a particular experience (depending upon one's individuality, previous experience and knowledge), the nature of the learning arrived through the knowledge construction phenomena may also differ from individual to individual. It is why there may exist wide individual differences among the learners with respect to the type of knowledge acquired by them through the knowledge construction mechanism in the similar learning situations.

Moreover, here while engaging in the knowledge construction task and deriving their own meaning and inferences from their experience of the things and events, children may go wrong by learning faulty concepts, and acquiring undesirable habits and skills. It is here the need of a proper elderly guidance and assistance arise. This need is also felt by the developing children when they are required to carry out their knowledge construction tasks on a higher level for learning relatively the higher level concepts, skills and applications than the simple ones carried out easily through their own reflections on day to day experiences.

At this level, the parents, teachers and elders are required to help the developing children to engage in the knowledge construction task by providing them needed opportunities, experiences and timely assistance. In no case, the all ready constructed knowledge should be directly poured in the minds of the children by making them a passive recipient of the knowledge.

As emphasized by Bruner, a prominent constructivist, in every teaching-learning situation earnest efforts should be made to make the child an independent and active enquirer and discoverer of the knowledge. He should be properly helped and guided in remaining engaged in the knowledge construction process, till he arrives at the desired solution of the problem through his own independent efforts. Here it is to be seen and watched by the elders that although the meaning derived and inferences reached through his knowledge construction efforts may be his own, yet the solution arrived or knowledge gained must be a representation of reality so that the knowledge construction efforts may always remain on track, proving their worth by being helpful in his proper education and development.

It has been arrived through experiences and established through researches in applied behavioural sciences that the learning reached through the mechanism of the "construction of knowledge", i.e., independent efforts of the learners to take stock of the situation and derive their own meaning is a real learning. It remains with them for encountering the similar situations in their future life. They can rely on their self-constructed knowledge and the habits of engaging in such independent or guided discovery pursuits may help them in gaining self-sufficiency for their adequate adjustment, development and progress in life.

In the end, as conclusion we can say the following things about the nature and advantages of the learning designed on the foot path of the construction of knowledge.

- In this mode of teaching-learning the learner plays a key role. He tries to learn, what he needs through his own independent efforts (although guided and supervised by the elders as the need may be).
- It is based on the principle that a learner learns best if he is provided proper opportunities, environment, timely help and needed guidance for the construction of knowledge he needs for adjustment, education and development.
- The beginning should be made to allow the child to construct or discover the knowledge by himself through his own independent efforts. He can take the help of the prior experiences and stock of the previous knowledge for facing the present realities and by reflecting

over them the present realities and by reflecting over them can arrive at his own decision for learning something new to meet the present situation and also get equipped for facing similar situations in life.

- Although, the knowledge construction is an individual phenomenon for an individual learner and one should go ahead for it single handed through his own independent efforts, yet there are occasions where every thing can't be discovered or know through own efforts. There are possibilities of drawing wrong conclusions, inferences and deductions from the first hand experiences, independent study and self pursuits. In such a situation, no time and energy should be unessentially wasted and efforts should be made by the parents, teachers, elders and also knowledgeable peers to make them available for the timely assistance and derived guidance to the struggling learners in their knowledge construction or reconstruction pursuits.
- The knowledge and skills so acquired and habits and interests so developed through one's own pursuit of knowledge construction task are selectively quite stable, enduring, effective and helpful to a learner in his further learning pursuits along with needed adjustment and development in his life. He can own this knowledge, by deriving his own meaning and purposes. It is not vanished from his mind like the memorized stock of the transmitted knowledge from the elders.
- It helps the learner to develop the ability of independent problem solving — an essential ability to face the necessities and eventuality of life.
- It helps the learners to provide needed opportunities and environment for expressing their self, opening up their inherent abilities and creative talents.
- Here the learning becomes a joyful activity a purposeful event and useful outcome for the learner as the command of his learning comes in his own hands rather being driven by others.
- In this mode of learning, teaching-learning process may be organized on the understanding and reflective level rather than merely on the knowledge level characterized with a one sided flow of communication and transmission of knowledge at the hands of the teacher or trainer.

With the discussions arrived at about the nature significance and merits/demerits of both the learning modes — Learning as a Construction of Knowledge and Learning as Transmission and Reception of Knowledge, one can easily conclude that learning as a construction of knowledge is advantageous to the learners in so many ways in addition to being quite in tune with the need of the time. Therefore, all efforts should be made to incorporate it in the teaching-learning process going on in our schools.

PROCESSES FACILITATING 'CONSTRUCTION OF KNOWLEDGE'

As discussed above knowledge acquisition on the part of a learner if to be proved fruitful, worthy and applicable, should essentially involve and demand from the learner to perform the task of constructing the needed knowledge by his own independent efforts. However, the task of constructing the knowledge for the learning or acquisition of one or the other thing is not so simple and easy as it may appear otherwise to those who have never put themselves to such task. The researchers and scholars have tried to think over the issue of suggesting some ways and means for facilitating the construction of knowledge on the part of learners. As a result, they have named a few, process quite useful for the 'construction of knowledge' on the part of the interested learners named as below:

A. Experiential learning and reflection
B. Social mediation
C. Cognitive negotiability
D. Situated learning and cognitive apprenticeship
E. Meta cognition

Let us, know about these processes with their respective roles in one's efforts in the knowledge construction task.

A. Experiential Learning and Reflection

What is Experiential Learning?

In its word meaning experiential learning stands for that type of learning which is based on the experiences (individual or in collaboration), *i.e.*, observing, doing and drawing inferences by getting actively involved in the learning process. For knowing more about its meaning and nature let us concentrate on some of the following definitions and view points expressed by various authorities in this connection:

Association of Experimental Education (1995): Experiential learning is learning through doing. It is a process through which individuals construct knowledge, acquire skills and values from direct experience.

ViljoKohonen (2001): The experiential learning is an educational orientation which aims at integrating theoretical and practical elements of learning for a whole-person approach, emphasizing the significance of experience for learning.

Kolb (1984): Experiential learning involves observing the phenomenon and doing something meaningful with it through an active participation. It emphasizes learning in which the learner is directly in touch with the phenomenon being studied, rather than just watching it or reading, hearing or thinking about it.

Karl Rogers (1969): Experiential learning is characterized by personal involvement of the learner. This self-initiated, self-directed and leaves a pervasive effect on the learner, i.e., whatever is learned can be used by him when and wherever needed.

Woolfe (1992): Experiential learning consists of the following four components:

(i) Awareness of the learning processes (The learner is aware of the processes which are taking place, and which are enabling learning to occur).

(ii) Involvement in a reflective experience (The learner is involved in a reflective experience enabling him to relate current learning to past, present and future, even if these relationships are felt rather than thought).

(iii) Personal Significance (What is being learned and how it is being learned have a special significance for the learner)

(iv) Involvement of the whole self (The learner is engaged as a whole person in the process of learning with his body, thoughts, feelings and actions, not just along with mind)

Nature and Characteristics of Experiential Learning

The view points of the different scholars outlined above may help us to derive following conclusions about the meaning and nature of the concept 'experiential learning'.

(i) Based on the personal experiences

Experiential learning is based upon the personal experiences of the learners (individually or in a group situation). Actually here the learning process is woven around an immediate personal experience in such a way as to help the learner to construct the needed knowledge through his own efforts.

(ii) Total Involvement of the Learners

Experiential learning requires on the part of the learner to have his total involvement (both intellectually and emotionally) in the process of learning rather than just watching it or reading, hearing or thinking about it.

(iii) Awareness of what, why and how of the Learning

For such involvement, it emphasizes that a learner should be quite conscious or aware of what and how of his learning along with its relevance and significance to his further learning development and progress.

(iv) Learner centered approach

Experiential learning is learner centered rather than the subject or teacher centered. Here the learner has to decide the type of experiences he wants to gain along with the way of their acquisition, he has to take change of his learning by taking all initiative and remaining actively involved for creating needed knowledge for his actual use and applications.

(*v*) *Integration of theory with practice*

Experiential learning lays much emphasis over the integration of the theoretical and practical elements associated with a learning situation by believing that theory without practice is lame and practice without theory is blind.

(*vi*) *Due emphasis over reflection*

In Experiential learning, the task of reflection performed by the learner for examining and studying one's own experiences carries a lot of significance.

Experience alone can not yield to the knowledge construction task and hence can't be turned as a sufficient condition for learning. For the acquisition of something new, the experiences related to it must be processed consciously through a deliberate mechanism of reflection.

(*vii*) *Usefulness of the end result*

The outcomes of experiential learning process carries a lot of significance and importance for the learners by enabling them to have a proper insight into the theory and practice of the things being learned. It helps them to construct the needed knowledge through their own efforts. As a owner of such self created knowledge they are fully powered to use and apply it in all its possible ways for their further learning, adjustment and development.

The things pointed out above about the meaning, nature and characteristing of experiential learning may lead us to realize that experience alone does not constitute experiential learning. It is just the beginning. It should be followed by reflection and concluding as well as acting upon the findings of the reflection that can help in selecting the outcomes of experiential learning. Such thinking on the point of scholars has made them to consider experiential learning as a four stage cyclic process. Let us have an idea about it.

Four-Stage Cycle of Experiential Learning

Experiential learning in its practical use and application may be termed as a continuously evolving process consisting of a four stage cycle named as:

(i) Concrete experience (ii) Reflection (iii) Abstract conceptualization or generalization and (iv) Active experimentation or practical action.

1. *Concrete Experience Stage:* It is the beginning stage of one's experiential learning that is focussed on gaining direct personal experiences about the things and phenomena to be studied. Here the learner is exposed to the phenomenon being studied by coming into its direct contact. He is required to gain direct concrete experiences about the phenomenon (things, events a processes) through his own independent efforts. The principle of learning by doing experiencing and natural observation are kept into consideration by the learners for gaining such concrete experiences about

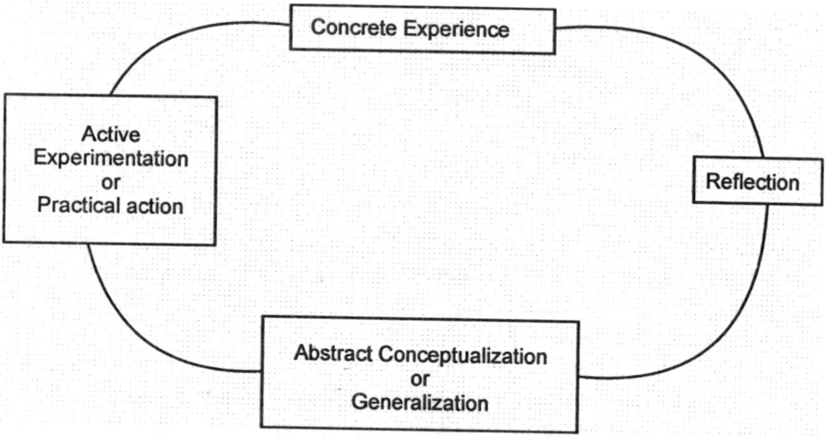

Fig. 12.2: Four-stage Cycle of Experiential Learning

the things and phenomena being studied. The learner is expected to involve his whole self, intellectually as well as emotionally, in the task of gaining the needed concrete experiences. In the classroom teaching-learning situations, we can make use of the activities like use of audio-visual aids and equipments, verbal examples and stories, small group discussions simulation and dramatic and playway activities, visits and excursions, etc. for helping the students to gain useful concrete experiences related to the content material of their syllabus.

2. *Reflection Stage:* Experience gives food for reflective thinking. Therefore in this second stage of experiential learning, what is gained in the form of concrete experiences, is put under deep thought, observation and consideration for deriving meaning and creating new information and knowledge from the concrete experiential material. Here the learner is mainly, concerned in judging and knowing how do the things actually happen by attempting to see them from different perspectives and for this purpose usually relies on his own thoughts, feelings and judgement by getting him involved fully as a whole person (intellectually as well as emotionally). In subjecting the gained concrete experiences under the close scrutiny of one's own reflection (a sort of introspective observation and evaluation), one may be seen to take a solid step for converting his experiences about the things or phenomena to be studied into experiential learning. It may lead him to the next step of the cyclic process of his experiential learning, named as abstract conceptualization.

3. *Abstract Conceptualization or Generalization:* In this third stage of experiential learning process, the output received from the second stage of reflecting thinking is utilized for arriving at the abstract conceptualizations and developing working hypothesis to be tested the next stage of the experiential learning. Practical experiences like feeling burning sensation while in getting touch of the burning flames or hot objects after being

subjected to reflection (deep thoughts and considerations) may help the child to build an abstract conceptualization in the form of keeping distance from the burning flames and hot objects. Similarly, the reflections on the experiences regarding the proper handling of the hot objects without getting harmed or getting cured after being harmed by them may help the individuals to develop the relevant conceptualization regarding the precautions taken first aid and treatment given to burning victims. For example "the use of common salt, iced water, and wet flour work as an effective first aid", such abstract conceptualization may be arrived at as the product of one's reflective thinking on the concrete experiences gained by the learner in one or the other learning situations.

4. *Active Experimentation or Practical Action:* At this fourth and final stage of experiential learning the abstract conceptualization made or workable hypothesis developed at the third stage are put to test through active experimentation *i.e.* what is generalized or concluded at the third stage is subjected to practical action at this stage. This practical action, in turn, yields concrete experimental material for further reflection and acceptance of the constructed knowledge or new learning (referred to as experienced leaning), as the new base for further learning, adjustment and progress in one's life

Experiential Learning and Reflection

Reflection involves deep sense of thought, understanding, involvement and insight about the things or phenomena observed or experienced by the individual concerned. It helps to give meaning to what has been experienced or being experienced by the learners in a particular learning situation. However the process of reflection comes into picture only when something is perceived or experienced by the learner. Experience provides food for reflection which in turn (as explained above in the cyclic process of experiential learning) leads to abstract conceptualizations or theoretical generalisations. In this way, reflection may be found to play an important role in the process of experienced learning by providing a connecting link or bridge, as it were, between experience and theoretical conceptualization. There is total involvement of the learner in experiencing and arriving at theoretical conceptualization through reflection on his own experiences. It is to be carried out both on the intellectual as well as emotional platforms.

In the traditional teacher centred teaching-learning process the students' learning is carried out mainly at an intellectual level. There is no involvement of the learners on emotional level. Therefore, they usually remain personally unaware of the effects of their own response (emotional reaction) to the subject material on themselves or on other people and intensify of such responses. This can lead to an inadequate application of knowledge in the use of the subject material in authentic real-life occasions (Kohonen, 2001).

On the other hand, experiential learning accompanied with a proper sense of reflection on the experienced objects or phenomena is likely to prove necessary meaningful to the learner. The learner can derive his own meaning from such learning for enabling him to use it in his own ways in the real life situations.

The Role of Experiential Learning in Knowledge Construction

The art of experiential learning enables the learner to learn the art of creating or constructing the needed knowledge for his use in his life. In fact, it is an essential component of a knowledge construction task. Let us see how?

The whole structure of an experienced learning lies on the two solid pillers known as experience and reflection. Experience provides starting base for an experiential learning. Afterward, what is being experienced or observed by the learner about an object or phenomenon is put to under close scrutiny, self examination and introspection through an useful mechanism known as reflection. It is this reflection that helps in the transformation of the experiences gained into some useful theoretical concepts readily available for use in one's real-life situations.

Knowledge construction task also begins with initiation and keenness. On the part of the learner to have his own experience about the object, event or phenomenon to be studied. For drawing valid inferences from the experiences gained, he needs the help of a proper reflection mechanism. What he gets as a result of the reflection on the experienced concrete material helps him to arrive at a new knowledge constructed or created through his own efforts. In this way, the processes employed for the knowledge construction task and experiential learning are almost identical in their nature and purposes served. In both of these mechanisms, learner or knowledge constructor is well aware of the need to learn or discover the knowledge. He is the incharge of the self-discovering or acquisition of knowledge gained through his self-efforts. Knowledge or learning he acquires, proves quite understandable and handy for him for the needed practical applications in his life. In view of such similarities shown in the acts of experiential learning and knowledge construction it can be safely concluded that art and skill learned in practising experiential learning may prove a quite significant facilitating factors in promoting the habits of knowledge construction on the part of the learners through their own independent efforts.

B. Social Mediation

The task of knowledge construction on the part of an individual is very much facilitated by a popular mechanism known as social mediation. Historically, in constructivism this concept was introduced by the famous Russian constructive psychologist Lev Vygotsky. Actually, the key premise of Vygotskian constructivism is often referred to as cultural or social mediation. In simple words it means that the cultural or social factors present in the child's environment play a role of an effective mediator between his self and the knowledge construction. His knowledge and development is always guided by the social and cultural factors present in his environment. The child becomes capable of constructing the knowledge needed for his desired adjustment and development with the active support and influences of the cultural and social factors present in his environment. Without such social and cultural mediation, he may remain handicapped in acquiring and using the needed knowledge and skills for his adequate adjustment development and progress in his life.

Piaget, a popular name in constructivism perspective, is known for his individual version of constructivism, i.e., assigning no role to social mediation or interaction in the process of knowledge construction on the part of a developing child. He emphasized that a child constructs the knowledge needed by him single handed with no outside help. Vygotsky opposed this notion by saying that child can't be deprived or alleniated from his social or cultural environment. The social or cultural forces directly or indirectly leaves their impact and come to his help for the knowledge construction on his part. Although he may try by himself to construct some knowledge in one way or the other with his independent efforts and in some cases of language and skill acquisition he may get partial success, but the acquisition and construction of knowledge and skills at some proper higher level may only be possible through social mediation — help and guidance from the parents, teachers, and elders. For example, take the case of the art of riding a bicycle or pouring a cup of milk. The child can't acquire/ construct such knowledge or skills without the help of social mediation. First he needs somebody as a role model for observing and imitating these behaviours and then practising these skill by himself. However, at each stage there must be active support, assistance and guidance from the peers parents or elders in helping the child to construct or acquire necessary knowledge and skills for doing these tasks. The mastery of such skills occurs through the activity of the child with in the society under social mediation. Cultural or social mediation thus may be taken as a type of social interaction (available in the form of socio-cultural environment and interpersonal communication) the presence of which, in view of Vygotsky and other social constructivists, is very much essential for allowing the children to construct or acquire the necessary knowledge for their needed adjustment, development and progress in their own ways.

The task of social mediation or social interaction is very much facilitated by the use of mediating tools and cultural art facts such as ways and means of communicating and interacting with each other. Acquisition of language on the part of children here now can play a major role in the art of interacting with their social and cultural environment, people and social institutions. He can now very well interact with his peers and elders including parents, teachers and other responsible members of the community. It can open a new dimension for the needed social mediation for his adequate adjustment, education and development. The communication and interaction with the elders and peers may now help him to get the needed timely help and guidance from the peers and elders for constructing his own knowledge, understand and apply it in his own ways and reflect upon it for its further creative and constructive output.

Social mediation-interaction with his social environment, peers and elders does not only help him to construct and acquire the knowledge and skills with in the parameter or paradigm of the shared knowledge of the society or culture, but also help him in constructing and using his knowledge in his own unique way. For example, helped in this way, a child does not confine the use of pencil in the way as used by others in his social and cultural environment but may go far beyond in using it very much for his own ends. The social mediation, thus here only plays the role of a necessary mediator or facilitator for helping the child in his knowledge acquisition or construction task.

C. Cognitive Negotiability

The term cognitive negotiability is composed of two separate terms or words cognitive and negotiability. Therefore to know about the meaning and concept of the term "Cognitive negotiability", we will have to know about the meaning of the words/ terms cognitive and negotiability.

Cognitive

The term cognitive as an adjective according to *Merrian Webster Dictionary* (1988: 257) stands for "relating to or involving cognition" and cognition is here defined as an act or process of knowing, including both awareness and judgement. In this way, we can take one's cognitive abilities as the capacities or abilities related to one's knowing about something.

Negotiability: In its dictionary meaning the term negotiability stands for one's ability to negotiate (to manage, to deal with some matter or attain that requires ability for its successful handling) — Merriam Webster, 1988: 791.

By understanding the meaning of the terms 'cognitive' and 'negotiability' now we can define the term cognitive negotiability in the manner given below:

Cognitive negotiability may be defined as the ability to negotiate or seek negotiations for knowing or searching about something. In making such negotiations one has to seek or discover the suitable alternatives getting success in finding the solution of a problem, handling of a situation or execution of a task in the most satisfactory way.

The Nature and Characteristics of Cognitive Negotiability

Cognitive negotiability as one of the important cognitive and constructivistic ability of an individual is characterised as below:

- It is essentially falls on the cognitive domain of one's behaviour.
- It helps an individual to think about alternate ways and means by substituting one technique with the other for knowing and discovering one or the other thing per requirement of a particular situation.
- It represents a type of cognitive strategy that facilitates the process of knowledge construction by enabling the learner to replace one way or means of knowing with the other.
- It helps a learner to construct his knowledge about a thing, person, idea or phenomena by himself on the basis of his own cognitive abilities, competencies, and motivation for doing so.

Relationship between Cognitive Negotiability and Knowledge Construction

Cognitive negotiability works as a bridge between one's knowing about a thing and his motivation for doing so for facilitating the task of knowledge construction by smoothening the way as under:

- It makes the learner realize that way of knowing about a thing is negotiable meaning that one should always try other ways for knowing or discovering about a thing.
- The use of cognitive negotiability on the part of the learner makes his thinking divergent. He can think out in many different ways for adopting work strategy by negotiating one with the other suitable one for arriving at the proper solution of his problem or adding something new in the stock of his knowledge.

D. Situated Learning and Cognitive Apprenticeship

Situated learning in its word meaning is the type of learning that is situation based or the learning that is undertaken or performed in the situations or contexts in which it is likely to be applied or being applied.

In such learning, the learners are made to learn and acquire the necessary knowledge and skills in the real life situations in the same way as being used and practised by the real life users and practioners in their usual ways. In this sense, if one has to acquire the knowledge and skills regarding agriculture and gardening, he has to learn the art of agriculture and gardening by learning it in the real life situations in the company, guidance and apprenticeship of those who are actually doing this task in their real life or are experts to teach it through modelling in real world situations. A tailor, thus while working in his tailor shop may provide lessons in situated learning to a learner interested in learning the knowledge and skills related to tailoring and a carpenter may provide valuable lesson on the trade of carpentry to the learner interested in the carpentary which allowing them to observe, imitate and practice the carpentary skills in his workshop or real life situations.

Situated learning thus may provide the learners appropriate opportunities to learn and acquire knowledge and skills under the guidance and supervision of the experts / real life users in the real life situations. The practice of apprenticeship employed for helping the learners to learn the art and skill of a profession or trade represents a good working example of the situated learning.

The situated learning perspective asks students to carry out tasks and solve problems in an environment that reflects the multiple uses to which their knowledge will be put in the future. As a whole, the situated learning here may be found to serve several purposes as mentioned below:

(i) Students are able to understand the purposes or uses of the knowledge they are learning.
(ii) They learn by actively using knowledge rather than passively receiving it.
(iii) They learn the different conditions under which their knowledge can be applied.
(iv) Learning in multiple contexts induces the abstraction of knowledge, so that students acquire knowledge in a dual form, both tied to the contexts of its uses and independent of any particular context. This unbinding of knowledge from a specific context fosters its transfer to new problems and new domains.
(v) Teaching-learning carried out in the situated learning perspective becomes quite useful, purposeful and motivating to the teacher as well as students. It helps in their proper interaction, making the teaching-learning process quite live and enjoyable.
(vi) In the context of situated learning perspective, the students find appropriate opportunities and conducive environment for engaging in the task of knowledge construction on account of finding reasons for getting engaged in the learning pursuit.

Cognitive Apprenticeship

What is Apprenticeship?

We all are quite familiar with the term apprenticeship. In this practice of learning or training a learner is required to learn the knowledge and skills associated with a particular vocation, profession or work area under the guidance and supervision of an expert or master of that profession or work area in a situational learning paradigm.

Apprenticeship was a quite popular way of teaching and learning in ancient times. Apprenticeship was the vehicle for transmitting the knowledge and teaching the skills needed for doing a number of tasks related to the fields from painting and sculpture to medicine and law. Infact, it was the natural way to learn for a learner interested in one or the other type of learning. In this type of teaching and learning the learner, in the capacity of an apprentice, was required: (i) to observe the processes of a task performed by the experts/masters in the execution of that task; (ii) perform the task himself exactly in the way as observed; (iii) allow the intervention of the expert or master for keenly observing his performance; and (iv) receiving direction and guidance from the expert/master for improving his performance until he becomes proficient enough to accomplish the task independently The basic notion of apprenticeship thus lies in showing the apprentice how to do a task and then helping him to do it.

What is Cognitive Apprenticeship?

Cognitive apprenticeship in its word meaning stands for the apprenticeship carried out in cognitive perspective: It allows the teacher / master to teach in a situated learning setup (real-life situations) the needed knowledge and skills for performing a task independently. Historically, the constructivist approaches especially related to social constructivism have led to the development of the notion of cognitive apprenticeship. It holds that masters of a skill often fail to take into account the implicit processes involved in carrying out complex skills when they are teaching novices. As an apprentice, thus, they can imitate the model behaviour of their masters without taking proper cognition of why and how of this behaviour. For example, while solving mathematics problems, they may try to copy the model problem solving on the part of their teachers/standard text books rather then getting acquainted with the actual task of learning problem solving strategies or intrinsic principles of the problems themselves. As a result when they encounter problems that fall outside these patterns (modelled behaviour), students are often at a loss for what to do.

To Combat these tendencies, cognitive apprenticeships ". . . are designed, among other things, to bring these tacit processes into the open, where students, can observe, exact, and practice them with help from the teacher" (Collins, Brown and Newman, 1987). The underlying video of cognitive apprenticeship is well in tune with Albert Bandura (1977), theory of modelling, which posts that in order for modelling to be successful, the learner must be attentive, must have access to and retain the information presented, must be motivated to learn, and must be able to accurately reproduce the desired skill.

Main Features and Characteristics of Cognitive Apprenticeship

Cognitive apprenticeship is said to be characterized with the features like below:

(i) Cognitive apprenticeship represents one of the type and form of situated learning. As a result it may be found to strive, first and foremost, to place teaching and learning practices within a rich and varied context that is meaningful and authentic to students. In cognitive apprenticeship, the activity being taught or experiences being gained are modelled in real life situations.

(ii) Cognitive apprenticeship emphasized on the learning and cognition that is situation or context based. It assumes that the context in which learning takes place is critical, the outcomes of the cognitive apprenticeship are therefore less effective when skill and concepts are taught independent of their real-world context and situation (Collins, Dugind and Brown, 1989).

(iii) By using processes such as modelling and coaching, cognitive apprenticeships also support the three stages of skill acquisition described in the expertise literature: the cognitive stage, the associative stage, and the autonomous stage. In the cognitive stage, learners develop declarative understanding of the skill. In the associative stage, mistakes and misinterpretations learned in the cognitive stage are detected and eliminated while associations between the critical elements involved in the skill are strengthened. Finally, in the autonomous stage, the learner's skill becomes honed and perfected until it is executed at an expert level. (Anderson, 2000).

(iv) Cognitive apprenticeship employs cognitive modelling in its execution. Here an apprentice is required to listen and watch the behaviour of the master/teacher very carefully. It may make him to conceptualize exactly what his master is doing and thinking. The apprentice then attempts to imitate those behaviours with the master observing and providing coaching.

(v) Coaching provides the needed assistance to an apprentice at the most critical level — the skill level just beyond what the apprentice could accomplish by herself. Vygotsky (1978) referred to this as the Zone of Proximate Development and believed that fostering development within this zone leads to the most rapid development. The coaching process includes additional modeling as necessary, corrective feedback, and reminders, all intended to bring the apprentice's performance closer to that of the master's. As the apprentice becomes more skilled through the repetition of this process, the feedback and instruction provided by the master "fades ' until the apprentice is, ideally, performing the skill at a close approximation of the master level. (Driscoll, 2000)

(vi) Cognitive apprenticeship, although, has its origin in the concept of traditional apprenticeship. Yet it differs from the same on account of its cognitive perspective. In cognitive apprenticeship, one needs to deliberately bring the thinking to the surface, to make it visible. There is no blind imitation or perfection of the skill on the part of the apprentice/learners he must have needed cognition of the how and why of the processes involved in the performance of the skill. As a result in cognitive apprenticeship the goal is not to acquire the knowledge but one must knew the way of acquiring the knowledge. The student should not merely produce the solution of the problem but should be able to know the very how and why of solving such problems for getting him full equipped for solving any of these problems belonging to the prescribed and other texts including the real life situations.

(vii) Cognitive apprenticeship for its execution in a proper way requires from the teachers (or coaches) to constantly attend to students' difficulties and problems. However, it does not require that the teachers permanently assume the role of the "expert". The goal here is to help the students in becoming independent by getting expertization in the field. In the tune of social constructivism, thus cognitive apprenticeship is aimed to facilitate the process of knowledge and skill acquisition/ construction on the part of the intended learners.

Benefits of Cognitive Apprenticeship

Cognitive apprenticeship practices can benefit learning in many ways summarized as below:

Cognitive apprenticeship encourages authentic activity and assessment: The most important emphases of the learning environment in cognitive apprenticeship are situated learning and the culture of expert practice (Collins, Brown, & Newman, 1989). Learners are engaged in learning activities that are similar to the practices of real-world experts.

Practices of cognitive apprenticeship are motivating and engaging for learners: Cognitive apprenticeship provides students with authentic tasks; it encourages them to think like and to be treated as experts (Collins, 1991). When students are actively engaged in authentic tasks and make discoveries on their own, they are motivated and experience a sense of ownership of their knowledge and tasks.

Cognitive apprenticeship may encourage greater levels of retention and transfer: Learning within the cognitive apprenticeship framework is situated in a context similar to that in which experts actually practice (Resnick, 1989). Situated, contextualized learning enables students to retain their knowledge until they encounter similar situations in the future.

Cognitive apprenticeship may facilitate higher order reasoning: In cognitive apprenticeship practices, students work with teachers and experts who use higher-level thinking processes; they are exposed to those processes through cognitive modelling (Hogan & Tudge, 1999). After receiving initial stages of support from teacher and experts, students actually explore new ideas and make discoveries using advanced reasoning processes.

Cognitive Apprenticeship and Knowledge Construction

Cognitive apprenticeship may prove quite helping hand to the students in facilitating the task of knowledge construction and skill acquisition under the guidance and supervision of a master/teacher in the situated learning and social constructivist paradigm.

Collins, Brown, and Newman (1987) have developed six teaching methods rooted in cognitive apprenticeship theory and claim these methods help students attain cognitive and meta-cognitive strategies for "using, managing, and discovering knowledge". Among these six methods the first three (modelling, coaching, scaffolding) are at the core of cognitive apprenticeship and help with cognitive and meta-cognitive development. The next two (articulation and reflection) are designed to help novices with awareness of problem-solving strategies and execution similar to that of an expert. The final step (exploration) intends to guide the novice towards independence and the ability to solve and identify problems within the domain in their own. Let us try to know about them in brief.

1. *Modelling:* While using this method/technique in cognitive apprenticeship, the expert/teacher act as a model to demonstrate a task (falling within the cognitive domain or subject area) to the learner for allowing him to experience and build a conceptual model of the task in hand. For example, a language teacher while making use of the modelling technique may try to model the reading process by reading aloud in one voice, while verbalizing her thought process in another voice (Collins and Smith, 1982) or a mathematics teacher may write out explicit steps and work through a problem aloud, demonstrating his heuristics and procedural knowledge.

2. *Coaching:* While using this method/technique in cognitive apprenticeship, the teacher is supposed to carryout his assistance/guidance task with his student on a little move promixty level for helping him to seek mastery over the task. For this purpose he keenly observes the task performed by the student as a result of the modelling and in doing so offers him the needed feedback and hints to do the task as masterly as possible. If required, he may again arrange for the demonstration of the performance of the task, observe the student's task and may structure the task accordingly as to help the student in learning and acquiring it in a proper way closer to expert performance. Specifically, coaching is immediately related to specific attempts to accomplish the target task at the hands of the learners.

3. *Scaffolding:* Scaffolding is based on Vygotsky's (1978) concept of the zone of proximal development (ZPD), which he defined as the distance between the "actual developmental level as determined by independent problem solving and the level of potential development as determined through problem solving under adult guidance or in collaboration with more capable peers" (p. 86). Vygotsky believed that when a student is at the ZPD for a particular task, providing the appropriate scaffolding would give the student enough of a "boost" to complete it. Further, once the student, with the benefit of scaffolding, masters the task, the scaffolding can be removed. Just as a building remains erect after its scaffolding is removed, a student should be able to achieve the task again without the aid of scaffolding.

Thus, scaffolding, as a method or technique utilized in cognitive apprenticeship, refers to the help and support provided by the teacher/expert for assisting the student in carrying out the task. It can be provided in the form of suggestions, guidance verbal directions or may take the form of physical supports. It is always provided at the time when it is needed most on the part of the student, *i.e.,* he is feeling difficulty in the execution of a skill or executing a particular part of a task such as committing error in putting decimal at a proper place. The use of scaffolding, thus requires from the teacher first to have an accurate diagnosis of the student's difficulty/his current skill level and then adopt the proper ways and means for guiding and helping the student in carrying out the target activity. In the learning of skills, such as riding a cycle or driving a car, the learner, thus, with the utilization of the technique scaffolding, may be provided the needed verbal and physical support as and when required by the learner for taking subsequent steps in the learning of the skill. This support should always be intended to remove the barriers and should be quite temporary in its shape and direction. It should be gradually removed as and when the learner shows symptoms of doing it by his own.

4. *Articulation:* Articulation is defined as "the act of giving utterance or expression (Merriam Webster's, 2001). In reference to cognitive apprenticeship, articulation as pointed out by Collin, Brown and Newmen (1987: 482) involves any method of getting students to articulate their knowledge, reasoning, or problem-solving process in a domain, particular field or subject area. Collins and Stevens (1982), have provided three distinct methods or forms of articulation, namely, enquiry teaching, thinking aloud, and critical student role.

Enquiry teaching refers to a strategy of questioning students to lead them to articulate and refine their understanding of concepts and procedures in different domains or area of the subjects. For example, while making use of the device enquiry teaching, a language teacher may systematically question students about one summary of the text is good but another is poor, to get the students to formulate an explicit model of a good summary.

The use of thinking aloud strategy demands from the students to articulate their thoughts while solving problems. The critical student role, on the other hand, demands from the students to assume the critic or monitor role in group or cooperative activities/ projects for articulating their ideas to other students.

5. *Reflection:* Mirriam Webster's (2001) defines reflection as "consideration of some subject matter, idea or purpose." In reference to cognitive apprenticeship, reflection as described by Collins, brown and Newman (1987:483) refers to a process that allows students to compare their own problem-solving processes with those of an expert / master; another student and ultimately, an internal cognitive model of expertise. It may be carried out by the use of various techniques for reproducing or "replaying" the performances of both expert and novice for comparison. For reading or writing, as example, methods of utilizing reflection strategy may consists of recording students as they think out loud and her replaying the tape for comparison with the thinking of experts and other students.

Whatever means may be applied, the goal of reflection, ultimately lies in making the students to look back and analyze their performance with a desire for understanding and improvement towards the behaviour of an expert.

6. *Exploration:* Exploration involves: (i) pushing students into a mode of becoming self dependent in the problem of solving or knowledge, construction task, and (ii) teaching students exploration strategies. In cognitive apprenticeship, to become independent problem solver on the part of the students is quite essential as without reaching it the true objective of cognitive apprenticeship can't be realized. One can be said to the master of a skill or field only when he is able to perform and execute it on his own. Besides this he should also be made capable of thinking and employing noble ways and means of improving the task performance and excelling in the exhibition of the variety of improved skills in the performance of that task. For this purpose, the students should not only be made an independent problem solver, by withdrawing the use of supports and scaffolds but should also be taught the way of exploring, researching and developing hypotheses for knowing the novel ways of performing the task and solving the problems.

Infact features of exploration are similar to those found in discovery learning and inquiry-based approaches. Exploration is not merely reading or listening; to a teacher presentation but obtaining knowledge for oneself. Nor it is simply students doing what they want to do; they perform directed and guided activities suggested by the teacher. The teacher poses general problems and allows students to move into specific problems of their own, instead of teaching how to solve a problem and providing materials to help students explore. Through exploration and other similar approaches, students discover new knowledge and learn general problem-solving skills (Bruner, 1961; Shunk, 2000).

Exploration in cognitive apprenticeship is pushing students to try out their hypotheses, methods and strategies with processes similar to those that experts use to solve problems (Collins, 1991). For this purpose students are usually engaged in two kinds of exploration:

1 Exploration of the world: Students explore and even play with facts, problems, phenomena, and properties of our world in a less structured learning environment (Rose, 1995).

2 Exploration of problem solving processes: When novel problems that require adjustment of pre-existing cognitive processes are presented to the students, the learners try different problem-solving processes.

The responsibilities of the teacher to foster students' explorations include gradual fading of support, encouraging students' autonomy, and transferring responsibility to students (Rogoff 1990). The goal of the students is to actually use their mental model of experts' cognitive processes on their own or as a group to find and solve problems, set achievable goals, test hypotheses, and make their own discoveries (Collins, 1991).

Conclusion about Cognitive Apprenticeship

Cognitive apprenticeship practices may prove a quite effective device, means and ways of helping the novice/students or learners to acquire the necessary knowledge and skills regarding the execution of a task, or subject areas. Their ultimate goal is to make the learner quite independent in the problem solving task or acquisition of mastery over the use of a skill. They become quite aware of the how and why of the task performance. Moreover it helps them in learning the ways of learning the task, i.e., constructing the needed knowledge by their own independent efforts, exploring the noble ways of solving the problems and doing the task as proficiently as possible. In this way, while following the foot steps of Vygotski social constructivism and Piaget individual constructivism cognitive apprenticeship may be seen to play the role of an effective facilitator in the knowledge construction and knowledge discovery task of a conscious and motivated learner.

E. Meta Cognition

Meta cognition as a concept and terminology used in the cognitive and construtivist perspectives of psychology of learning and living has been defined in a number of ways by the scholars and authors. Let us reproduce a few of these definitions for knowing about the meaning and nature of meta cognition.

1. *Collins English Dictionary (2009):* Meta cognition refers to "the process of one's thinking about one's own mental processes."
2. *Flavell (1976: 232):* Meta cognition refers to one's knowledge concerning one's own cognitive processes or anything related to them, e.g., the learning-relevant properties of information or data. For example, I am engaging in metacognition, if I notice that I am having more trouble learning A than B; if it strikes me that I should double check C before accepted it as fact.
3. *Livingston (1977):* Meta cognition refers to higher order of thinking which involves active control over the cognitive processes engaged in learning. Activities such as planning how to approach a given learning task, monitoring comprehension, and evaluating progress towards the completion of a task are meta cognitive in nature.
4. *Metealfe & Shimamura (1994):* Meta cognition is defined as "cognitive about cognition", or "knowing about knowing". It can take many forms; it includes knowledge about when and how to use particular strategies for learning or for problem-solving.
5. *Hacker (1997):* Meta cognitive is often referred to as "thinking about thinking" and can be used to help students "learn how to learn."

The definitions of the term metacognition cited above may help us to know about the meaning, nature and characteristics of the concept "meta cognition" in the manner given below:

- Meta cognition is relatively a much higher and deeper concept than the cognition. Cognition in simple words stands for awareness or knowing. Meta cognition as a higher concept stands for "knowing about knowing" or "cognition about cognition". It tells us that merely knowing or getting aquainted with a piece of knowledge somehow is not sufficient. One should know the 'why' and 'how' of the acquired knowledge, experience or skill. One should therefore be fully acquainted with the knowledge getting process and should be equipped with the skill of knowledge construction through his own independent efforts.
- Metacognition helps one to have the desired cognition about his own cognitive functioning *i.e.*, subject of his cognition or thinking; the tools or strategies applied in carrying out this thinking; the direction of the present thinking; the help received from the present thinking in achieving the target (such as problem solving, acquisition of certain knowledge or skill, etc.) ; desirability or non-desirability of bringing change in plan of action, learning or problem solving strategies, etc.
- Meta cognition helps in seeking full awareness and self-regulation of one's own thinking and learning. It represents a system of active monitoring and regulation of an cognitive processes. In other words, it helps us to exercise active control over our process of thinking and cognition that we make use for our new learning, construction of knowledge or ways of discovering the solution of our problems.
- Meta cognition as a higher order thinking skills are very much utilized by us in the execution of our tasks and solving of our problems involving complex cognitive abilities. The planning, execution, monitoring and evaluation of the strategies used for carrying out such higher order mental tasks are very much regulated through the variety of meta cognition skills possessed by us as the human beings.

Knowing in this way, we can now functionally define the term metacognition as a process or ability possessed by us in the form of self awareness and self-regulation of our thinking and cognitive functioning for helping us to know or discover the way of acquiring or constructing a piece of knowledge or solving a particular type of problems in a most effective way.

Components or Elements of Meta Cognition

According to Flavell (1987), meta cognition in said to involve the following constituents or elements in its functioning.

1 Meta cognitive knowledge or Meta cognitive awareness
2. Meta cognitive experiences or regulation.

Let us know about these components of our meta cognition.

Meta Cognitive Knowledge or Meta Cognitive Awareness

It is concerned with what an individual knows about him and others as cognitive processors. Such meta cognitive knowledge, according to Flavell (1987) may be further divided into three categories: knowledge of person variables, task variables and strategy variables.

Stated very briefly, knowledge of person variables refers to general knowledge about how human beings learn and process information, as well as individual knowledge of one's own learning processes. For example, you may be aware that your study session will be more productive if you work in the quiet library rather than at home where there are many distractions. Knowledge of task variables include knowledge about the nature of the task as well as the type of processing demands that it will place upon the individual. For example, you may be aware that it will take more time for you to read and comprehend a science text than it would for you to read and comprehend a novel.

Finally, knowledge about strategy variables include knowledge about both cognitive and metacognitive strategies, as well as conditional knowledge about when and where it is appropriate to use such strategies.

Metacognitive Regulation or Experiences

Metacognitive experiences involve the use of metacognitive strategies or metacognitive regulation (Brown, 1987). Metacognitive strategies are sequential processes that one uses to control cognitive activities, and to ensure that a cognitive goal *(e.g.,* understanding a text) has been met. These processes help to regulate and oversee learning, and consist of planning and monitoring cognitive activities, as well as checking the outcomes of those activities. For example, after reading a paragraph in a text a learner may question herself about the concepts discussed in the paragraph. Her cognitive goal is to understand the text. Self-questioning is a common metacognitive comprehension monitoring strategy. If she finds that she cannot answer her own questions, or that she does not understand the material discussed, she must then determine what needs to be done to ensure that she meets the cognitive goal of understanding the text. She may decide to go back and re-read the paragraph with the goal of being able to answer the questions she had generated. If, after re-reading through the text she can now answer the questions, she may determine that she understands the material. Thus, the metacognitive strategy of self-questioning is used to ensure that the cognitive goal of comprehension is met.

Meta Cognitive Skills

Metacognition, the process of knowing about knowing is said to involve a number of specific skills named as meta cognitive skills. A few of these skills may be outlined as below:

- Skill of planning a cognitive task
- Skill approaching or executing a cognitive task
- Skill of monitoring, comprehension and evaluating the progress towards the complication of a cognitive task.
- Skill associated with the maintenance of motivation to see a cognitive task to completion.
- Skill of identifying blocks to learning or problem solving as early as possible.
- Skill of changing tools or strategies to ensure goal attainment.
- Skill of being aware or conscious of one's own strengths and weaknesses in relation to the execution of a cognitive task.
- Skill of being above of the nature of the cognitive task.
- Skill of being aware of the 'tools' or skills needed for the execution of the task in hand.
- Skill of self-regulating one's own thinking and learning.
- Skill of bringing learning from off-the-situational learning to on-the-situational learning.

Meta Cognition and Intelligence

Metacognitive enables us to be successful learners and problem solvers and therefore is essentially associated with our cognitive abilities and intelligence. Robert Sternberg (1985), propagator of the "Information Processing or Triarchic Theory of Intelligence" refers to the executive processes related to the controlling of one's cognitive processes (self regulation) involved in meta cognition as "metacomponents". In his theory, Sternberg treats metacomponents as the executive processes that control other cognitive components as well as receive feedback from these components. According to Sternberg, metacomponents are responsible for "figuring out how to do a particular task or set of tasks, and then making sure that the task or set of tasks are done correctly" (Sternberg, 1986b, p. 24). These executive processes involve planning, evaluating and monitoring problem-solving activities. Sternberg maintains that the ability to appropriately allocate cognitive resources, such as deciding how and when a given task should be accomplished, is central to intelligence. It can be seen here that ability to appropriately allocate cognitive resources is nothing but the process of self regulation or exercising proper control over one's thinking process. Therefore, it can be safely concluded that meta cognition is essentially linked with one's cognitive potential and intelligence.

Cognitive vs. Metacognitive Strategies

The question here may arise what is the difference between the term cognition and meta cognition or what is the difference between a cognitive and metacognitive strategy?

Can declarative knowledge be metacognitive in nature? For example, is the knowledge that you have difficulty understanding principles from biochemistry cognitive or metacognitive knowledge? Flavell himself acknowledges that metacognitive knowledge may not be different from cognitive knowledge (Flavell, 1979). The distinction lies in how the information is used. Recall that metacognition is referred to as "thinking about thinking" and involves overseeing whether a cognitive goal has been met. This should be the defining criterion for determining what is metacognitive. Cognitive strategies are used to help an individual achieve a particular goal (e.g., understanding a text) while metacognitive strategies are used to ensure that the goal has been reached (e.g., quizzing on self to evaluate one's understanding of that text). Metacognitive experiences usually precede or follow a cognitive activity. They often occur when cognitions fail, such as the recognition that one did not understand what one just read. Such an impasse is believed to activate metacognitive processes as the learner attempts to rectify the situation (Roberts & Erdos, 1993).

Metacognitive and cognitive strategies may overlap in the same strategy, such as questioning, could be regarded as either a cognitive or a metacognitive strategy depending on what the purpose for using that strategy may be. For example, you may use a self-questioning strategy while reading as a means of obtaining knowledge (cognitive), or as a way of monitoring what you have read (metacognitive). Because cognitive and metacognitive strategies are closely interwined and dependent upon each other, any attempt to examine one without acknowledging the other would not provide an adequate picture.

Knowledge is considered to be metacognitive if it is actively used in a strategic manner to ensure that a goal is met. For example, a student may use knowledge in planning how to approach a math exam: "I know what I (person variable) have difficulty with word problems (task variable), so I will answer the computational problems first and save the word problems for last (strategy variable)." Simply possessing knowledge about one's cognitive strengths or weaknesses and the nature of the task without actively utilizing this information to oversee learning is not metacognitive.

Metacognition as Facilitator of Knowledge Construction Task

Metacognition defined as "cognition about cognition" and "thinking about thinking" is credited of paving a smooth road for the knowledge construction on the part of an intended learner. Metacognition processing aided by one's metacognitive skills helps him:

- to become aware of his thinking processes being employed in his learning or problem solving acts.

- to take needed control of his cognitive process for planning, executing, evaluating and bringing changes in his cognitive strategies for accomplishing the desired end.
- to strive for learning the way of acquiring or constructing the knowledge rather than merely acquiring knowledge.
- some how to make use of his cognitive abilities and intelligence at his disposal for discovering the solution of the problem and disposal for discovering the solution of the problem and construction of knowledge by himself as needed in one or the other situations of learning or problem solving.

13

Cognition and Learning

MEANING OF COGNITION

In terms of its etymological derivation, the word cognition comes from the Latin verb 'Cognoscere' meaning the act of knowing or perceiving. In the available dictionaries, however, it has been defined and explained as below.

1. *Dictionary.com* (on line) has defined and explained it as below:
   - (i) The mental act or process by which knowledge is acquired, including perception, intuition and reasoning.
   - (ii) The knowledge that results from such an act or process.
2. *Webster Seventh New Colligiate Dictionary (1970: 161)* has defined and explained it as below:
   - (i) The act or process of knowing including both awareness and judgement.
   - (ii) The product of this act.

Explained and defined in this way cognition may be adjudged as a process as well as product of knowing about one thing or the other existing in one's environment.

The question here may arise when a student is provided information and knowledge directly by a teacher through lecture method *i.e.* telling about something then the knowledge/information gained through this mode may be included in the definition of cognition or not. The answer is simply 'no'. A process of cognition essentially involves one's own experience carried out through the use of one's senses, intellect or brain. It makes use of the process of sensation, perception and construction of knowledge on the part of the learners instead of receiving it through the direct transmission on the part of a source of knowledge. Direct transmission provides the students purely a memory level of learning and acquiring the new information without the involvement of their cognitive abilities like thinking and reasoning, analysing and synthesizing, generalization and inference drawing or critical evaluation, etc. We can't term such knowledge gathering process a cognitive process and also the product of such learning or acquiring an information or knowledge can't be termed as cognition.

The process of cognition always involves the use of one's sensory and perceptual abilities, and cognitive capacities for getting aware as well as taking judgement about a thing sensed and perceived by him. The acquisition of information or knowledge here thus does not rest at the memory level alone but is necessarily carried out at one's understanding and reflective level. The knowledge gained through the process of cognition is properly understood and grasped by an individual for its proper use on the part of the learner. He is in a position to take his own judgement about its use and worthwhileness and can reflect on it in the way he likes.

Understood in this way, now we can provide an operation definition of the term cognition in the following words:

Cognition is a process as well as product of knowing about one thing or the other existing in one's environment at the understanding and reflective level. In other words, we can also term it as a process or product of acquiring knowledge at the understanding and reflective level necessarily with the use of one's sensory, perceptual and mental abilities.

ROLE OF COGNITION LEARNING

Cognition as we have defined it essentially involves a process of acquiring knowledge through one's sensory, perceptual and mental abilities. In its true sense it is nothing but the process of learning carried out at the understanding and reflective level. It is why more often cognition and learning are taken as awfully similar in terms of their processing as well as product. Learning of a thing in a useful way always requires cognition and taking cognizance of a thing involves the process or product of learning.

School of behaviourism and learning theories propounded on the philosophy of behaviourism like trial and error theory, classical and operant conditioning, etc. do not assign any substantial role for the cognition or mental abilities in the acquisition of knowledge or learning on the part of human beings. They consider learning either as a machine like stimulus-response mechanism or habit formation function. Such type of learning usually operates at the memory level and thus can't be adjudged appropriate for its proper grasping and use in the desired way. As we know really speaking that type of knowledge gathering or learning does not fit into our definition of cognition. It is also openly criticized, opposed and decried in the world of teaching-learning. Gathering knowledge in the absence of cognitive processing serve no useful purpose for the learner. It is a useless burden on the part of the learner. Knowledge is useful for the knowledge seeker only when he is fully capable of making its proper use. However, it can be useful or serviceable only when it is acquired by the learner through his own efforts with the use of his own sensory, perceptual and mental abilities *i.e.* through cognition input and processing. The cognitive theories of learning like theory of insight or Gestalt learning, as well as theories involving information processing, constructivist learning all support the notion that the true and proper learning in the human beings always involves one's cognition. We can say the things like below in support of this assertion.

1. According to Gestalt or Insightful approach one is helped by his insightful thinking (cognition) in learning the solution of a problem

similarly as Kohler's apes learned to pick up the bananas hanging on the top of the cage or lying outside the cage. A student's cognition in the form of perceiving the situation as a whole supported by his intellectual abilities helps him in finding the solution of a mathematical problem.

2. According to information processing approach we learn or gain understanding of a number of things lying in our environment by a particular cognitive process named as information processing. When one sees or hears something new such input provided through his sense of sight and hearing travels to his mind/brain where it is being processed for its clear perception *i.e.* deriving proper meaning. In this way, a cognitive process in the shape of information processing helps one in acquiring proper knowledge (learning) about a thing seen or heard by him.

3. According to constructive approach one can acquire knowledge or is helped in the learning of one or the other things by constructing knowledge through his own efforts (guided or supported by his cognitive abilities). Let us illustrate this view point of constructivist learning in the light of the theoretical notions of constructivist Jean Piaget. According to Piaget knowledge or cognition about one or the other things lying in one's environment rests in the child in the form of one or the other schema. In this way, he may have some funds of knowledge already lying with him in the form of previous knowledge (cognition) at the time of learning a new thing. This previous knowledge (existing schemas) helps him in the proper assimilation (acquisition) of the related new knowledge. However, when he encounters a totally new information for the learning for which he has no previous knowledge (schema in which new information can be assimilated) he gets engaged in constructing a new schema for its accommodation or understanding. With the use of his cognitive abilities (the abilities related to cognition). In this way, the task of acquiring and understanding a new information *i.e.* learning according to Piaget is always facilitated and helped by one's own cognition and cognitive abilities. The more a child gets cognitively matured the more capacity and abilities he accumulates for understanding and learning new things.

Such assertion about the role of cognition learning may be clearly visible in our life when we find that whatever we want to learn in terms of knowledge, skills, and applications are always helped by the power of cognition (knowledge we all ready possess) as well as cognitive processes supported by our sensory, perceptual and mental abilities. Hence, in the end we can properly conclude that cognition as a process or product always works for bringing positive results or outcomes for our learning.

SOCIO-CULTURAL FACTORS AFFECTING COGNITION AND LEARNING

Cognition (knowing and understanding about a thing) and learning (acquiring knowledge through experience or training) as we have seen are found to co-exist. Cognition *i.e.* cognizance of a thing helps in its learning and learning adds to one's cognition. Both are also found to be a function of one's experience (direct or indirect, formal or informal) social exposure *i.e.* experiences gained by a developing child through his interaction with the socio-cultural forces present in his environment help him much in the task of cognition and learning. He understands and gains knowledge about the things, ideas and processes going on around him through the interaction and experience available to him in his socio-cultural environment. As a result, the processes and product of his cognition and learning are very much affected and influenced by a number of socio-cultural factors like home and family, school, community, mass media, cultural diversities and religion etc. Let us see how such socio-cultural forces are responsible for affecting the cognition and learning of the developing children

Role of Home and Family : living conditions, food habits, healthy discussion and entertainment, bonding with parents, attitude and behaviour of parents, size of family, socio-economic status, traditions, cultural values, educational level of parents, change in status due to economic or natural disasters

Role of School : Educational and professional qualification of teachers, relationship with teachers, mental and physical health of teachers, sincertiy and devotion of teachers, Leadership qualities of head, relationships with other students, nature of discipline, nature of organization and academic programmes, co-curricular activities organized, nature of additional facilities, physical environment and adequacy of resources, proper evaluation, provision for guidance and counselling

Role of Society and Community: Physical means and facilities, nature of local, state and national government, type of neighbours and neighbourhood, interrelationship with community and society, personality traits of members, effects of interaction with community, presence or absence of social evils, level of urbanization, education, nature of affective, conative and cognitive development of members, presence or absence of disputes, crimes etc.,

Role of Mass media: Reading about things and events shaping the thought processes of children, audio-visual and multimedia, computer shaping there verbal comprehension, personality, behaviour, thnking, behaving etc., increasing awareness about environment, regional, national and international happenings, offering wide opportunities for social relationships, breaking stereotypes, old traditions, negative influences as well on youngsters.

Role of Different cultures and religion: Values, norms, practices, migratory practices and trends, superstitions, misbeliefs, cultural segregation, marginalization, exposure to different cultures etc., imbibing good charcteristics of particular religion, worshiping diety, places of religious gatherings, rituals and practices of particular religion, etc.

Fig. 13.1: Socio-cultural Factors Affecting Cognition and Learning

Role of Home and Family

Mother, father, siblings and other members of the family may be found to exercise great influence over shaping the cognitive structure and ways of behaving and learning of the developing children. This influence cast a significant impact over their development in a positive or negative way depending upon the personality characteristic, behaviour and nature of interaction or relationship's existing among the members of the family among themselves as well as with the other segments of the society. All the earlier lessons regarding the shaping of behaviour and development of personality are well learned on the part of developing children in the company and direction of their parents, caretakers, siblings and other members of the family. How well a child grow and develop in form of his physical, motor, mental/cognitive, emotional, social or moral development depends upon the type of favourable or unfavourable environment available for his living and developing at his home. The things and factors like below present in one's home and family environment may play a quite decisive role in setting the course of child's cognitive, affective and conative development.

- The healthy or unhealthy living conditions, food habits, availability of nutritious and balanced diet, play and healthy entertainment facilities at home.
- Type of bond and relationship existing between parents.
- The attitude and behaviour of the parents and members of the family towards the child showing over-affection, partiality, neglect, hatred, prejudices, over-anxiety and over-security, strictness or carelessness etc.
- The size of the family and birth order of the child.
- Relationships among the members of the family.
- Socio-economic status and position of the family in the society.
- The traditions, cultural values and ideals of the family.
- The education level of the parents, their interest and attention in bringing up of the children and their abilities and capacity for this purpose.
- The organised or broken homes.
- The individual behaviour, habits, temperament and other personality characteristics of the parents and other members of the family.
- The attitudes and ideals of the parents and members of the family towards social norms, ethical, moral and human values,
- The changes introduced in the set up and status of the family on account of the extreme variations of the conditions like sudden losses in terms of human lives, natural calamities, economic disasters, etc. or gain in positive side like increase in wealth, social status and power equations, etc.

All of the above things and situations prevalent in the home and family environment cast a considerable impact in influencing and providing a definite direction to the growth and development of the child including his personality make-up and behavioural traits.

In the homes, where the children get a desirable stimulating and enriched environment for the development of their linguistic ability, communication skills, creative potential and mental faculties they may be found proceeding well on the path of their proper language and cognitive development in comparison to those who are deprived with such facilities and congenial home conditions. Similarly, the children who are privileged to have conditions at their home quite congenial to their physical or motor development may be found to go far ahead in terms of the acquisition of motor skills and physical development in comparison to the children being deprived of such congenial conditions. Actually every child learns and acts what is observed and imitated by him through the behaviour of his parents, elders, siblings and other members of the family. Therefore, all what is there in child's behaviour and development with respect to his habits, temperament, emotional expressions, social traits, morality, etc. are mostly learned and reflected in his behaviour through the impact or influence of the home and family environment. The satisfaction of basic needs — physical and socio-psychological is very much essential for the proper cognitive, conative and affective development and adjustment of a child. As far as the home and family environment remains congenial and helpful for the child in the realization of his desired needs, the child may remain on a proper track, of his adequate adjustment and development but as soon as things drift on the other side, the child begins to feel despair and frustration, become maladjusted to his self and the environment and consequently may lag behind in his cognitive, conative and affective development or may learn maladapted or socially undesirable behaviour in the chain of his doomed future. In this way, the uncongenial or defective home and family environment may prove not only a great obstacle in the proper development of children but it may also provide all what is needed for the full growth and nourishment of unsocial or immoral behaviour. The development of proper or improper and good or bad behaviour, thus may have its origin as well as its further stimulation and reinforcement from what is available to it from the family and home environment.

Role of School

The other most important social agency to influence the development and behaviour of the adolescents after the home and family is the school. It is the center of learning for the child and therefore the learning experiences — formal or informal — he gets inside the school, control and shape his behaviour. There is no exaggeration in saying that a man can be identified and known through the names of the institutions from where he gets his education. It is also true that every institution or school has its own impression or reputation for being relatively good and bad. These are labelled so on account of what is being done there through their curricular and co-curricular experiences and the ways of administration for the growth and development of the personality of their students making them to — acquire the desirable or undesirable behaviour and styles of living. Then the head of the institution, teachers, employees and the fellow students play their roles in influencing the development pattern and behaviour of the students in the same way as played by the parents and members of the family in the home and family set-up.

Apart from the human factors, the nature and quality of the material resources, psychological, social and cultural environment of the school also work as a great deciding factor in influencing and controlling the developmental direction and behaviour of the students. Some of the things, situations and factors inherent in the overall environment of the school which work as the determinants of the students' cognitive, affective and conative behavioural development may be named as below:

- The educational and professional qualification of the teachers, their teaching experience, personality and behavioural make-up.'
- The sweetness or bitterness in the relationships among the teachers and other employees.
- The mental and physical health of the teachers.
- The sincerity and devotion of the teachers towards their duties and profession.
- The abilities and competencies of the head of the institution, his personality and behavioural traits, his relationship with the fellow teachers, students, employees of the institution and parents of the students.
- The nature of the relationship between the teachers and students.
- The nature of the relationship existing among the students of a particular class or the school in general.
- The nature of the discipline and administrative arrangements prevalent in the school.
- The nature of the organisation of the academic programmes and the educational standards maintained by the school.
- The provision for co-curricular activities and the nature of their organisation.
- The examination results of the school.
- The place, status, name and fame of the school with respect to the achievements in games and other co-curricular activities.
- The nature of the facilities available in the school for the organisation of various cocurricular activities, hobbies and other talents development programmes.
- The nature of the facilities regarding library, reading room, museum,

laboratories, work places, etc. available in the school.

- The nature of the arrangement for mid-day meal, canteen, common-room, drinking water, laboratories, etc.
- The appropriateness or inappropriateness of the things and situations related to the physical environment of the school like adequacy of the school building, sanitation, pollution free environment, seating arrangement, proper ventilation and lighting, etc.
- The provision and adequate arrangement for the education and adjustment of the gifted, the creative, the backward, the problematic and the handicapped children with their special problems.
- The nature of the provision and arrangement for guidance and counselling services to the students.
- The adequate arrangement with regard to the evaluation of the progress of the children in quite an objective and impartial way.

Besides the things pointed out above, we may include many other things, attributes or factors related with the physical, educational, administrative, social or cultural environment of the school in this list which may directly or indirectly influence and control the cognitive affective and conative development of the adolescents including their learning potential and ways of behaving. In fact, what we appreciate in our children and adolescents with regard to their good habits, temperament, desirable personality traits and ways of behaving, to a large extent, is the sole product of the school environment. The students learn and grow in the way they are shaped and moulded by the presence and interaction of the various things, situations and factors present in their school environment. A single factor, incident or accident may make and mar the whole life of an innocent child. A sympathetic, affectionate and inspiring behaviour of a teacher may bring in the child the needed enthusiasm, motivation, confidence and will power to develop in a desired way. On the other hand, the partiality shown and injustice done to the child may vitiate his mind to such an extent that he may be forced to adopt reactive and maladapted behaviour patterns first by developing hate towards the teacher and his subject and then by isolating himself completely from the class and the school for playing truancy and engaging in other deviant behaviour.

In this way what goes inside the school and how the students react to the school environment, may definitely work as a potent determinant of their present and future development with respect to their cognitive affective and conative behaviour.

Role of Society or Community

Apart from home and school, society/community through its various institutions, components or instruments like neighbourhood, social clubs, religious institutions, means of transport, means of communication and entertainment, news papers and reading literature, the type of Government ruling state, country or local machinery, social, cultural and community fairs and festivals, etc. may play a quite decisive role in providing direction and magnitude to the cognitive, affective and conative behavioural development of the children. Here the things and features like below present in the available social/community environment may be found to mould the children's development in a particular way:

- Nature of the physical means and facilities related to transport and communication, sanitation and cleanliness, level of pollution, medical facilities, electricity facilities, means of entertainment, social company and interaction, etc.
- Nature of the local, state and national level of government and its functioning for the welfare of the citizens.
- The type of neighbours and neighbourhood influences available to the developing children.
- The nature of the interrelationships carried out with the meaning of the community and society.
- The nature of personality traits and behaviour patterns orders members of the society/community — children as well as adults.
- The socio-economic states, cultural traditions and religious faiths of the community and society to which the child and his family belongs.
- The good and evil effects of the company and interaction with the members of the community/society on the child and his family.
- Nature of the role played by religious institutions and social organization in the development and welfare of the developing children and community as a whole.
- The presence or absence of stereotyping, social evils, traditions, practices and restrictions affecting the cognitive, conative and affective development of children.
- The attitude of the society/community towards children with special needs or different abilities and facilities available for inclusive setup.
- The level of education, thinking and outlook of the society/ community to which the child belongs.
- The level of urbanization, industrialization or ruralization of the society or community.
- The nature of conative, affective and conative development of the peers and older children of the community/society in which child is developing.
- The presence or absence of the disputes and conflicts, fear and phobias, crimes, terror activities and war like situation in the community/society.

Where the favourable impact of the positive factors or things available in the form of human capital and resources of the society help much in shaping the children's cognitive, affective and conative development in a healthy and desirable way, the negativity breeds negative and damaging effect to their development and wellbeing. Where the favourable factors help in the healthy well being of the developing children, the unfavourable one's lead to the deficiency, ailment and impairment in the motor, physical, emotional social and moral development of the children. The society or community ridden with superstitious, stereotypes, rigidity, social evil is bound to imbibe the developing children with closed thinking, misbeliefs, emotional instability and a variety of educational, and socio-psychological deprivation or behavioural problems while a progressive democratic society may help the children to grow in a useful way contributing towards their healthy and desirable well being.

Role of Mass Media

The Meaning of the Term Mass-media

In its word meaning, the term mass-media stands for the media (means and mode of communication) for the masses. It can thus represent all channels, means and modes that can be used for conveying information, messages or appeal simultaneously to a number of people breaking the barrier of location, places and timings. It can exist in audio, video or multi sensory forms and thus may appeal a number of senses for producing lasting effects or impressions on the minds and hearts of the individual. The means and modes like blow may be properly included in the term mass-media.

1. News papers and magazines
2. Books (Printed and e-form)
3. Advertisement
4. Radio Broadcast
5. Telecasts
6. Films and Movies
7. Internet and Web material
8. The modern communication means like messages and audio-video material loaded on smart phones, Facebook, Blogs, Twitter etc.

Role of Mass Media in Influencing Behaviour and Development

Mass media play a quite dominant role in influencing behaviour and development of the children and adolescents in a number of ways and forms. What they read, listen and watch through the mass media appeal to their senses and goes deeply in the minds and hearts in a great way and as a result they may learn and imbibe so many things in their habits, ways of behaving and doing that may go to shape the events of their life in a particular way. Let us see how it happens.

1. When the children and adolescents read about the things and events in newspapers, pamphlets, magazines and books, etc., it may catch their

attention and get them acquainted with so many things — positive as well as negative. It can add to broaden their mental horizon and learn so many things. Learning as you know can result in the desirable or undesirable developments of interests, attitudes, habits, temperament and so many other personality traits. It happens also in the case of the children's exposure to reading material. They may not only get acquainted with the goods and evils, virtues and vices but also consciously and unconsciously try to imbibe them in their behaviour.

2. The audio-visual and multi-media means like radio and television, films and movies and what is available to them on their computer and mobile screens, exercise much greater influences in shaping their behaviour and personality then their verbal comprehension of the material available in the newspapers, magazines and books. Here, the learning takes place in a more organized way. It is multi-sensory and observational learning much superior to the verbal. When a child observes his most liked actor or actress to perform or do certain types of acts or behaviour, he can't resist the desire to get it copied in his behaviour. It is nothing but hero worship that is most common among children and especially in adolescents. As a part of social learning as advocated by Bandura (1977), all such observations on their part are imitated, practised and assimilated in their behaviour on the part of children and adolescents who get exposed to such type of mass media experiences. The easy and unlimited availability of such multimedia exposure to the youngsters through the developed electronic and computer means has almost revolutionized such type of social learning. As a result we may find tremendous changes in the interests, attitudes, ways of thinking, feeling and behaving of the youngsters-affecting the task of shaping and developing their personality in a positive or negative way. The much observed and talked influences of the mass media (included printed material and multimedia) as a whole may be summarized as below.

(i) The exposure to available mass media resources has resulted in increasing awareness towards the things and events concerning one's environment. The children and adolescents of today have much opportunities to get exposed to their physical, social and cultural environment-local, regional national and international in comparison to a few decades ago. Hence much credit for the development in the cognitive behaviour of the children goes to the mass-media.

(ii) Mass media is also credited for bringing rapid changes in social, emotional, language, communication and aesthetic development of the youngsters. Today they enjoy more opportunities for developing social relationships with each other and getting better connected in comparison to the olden days. Mass media have given them enough opportunities for getting acquainted with the social and cultural life of their own and others. They may know how people behave and live in their own region, country, or other parts of the Globe. It has thus contributed in understanding the people living on this earth, developing global understanding, cooperation and collaboration.

(iii) Mass media is also credited for removing a number of social barriers, stereotypes, social evils, discriminations, marginalization and misunderstandings among the members of a community, regions and nations. Children and youths of today are proceeding towards a global society or community, having less rigidity and bondage of caste, colour, religion, language, nationality, etc. They are having inter-caste, inter-religion and international relationships, friendships and marriages. It is all happening with the services of the developed mass media platforms and related technologies.

(iv) The exposure to available mass media in contrary to its valuable advantages and contributions is also decried and criticised for a number of its negative influences on the behaviour and development of the youngsters. In this concern particularly we note that mass media is held responsible for exposing the youngsters to the world of crime, hate, violence and sexual exploitation. There is too much violence, sex and other type of immoral, illegal and inhuman behaviour reported in the newspapers and shown in the new channels, episodes of television serials and movies. The Internet, web and other sources of social media are also loaded with such evil as influencing material, adult and child porn is freely available on Internet.

Children and adolescence here have many chances to get drifted from their welfare path. Many of them can waste their time, money, energy and mar their future for indulging in socially undesirable acts, violence and crimes. They may also get victim at the hands of culprits, criminals terrorist groups and sexual offenders since the mass media many times is used by notorious people for serving their vested interests.

In this way, it can be observed that mass media has a powerful capacity to influence the development of the children and adolescents in a positive as well as negative way.

Role of Different Cultures

Culture of a society or community reflects the mode of living and behaving of the members of that community prevailed in the community since a number of decades or centuries. The community or people belonging to a particular culture may be found to adopt uniqueness in their dress, make up, food choices, social and cultural values, ethics, ideas, religious beliefs, social norms, moves, rituals, stereotypes, celebration of festivals and philosophy of life. Each culture has a great potential to cast a strong impact over the growth and development of the children.

Adolescents and youths adopt the ways of living and behaving of their culture from the quite early age. They have proper respect for their cultural and social values, traditions and practices.

Influenced by the culture of their community, they may be found to a great fan and devotee of their cultural norms, values and practices and it really matters the way they are developed in physical, mental, emotional, social, moral, linguistic and aesthetic dimensions of their personality. However, in a multi-cultural society, there comes a great change. The children and adolescents are exposed to the ways of behaving and living of the persons belonging to other cultures. It may bring a great change in their life styles, ways of behaving and living. The task of their growth and development and shaping of their personality is also greatly affected by their exposure to the world of multiculturalism or the culture of the place and community to which they are migrated.

For example, when a child and his family get migrated from a rural area to urban one, his growth and development is very much affected by coining into the urban culture of the migrated place. As Bruner (1996) says "culture shapes the mind and it provides us with a tool kit by which we construct not only our worlds, but our very conceptions of ourselves and our powers".

The overall development and progress of a migrated child or adolescent is thus very much affected when he comes into contact of a particular culture or different cultures prevailing at his place of migration. He gets more opportunities for the cognitive, social, emotional and linguistic development. He may be helped to get rid of many superstitions, misbelieves, stereotypes coming in the way of his development and progress. It is why we may see a lot of overall improvement in the rate of growth and development when they get entry into a privileged social or multi-cultured environment. However it is not be understood that exposure to different cultures always bring positive results. The wind may blow both ways. In brief their exposure to different cultures may be found to affect their growth and development in the ways given below:

- It may affect their physical growth and development, health status and conditions as and when they pick up the healthy or unhealthy habits of eating and drinking, and living inherent in other cultures.
- It may affect their social and cultural development. It may help them to break the barriers related to gender, race, caste and cultural segregation or marginalization and get better opportunity for their overall growth and development.
- The cultural integration may affect their moral and ethical development in a great way. However, it may drift them in both the ways. They may get imbibed with desirable values or may lost in the blind race of individualism, fashion and exhibitionism and pleasure seeking motives. It is here a little precaution and guidance is needed to them on the part of elders, teachers and parents.
- The exposure of multi-cultures may help the children to get in touch with the goodness of other cultures and develop closeness to the followers of different cultures. It may help in seeking unity in

diversity and learn the lesson of "peaceful coexistence" with the others. The imbibing of such virtue may prove helpful to the children and adolescents in a great way in the task of their overall development and wellbeing.

Role of Religion

Religion occupies a quite significant place in the life of human beings. It is enshrined deeply in their culture and day to day functioning. By virtue of our living in a society, every one of us is a devotee and follower of one or the other religion. Whatever religion, Hinduism, Islam, Christianity, Jainism, Buddhism, Sikhism we follow every religion is engrained with the virtues and ethics helpful in the wellbeing of its followers, society and humanity at large. It shows us a way of life and helps us leading our life in a balanced way. Its impact on our behaviour and personality is also quite impressible. Whenever, one visits a place of worship (temple, masjid, church or gurudwara) he or she feels a unique sense of inner satisfaction and mental peace. All the evil feelings and negative thoughts just pump out from one's inner self and the mind and heart begins to get fresh air of positive thoughts and divine feelings. Moreover, the rituals and ceremonies performed, rules and regulations observed, code of ethics and conduct followed, religious practices adopted, may prove a quite decisive force in moulding and shaping the behaviour and personality of the individuals.

Adolescence in the human beings is marked as the age of intensive growth and development in all the personality dimensions. Here one learns and develops maximum for attaining maturity in every aspects. By coincidence this age is not only marked as the age of friendship and social relationships but it is also dominated with intensive flow of emotions. The adolescents due to too much physical energy and almost uncontrollable flowing of the emotional current seriously need some ways for the channelization and redirection of their energies to the constructive, healthy and socially desirable outlets. Religion with all its formalities may come here to their help in a suitable way as laid down below:

1. A religion helps the children and adolescents to learn a number of good habits leading to get imbibed with good physical health involving cleanliness, consumption of uncontaminated hygienic *sativic* food, healthy sleeping and awakening habits, maintaining fitness of the .body and health by keeping fasts and rozas, and practising *asanas*, *pranayama*, *surya namaskar*, Namaz postures, *ardas* etc.

2. It can help the children to learn a number of good habits and engage in healthy practices helpful for their needed cognitive development and contributing towards their mental health.

3. Religion in all its shades and forms teaches us to have a considerable faith in the absolute power of Almighty God. God is watching, such perception saves the children from being socially or morally deviant.

4. The religious belief that "God, Allah or Guru is with me" fills in children with an unquestionable sense of self-confidence. It makes them fearless and courageous to face any eventualities in life and engage in challenging and risk taking behaviour.

5. The visit to the places of worships, participation in religious gatherings, festivals and rituals provides enough opportunities to the children for the social contacts and inter-action, cooperation and collaboration leading to get imbibed them with appropriate social manners, habits and virtues.

6. A number of rituals and practices (e.g., meditation, worship rituals, etc.), adopted in the religions, help the children in learning the ways and means of getting focused on the target, sustaining their attention over the focused objects, and performing their tasks in a quite systematic and desirable ways.

14

Role of Teacher in a Teaching-Learning Context

INTRODUCTION

The teaching-learning process in its variety of ways and situations always stands for helping the learners in their learning tasks and contributing towards the development of their abilities and capacities. A teacher occupies quite a key place and plays a substantial role in the realization of teaching-learning objectives in one or the other teaching-learning situation. Although, in all the teaching-learning situations his goal to help the students in their learning and development is the same, yet the ways and means adopted and the nature of role played may differ from situation to situation. As a result the teachers may be found to play different roles depending upon the needs of the teaching-learning situations and their own styles of teaching. With the changed scenario in the teaching-learning areas, it has become quite essential for the teachers to resort to techniques and strategies of teaching other than involving direct transmission of knowledge and skills. He has thus now to play many other roles besides the transmission of knowledge to his students. In this chapter, we would like to throw light on the different types of roles usually played by the teachers in the changed scenerio of a teaching-learning context.

A. ROLE OF TEACHER AS TRANSMITTER OF KNOWLEDGE

In playing such role a teacher may be found to focus on direct transmission of knowledge to the students by making use of the direct methods and strategies of teaching like lecture, demonstration, narration, exposition, explanation, illustration, description, etc. The basic assumptions lying in the minds of the teacher while resorting to such role may be briefed as below:

- Children can't acquire knowledge or skills through their own efforts. Needed knowledge and skills should be given to them by the teachers.
- Knowledge and skills should be directly told and demonstrated to the children with the use of direct method like lecture or demonstration.
- There is too much to be known by the children. The knowledge of the contents regarding their curriculum can only be furnished through direct transmission of knowledge to them.

- Children can learn well when knowledge and skills are transmitted directly by the elders/teachers to them.

With such assumptions, teachers then try to equip them with the needed knowledge and information regarding their subjects of teaching and then try to pour the knowledge in the minds of the students by adopting purely a teacher and subject centered approach. They transmit the knowledge and information and expect from the students to listen and watch, grasp the delivered contents, memorize and reproduce it in the manner transmitted to them on the part of teacher. It is purely a knowledge level of teaching-learning. Knowledge is transmitted by the teacher, received by the students, kept in their memory and get reproduced at the time of assessment and examination. The understanding and reflective level of learning on the part of the students thus can hardly be possible with the adoption of the role of a transmitter on the part of the teacher in the ongoing teaching-learning situation.

B. ROLE OF TEACHER AS A MODEL

In such a role teachers are found to act as a role model for being observed, and imitated on the part of their students to the required learning and modification in their behaviour.

The famous psychologist Bandura through his theory of social learning has proposed that children learn well when they are given opportunity to learn through modelling *i.e.* when they happen to observe the behaviour of their role model and begin to imitate and practice the observed behaviour. A teacher here thus in his role as a model, may provide needed opportunities for his students to learn the desired behaviours being modelled by the teacher. A number of desirable habits, interests, attitudes and likewise personality traits thus may be imbibed by the students well with the inspirational role of the teacher as model. Encouraging results are also received in the skill acquisition areas. The model behaviour and actions of the teachers are properly imitated by the students in many of the skilled areas such as games and sports, performance in laboratory work, home science classes, arts and crafts, dance, dramatic activities, art and painting, etc. Much of what we know as problem solving ability may also be witnessed more in the students who carefully observe the problem solving behaviour of their elders particularly the teachers. In this way, a teacher through his role playing as model may help the students in learning and imbibing so many desired things in their behaviour consciously or unconsciously in a variety of ways. However, in such a role playing situation the teacher always remains in a dominant position and thus invariably, the approach involved in this type of teaching-learning is absolutely a teacher centred approach. Through his unique specific position in the eyes of the students, a teacher's behaviour and actions related to cognitive, conative and psychomotor domains always remains a thing to be closely watched and imitated at the hands of the students. In such a role the teacher always needs to be quite conscious about his behaviour and actions. He should not do, say or demonstrate in his behaviour anything negative and harmful for the proper learning and development of the students. What he does not intend to be in the behaviour and action of his students, it should not also be visible in his own behaviour.

C. ROLE OF TEACHER AS FACILITATOR

In such a role teacher neither demonstrates his ability and strength by playing the role of a knowledge transmitter nor imposes his personality, behaviour and actions as a model for the keen observation and imitation on the part of his students. From a dominating position now he switches over his role to a well wisher, facilitator and helper always standing by his students for arranging what is needed by them in their tasks of learning and development. The students themselves have to learn and make efforts from their side. No direct instruction or demonstration is available from the teacher's side. However, the path of their learning or imbibing desirable behaviours get smoothened and facilitated with the total commitment of the teacher for the learning and development of his students. As a facilitator he has to help them in setting their learning goals, arranging better teaching-learning situations, selecting appropriate learning styles, using appropriate devices, aids and equipments much in tune with their own capacities, and potential for learning and striving. He is there to guide their path and assist them in their learning. In no case he takes the driver seat and own the whole responsibility of making them to learn what he thinks better for them as happens in the case of his playing the roles of knowledge transmitter and role model.

Actually there is a total paradigm shift in the scene where teacher is supposed to play the role of a facilitator instead of transmitting the knowledge or personalizing his figure as a model. Here cognitivism and constructivism emerge on the teaching-learning scene in place of the traditional behaviouristic perspective. The child centered approach takes the front seat leaving behind the teacher and subject centred approaches. The responsibility of learning is to be owned by the learner himself. He has to know, discover and construct the knowledge he needs or aims at with his own efforts. However, in doing so he may need timely assistance, guidance and help from the teacher. He wants the needed facilities, aids and equipments and necessary enlightenment for his learning path and it is here the teacher may come to his help in his knowledge constructional task in the capacity of a facilitator, guide and helper. The role of the facilitator played by the teacher thus may result in guided discovery as proposed by Jerome Bruner in his guided discovery approach and scaffolding as suggested by Lev Vygotsky in his social constructionist learning.

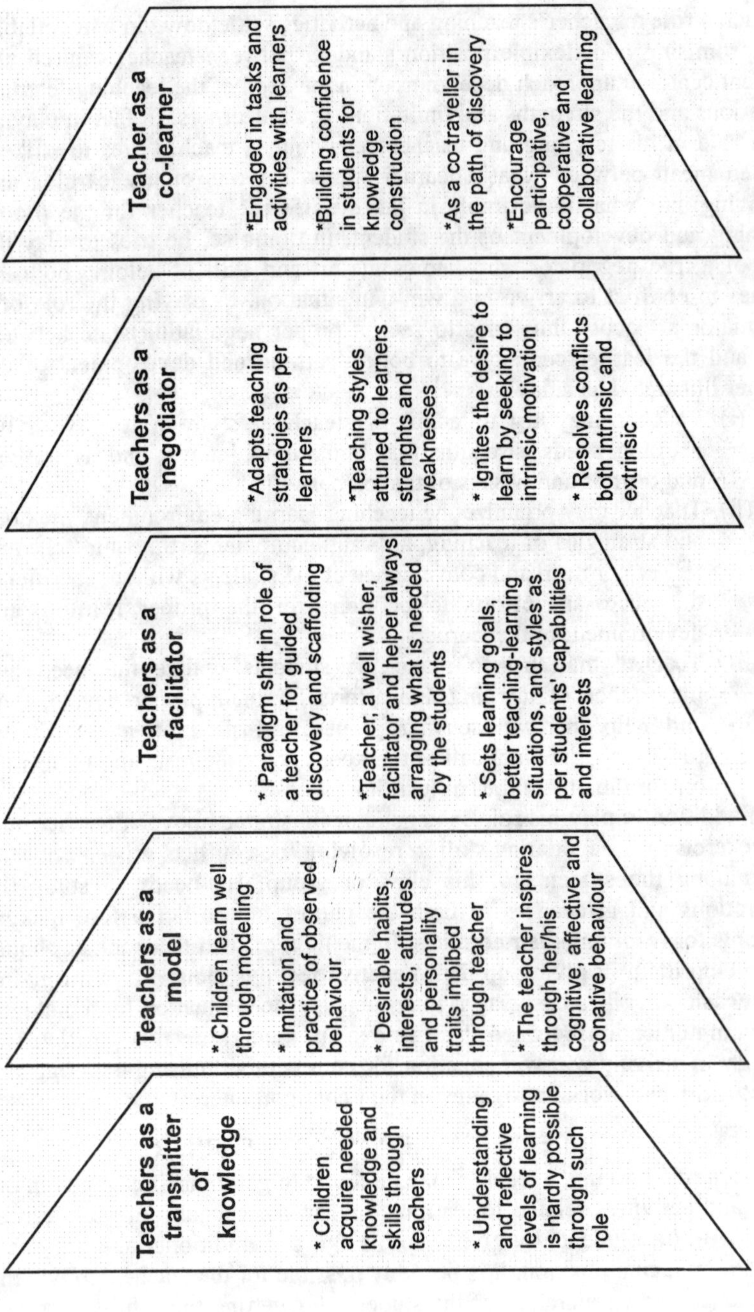

Fig. 14.1: Various Roles of a Teacher

D. ROLE OF TEACHER AS NEGOTIATOR

In such a role a teacher's teaching and activities settle down in a negotiable, compromising and flexible position standing between teacher centred and student centered approach depending upon the need of the teaching-learning situations and the strengths and limitations of the learners. In fact in playing such role in his teaching and teacher behaviour, a teacher tries to strike a golden mean between what a learner wants in terms of his learning and behaving and what is desirable in the eyes of the teacher for the proper learning and development of the student. In doing so, he tries to play the role of a true negotiator who knows the art and skill of helping both the parties in conflict to arrive in a win-win situation. In playing the role of a negotiator a teacher thus tries to seek a proper negotiating state between him and the learner conducive to better learning and development of the learner illustrated as below:

(i) Teacher may try to adapt his teaching style in tune with the learning needs, strengths and limitations, interest and aspirations and desires and wishes of the learners.

(ii) Teacher may organize the teaching-learning environment, methods and strategies of teaching, aids and equipments, time and schedule etc. as per need and convenience of the students without sacrificing the necessary efforts to be done for the proper learning and development of the learners.

(iii) Teacher may try to make the students realize the need and importance of learning and efforts for their proper development and help them in seeking proper intrinsic motivation without sacrificing the inner call of their conscious, interests and likings for one or the other types of learning.

In addition to play his role as negotiator illustrated above, a teacher may also exercise his negotiating skill in resolving the conflicts arising between and among the students of his class or group. He needs to study the frustrations and grievances of both the parties in conflict before making attempts for resolving their conflicts. In the light of such feedback he should try to help them in giving up their negative feelings, doubts and misgiving about each other The best way is to arrange a proper situation for a dialogue and communication between them to explain their respective position and then try to arrive a win-win situation for both without hurting their ego and self-identity and working together in their common interest.

E. ROLE OF TEACHER AS A CO-LEARNER

In such a role playing, a teacher may be found to get himself engaged in the tasks and activities related to learning well in the capacity of a co-learner along with his students by giving up his ego and traditional authority as a teacher. In such a position, it is properly possible for the teachers to win the confidence and cooperation of the students for getting them fully involved in the ongoing teaching-learning process in the proper lime light of the following saying:

> "Tell them they will forget. Show them, they will remember. Involve them, they will learn."

In fact such role playing on the part of teacher fulfills the requirements needed for playing a proper role on the part of teachers in a constructive paradigm making students to learn and construct their knowledge at their own with their efforts. The teacher here remains in a position to convince a learner that he is with him in the journey of his learning as a con-traveller. In this connection, the things like below may prove quite fruitful for a teacher in playing the role of a co-learner in a proper way.

1. At the introductory stage of the teaching a topic related to his subject, a teacher should always conclude the introduction of his topic by declaring that "Well students we will be studying about . . . (topic) or try to learn or know about . . . (topic). By declaring the objective of the current teaching-learning task in such a way, he will be in a position to convince or convey that he will be a co-traveller in the learning journey aimed to know and learn about the topic in hand.

2. While resorting to such role playing, a teacher should essentially remind himself that his goal is not to show his students how much he knows but to inspire, encourage and allow his students to show him how much they know.

3. Instead of telling or demonstrating about the knowledge and skill gaining related to the topic of the study by themselves through direct instruction—lecture or demonstration, they should try to work for providing the students full opportunity to know, discover and construct the knowledge related to the topic with their own attempts. In this venture, for playing the role of a co-learner, he should always insist that true we don't know much about this topic but let us work together for knowing what it is in its appropriate way.

4. As a co-learner (but at the same time enjoying a leadership position on account of his status) the teacher here should always strive to give his students the necessary confidence and learning tools needed by them for the discovery or knowledge construction related to the topic. However, in doing so, he should remain reminding the students that he does not have all the answers for them, but he is with them and let us work together for knowing all related to the topic in hand.

5. Teachers should remember that it is the students who need to learn about the concerned topic, seek answers to the raised curiosity and apply the skills at the time of need. Therefore, they should be given opportunity to know and learn by themselves by owning the full responsibility for their learning. But since they are noble and novice in this discovery path, they may need a knowledgeable co-traveller in the path of their learning journey and it is here the teachers are needed to play a role of a true co-traveller for

jointly sharing the quest for knowledge, understanding and application of the topic in hand.

6. As a co-learner, when needed so they may often play a part of more knowledgeable peer, a wise leader for guiding and illuminating the learning path of the travelled journey. They should however tell and guide only what is urgently and essentially needed in a teaching-learning situation and not snatch the opportunity of knowing and discovering the things with their own attempts by remembering that they are along with the students in their learning journey as a co-learner and not at all in the capacity of knowledge transmitter or role model.

7. For providing better platform and opportunities for playing the role of a co-learner, teachers should try to encourage the use of such teaching-learning strategies, methods and devices that encourage participating, cooperative and collaborating learning as well as constructivist learning with independent efforts. The use of problem solving method, heuristic method, project method, assignment method, collaborative approach, seminar and group discussion strategies, brain storming strategy, inductive thinking or teaching model etc. may prove quite beneficial for a teacher to play the role of a co-learner in one or the other teaching-learning situations in an effective way.

15

Intelligence: Concept, Theories and Measurement

INTRODUCTION

In contrast to animals man is considered to be endowed with certain cognitive abilities, which make him a rational being. He can reason, discriminate, understand, adjust and face a new situation. Definitely he is superior to animals in all such aspects of behaviour. But human beings themselves are not all alike. There are wide individual differences. A teacher easily discovers these differences among his pupils. Some learn with a good speed while others remain lingering too long. There are some who need only one demonstration for handling the tools properly while for others even the repeated individual guidance brings no fruitful result.

What is that causes one individual to be more effective in his response to a particular situation than another. No doubt, interest, attitude, desired knowledge and skill, etc. count towards this achievement. But still there is something that contributes significantly towards these varying differences. In Psychology it is termed 'Intelligence'. In ancient India our great Rishis named it 'Viveka'.

CONCEPT OF INTELLIGENCE

Since time immemorial attempts have been made to have understanding about the concept of intelligence. Let us be acquainted with the concept and meaning of intelligence by throwing light on the following aspects:

A. Meaning and Definition of Intelligence.
B. Some established facts about Intelligence.
C. Misconception about Intelligence.

A. Meaning and Definitions of Intelligence

As discussed earlier, in a day to day conversation an individual is said to be intelligent in proportion as he is successful in meeting general life situations. What is there in intelligence that contributes towards this success, is a question which has been attempted by psychologists in different ways resulting in so many varied definitions. Below we give some of these important definitions.

Woodworth and Marquis. *"Intelligence means intellect put to use. It is the use of intellectual abilities for handling a situation or accomplishing any task."* (1948. p. 33)

Stern. *"Intelligence is a general capacity of an individual consciously to adjust his thinking to new requirements. It is general mental adaptability to new problems and conditions of life."* (1914, p. 3)

Terman. *"An individual is intelligent in proportion as he is able to carry on abstract thinking."* (1921)

Wagnon. *"Intelligence is the capacity to learn and adjust to relatively new and changing conditions."* (1937, p. 40)

David Wechsler. *"Intelligence is the aggregate or global capacity of an individual to act purposefully, to think rationally and to deal effectively with his environment."* (1944, p. 3)

Analysis of these Definitions

Above we have given some definitions, more of such definitions can further be cited. All these definitions when taken separately, give an incomplete picture because they partly emphasize that—

(a) intelligence is the ability to learn.

(b) it is the ability to deal with abstraction,

(c) it is the ability to make adjustment or to adapt to new situations.

The definition given by Wechsler seems to combine all three view points presented above but this definition too has come under criticism due to difference of opinion among Psychologists. Several attempts have been made to reach some general agreement but all have been in vain. However, the British psychologists are said to have reached some measures of agreement regarding a suitable definition of intelligence.

To them intelligence consists of the ability:

(a) to see relevant relationships between objects or ideas and

(b) to apply these relationships to novel situations.

It makes us conclude that intelligent behaviour is divided into two categories — theoretical and practical, abstract and concrete. The theoretical operations make an individual capable to face and solve the actual life-problems and make adjustment to the environmental situations. If we try to analyse the factor which determines the success of an individual's activities we can by all means say that cognitive or mental abilities have a dominant role to play in the success or failure. "Intelligence," as Rex and Margaret Knight have put it *"is the factor that is common to all mental abilities"* (1952, p. 124) and therefore, the judgement about intelligence can ever be taken with the evaluation of the task one performs, how he reacts and responds to a situation. In this way if we try to come to the practical ground, we can define intelligence as follows:

Intelligence consists of an individual's those mental or cognitive abilities which help him in solving his actual life-problems and leading a happy and well contented life.

B. Some Established Facts about Intelligence

1. *The relation of intelligence with nature and nurture:* There have been too many attempts on the part of psychologists to weigh the relative importance of nature and nurture. The conclusion of their studies reveals that intelligence is the product of heredity and environment. Both are necessary for the intellectual growth of an individual, neither can be considered more necessary than the other.

2. *Distribution of intelligence:* There are individual differences with regard to the distribution of intelligence in nature like wealth, health, etc. This distribution is governed by a definite principle that is "the majority of the people are at the average, a few very bright and a few very dull."

3. *Growth of intelligence:* As the child grows in age, so does the intelligence as shown by intelligence tests. Now the question arises — at what age does this increase cease? The age of cessation of mental growth varies from individual to individual. However, in majority of cases, intelligence reaches its maximum, somewhat at the age of 16 or 20 in the individual. After that the vertical growth of intelligence ceases. But the horizontal growth—accumulation of knowledge and acquisition of skills — continues throughout the life span of an individual.

4. *Intelligence and Sex differences:* Various studies have been conducted to find out whether women are less intelligent than men and vice-versa. The result of these researches hangs in one way or the other. In some of the cases, no significant difference has been found. Therefore, it is proper to think that difference in sex does not contribute towards difference in intelligence.

5. *Intelligence and racial or cultural difference:* Whether a particular race, caste or cultural group is superior to other in intelligence — the hypothesis has been examined by so many research workers. In U.S.A. it has been a burning problem for centuries. The results of earlier studies which take the whites to be a superior race in comparison to the Negroes have been questioned. Now it has been established that intelligence is not the birth right of a particular race or group. The 'bright' and the 'dull' can be found in any race, caste or cultural group and the differences which are found can be explained in terms of environmental influences.

C. Misconception about Intelligence

There are a number of misconceptions prevalent about the nature and concept of intelligence. For the clarification let us be clear that what is not meant by intelligence.

1. Intelligence is not knowledge, though acquisition of knowledge depends, to a great extent, on intelligence and vice-versa.
2. Intelligence is not memory. A very intelligent person may have a dull memory and vice-versa.
3. Intelligence is no guarantee against abnormal behaviour, backwardness and delinquency inspite of the fact that it is one of the major factor contributing towards achievement, adjustment and character formation.

THEORIES OF INTELLIGENCE

With the help of definitions of intelligence, we can be able to understand how intelligence operates, what type of behaviour of an individual makes him intelligent or unintelligent person. But these do not tell about the structure of intelligence or in other words, the different components or elements involved in one's intelligence. The theories of intelligence propagated by psychologists from time to time have tried to answer this question. These theories can be grouped under two heads, namely, factor theories and cognitive theories. However, in this text we will limit our discussion to factor theories.

Factor Theories of Intelligence

Let us try to discuss some of these theories below:

1. Unitary Theory

This theory holds that intelligence consists of one factor: simply a fund of intellectual competency, which is universal for all the activities of the individual.

A man who has vigour can move so much to East as to the West in a similar way if one has a fund of intelligence, he can utilize it to any area of his life and can be as successful in one area as in the other depending upon his fund of intelligence. But in actual life situations, the ideas propagated by this theory do not fit well. We find that the children who are bright in Mathematics may, despite serious interest and hard work, not be so good in Civics. A student very good in conducting Science experiments does not find himself equally competent in learning language. This makes us conclude that there is nothing like one single unitary factor in intelligence. Therefore, the unitary theory stands rejected.

2. Anarchic Theory or Multi Factor Theory

The main propagator of this theory was E.L. Thorndike. As the name suggests this theory considers intelligence a combination of numerous separate elements or factors, each one being a minute element of an ability. So, there is no such things as general intelligence (a single factor) and there are only many highly independent specific abilities which go into different tasks.

In this way, Monarchic and Anarchic theories hold the two extremes. Just as we cannot assume good intelligence, a guarantee of success in all the fields of human life, we cannot also say with certain specific type of abilities one will be entirely successful in a particular area and completely unsuccessful in the other areas. Actually as Gardner Murphy puts it, *"There is a certain positive relationship between brightness in one field and brightness in another and so on."* (1968, p. 358). This brings us to the conclusion that there should be a common factor running through all tasks. The failure to explain such phenomena gave birth to another theory named Spearman's two factor theory.

3. Spearman's Two Factor Theory

This theory was advocated by Spearman. According to him every different intellectual activity involves a general factor 'g' which is shared with all intellectual activities and a specific factor 's' which it shares with none.

Fig.15.1: Spearman's Two Factor Theory

In this way, he suggested that there is something which might be called general intelligence, a sort of general mental energy, running through all the different tasks but in addition to this general factor there are specific abilities, which make an individual able to deal with particular kinds of problems. For example, an individuals performance in Hindi is partly due to his general intelligence and partly to some kind of specific ability in language which he might possess *i.e.,* $g + s_1$ *or* in Mathematics his performance will be due to $g + s_2$; in drawing it will be due to $g + s_3$ and so on and so forth. The factor g (in lesser or greater degree) will enter in all specific activities. The total ability or intelligence of such an individual (symbolized as A), thus, will be expressed by the following equation schedule.

$$g + s_1 + s_2 + s_3 + \ldots = A.$$

This two factor theory of Spearman has been criticized on various grounds. The main reasons are given below:

(a) Spearman said that there are only two factors expressing intelligence but as we have seen above there are not only two but several factors (g, s_1, s_2, s_3 ... etc.)

(b) According to Spearman each job requires some specific ability. This view was not proper as it implied that there was nothing common in the jobs except a general factor and profession such as those of nursery, compounders and doctors could not be put in a group. In fact the factors s_1, s_2, s_3, s_4,...etc. are not mutually exclusive.

They overlap and give birth to certain common factors.

This idea of overlapping and grouping has given origin to a new theory called Group Factor Theory.

4. Thurstone's Group Factor Theory

For the factors not common to all of the intellectual abilities, but common to certain activities comprising a group, the term 'group factor' was suggested. Prominent among the propagators of this theory is L.L. Thurstone. While working on a test of primary mental abilities, he came to the conclusion that certain mental operations have in common a primary factor which gives them psychological and functional unity and which differentiates them from other mental operations. These mental operations constitute a group factor. So, there are a number of groups of mental abilities each of which has its own primary factor. Thurstone and his associates have differentiated nine such factors. They are:

(a) Verbal factor (V): concerns with comprehension of verbal relations, words and ideas.
(b) Spatial factor (S): involved in any task in which the subject manipulates an object imaginatively in space.
(c) Numerical factor (N): ability to do numerical calculations, rapidly and accurately.
(d) Memory factor (M): involving the ability to memorize quickly.
(e) Word Fluency Factor (W): involved whenever the subject is asked to think of the isolated words at a rapid rate.
(f) Inductive reasoning factor (RI): ability to generalize through specific examples.
(g) Deductive reasoning factor (RD): ability to make use of generalized result.
(h) Perceptual factor (P): ability to perceive objects accurately.
(i) Problem-solving ability factor (PS): ability to solve problems independently.

The weakest link in the group factor theory was that it discarded the concept of common factor. It did not take Thurstone very long to realise his mistake and to reveal a general factor in addition to group factors.

5. Guilford's Theory Involving a Model of Intellect

J.P. Guilford and his associates have developed a model of intellect on the basis of the factor analysis of several tests employed for testing intelligence of the human beings. They have come to the conclusion that any mental process or intellectual activity of the human being can be described in terms of three basic dimensions or parameters known as operation (the act of thinking or way of processing the information), contents (the terms in which we think or the type of information involved) and products (the ideas we come up with *i.e.* the fruits of a thinking).

Each of these parameters — operations, contents and products — may be further subdivided into some specific factors or elements. As a result operations may be subdivided into 5 specific factors, contents into 5 and products into 6. The interaction of these three parameters, according to Guilford, thus results into the 5 x 5 x 6 = 150 different elements or factors in one's intelligence. In a figural form, these 150 factors or independent abilities of the human beings along with the basic parameters and their divisions can be represented through a model named as Guilford's Model of Intellect or Intelligence (See figure 15.2).

GUILFORD'S MODEL OF INTELLIGENCE

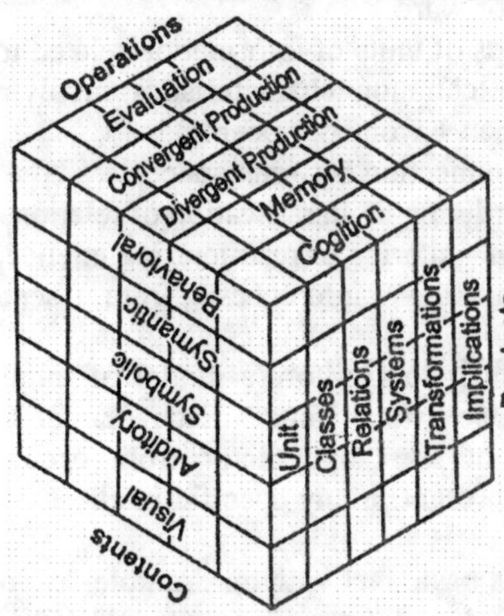

Fig. 15.2: This model proposes that intelligence consists of 150 independent abilities that result from the interaction of five types of contents, five types of operations and six types of products (after Guilford, 1982)

What is implied by these contents, operations and products can be understood through the following brief description:

Contents (The Type of Information involved)

- *Figural (visual)* — The properties of stimuli we can experience through the visual senses *e.g.* colour, size, shape, texture and other visual characteristics of figure.
- *Figural (Auditory)*— the properties of stimuli we can experience through the auditory senses *e.g.* voice and sound.
- *Symbolic*—numbers, letters, symbols, designs.
- *Semantic*— the meaning of words, ideas.

- *Behavioural*—the actions and expressions of people.

Operations (The Way of Processing the Information)

- *Cognition*—recognizing and discovering.
- *Memory*—retaining and recalling the contents of thought.
- *Divergent production*—producing a variety of ideas or solutions to a problem.
- *Convergent production*—producing a single best solution to a problem.
- *Evaluation*—taking decisions about the nature of the intellectual contents or gathered information whether it is positive or negative, good or, bad, etc.

Products (The results obtained through Operations)

- *Units*—Individual pieces of information limited in size *e.g.* a single number, letter or word.
- *Classes*—groups of units of information related to each other on the basis of some common characteristics involving a higher order concept (*e.g.* men + women = people).
- *Relations*—a connection between concepts.
- *Systems*—an ordering or classification of relations.
- *Transformation*—altering or restructuring intellectual contents.
- *Implication*—making inferences from separate pieces of information.

In this way according to Guilford's model of intellect, there are 150 factors operating in one's intelligence. Each one of these factors has a trigram symbol, *i.e.* at least one factor from each category of three parameters has to be present in any specific intellectual activity or mental task.

Let us illustrate this basic fact with an example. Suppose in case a child is asked to find out the day of the week on a particular date with the help of a calendar. In the execution of this mental task he will need mental operations like convergent thinking, memory and cognition. For carrying out these operations, he has to make use of the contents. In this particular case, he will make use of semantics, *i.e.* reading and understanding of the printed words and figures indicating days and dates of a particular month in the calendar. By carrying out mental operation with the help of contents he will finally arrive at the products. The day of the week to which the date in questions refers, represents the factor known as "relations". He may further transform and apply this knowledge to identify the days for contiguous dates or vice-versa.

Conclusion about the Factor's Theory of Intelligence

Each of the seven theories of intelligence described above attempt to provide a structure of intelligence in term of its constituents or factors.

These theories exhibit wide variations in terms of the numbers of factor that they consider important. The range of all such factors also varies from 1 (Unitary theory) to 150 (Guilford's Intellect Model). However, for understanding what goes on inside one's intelligence we must try to build an eclectic view by incorporating the essence of all the workable theories of intelligence. Consequently, any intellectual activity or mental task may be said to involve the following three kinds of basic factors, (arranged in the order as suggested by Vernon or in the form of model suggested by Guilford).

1. General Factor 'g' (Common to all task).
2. Specific Factors s_1, s_2, etc. (Specific to the task).
3. Group Factor 'G' (Common to the task belonging to a specific group).

Cognitive Theories of Intelligence

Apart from the above mentioned theories of intelligence grouped as factors theory of intelligence psychologists have also propagator number of theories explaining the mechanism of human intellect grouped as cognitive theories of intelligence. Here at present we would like to discuss in this chapter a few of such important theories named as below:

(i) Cattel and Horn's Theory of Intelligence
(ii) Sternberg's Information Processing Theory
(iii) Howard Gardner's Theory of Multiple Intelligence.

Cattell and Horn's Theory of Intelligence

Cattell (1965) and Horn (1978) proposed a theory of intelligence by distinguishing between two types of intelligence, i.e. *fluid intelligence* and *crystallized intelligence.* Although viewed as different and distinct, these two types of intelligence intermingle and interact to produce overall intelligence.

Fluid intelligence is considered to be the mental capacity of an individual, which is required for learning and problem solving. It is dependent on neurological development and is relatively free from the influences of education and culture. In other words, it is derived more from biological and genetic factors and is less influenced by training and experience. This type of intelligence is put to use when facing new and strange situations requiring adaptation, comprehension, reasoning, problem solving and identifying relationships, etc. It reaches full development by the end of an individual's adolescence.

Crystallized intelligence, on the other hand, is not a function of one's neurological development and therefore is not innate or unlearned like fluid intelligence. Rather, it is specially learned and is, therefore, dependent on education and culture. It involves one's acquired fund of general information consisting of knowledge and skills essential for performing different tasks in one's day-to-day life. It can be identified through one's fund of vocabulary, general knowledge of the world affairs, the knowledge of customs, traditions and rituals, manner of behaving in the society, handling of machines and tools, craftsmanship and art, computation and keeping of accounts and various other such tasks requiring knowledge, experience and practice.

Thus, while fluid intelligence is characterized by a relatively high degree of culture, education, experience and training-free performances in abstraction, thinking, reasoning and imagination, crystallized intelligence is known for its evolution through experience, training and interaction with of one's environment over a number of years. That is why it is found to continue to increase throughout one's life span.

Sternberg's Information Processing Theory of Intelligence

Robert Sternberg is distinctively known for his information processing theory of intelligence popularly named as Triachic Theory of Intelligence developed by him in as below.

A. Component or Analytical intelligence (analysis of information to solve problems)
B. Experiential or Creative intelligence (using prior knowledge as information in problem solving and creating new ideas)
C. Contextual or Practical intelligence (using intelligence to adapt to environmental demands or practically using cognition in doing day to day work).

He also added that each component is a basic unit of information processing and the task of information processing the following major steps.

- Encoding (identifying the relevant available information in the mind)
- Inferring (drawing the necessary inference)
- Mapping (establishing the relationship between a previous situation and the present one)
- Application (applying the inferred relationship)
- Justification (justifying the analyzed solution of the problem)
- Response (providing the best possible solution)

Let us now know what he has theorized about all the three components/types of intelligence.

A. Component or Analytical Intelligence (analysis of information to solve problems)

This type of intelligence demonstrated by an individual reflects how an individual relates to his internal world. It is demonstrable through the capacity of an individual to analyze the available information for sorting out away of solving a problem or performing a given cognitive act. People of such intelligence perform excellently on the standard intelligence tests and in displaying rational behaviour. Sternberg believes that componential or analytical Intelligence is based on the joint operations of three types of components namely (i) meta-components (ii) performance components and (iii) knowledge acquisition components of intelligence.

Meta-components control, monitor and evaluate cognitive processing going in one's mind. They prepare a theoretical ground work for the execution of a task in the form of analysis of the problem, selection of the strategies, monitoring of the possible solutions and interpretation of the feedback about performance etc. In fact, as a higher order processes, they carry out executive functions and decide for the performance and knowledge components what to do. Their contribution helps the performance and knowledge components to carry out the responsibilities enshrined on their shoulders.

Performance components execute the directions and strategies provided by the meta-components. They are the action centers and thus represent the actual mental processes used for the execution or completion of a cognitive act such as problem solving. Cognitive processes associated with this component enable one to encode stimuli, hold information in short-term memory, make calculations, perform mental calculates, mentally compare different stimuli, retrieve information from long-term memory etc. Performance components go beyond meta-components in that they perform the function also of weighing the merit and or consequences of actions in comparison to other options rather than simply identifying options.

Knowledge-acquisition components represent the mental processes used in gaining and storing new knowledge, *i.e.,* the ability to learn new information in order to solve a potential problem or doing a cognitive act. This type is much more abstract and mayor may not be directly related to a current problem-solving task (Driscoll, 2001). The strategies you use to help memorize things exemplify the processes that fall into this category.

B. Experiential or Creative intelligence (using prior knowledge as information in problem solving and creating new ideas).

This component of intelligence focuses experience. It is involved in using the past experience creatively to solve new problems. Thus, experiential intelligence is reflected in creative performance. Persons who are high in this component quickly find what information is crucial in a given situation, and how the information is to be used to reach the target. This is the kind of intelligence shown by many scientific genius and inventors such as Einstein, Newton, Freud, C.V. Raman and J. C. Bose or artists and cartoonists like Michael Angel and R.K. Laxman.

C. Contextual or Practical Intelligence

This component of intelligence is associated with the contextual aspect or practical application of one's intelligence and reflects how one relates to the external world about him or her. In its basic operation contextual or practical component of one's intelligence involves the ability to grasp, understand and deal with the practical management of day-to-day life affairs, *i.e.,* how to get rid of trouble, how to face the environmental demands, and how to get along with the society. Sternberg (1985) has termed it as "mental activity directed toward purposive adaptation to, and selection and shaping of, real world environments relevant to one's life."

In seeking purpose or goals of his life, thus one has to make use of his contextual intelligence working in a real way in that particular context or situation. For this purpose his practical intelligence may persuade him for *(a)* adaptation to present environment *(b)* selection of a relatively favourable environment instead of the existing one, and (c) modifying the present environment to fit to one's skills, needs, and value.

Contextual or practical Intelligence can be said to be intelligence that operates in the real world. Sternberg believes that this kind of practical intelligence is the tacit knowledge or street smartness. It consists of all of the important information about practical reality of the world about which one is taught neither in schools nor in colleges. According to him, tacit knowledge is more important for success than the obvious "bookish" knowledge. The standard IQ tests are unable to tap contextual or practical intelligence. In measuring this facet, not only mental skills but attitudes and emotional factors that can influence intelligence are also measured.

Conclusion and Significance

In this way, the concept, and structure of intelligence proposed by Robert Sternberg through his information processing theory of intelligence thus went beyond the concept of IQ measurement and traditional cognitive processes as it gave greater freedom and power to an individual to solve his day to day problems and to become the master of his destiny.

Moreover, Sternberg's theory is also credited in brining into limelight the impact of social interaction on one's cognitive development. In fact, one of the three parts of his theory is based on the context in which learning takes place; this subpart of the theory specifies that intelligent behaviour is defined by the socio-cultural context in which it takes place and involves adaptation to the environment, selection of better environments, and shaping of the present environment. The addition of social context as a factor in cognitive development links Sternberg to the interactional theories of development given by Bruner (1977, 1986) and Vygotsky (1978). These theories, and others of this type, are premised on the assumption that learning does not occur in a vacuum. Therefore, one must discuss the social and cultural contexts of learning and as a result the curriculum and teaching learning experiences given to the children must be essentially linked with the essential social interaction and socio-cultural influences.

Howard Gardner's Theory of Multiple Intelligence

Howard Gardner's theory of multiple intelligence represents a family of the cognitive theories of intelligence (other than the factorial theories). These theories provide a workable cognitive base for the understanding and explanation of human intelligence. Howard Gardner of Harvard University proposed such a cognitive theory of intelligence in the name of "Theory of Multiple Intelligence". His theory first appeared in his 1983 book "Frames of Mind: The Theory of Multiple Intelligences". Where he suggested that all people have different kinds of "intelligences". Through his views expressed in his theory Gardner tried to challenge the traditional views and notions regarding the composition and functioning of human intelligence. Gardner questioned the validity of the functioning of one's intelligence as a composite unit capable of performing all cognitive functions according to the degree of intelligence possessed and measured through a composite intelligence test. He asserted that there is no unitary or single intelligence like 'g' operating or running in the functioning of human minds but there are several or multiple intelligences functioning in their own ways for directing and operating the human cognitive functioning and it is why some may be found to excel in one or the other areas of their cognitive functioning *i.e.* learning the language, mathematics, music, dance, painting or maintaining intra-personal or inter-personal relationships. He raised his voice regarding the use of the so called composite intelligence tests for testing the intelligence of human being. He asked how an individual's intellectual capacities could be captured in a single measure of intelligence while it has been properly seen that people do not have just a intellectual capacity, but have many different intelligences very much associated with different areas or fields of their cognitive functioning. Believing in the natural phenomenon of individual differences found in the human beings, he strongly asserted that people in general possess different kinds of minds and intellectual capacities to learn, remember, perform and function in the different types of life situations. Therefore, it is quite absurd to assume a single type of intelligence or intellectual current flowing in the minds of the human beings. Rather, there are multiple sets of varying intelligences owned by the people depending upon their hereditary and environmental composition. Every one of us possesses a unique set of multiple intelligences that distinguishes us from one another.

What are Multiple Intelligences?

Gardner tried to give a quite broad base to the concept of intelligence and its measurement by providing a multiple frame. He suggested that human intelligence or cognitive competence can be better described as a set of an individual's multiple abilities, talents and mental skills related to a multiple number of domains of knowledge in a particular cultural setting. Elaborating his pluralistic view of intelligence, further, he concluded that there are seven independent types of intelligence that grow and develop differently in different people, depending upon their hereditary characteristics or environmental experiences. These different types of intelligence named as multiple intelligences by Gardner were outlined as below.

1. Linguistic-Verbal Intelligence
2. Logical-Mathematical Intelligence
3. Spatial Intelligence
4. Musical Intelligence
5. Bodily-Kinaesthetic Intelligence
6. Intrapersonal Intelligence
7. Interpersonal Intelligence

Let us know about these intelligences one by one.

1. *Linguistic-verbal intelligence:* This type of human intelligence is responsible for all kinds of linguistic competence-abilities, talents and skills, available in human beings. It can be best broken down into components like syntax, semantics and pragmatics as well as more school-oriented skills such as written or oral expression and understanding. This type of intelligence is most visible in professionals like lawyers, lecturers, writers and lyricists, and a number of other professionals exploiting linguistic intelligence.

The students loaded with this type of intelligence may be seen to demonstrate the features like below.

- Good at remembering written and spoken information
- Enjoys reading and writing
- Good at debating or giving persuasive speeches
- Able to explain things well
- Often uses humour when telling stories

2. *Logical-mathematical intelligence:* This type of intelligence is responsible for all types of abilities, talents and skills in areas related to logic and mathematics. It can be broken down into components like deductive reasoning, inductive reasoning, scientific thinking including solving of logical puzzles, carrying out calculations and the like. Professionals like mathematicians, philosophers, physicists, etc. are found to exhibit this type of intelligence in abundance. The students possessing this intelligence may be seen to demonstrate the features like below in a good amount.

- Excellent problem-solving skills
- Enjoys thinking about abstract ideas
- Likes conducting scientific experiments
- Good at solving complex computations

3. *Visual-spatial intelligence:* This type of intelligence is concerned with the abilities, talents and skills involving the representation and manipulation of spatial configuration and relationship. Many of us as adults make use of this kind of intelligence in the sphere of our work. For example, painters may be seen to demonstrate spatial intelligence through their use of space when applying pigments to a canvas. This is also true of professionals like land surveyors, architects, engineers, mechanics, navigators, sculptures and

chess players — who are found to rely upon the spatial intelligence in their own way. The students having this type of intelligence have been found to possess the following characteristics in a good amount.

- Enjoys reading and writing
- Good at putting puzzles together
- Good at interpreting pictures, graphs and charts
- Enjoys drawing, painting and the visual arts
- Recognizes patterns easily

4. *Musical intelligence:* This type of intelligence covers the abilities, talents and skills pertaining to the field of music. It may be well demonstrated through one's capacity for pitch discrimination, sensitivity to rhythm, texture and timbre, ability to hear themes in music; and in its most integrated forms, the production of music through performance or composition. It is visible in a quite large proportion in professionals like musicians and composers. The students possessing this type of intelligence may be seen to demonstrate the features like below in a good amount.

- Enjoy singing and playing musical instruments
- Recognizes musical patterns and tones easily
- Good at remembering songs and melodies
- Rich understanding of musical structure, rhythm and notes

5. *Bodily kinesthetic intelligence:* This type of intelligence is concerned with the set of abilities, talents and skills involved in using one's body or its various parts to perform skillful and purposeful movements. A child may be seen to demonstrate such intelligence in moving expressively in response to different musical and verbal stimuli or bending different body parts in organised sports. Among professionals, dancers, athletes and surgeons may be seen to demonstrate a high degree of bodily-kinesthetic intelligence in their respective fields. The students possessing this type of intelligence may be found to imbibe with the following features in a good amount.

- Good at dancing and sports
- Enjoy creating things with their hands
- Excellent physical coordination
- Tends to remember by doing, rather than hearing or seeing

6. *Interpersonal intelligence:* The counterpart of intrapersonal intelligence in one's cognitive structure is interpersonal intelligence. It consists of the abilities to understand individuals other than one's self and one's relations to others. In addition, it includes the ability to act productively, based on the understanding of others. The knowledge and understanding of others is the quality that is needed for social interactions in one's day-to-day life. In practical life, this type of intelligence is most visible among psychotherapists, teachers, sales people, politicians and religious leaders. The students having this typing intelligence may be found to possess the following features in a good amount.

- Good at communicating verbally
- Skilled nonverbal communicators
- See situations from different perspectives
- Create positive relationships with others
- Good at resolving conflict in groups

7. *Intrapersonal intelligence:* This type of intelligence consists of an individual's abilities to enable him to know his self. It includes knowledge and understanding of one's own cognitive strengths, styles and mental functioning, as well as one's feelings, range of emotions and skills to utilize one's fund of knowledge in practical situations. In brief, intrapersonal intelligence helps an individual to understand his own self by providing an insight into his total behaviour — what he feels, thinks or does. It is, therefore, said to be the most private of the intelligences that a person possesses. On account of its secret and private nature, the access to this type of intelligence in an individual is available only through self-expression, *i.e.* language, music, visual art and similar other forms of expression. In our practical life, this type of intelligence is demonstrated by yogis, saints and masters of Zen. The students possessing this type of intelligence may be found to have the features like below in a good amount.

- Good at analyzing their strengths and weaknesses
- Enjoys analyzing theories and ideas
- Excellent self-awareness
- Clearly understands the basis for their own motivations and feelings

In addition to the seven intelligences discussed above, Gardner in the later years of his research study arrived with his "eighth intelligence" named as naturalistic intelligence. Now Gardner's theory of multiple intelligence is known to consist of eight intelligences instead of the seven as laid down earlier. Throwing light on his 'eighth intelligence' Gardner writes as under "The naturalist intelligence refers to the ability to recognize and classify plants, minerals, and animals, including rocks and grass and all variety of flora and fauna. The ability to recognize cultural artifacts like cars or sneakers may also depend on the naturalist intelligence. Some people from an early age are extremely good at recognizing and classifying artefacts. For example, we all know kids who, at 3 or 4, are better at recognizing dinosaurs than most adults."

According to Gardner, thus individuals who are high in this type of intelligence are more in tune with nature and are often interested in nurturing, exploring the environment and learning about other species. These individuals are said to be highly aware of even subtle changes to their environments.

The students having such type of intelligence may be found to possess the characteristics like below in a good amount.

- Interested in subjects such as botany, biology and zoology
- Good at categorizing and cataloging information easily

- May enjoy camping, gardening, hiking and exploring the outdoors
- Doesn't enjoy learning unfamiliar topics that have no connection to nature

Implications of Gardner's Theory of Multiple Intelligences

Gardner's theory of Multiple Intelligences carries a quite wide and useful applications in terms of its use in the education of the learners with a number of variations and differences in their intelligences (abilities, strengths, talents and capacities) and learning needs. We can summarize it in the ways mentioned below:

1. Gardner's concept of multiple intelligences tells the teachers and parents in a clear way that the concept of overall general intellectual capacity 'g' is at best limited and at worst educationally misleading. It is not at all essential that an individual highly loaded with linguistic and / or logical mathematical abilities will also display exceptional ability (or even interest) in all or any remaining domains, *i.e.* spatial and musical abilities, etc. It happens on account of a sort of autonomy maintained by each type of the seven different human intelligence which are said to be quite capable of developing independently of each other and also quite independently or an all-encompassing general intelligence, "g".

2. Gardner's theory of intelligence emphasizes that a person needs all eight types of intelligences for his useful and productive functioning in society. Therefore, in our schools these should be an equal emphasis on the development and use of all these types of intelligences instead of verbal and mathematically intelligences usually taken care of in our traditional classroom setting.

3. Since every learner is supposed to have a unique set of multiple intelligences (with variation in abilities and learning needs), teachers are required to present the subject material in a way suiting to most or all of the intelligences. For example, when teaching about the revolutionary war, a teacher can show students battle maps, play revolutionary war songs, organize a role play of the signing of the Declaration of Independence, and have the students read a novel about life during that period. This kind of presentation not only excites students about learning, but it also allows a teacher to reinforce the same material in a variety of ways. By activating a wide assortment of intelligences, teaching in this manner can facilitate a deeper understanding of the subject material.

4. Everyone is born possessing the seven intelligences. Nevertheless, all students will come into the classroom with different sets of developed intelligences. This means that each child will have his own unique set of intellectual strengths and weaknesses. These sets determine how easy (or difficult) it is for a student to learn information when it is presented in a particular manner. This is commonly referred to as a learning style. Many learning styles can be found within one classroom. Therefore, it is impossible, as well as impractical, for a teacher to accommodate every

lesson to all of the learning styles found within the classroom. Nevertheless the teacher can show students how to use their more developed intelligences to assist in the understanding of a subject which normally employs their weaker intelligences (Lazear, 1992). For example, the teacher can suggest that an especially musically intelligent child learn about the revolutionary war by making up a song about what happened.

5. Gardner's theory of multiple intelligence suggests to bring changes in the ways and means of assessing the students' success. The things conveyed in this connection may be summarized as below.

- As the education system has stressed the importance of developing mathematical and linguistic intelligences, it often bases student success only on the measured skills in those two intelligences. Supporters of Gardner's Theory of Multiple Intelligences believe that this emphasis is unfair. Children whose musical intelligences are highly developed, for example, may be overlooked for gifted programs or may be placed in a special education class because they do not have the required math or language scores. Teachers must seek to assess their students' learning in ways which will give an accurate overview of their strengths and weaknesses.
- As children do not learn in the same way, they cannot be assessed in a uniform fashion. Therefore, it is important that a teacher create an "intelligence profiles" for each student. Knowing how each student learns will allow the teacher to properly assess the child's progress (Lazear, 1992). This individualized evaluation practice will allow a teacher to make more informed decisions on what to teach and how to present information.
- Traditional tests *(e.g.* multiple choice, short answer, essay...) require students to show their knowledge in a predetermined manner. Supporters of Gardner's theory claim that a better approach to assessment is to allow students to explain the material in their own ways using the different intelligences. Preferred assessment methods include student portfolios, independent projects, student journals, and assigning creative tasks. An excellent source for a more in-depth discussion on these different evaluation practices is Lazear (1992).

6. Gardner's theory of multiple intelligence has a huge potentiality to help the students in developing more successful and functionable adults in their social life and cultural settings by providing a more authentic theoretical foundation for recognizing the different abilities and talents of the students. This theory acknowledges that while all students may not be verbally or mathematically gifted, children may have an expertise in other areas, such as music, spatial relations, or interpersonal knowledge. Approaching and assessing learning in this manner may allow a wider range of students to successfully participate in classroom learning. It is therefore needed on the part of school authorities to have variations in their activities

and programs (curricular and co-curricular) to meet the needs and potentials of the learners in view of their cognitive structure (set of multiple intelligence possessed by the individual learner).

7. Gardner's theory of multiple intelligence advocates to make use of different types of tests and assessment devices for assessing the cognitive development or intellectual functioning of the students with regard to all the eight types of intelligences instead of making a single composite test for assessing one's level of intellectual functioning.

8. Gardner's concept of multiple intelligences has provided a great relief and opportunities to the learners for their adequate learning and accomplishments despite their weaknesses in the learning and use of language and mathematical skills.

The other skills related to six other intelligences namely visual-spatial, musical, bodily kinesthetic, interpersonal and intrapersonal carry essential significance and importance for the accomplishment and success in one's life. Therefore, the students should never be discouraged, neglected or denied opportunity to learn and progress by getting engaged in the activities and learning areas not dominated by verbal or mathematical abilities.

In this way, the path shown by Gardner's theory of multiple intelligences may prove a big guiding factor and helping hand in arranging or organizing learning experiences for the learners characterised with wide individual differences, variations, styles and learning needs.

MEASUREMENT OF INTELLIGENCE

We are only familiar with that intelligence of an individual which is manifested by him on an intelligence test or tests. Psychologists have devised so many such tests for the measurement of intelligence.

Classification of Intelligence Tests

1. As far as the administrative point of view is concerned the intelligence tests can be classified into two broad categories namely—

(a) *Individual Test*: In which only one individual is tested at a time.

(b) *Group Test*: In which a group of individuals is tested at a time.

2. Another way of classifying the intelligence tests is based on the form of the test. Accordingly there are two types of tests:

(a) *Verbal or Language Tests:*

These tests make use of language. Here the instructions are given in words (either in written or oral form or both). Individuals are required to use language as well as paper and pencil for giving the responses. The test content is loaded with verbal material.

(b) *Non-Verbal and Non-Language Tests:*

These tests involve such activities in which the use of language is not necessary. The use of language is eliminated from test content and response except in giving directions.

The typical examples of such non-verbal tests are Performance

Tests. The principal characteristics of these tests are given below:

(a) Test contents of these tests are in the form of material objects.

(b) What an individual has to do is indicated by the tester either through oral instructions or by pantomime or signs.

(c) Individual's responses depends upon what he does or performs rather than by anything he says or writes.

(d) Generally these tests are individual tests. As Dr. Filial observes, *'These cannot be used as group tests, chiefly because it is necessary to supervise the individual testee at work and give him necessary direction."* (1972, p. 265).

If we try to have a final picture of all types of tests in intelligence we will have to keep in view both the ways of classifying them as mentioned above. All these types of intelligence tests can be represented — diagrammatically as follows:

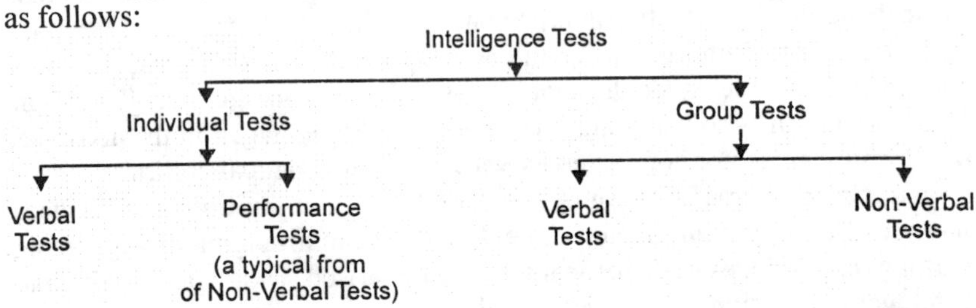

Now we will discuss these types one by one.

Individual Verbal Tests

The tests involving the use of language and administered to an individual at a time belong to this category. As an example of such tests we can quote Stanford-Binet Scale. It is the revised form of the Binet-Simon test. Actually, French Psychologist Alfred Binet is the father of intelligence test construction movement. He, along with Theodore Simon prepared a test as early as in 1905, containing of 30 items (arranged in order of increasing difficulty) graded for different levels. The test included such items as:

At age 3-Point out to nose, eyes and mouth.

At age 7-Tell what is missing in the unfinished picture.

In 1931, the first American revision of this test was published by Terman at Stanford University and in 1937 another revision was carried on with the help of Maud A. Merrill. This as well as 1960's revision is called *Stanford Binet Scale* and widely used as an individual intelligence test.

The tests in this scale are grouped into age levels, extending from age 2 to 22 years. The tasks to be performed by the testees in these various tests range from simple manipulation to abstract reasoning.

Binet Tests have been adopted in India too. The first such attempt was made by Dr. C.H. Rice in 1922 when he published his "Hindustani Binet Performance Point Scale." This was an adaptation of the Binet test along with some performance tests in addition. The State Manovigyan Shala of Uttar Pradesh has made a Hindi Version of Standford Binet test. This test is divided into several age-groups and named as Budhi Pariksha Anooshilan.

The other common Verbal Individual Intelligence test (used in India) is Samanya Budhi Pariksha (Pt. 1 and 2). This test is an Indian adaptation of the well known test of William Stephenson. It has been prepared by State Bureau of Educational and Vocational Guidance, Gwalior (M.P.).

Individual Performance Tests

As said earlier, the complete non-verbal or non-language tests of intelligence for testing an individual at a time come into this classification. In these the contents and responses are in the form of performance and language is not used at all. In these tests the items which require responses in terms of motor activities are included. Generally the activities, on which the performance of an individual is tested, are of the following types:

(*i*) *Block building cr cube construction:* Where the subject is asked to make a structure or design by means of blocks or cubes supplied to him. The examples of the tests, involving such type of activities are Merril Palmer Block Building, Koh's Block Design Test, Alexander's pass-along Test etc.

(*ii*) *To fit the blocks in the holes:* Test material of such types provides numerous blocks and a board in which there are holes corresponding to these blocks. The subject has to fit the blocks in these corresponding holes (in the board). Examples are Seguin Form Board Test and Goddard Form Board Test.

(*iii*) *Tracing a maze:* Test material consists of a series of mazes of increasing difficulty, each printed on a separate sheet. The subject is required to trace with pencil, the path from entrance to exit. Porteus Maze Test is an example involving such type of activities.

(*iv*) *Picture arrangement or picture completion:* In picture arrangement test the task is to arrange in series the given pictures whereas in picture completion test the subject is required to complete the pictures with the help of given pieces cut of each picture. The Healy pictorial completion test is a good example of such test which provides a good estimate of the intelligence of the subject without making use of language.

As seen above, these tests try to emphasize upon one or the other types of performance. Instead of using one or two tests a group of performance tests, organised either into a scale or battery, are used for a comprehensive picture of an individual's mental ability. Some of the popularly known scales are:

(a) The Pinter Patterson Scale.
(b) The Arthur Point Scale.
(c) Alexander's Battery of Performance Tests.

In India too the attempts for constructing such batteries have been made. Dr. Chander Mohan Bhatia's work, in this regard, deserves special mention. He has developed a battery of performance tests known as 'Bhatia's Battery of Performance Tests.'

It contains the following five sub-tests:

(a) Koh's Block Design Test.
(b) Alexander's Pass-along Test.
(c) Pattern Drawing Test.
(d) Immediate memory test for digits (with an alternative form suitable for illiterates).
(e) Picture Construction Test.

Last three tests in this battery have been constructed by Mr. Bhatia himself while the former two have been borrowed.

Wechsler Bellevue Intelligence Scale

This scale is available in two forms. The one form WISC is used for children and the other WAIS for adults. It is an individual test which has a unique quality of being named as verbal and performance scale simultaneously.

The scale consists of eleven sub-tests. Six sub-tests make up a verbal scale and five performance scale. These tests are listed below in the order in which they are administered. Verbal Scale:

1. Test of General information.
2. Test of General comprehension.
3. Test of Arithmetic reasoning.
4. Test of distinction between similarities.
5. Test of Digit span.
6. Test of Vocabulary.
7. Digit symbol test.
8. Picture completion test.
9. Block Design test.
10. Object assembly test.

The scores on these sub-tests are added to give an idea of an individual's intelligence.

The Group Vertical Intelligence Tests

The tests which necessitate the use of language and are applied to a group of individuals at a time come under this category. Some of the earlier tests belonging to this category are:

(a) Army Alpha Test (developed in World War).
(b) Army General Classification Test (developed in World War II).

Today we have so many group verbal tests. In India too, the attempts have been made to construct such tests. Some of the popular tests of this nature are:

1. C.I.E. Verbal Group Test of Intelligence (Hindi) constructed by Prof. Uday Shankaı.

2. The Group Test of General Mental Ability (Samuhik Mansik Yogyata Pariksha) constructed by Dr. J.S. Jalota (Hindi).
3. Group Test of intelligence, prepared by Bureau of Psychology, Allahabad (Hindi).
4. Prayag Mehta's Group Intelligence Test (Samuhik Budhi Pariksha, Hindi). This test has been published by Mansayan, Delhi.
5. General Mental Abilities Test prepared by Dr. P. S. Hundal of Punjab University (Punjabi).
6. Group Verbal intelligence test prepared by Dr. P. Gopala Pillai of the Kerala University (Malayalam).
7. Samuhik Budhi Pariksha (Hindi), prepared by Sh. P. L. Shrimali of Vidya Bhavan G.S. Teacher College, Udaipur.
8. Samuhik Budhi Ki Jaanch (Hindi), prepared by Shri S.M. Mohsin, Educational and Vocational Guidance Bureau, Bihar, Patna.

The Group Non-Verbal Intelligence Tests

These tests do not necessitate the use of language and are applicable to the group of individuals at a time.

The difference between performance test (used for an individual) and non-verbal tests (used for a group) is of degree as far as their non-verbal nature is concerned. The performance tests require the manipulation of concrete objects or materials, supplied in the test, by the subject. Responses are purely motor in character and seldom require the use of paper and pencil by the testee (except in a case like Maze test etc.). Where the test material in the non-verbal tests, used for group testing, is provided in booklet and requires the use of pencil by the tests.

Still in these tests material does not contain words or numerical figures. It contains pictures, diagrams and geometrical figures etc. printed in a booklet. The subject is required to do such activities as to fill in some empty spaces, to draw some simple figures, to point out similarities and dissimilarities etc. In this way although the subject uses paper-pencil he does not need to know words or numerical figures. What he is to do is explained clearly by the examiner usually through clear demonstrations so as to make the least possible use of language.

The examples of such type of tests are:

1. *Army Beta Test.* It was developed in World War I, in U.S.A. for testing the intelligence of those soldiers who were either illiterates or were not used to English language.

2. *Chicago Non-verbal Test:* This non-verbal test has been proved most useful for the young children aged 12 and 13 years.

3. *Raven's Progressive Matrices Test:* This test was developed in U.K. It is a very much popular non-verbal group test of intelligence. The test has been designed to evaluate the subjects' ability:

(a) to see relationship between geometric figures or designs.

(b) to perceive the structure of the design in order to select the appropriate part for completion of each pattern.

4. *C.I.E. Non-verbal Group Test of Intelligence:* Originally prepared by J.W. Jenkins, the test is printed by C.I.E. for adaptation into Hindi medium schools. The test contains such terms as instructed below:

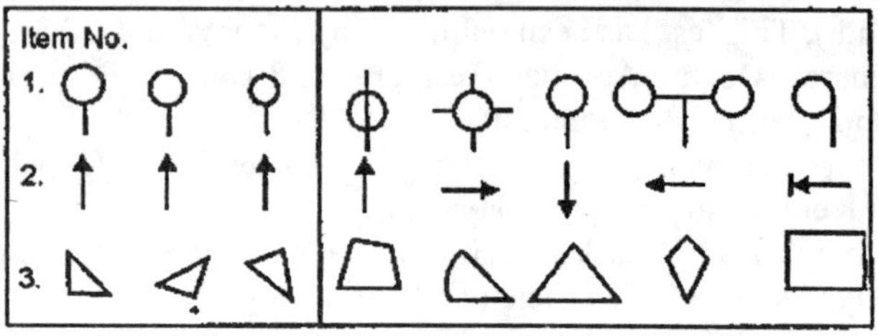

Fig. 15.3: An Item from C.I.E. Non-Verbal Group Test of Intelligence

Individual v/s Group Tests

Individual and group tests have their advantages as well as disadvantages. We can compare them on the following lines:

Individual Tests	*Group Tests*
1. With these tests only one individual is tested at a time. They cannot be administered to a group and this makes them costly in terms of time, labour and money.	1. These tests have two fold advantage. In addition to their applicability in testing a group of individuals at a time, they can also be administered to the individuals separately. Testing of so many individuals at a time gives them the advantages of saving time, money and labour.
2. Individual tests have the unique advantage of being used for children as well as adults.	2. Group tests cannot be given to young children below 9 or 10 years of age.
3. As examiner has a close contact with the subject, he can take into account all personal and emotional factors and like wise have all those additional pieces of information which may prove useful for the interpretation of an individual's test scores.	3. The examiner does not have a desirable contact with the subject. He cannot detect and rectify influence of such factors as ill health, mood, poor social background or practice and coaching that might have been given to a subject for boosting his scores. What the examiner gets at all is the numerical score and nothing of additional information as obtained in individual tests.
4. Individual tests are not as objective and standardized as group tests. Their administration, scoring and interpretation require well trained and competent examiners.	4. Group tests are more objective and standardized in comparison to individual tests. The manuals and instructions provided with these tests make their administration, scoring

	and interpretation so easy that a need of such trained personnel is seldom felt.

Verbal Test V/s Non-Verbal and Performance

What led to the construction of non-verbal and performance tests, when verbal tests were there for testing the intelligence, is a relevant question to be asked. Verbal tests as already said, gave emphasis on linguistic ability. They were loaded with verbal material-words and numerical. Hence, the persons having linguistic superiority were always on the side of advantage in comparison to the persons having language weakness. To do away with such evils, non-verbal and performance tests were put to use. In brief the advantages of these tests over verbal tests are as under:

1. Performance tests are useful for those who have language handicaps due to some of the following reasons:

(a) They may belong to the foreign language speaking groups.

(b) They may be illiterates not knowing how to read and write.

(c) They may have difficulties in reading, writing and listening due to defects in their sense organs (persons like deaf, dumb etc.),

(d) They may be younger children who are not yet able to read and write well.

(e) They may be mentally retarded or mentally deficient children and therefore, are very slow in grasping and responding to the verbal items.

(f) They may belong to unprivileged class or strata of the society and hence have got limited educational opportunities.

2. Verbal test belonging to one region contains the material which has a direct relationship with the language or culture of that region or country. Non-verbal and performance tests are more or less language and culture free and hence can be used for cross cultural and linguistic study of intelligence.

3. They can be proved useful in the efforts to determine aptitude and promise in shop work, mechanical job, etc.

Limitations of Non-Verbal and Performance Tests

1. They may not be able to predict scholastic success in schools as do the verbal tests simply because school work itself is predominantly verbal.
2. They, specially performance tests, are very costly and pose difficulty in carrying from one place to another.
3. They are more susceptible to practice-effects and chance successes are more frequent than in the case of verbal tests. Therefore, they are less reliable than verbal tests.
4. These tests are limited in a range of mental functioning tested, such as they do not require much use of the ability to make abstractions

and to deal with concepts. That is why they are not able to differentiate among above-average individuals.

In this way, we come across the merits and limitations of these tests. In fact the testing of mental ability is a comprehensive task and cannot be solely left either to the verbal or performance tests. For taking a reliable view of a person's intellectual ability the following things should be kept in mind:

(a) Performance test should be taken as a supplement to verbal tests and vice-versa.

(b) No single test or tests is suitable for this purpose. There should be an attack from so many angles.

CAN INTELLIGENCE BE MEASURED LIKE A PIECE OF CLOTH?

Measurement of intelligence is not possible in the same way as we measure a piece of cloth or temperature of our body. Why it is not possible can be understood through the following discussion:

1. *Nature of the thing we want to measure*: Intelligence is not a thing. It is only an idea, an abstraction. Therefore, its measurement is not possible like the measurement of a piece of cloth, wood or land, etc.

2. *Nature of the instrument or the scale by which intelligence is measured*: In measuring piece of cloth we use scales made up of absolute units. For measuring temperature of the body we use thermometers having degrees as units of measurement. In such measurement we use scales made up of absolute units and the instruments give somewhat reliable and valid results. But in case of intelligence measurement we don't have such scales. Here, as Griffith observes *"the standard of measurement is a group performance"*. (1993, p. 138).

Therefore, when we measure intelligence of an individual with the help of an intelligence test we try to interpret the resulting score in the light of norms established (group performance) by the author of the test. In this way, one's intelligence is determined relatively to the classified group to which he belongs. So, where in the case of a piece of cloth absolute measurement is possible, here in case of intelligence measurement we have relative measurement.

With the differences in the nature of measuring instruments, we can observe that whereas in case of a piece of cloth and temperature of the body it is convenient to use the measuring instrument when and where we require its need, it is difficult to use intelligence test with the similar convenience and ease. The administration as well as interpretation of these tests requires sufficient competency, skill and labour on the part of the examiner.

In this way, we can see that the measurement of intelligence is not so simple, definite, reliable and valid task as the measurement of a piece of cloth or the temperature of a body.

CONCEPT OF MENTAL AGE AND INTELLIGENCE QUOTIENT

As we have used above the term mental age and I.Q. in the interpretation of intelligence test results, it is worth-while to know something about them.

Mental age: The term mental age was used for the by Binet. What is this concept can be clarified through the following example.

Suppose there is a test which has 100 questions (like Jalota's test) and suppose the majority of the subjects whose age is 13 years 6 months, answer successfully 48 questions, then any individual who earns a score of 48, regardless of his chronological age, will be said to have a mental age of 13 years 6 months.

Intelligence Quotient (I.Q.): This term was initiated by the German Psychologist William Stern and put into wide practice by Terman. It appeared to Stern that if a child was 6 years old (chronologically), but could do what an 8 years old normally does he $\frac{M.A.}{C.A.}$ would be 8/6 or 1.33 as bright as the average. And in this way he made the ratio, measure of the rate of mental development of an individual. The ratio was given the name of Intelligence Quotient (I.Q.). To do away with the decimal point the ratio was again multiplied by 100 and thus the formula to calculate I.Q. was known as

$$\text{I.Q.} = \frac{\text{Mental Age (M.A.)}}{\text{Chronological Age (C.A.)}} \times 100 \text{ (as used in Standford Binet Scales).}$$

$$\text{or I.Q.} = \frac{\text{Attained or actual score}}{\text{Expected mean score for age}} \times 100 \text{ (as used by Wechsler).}$$

CLASSIFICATION OF I.Q.

By making use of the formula of I.Q. given by Stern, Terman tried to classify the individuals into certain specific categories on the basis of the data collected through the administration of his intelligence tests for terming them average, below average and above average as given below:

I.Q.	*Level of Intelligence*
140 and above	Gifted or Genius
120 -140	Very Superior
110 -120	Superior
90 -110	Normal or Average
75 - 90	Border Line and Dull
50 -75	Morons
25 - 50	Imbecile
Below 25	Idiot

However, as far as, the classification based on the intelligence tests suitable to the Indian conditions, is concerned the, following one presented by professor Udai Shanker may work well.

I.Q.	*Level of Intelligence*
140 and above	Genius
120-140	Very Superior
110-120	Superior
90-110	Average
75-90	Border Line and Dull
50-75	Morons or Feeble minded
25-50	Imbecile
Below 25	Idiots

THE CONSTANCY OF I.Q.

As mentioned earlier, intelligence goes on growing upto 16 or 18 years of age, but I.Q. for most of the individuals remains constant. Primarily I.Q. provides a ratio for knowing how bright an individual is as compared with some of his own age. Actually, it is an index which is independent not only of the particular score which an individual makes on a particular scale but also of the particular age at which he happens to make it. It is thus a measure which acquaints us with the relative brightness or intellectual possibilities of an individual, more or less permanently.

It is true that an individual grows in intelligence but the whole group (the other individuals of his own age) also grow at the same rate as that particular individual does. Thus I.Q., a measure of defining relative brightness or intellectual possibilities of an individual remains practically constant. Under ordinary circumstances (accident or disease exempted) an individual's I.Q. is supposed to remain constant throughout life or at least throughout the age limits covered by the scale. This property of I.Q. is referred to as constancy of I.Q. by psychologists.

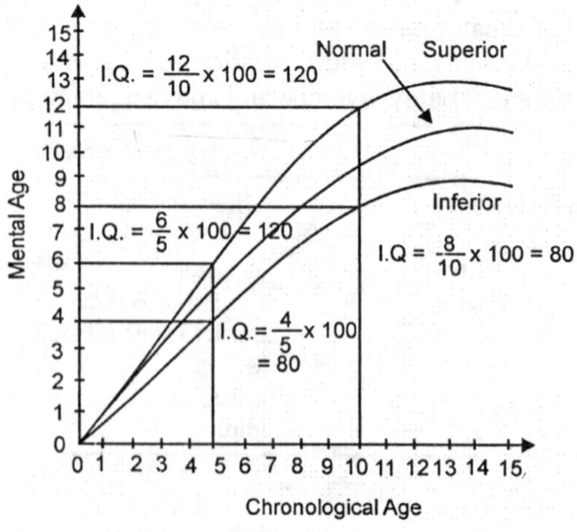

Fig. 15.4: Hypothetical Growth Curves which give a Constant I.Q. from H.E. Garrett's and M.R. Shneck.

USES AND LIMITATIONS OF INTELLIGENCE TESTS

Intelligence tests have their advantages as well as drawbacks. Below we list them one by one.

Uses of Intelligence Tests

1. *For the purpose of selection:* Intelligence tests are often used for the purpose of making selection of the suitable candidates for activities like.
   (i) admission in a particular course of instruction.
   (ii) deciding the cases of scholarships.
   (iii) choosing candidates for assigning some specific responsibilities.
   (iv) selecting candidates for participation in various co-curricular activities etc.

2. *For the purpose of classification:* Intelligence tests help the teacher to classify the students as bright, dull or average and hence make possible putting them into more homogeneous groups in order to bring efficiency in teaching-learning process.

3. *For the purpose of promotion:* Intelligence tests can prove themselves as one of the useful instruments in promoting the individuals not only in educational fields but in all other occupational and social situations where one studies to go higher on the ladder.

4. *For knowing one's potentiality:* Intelligence tests help in revealing the potentialities of an individual and in this way make possible the predication of one's success in a particular field. The knowledge of such potentiality helps the teacher in the following ways:
   (i) Giving guidance. Teacher or a guidance personnel can give guidance to the pupils in the selection of various courses of instruction and occupations.
   (ii) Helps in learning process. Teacher can plan teaching-learning activities with the help of this knowledge. "*Results of intelligence tests,*" as Crow and Crow write, "*can help a teacher to discover what the child can learn and how quickly he can learn, as well as the teaching methods that should be applied and the learning content that should he utilized to guide the learner to use his mental potentialities to their utmost.*" (1964, p.484)
   (iii) To establish a proper level of aspiration. As Sawrey and Telford write, "One of the most important ends served by intelligence testing is that of the assisting of the individual to establish a level of aspiration that is realistic in terms of intellectual potential." (1964, p.484)

5. *For diagnostic purpose:* Exceptional children like gifted, backward and the mentally retarded children can be detected with the help of intelligence tests. Moreover, the intelligence tests help in the diagnosis of the root causes of problematic behaviour of the child and likewise suggest the possible remedy.

6. *Helps in Research work:* Intelligence testing has been proved very useful in Psychological, Sociological and Educational research. For example, in deciding the relative role of heredity and environment in the process of growth and development, research workers have made much use of intelligence testing.

Limitations of Intelligence Tests

Intelligence tests have given birth to so many problems due to their limitations and shortcomings. We can list them as follows:

1. *Intelligence tests and students:* Intelligence tests label some students as superior and the others as inferior. This type of knowledge creates so many problems. Children who are slightly dull are still brilliant enough to realise through the results of intelligence tests that they are slow to learn. It makes them disappointed and causes inferiority feelings and ultimately mars their future. On the other hand, the students with a slight more I.Q. may create over-confidence in them. There is very possibility that these students may not give serious attention to their work. Also the consciousness of their superiority may result in misbehaviour on their part and can turn them into problem children.

2. *Intelligence test and teachers:* Teachers, after knowing the I.Q. of the child make a permanent idea of the child's potentialities and abilities. They try to see him through his I.Q. They leave no attempt to discourage or to create over-confidence in the students according to the level of their intelligence announced by these tests. Moreover, the knowledge of the intelligence of the pupils for a teacher may result in slackness on his part. He may put the entire responsibility of a pupil's failure on his inferior intelligence and for a bright pupil he can think that he would be able to do himself. In this way the knowledge of intelligence supplied by these may bring disastrous results to the teacher.

3. *Given birth to Segregation and conflicts:* Intelligence test results have been misused to uphold the theory of royal blood, segregation and sectarian outlook. In U.S.A. it has led to a conflict between the Negro and the white populations. The conflict, in actual sense, is the result of misconception about the predictive value of these tests and their correlation with hereditary factors. In defence we can put the following points:

(a) No intelligence tests, including most refined performance tests, can be claimed as completely free of practice or coaching effects and independent of cultural, social, racial and other environmental factors. Hence, they cannot be claimed as a measure of initial mental abilities and capacities of the individual and therefore it is quite unjust to deny or uphold the right of admissions or job opportunities to the people on the basis of these tests. Now the contemporary researches in this direction have proved that intelligence tests results always show favour towards healthy environmental conditions like improved sanitation, family atmosphere, education of parents, cultural background, socio-economic conditions and better educational opportunities, etc.

(b) In fact, intelligence test helps in knowing very little about the total make-up of the child's potentialities. Only cognitive (mental functions) domain can be said to be touched by these tests. They leave untouched many important aspects like interests, attitudes, motives, etc. Hence, they cannot be relied as the predictor of the future success of an individual.

(c) "*The results of all such tests,*" as Crow and Crow put it, "*may be effected by many factors inherent in the testing conditions, the child's background of experience and other favourable or unfavourable elements. Hence, no administrator, teacher or student of education should accept test results as the only measure of an individual's ability to learn.*" (1973, p. 160)

In this way, it is not proper to give over weightage to intelligence tests. They should not be accepted as the only measure of an individual's degree of ability to learn. They should not be made an instrument of creating complexes among the students and misunderstanding among the teachers. In a nut-shell, the results of these must be interpreted and used intelligently. They should be taken as the means and not the end in themselves.

16

Motivation

MOTIVATION — NATURE AND MEANING

A small bird collects the material to build its nest in the upper corner of our drawing room. After looking at it we try to remove it. But the bird again brings the small pieces of straws leaves etc. and engages itself in building its nest. What makes it so much hard working? Why did it learn to build the nest? Similarly, we see a student burning mid night oil during the examination days, a boy constantly busy in learning how to cycle even after getting many cuts and bruises. What makes them to engage in one or the other types of learning and continue their efforts while facing even so many handicaps and obstacles?

Such questions related to 'why of learning' are always answered through a key word 'motivation'. The bird, which is building its nest, the student, who is studying hard and the boy, who is learning how to cycle; all do so because of the 'Motivation'. They learn because they are motivated to learn. They act because they are persuaded to act in order to satisfy their basic needs and attain the desired goals. There is something which energies or compel them to act and behave in a specified way. The question arises what is that which pushes and pulls an individual to move or act in such a specified way to attain the desired objectives. In psychology, it is named as motive. A motive drives our behaviour in the same way as a motor vehicle is driven by the fuel in its tank. There are a number of motives in our personal and social life which are responsible for energizing and motivating our behaviour. These motives can be broadly classified into two categories named below:

1. Primary motives
2. Secondary motives.

1. *Primary Motives:* These motives are linked with the basic primary needs associated with the biological or physiological well-being of the individual. That is why these motives are often named as biological or physiological motives. These motives ensure the preservation of life for the individual and for his race. Examples of such motives are hunger, thirst, sex, avoidance of pain, elimination of body wastes, sleep and rest, etc. The primary motives are universal motives; they are found in all organisms human or non-human, in one form or the other. They serve the basic

physiological need of the organism. They are inborn and innate.

2. *Secondary Motives*: These are linked with one's socio-psychological needs and hence are named as the psychological or social motives. They are acquired like other forms of learned behaviour in the course of satisfaction of the needs. Examples of such motives are Power motives, Achievement motive, Self-actualization motive, Security motive, Application motive, Affiliation motive, etc.

At any occasion when a primary or secondary motive is attached with one's action or behaviour, then his behaviour patterns get dominated by such motive. His behaviour is termed as motivated behaviour forcing and compelling the individual to behave in a particular way at the command of the involved motive.

Such motivated behaviour of an individual possesses the following characteristics:

1. A motive works as a source or energizer for pushing and pulling the motivated behaviour.
2. It is in fact aimed towards the satisfaction of one or the other basic need.
3. One's behaviour can be properly initiated and its continuity can be properly assured in the shape of his motivated behaviour.
4. Motivated behaviour is quite selective. Here one tries to respond to the environmental stimuli strictly in view of the satisfaction of the desired needs linked with the motivated behaviour.
5. Motivated behaviour has dynamicity and flexibility in its nature. In the course of behaving, if there is some alteration in the nature of the further requirements of satisfaction of the need, it may bring change in one's motives of behaving. As a result, the shape or direction of the motivating behaviour may altogether be changed as per demands of the new situation.
6. Motivated behaviour is goal directed. The individual is totally engaged in the realization of the goals of his motivated behaviour. The realization of one goal may further put him in the cycle of motivated behaviour as he may feel the necessity of the realization of his further needs in the path of his progress or cycle of his life.
7. Motivated behaviour helps us in seeking equilibrium between our needs and their satisfaction. It lies in between one's need and its satisfaction. Since, the key to our adjustment lies in the satisfaction of our needs, the motivated behaviour proves an important tool and means for making ourselves adjusted and integrated.

In this way, with what we have discussed in the above lines, we may be now in a position to have a workable definition of the term motivation or motivated behaviour in the following way.

Motivation as a process or behaviour refers to a reinforced, selective and goal directed behaviour initiated and energized by a motive which aims to maintain and balance the equilibrium of the person in relation to his environment by keeping his basic needs in the process of satisfaction.

THE MOTIVATIONAL CYCLE

Motivation, as we have discussed earlier stands for the state of an organism which involves the existence of a need that moves or drives him from within towards a goal for the satisfaction of the desired need.

As visualized from Fig. 16.1, the motivation or motivated behaviour functions as a continuous flow in the shape of a cycle named motivational cycle explained below:

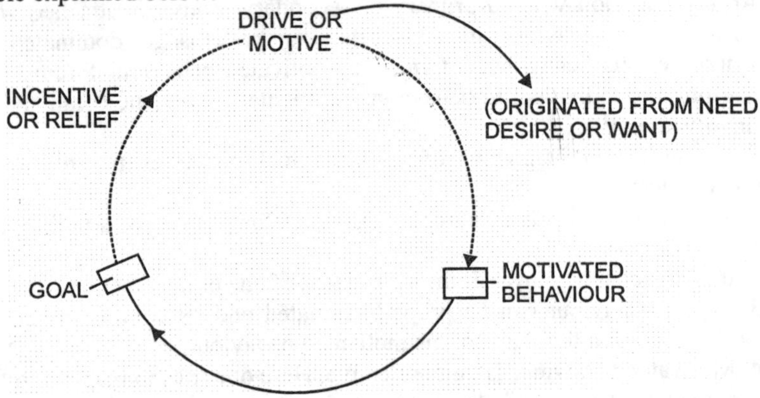

Fig. 16.1: The Motivational Cycle

1. The behaviour is initiated on account of some inherent need. Thereby, the first stage or the starting point of the motivation cycle is the birth of a desire, want or need in the individual. This desire, want or need, makes an individual to think about the ways and means of its satisfaction. He may become now quite anxious and perturbed for the satisfaction of his desire or need, such that the stage of his mind and body becomes a germinating point for the birth of a drive or motive.

2. The drive or motive so produced on account of the felt need or desire, now becomes a driver, persuader and energizer of one's behaviour. It initiates one's behaviour to a goal directed path, provides sufficient inputs for the continuation of such behaviour till the goal in terms of the realization of the desired need, desire or want is not attained. Thus, in the end the organism becomes able to reach the desired goal and feel satisfied in terms of the satisfaction of his need or motive. It enables him to get relief from the anxiety and tension related to the satisfaction of his need and motive.

3. However, what one gets through the satisfaction of his felt need or desire through his motivated behaviour, provides a temporary halt to his behavioural activities. The journey is not at all completely stopped but in fact advances further with a new zeal and enthusiasm for the realization of some other needs and desires. Satisfaction of a need through a motivated behaviour reinforces one's behaviour to work for the realization of another goal i.e. satisfaction of other needs or desires accompanied with new

motives. In this way, one motivated behaviour gives birth to the next motivated behaviour in the shape of a motivational cycle. Originated from the felt needs, energized and directed by one's motives, reinforced by the progress in the satisfaction of the need or other external reinforcement, the motivation behaviour thus helps in the satisfaction of one's needs or motives. It further energizes an individual to remain in the cycle of motivation by creating new desires, ambitions and needs, the satisfaction of which further requires a new set of motivation behaviour and motivation cycle.

TYPES OF MOTIVATION

The motivation can be broadly classified into two types:

1. Natural Motivation or Intrinsic Motivation.
2. Artificial Motivation or Extrinsic Motivation.

1. *Natural Motivation or Intrinsic Motivation:* The type of motivation is directly linked with the natural instincts, urges and impulses of the organism. The individual, who is intrinsically or naturally motivated, performs an act because he finds interest within the activity. He is engaged in learning something because he derives pleasure within the learning of that thing. The activity carries its own award and the individual takes genuine interest in performing the activity due to some outside motives and goals.

When a student tries to solve a mathematical problem and derives pleasure in the task of solving it or tries to read poetry and the reading itself gives him pleasure, we can say that he is intrinsically motivated. In these cases the source of pleasure lies within the activities. He solves the problems or reads the poetry for its own sake. Such type of motivation has real values in the learning task as it creates spontaneous attention and interest and sustains it throughout.

2. *Artificial Motivation or Extrinsic Motivation:* In such motivation, the source of pleasure does not lie within the task. Such kind of motivation has no functional relationships to the task. Here the individual does or learns something not for its own sake, but as a means of obtaining desired goals or getting some external reward. Working for a better grade or honour, learning a skill to earn the livelihood, receiving praise and blame, rewards and punishment, etc. all belong to this category.

In comparison to extrinsic motivation, intrinsic motivation, as a source of spontaneous inspiration and stimulation, brings better results in the teaching-learning process. Therefore, it is always better to make use of intrinsić motivation, whenever it is possible to do so. But in case, when it is not appropriate to make use of intrinsic motivation, the use of extrinsic motivation should not be suspended. Depending upon the learning situation and the nature of the task, the choice for providing appropriate motivation should be made by the teacher so that the learner may take proper interest in a learning activity.

NEED OF MOTIVATION FOR THE LEARNERS AND TEACHERS

The knowledge regarding the phenomenon and mechanism of motivation along with the technique of its enhancement among the learners may probe quite beneficial to the teachers and learners in the variety of ways like below:

1. Motivation carries a great significance to the learner. It results into proper readiness for learning. According to Thorndike's law of readiness, a learning take place well when the learner has proper willingness or readiness for the learning of a thing. Motivation helps the child in making him ready and willing for a particular learning. If it is done, then a great work is automatically performed in the direction of teaching work performed by the teacher and learning task carried out by the learner.

2. Motivation helps the learners to take interest in his learning, capturing his interest and gets focused on the learning task relatively for a longer time. Interest, attention and sustaining of attention are quite vital for the effectiveness of learning and a learner can reap their benefits well by getting him motivated for the learning of a task. The learners who seem quite motivated to learn are bound to get desired success in the accomplishment of their learning objectives.

3. A teacher should learn the art and techniques of motivating his students for a target learning. He should also learn to help his students to seek intrinsic motivation in place of extrinsic motivation. However, he should not also feel hesitation in getting his students motivated through extrinsic means like praise, appreciation, certificates, medals, etc. He should try to avoid punishment, reproof or blaming as a method of instigating on compelling the students for a particular learning and always prefer positive means like appreciation and rewards over the negative means.

4. A teacher should try to the learning experiences and learning opportunities in tune with the needs, motives, interests, goals and aspirations of the learners for seeking means of intrinsic motivation to his learners.

5. While delivering his lesson to the students in the class, a teacher must begin his journey of teaching by seeking proper motivation of the students towards his lesson. For this purpose he should try to get their attention focused and interest maintained in his delivered lesson by adopting a variety of means and techniques. In all cases, he should make the students feel the importance or genuine need of studying the topic to be presented by the teacher in the class or an activity performed by the students on an individual or collective basis.

THE CONCEPT OF NEEDS, DRIVES AND INCENTIVES

While discussing the process of motivation through a motivation cycle we have used the terms needs, drives and incentives etc. All these concepts need a necessary explanation for knowing about their true nature and role in the process of motivation. Let us have a brief discussion about all of them.

Needs

Meaning of the term Need: We make use of the term need in our day to day life in many ways. When we desire or wish to have food, we say that we are in need of the food, some eatable. We need water for quenching our thirst, sex objects for the satisfaction of our sex needs, companions and friends in the hours of loneliness and loneliness or rest after being tired from the busy schedule. We have a craving for being loved or to love and also remain struggling for achieving some status, recognition and appreciation for our work and duties. In this way, the term 'need' is very often used as synonymous to the terms 'want' and 'desire'. We are always in a state of anxiety, eagerness and temptation for fulfilling our desires or wants. In fact these desires or wants (psychologically named as needs) prompt or persuade us to behave in a specific way.

In the light of the above discussion, thus now we may have a workable definition of the term need in the following way.

> *Need refers to a condition or state of our mind that prompts or persuade us to act or behave in a specific way.*

What are the Basic Needs?

There is no end of our derives or wants in our life. As a result it is difficult to name or tell the number of the individual needs. However, there are needs which are quite essential for an individual in terms of his remaining alive, maintaining proper physical and mental health, leading a social life and getting well in terms of personality development, etc. Such essential needs are referred to as individual's basic needs. These basic needs for their proper understanding may be broadly classified into the following two categories:

A. Physiological or Biological Needs
B. Socio-psychological Needs.

A. Physiological or Biological Needs: All our bodily or organic needs fall into this category. They may be further categorised as under:

(i) In this first category of biological needs, we have need for oxygen, water and food. These needs are most fundamental for our survival and existence. Without them we can hardly survive.

(ii) In the chain of our survival and existence the other category of the biological needs include needs like:

(a) Need for rest when tired.
(b) Need for being active when rested.
(c) Need for sleep when deprived of it for long.
(d) Need for regular elimination of waste products from the body.
(e) Need for having an even internal body temperature.
(f) Need for protection from the threats of physical environment like hazards of weather, natural calamities, wild animals, etc.

(iii) In the third category of biological needs, we can place the need for satisfaction of sex urge or desire to seek sex-experiences. Although sex urge is not essential for the survival of an individual, it is the strongest human urge in the satisfaction of which lies his proper growth, development, adjustment and well-being. Moreover, the satisfaction of this need and normal sex behaviour are most essential for a happy family life and the continuity and survival of the human species.

(iv) In the last category of biological needs, we have needs that are associated with the demands of our senses. These sensory needs include the need for physical contact, sensory stimulation and stimulus variability and manipulation. Although we may not die if deprived of these needs, they are supposed to be quite essential for our general welfare and optimal growth.

B. *Socio-psychological Needs*: Under this category, we can list all those needs that are associated with the socio-cultural environment of an individual. They are acquired through social learning. Although such needs are not linked with the survival of the organism or species, their deprivation may lead to a psychological state seriously affecting his survival and welfare. These needs for the sake of clarity may be classified as follows:

1. *The need for freedom or gaining independence*: An individual possesses a craving for independence. Nature has created us free and independent as individuals and requires us to remain so. Therefore, all human beings have an urge to remain free and independent.

2. *The need for security*: Every one of us needs to feel secure not only to save ourselves from the physical dangers but also from socio-psychological angles. One needs desirable emotional, social and economical security for his well-being.

3. *The need for love and affection*: Every one of us, irrespective of age, caste, colour and creed, has a strong desire to love and be loved. Depending upon one's age and circumstances, it may vary in kind and nature, but a sort of emotional craving for the satisfaction of this need is exhibited universally by all living organisms.

4. *The need to achieve*: Every human being has a strong desire to achieve some or other things like money, fame, reputation, degree, merit, position, medals, good life partner, spiritual attainment, etc., not only for raising his status in the eyes of others but also for the satisfaction he gets out of his own accomplishment.

5. *The need for recognition or social approval*: Each one of us has an inherent desire for gaining recognition, appreciation and esteem at the hands of others. An artist may thus desire to be known for his art, a young woman may desire to be appreciated for her beauty, good manners or house-keeping by fellow human beings especially the members of the group to which she belongs. A student may show this desire in surpassing other students of his class and thus gaining required social status, prestige or approval from his fellow students, teachers and parents.

6. *The need for social company*: Man is referred to as a social animal in the sense that he has a strong urge to be with his own kind and maintain social relations with them. The real strength of this need can be felt by those individuals who are faced with social rejection or solitary confinement.

7. *The need for self-assertion*: Every one of us has an inherent desire to get an opportunity to rule or dominate others. It may vary in intensity from person to person but it is surely exhibited by all of us in one or other situation irrespective of age, strength and status. Some may show it to their juniors, servants, life partner or children while others may exhibit it towards their pet animals, birds and even inanimate things like dolls or pictures. This need of asserting oneself gives birth to an important motive called power motive that works as a strong determiner of one's personality and behaviour.

8. *The need for self-expression or self-actualisation*: We all have an inherent craving for the expression of our self and actualisation of our own potentialities. An individual may have a hidden poet, musician or painter in his self and thus may have a strong desire to get his talent exhibited or nurtured. In this way one wants to get adequate opportunities for the expression and development of his potentialities and subsequently he strives for it and is not happy until he gets opportunities for such expression and self-actualisation.

Drives

A need gives rise to a drive *which may be defined as an aroused reaction, tendency or a state of heightened tension that sets up activities in an individual and sustains them for increasing his general activity level*. The existence of a need moves or drives the individual from within and directs its activities to a goal that may bring about the satisfaction of the need. The strength of a drive depends upon the strength of the stimuli involving the related need.

Drives of any nature are divided into two categories. In the first category we have biological or primary drives such as hunger, thirst escape from pain and sex drive. In the second category we have socio-psychological or secondary drives such as fear or anxiety, desire for approval, striving for achievement, aggression and dependence. These drives are not related to our physiological needs and, therefore, do not arise on account of imbalances in the body's internal functioning. They arise from the socio-psychological needs and are said to be acquired through social learning as a result of one's interaction with his socio-cultural environment. These drives move an individual to act for the satisfaction of his socio-psychological needs which in turn proves as a reinforcer of the behaviour for the continuity and maintenance of the behaviour.

Contrary to the socio-psychological or secondary drives the biological drives are basically unlearned in nature. They arise from our biological needs as a result of an attempt to satisfy these needs.

Incentives

Needs and drives, as we have studied in the above pages, reveal and represent the inner state of an individual's behaviour. When there is deficiency or shortage of water and food in our body, we feel the need for their satisfaction. The need gives birth to thirst and hunger drives. But sometimes it may happen that we feel the necessity of getting some eatables or drinks in spite of the fact that our body does not require them. There is no shortage of water or food and hence there is no biological or physiological need that is to be gratified by our behaviour. In this case such need is produced on account of our excessive liking for a particular type of food or drink or on account of its smell, taste and other perception, instead of its natural demand or necessity to our body. Such external factors, affecting our needs are usually referred to as incentives. Not only our needs but drives — physiological and socio-psychological are also influenced and guided by incentives. If one gets incentives in terms of the food of his choice and taste, he may be attracted and feel necessity of getting it more and more. The drive of hunger here gets a new source of energy and backing through such incentives.

As the examples of incentives we may cite the name of praise, appreciation, rewards, bonus, fulfilment of one's needs and getting the desired objectives.

Any type of incentive always works as a reinforcing agent as it adds more force to a new attached drive like adding fuel to the already ignited fire. As a result the individual behaves with a new zeal and enthusiasm for achieving his need based objectives. For example, let us take the case of providing bonus to the workers of a factory. Here bonus is an incentive. It provides an additional backup and energy to the workers for doing hard or extra work for attaining the production targets of the factory. It works as a reinforcing agent to activate their behaviour and creates an extra drive for bringing efficiency in their work. The same may be perceived in the case of any individual where we may find a tremendous change in his behaviour through the incentives received by him during the course of his behaviour. For example, a piece of toffee, chocolate or ice-cream or a playing toy may work as an incentive for a boy to give more strength to his drive and as a result he may be further motivated to act or behave in a desirable way. Similarly, a favourite food may provide an incentive for an individual to eat or a favourite movie may compel other individuals to go and see it. In this way needs and drives, whether primary or secondary, are greatly affected and directed by the incentives.

It is not essential for these incentives to remain external. The internal incentives, around from within also have the same effect of directing and influencing one's drive for the satisfaction of one or the other need. During the course of his activity if one feels satisfied with his progress in work or gets success in achieving his objectives, he gets a lot of incentive from his own self for providing fresh energy to put his heart and soul in the work.

STRATEGIES OR TECHNIQUES FOR MOTIVATING THE STUDENTS

Motivation, as discussed earlier, occupies a central place in the teaching-learning process. It is, in fact, indispensable to learning. Every teacher, at one time or the other, is faced with the problem of motivating his students to learn. Therefore, it is essential to think of the ways and means for achieving motivation in the class room situation. The principles of motivation described earlier may provide necessary guidelines for this purpose. However, in brief, we can adopt the following techniques in this regard.

1. *Child-centred approach:* It is the child who has to learn. The teacher only helps him to learn. Therefore, what the child has to learn, the teacher is only to help him in learning that. But, what child has to learn, should be judged according to the ability, interest, capacity and previous experience of the child. Is he mature enough to understand the new material or do the assigned task? Does he possess necessary skills and abilities for doing the present task? Is he mentally prepared for the present learning? These are some of the questions which should be kept in mind while asking the child to learn something new or perform some assigned task. The learning material or experiences should always be assigned according to the needs, interests and abilities of the child.

2. *Linking the new learning with the past:* Experience is a great teacher. What has been learned or experienced in the past, proves a good base for the present learning. The assigned task seems to be interesting, easy and within the capacity of an individual, if it is properly related with the past experience. The child is easily motivated to learn the new material if he thinks that he knows all that which is required as a base for the new learning. Therefore, it is the duty of the teacher to base his present teaching upon the previous learning experiences acquired by the pupil.

3. *Use of effective methods, aids and devices in teaching*: Whatever the subject-matter may be, a good teacher with his art of teaching can stimulate the students for learning. Old dogmatic methods kill the initiative and interest of the learner while the progressive methods based on the psychological principles, keep him motivated. The use of audio-visual aids and the service rendered by museum, library, visit of places, etc., directly help the teacher in motivating his students. Therefore, a wise teacher should make use of the suitable methods, devices and aid-material in his teaching.

4. *Definiteness of the purposes and goals*: One cannot feel interested in a task if one is not aware of the purpose served by doing that. Definiteness of the aims and goals makes the learner interested and sets him to work in a desirable direction. The students must be acquainted well with the aims and objectives of studying a subject or topic. They must be told the purpose of acquiring a new skill or experience so that a clear perception of the goals may motivate them and bring required results.

5. *Knowledge of the results and progress:* Every learner wishes to know the result of his striving. When we make ourselves engaged in doing some task, it is natural to have curiosity about the progress made in completing that task. The knowledge that we are progressing satisfactorily, gives us proper incentive. The child, who is attempting Mathematical problem concerning with a particular topic, gets constant motivation if he is well acquainted with his progress. Immediate knowledge of the results provides sufficient feed-back to the learner. It does not only acquaint him with his success or failure but makes him able to plan his further attempts in reaching towards specific goals. The proper critical evaluation of the pupil's work, in terms of specific defects, errors and good points, etc., proves an effective incentive for the desirable improvement. Teachers should make provision for acquainting the students well with their progress. For this purpose, proper Record-cards, Graphs and Charts should be maintained in the schools.

6. *Praise and Reproof*: Both praise and reproof are the potent incentives. They can be safely used for the achievement of desired motivation in the class-room situations. Which one of these incentives will prove more effective depends upon the personality of the learner as well as of the person who gives them. In the case of some individuals, both praise and reproof work well while others respond best to one or the other. Generally, those having feelings of inadequacy respond more favourably to praise and those who are self-assured, work harder after criticism. The way, in which these incentives are given or repeated by the teacher, also counts much. The essential condition for the effectiveness of these incentives, is that they must either satisfy or threaten our security or one or more of our other motives. In this way, the teacher must try to recognize the nature of the students and consequently make use of the praise or reproof in motivating and inspiring them.

7. *Rewards and Punishment*: Rewards and punishment bring the same results as praise and reproof. Both of these are powerful incentives and try to influence the future conduct or learning of an organism favourably. While punishment as a negative motive is based on fear of failure, fear of losing prestige, fear of insult on rejection, fear of physical pain and so on, the reward as a positive motive seeks to influence conduct favourably by associating a pleasant feeling with the desired act.

As far as possible, the use of punishment as a motivating agent should be avoided as it kills initiative, leadership, resourcefulness and the spirit of free thinking and adventurous living. On the other hand, the rewards like prizes, honours, certificates, medals, etc. have psychological value and develop in the students creative abilities, spirit of emulation, self-confidence and self-respect and other democratic feelings.

With this discussion, it should not be taken that punishment as a rule should be decried in all circumstances and never be given to anybody. In some cases, it brings more improvement than reward. On the other hand indiscriminate and unqualified use of reward proves harmful as it sometimes tends to become an end in itself. For an example, a student may strive hard to get the Gold medal but in doing so he may be interested, not in learning but in the medal. Therefore, the teacher should be very careful in using rewards or punishment as an incentive to motivate his students.

8. *Competition and Co-operation*: Competition as a source of motivation is universally recognized. In a simple language, it indicates the desire to excel others. Now-a-days we find too much competition in all walks of life. In the field of education, this spirit can be used as a powerful motivating force. We can create learning situations, where the students of a class are engaged in a healthy competition. Competition may take one of the two forms — competition against another person or competition against one's own record. In the former form of the competition there lies a danger of developing undesirable habits in the individual as he may resort to unfair means for excelling others. The other form of competition stimulates the learner to compete with his own past record. It sets him on the path of self-learning and provides an intrinsic motivation. Therefore, the teacher should try to inculcate the feeling of self-improvement in the learner.

Competition, particularly, the group-competition may give birth to bitter criticism, improper rivalry, enmity and conflicts, etc. For removing these bad effects, the remedy is often suggested in the form of cooperation. The co-operation as well as competition are used in combination. In this process, the members of a group may co-operate with each other, while the group competes with other groups and so on. This type of co-operation and friendly competition develop team-spirit, community feeling, thinking for a common cause, a sense of unity and other socially desirable habits. A wise teacher should try to make use of the competition based on co-operation and 'we feeling'.

9. *Ego-involvement*: The ego consists of attitudes relating to the self. Every one of us tries to maintain status and self-respect. We like those people, objects and situations that make us feel important and dislike those that make us feel inferior. Teachers, generally, are in the habit of ridiculing and snubbing their students. It is not the proper way of motivating them, Instead of using such means, the teacher should try to motivate his students by appealing to ego maximization. He should engage them in the activities which can appeal to his self-respect and raise his status among his class-mates or peers.

10. *Development of proper attitude*: Attitude is defined as ones set to react in a given way in a particular situation. It is closely related to attention and interest. A child, who has developed a healthy attitude towards manual work, takes genuine interest in working with hands, while the other one who has developed a negative attitude, shirks away from it. In this way, a favourable attitude helps the learner in setting of his mind or preparing him mentally for doing a particular task or learning something. Therefore, the teacher should try to develop proper attitude of his students towards the desired act or learning.

11. *Appropriate learning situation and environment*: The situations and the environment, in which the learning is to be made by the learner, influences the learning process. A well equipped, healthy class-room environment proves a motivating force. The child likes to read, write or listen to the teacher carefully if he finds favourable environment and appropriate learning situations. The suitability of the school building, the seating arrangement and other physical facilities available and affection he gets from his teachers, the mutual cooperation and help, he gets from his class-mates, the opportunity of participation he gets in the school co-curricular activities etc. — all influence and motivate the learning behaviour of the child. Therefore, efforts should be made to provide suitable learning situations and environment for effective learning.

TEACHER'S ROLE IN MOTIVATING, STRENGTHENING AND SUSTAINING MOTIVATION LEARNERS

In a teaching-learning process, a teacher can play a quite substantial role not only in motivating his students for the classroom learning but he may be found to remains in a position to strengthen and sustain such aroused motivation among them. Let us see if it can be done by a teacher:

1. A teacher should try to be alert and conscious of getting motivated to the topic of his lesson delivered in the class from the very beginning. He should try to introduce his lesson before the students in such a way as to capture their needed attention and arousing interest and curiosity about studying the topic to be taught to them in the class. For this purpose, he should try to link the introduction of his lesson to the previous knowledge and learning of the topic, their day to day experiences and their curiosity to know about new things. He should also try to seek and arouse motivation of the students by linking his lesson with one or the other motives of the students. They should be realized the importance and significance of the topic being taught to them. How are they going to be benefitted with the study of the things or learning experiences given to them by the teacher in the class should be clearly known to the students for motivating them towards classroom learning.

2. Once students are motivated, their attention is drawn interest in created towards the studying of the topic, the next essential thing in this direction is to attempt for strengthening and sustaining of the motivated behaviour of the students. For this purpose the things like below may be done on the part of a willing teacher.

(i) The learning experiences or content material presented before the students should be well integrated, organized in a quite logical as well as psychological way. What follows should be linked with the previous things delivered or understood by the students as well as it should help in building the base of future presentation of the content material/learning experiences before the students. It should follow the principle of simple to complex, concrete to abstract and examples to generalization in its organization as well as delivery.

(ii) Methods of teaching, strategies and devices, media and mode should be so chosen and applied for the classroom teaching-learning as to help the students in maintaining their interest and motive towards class-room learning.

(iii) Teaching-learning process should work on an interactive learner centered and sharing basis rather than on a teacher dominated single track. The students should be given proper opportunity for providing their active involvement and participation in the teaching-learning process. They should be inspired and encouraged for putting questions, satisfying their curiosity and meeting their constructive and creative needs.

(iv) Use of audio visual aids, multimedia and ICT should be in corporated well in the classroom teaching for keeping up a sufficient level of motivation of the students as well as helping them to derive maximum educational benefits with the use of such aid material and equipments.

(v) A motivated behaviour can be strengthened and sustained well if necessary attention and efforts are made for getting it properly reinforced through an appropriate schedule and method of reinforcement. A teacher therefore should try to make use of a proper combination of priase and blame, competition and cooperation, rewards and punishment, for strengthening and sustaining motivated spirit of the students towards classroom learning. The measures like putting questions to the students in the class, engaging them in dull and practice work, evaluating their classroom performance and getting them acquainted immediately with the outcomes or results of their performance may also bring quite a positive consequence towards strengthening and sustaining of their motivation.

17

Personality — Meaning, Nature and Theories

In Educational world the term 'personality' has a wide significance. Education is concerned with an all round development of the personality of a child. Therefore, it is quite essential for a pupil teacher to know about the term personality. Here, we are going to focus our attention on the issue, the meaning and the nature of the term Personality.

THE MEANING AND NATURE OF PERSONALITY

To reflect light on the meaning and nature of personality, we can consider this issue in the following steps:

A. Wrong notions and misconceptions about personality.
B. Meaning and definitions of the term personality.
C. Some glaring facts about personality.

Let us take them one by one.

A. Certain Wrong Notions and Misconceptions about Personality

Let us first make ourselves acquainted with the wrong notions and misconceptions about the term personality.

Etymologically; the word personality has been derived from the Latin word 'persona'. At first this word was used for the mask worn by the actors to change their appearance but later on it began to be used by the actors themselves. Since then, the term personality has been used to depict outward appearance or external behaviour, etc. It is in this sense we have developed a wrong notion about the term personality. We often listen to such comment as this man has a fine or magnetic personality or that man has a poor personality. We try to paste such labels as fine, good or poor on the individuals on the basis of their physical make-up, manner of their walking, talking, dressing and host of other similiar characteristics.

Sometimes, we use personality as equivalent to one's character. It is also a wrong notion. Character is, by all means, a moral or ethical term which refers to the standards of right and wrong. While personality is purely a psychological term and hence it is not proper to use it in reference to the study of ethical values.

Thus, we cannot take personality as an equivalent word for outward appearance or behaviour. It is a very superficial approach. We cannot ignore the inner aspect of one's personality. Personality includes the totality of one's behaviour and hence, both inner and outer (covert as well as overt) behaviour should be taken into consideration.

B. Meaning and Definitions of the Term Personality

Psychologically speaking personality is all that a person is. It is the totality of one's behaviour towards oneself and others as well. It includes everything about the person, his physical, emotional, social, mental and spiritual make-up. It is all that a person has about him.

In this way, definitely, the term personality signifies something deeper than mere appearance or outward behaviour. How should it be given a proper meaning or definition is a difficult problem. Actually its subjective nature does not allow to reach a clear-cut, well agreed definition. That is why, it has been defined by so many psychologists in so many ways according to their own points of view. Some of these well known attempts at defining personality are presented below:

Watson. "Personality is the sum of activities that can be discovered by actual observations over a long enough period of time to give reliable information." (1930)

In this manner Watson gives emphasis upon the behaviour of an individual and say that personality is nothing but the useful effect one makes upon the person coming into his close contact.

Morton Prince. accepting the role of both heredity and environment, defines it as—

"Personality is the sum total of all the biological innate dispositions, impulses, tendencies, appetites and instincts of the individual and the dispositions and tendencies acquired by experience." (1929, P. 532)

Allport. After evaluating 49 definitions of personality written by so many eminent persons, Allport summarizes his own concept in the following words:

"Personality is a dynamic organisation within the individual of those psychophysical systems that determine his unique adjustment to his environment." (1948, p.28)

Although Allport has tried to give a comprehensive definition of the term personality including the words organisation, dynamic, psycho-physical system, unique adjustment and environment etc. yet he, like other previous ones, only describes it. By emphasizing merely on theoretical aspect and describing it in terms of behavioural or dynamic concepts the true nature of personality cannot be understood. The contemporary psychologists like R.B. Cattell and Eysenck are of such opinion. They feel very strongly that if personality cannot be demonstrated, measured and quantified it should be called philosophy or art and not personality theory in psychology.

Below we give their ideas in connection with the meaning of the term personality.

R.B. Cattell. "Personality is that which permits a prediction of what a person will do in a given situation." (1929, p. 532)

Eysenck. "Personality is the more or less stable and enduring organisation of a person's character, temperament, intellect, and physique, which determine his unique adjustment to the environment." (1971, p. 2)

He has tried to make certain terms clear in the following way:

Character denotes a person's more or less stable or enduring system or organisation of conative behaviour ("Will").

Temperament denotes a person's more less stable or enduring organisation of affective behaviour ("Emotions").

Intellect denotes a person's more or less stable or enduring organisation of cognitive behaviour ("intelligence").

Physique denotes a person's more or less stable or enduring organisation of bodily configuration and neuro-endocrine endowment (glands + nervous system + bodily configuration).

Evaluation of the Definition

(i) This definition gives a balanced consideration to heredity and environment in building one's personality.

(ii) Eysenck stresses the concept of structure and organisation and criticises just naming of some of the behavioural characteristics like bricks in describing a home.

(iii) This definition gives personality a physiological base.

(iv) It gives a complete picture of the human behaviour patterns by including cognitive, conative, affective and somatic (constitutional) aspects.

(v) This definition aims at making personality somewhat measurable and assessable and thus gives it a scientific base.

The above mentioned characteristics do not suggest that Eyrenck's definition has explained everything about the term personality or it does not have any weak point. Like other definitions, this also suffers from some limitations and drawbacks, which are given below:

(i) Eysenck advocates that personality must have a physiological base, but it is not a case always. Every time we cannot have a physiological base due to the very complex nature of personality.

(ii) His definition leads us to form an opinion that personality is fixed and cannot be changed.

This is an extreme approach. It is true that personality should be evaluated on the basis of generality of the behaviour (the behaviour must be consistent in a number of situations) but on the other hand, changes cannot be denied. The person who is extrovert may turn into introvert depending upon so many intervening factors.

In this way, for understanding of the concept of personality, the evolution of an ideal definition still needs further research. In fact, the concepts like personality are difficult to be explained as they have the identity like sound, electricity etc. the impact of which can be felt but the real nature of them is always a matter of secrecy. Something about them can be known by their utility or describing some of their characteristics and distinguishing features. Let us seek the meaning of the term personality also on similar lines.

C. Some Glaring Facts regarding Personality

With all what has been said above we can conclude the given ahead things about personality:

1. Firstly, the personality is something unique and specific. Every one of us is a unique pattern in ourselves. No two individuals, not even the identical twins, behave in precisely the same way over any period of time. Everyone of us has specific characteristics for making adjustments.

2. The second main characteristic of personality is self-consciousness. The man is described as a person or to have a personality when the idea of self enters into his consciousness. In this connection H.R. Bhatia writes, *"We do not attribute personality to a dog and even a child cannot be described as a personality because it has only a vague sense of personal identity"* (1968, p. 371)

3. Personality includes everything about a person. It is all that a person has about him. It includes all the behaviour patterns *i.e.,* conative, cognitive and affective and covers not only the conscious activities but goes deeper to semi conscious and unconscious also.

4. It is not just a collection of so many traits or characteristics which is known as personality. By counting the bricks only how can we describe the wall of a house? It needs something more and actually personality is more than this. It is an organisation of some psychophysical systems or some behaviour characteristics and functions as a unified whole. Just as to tell what an elephant is, we cannot say that it is like a pillar only by examining its legs. In the same way by looking through one's physique or sociability, we cannot pass judgement over one's personality. It is only when we go carefully in all the aspects — biological as well as social — we can make an idea about his personality.

5. Personality is not static, it is dynamic and ever in process of change and modification. As we have said earlier that personality is all that a person has about him. It gives him all that is needed for his unique adjustment in his environment. The process of making adjustment to environment is continuous. One has to struggle with the environmental as well as the inner forces throughout the span of his life. As a result one has to bring modification and change in one's personality patterns and it makes the nature of personality dynamic instead of static one.

6. Every personality is the product of heredity and environment. Both contribute significantly towards the development of the child's personality.

7. Learning and acquisition of experiences contribute towards growth and development of personality. Every personality is the end product of this process of learning and acquisition.

8. Every person's personality has one more distinguishing feature that is, aiming to an end — towards some specific goals. Adler asserts this view frankly in his book 'Individual Psychology'. He is of the opinion that a man's personality can be judged through a study and interpretation of the goals he has set for himself to achieve and the approaches he makes to the problems of his life. In this way he gives very concise meaning to the personality of an individual by calling it by the name 'lifestyle of an individual'.

Indeed this short and concise explanation of the term has a wide meaning. It draws a beautiful portrait of an individual's totality. It may be understood to mean as the sum total of one's way of behaving towards oneself and others as well. It also predicts one's nature of behaviour as how one will behave in a particular situation and one's pattern of adjustment to the every changing forces of environment.

THEORIES OF PERSONALITY

The search for the nature of personality will be rather incomplete if we do not mention some important theories of personality. This helps us in classifying the people into some categories according to their personality characteristics and gives a base for the assessment of their personality. The theories of personality, in general, can be classified into four broad categories according to their modes of approach.

(A) The theories which adopt Type-approach: The viewpoint of Hippocrates, Kretschmer, Sheldon and Jung belong to his category. They hold that human personalities can be classified into a few clearly defined types and each person can be put in one or the other types according to his personality traits.

(B) The theories which adopt Trait-approach: Worth mentioning in this category is Cattell's theory of personality. This approach believes in the mathematical analysis and quantification of the personality constituents and helps in the prediction of human behaviour in a particular situation.

(C) The theories which adopt Type as well as Trait approach: Eysenck's theory of personality belongs to this category. He goes a step ahead to the approach adopted by Cattell. He does not only mention the personality traits for assessing one's personality but also tries to give definite personality types.

(D) The theories which adopt Psycho-analytic approach: These are the theories which try to explain the growth and development of personality by adopting the ideas and approaches propagated by the school of

psychoanalysis. The psychoanalytical theory of Freud and theory of individual psychology by Adler fall into this category.

(E) The theories which adopt Humanistic approach: These are the theories which try to explain the development of human behaviour and personality through the ideas and approaches propagated by the school or philosophy of humanism. The theories like the self-actualization theory of Abraham Maslow and Carl Roger's self theory fall in this category.

(F) The theories which adopt Learning approach: These are the theories which try to explain the development of one's behaviour and personality by advocating that personality in shaped and developed by acquiring social experiences through indirect and direct learning. The theories named as Dollard and Miller's learning theory of personality and Bandura & Walter's social learning theory fall in this category.

Let us summarize the view points of above mentioned theories.

(A) Type Approach

(1) *Hippocrates' classification*: He tried to classify all human beings into four characteristics groups according to their temperaments as:

(i) Choleric
(ii) Melancholic
(iii) Phlegmatic
(iv) Sanguinic

The following chart explains the classification:

Temperamental characteristics and the associated personality types:

Choleric (– +) (Emotionally weak but bodily strong) Active but irritable (easily angered)	Sanguinic (++) (Bodily strong and Emotionally Stable) Excessive blood, cheerful energetic and optimistic
Melancholic (– –) no energy & no happiness Pessimistic (Emotionally as well as bodily weak)	Phlegmatic (+ –) (Emotionally strong but bodily weak) Happy but lazy

(2) *Kretschmer's classification*: Kretschmer classified all human beings into certain biological types according to their physical structure and has allotted definite personality characteristics associated with each physical make-up as follows:

Personality Types	*Personality Characteristics*
I. Pyknic (having fat bodies)	Sociable, jolly, easy going and good natured.
II. Athletic (balanced body)	Energetic, optimistic and adjustable.
III. Leptosomatic (lean and thin)	Unsociable, reserved, shy, sensitive and pessimistic.

(3) *Sheldon's classification.* He too like Kretschmer, classified human beings into certain types according to their physical structures and attached certain temperamental characteristics to them as under.

Personality Types	*Somatic or Body Structure*	*Personality Characteristics*
Name	*Description*	*Description*
(i) Endomorphic	Person having highly developed viscera but weak somatic structure (Like Kretschmer's Pyknic type).	Easy going, sociable and affectionate.
(ii) Mesomorphic	Balanced development of viscera and somatic structure. (Like Kretschmer's athletic type).	Craving for muscular activity, self assertive, loves risk and adventure.
(iii) Ectomorphic	Weak somatic structure as well as undeveloped viscera (Like Kretschmer's Lepto-somatic).	Pessimistic, unsociable, and reserved.

Fig. 17.1: Sheldon's Personality Types

The approach adopted by the above psychologists to have classification on the basis of seeking correlation between structure of the body and personality characteristics, is only lopsided. It is somewhat misleading. There does not exist such perfect body mind or body-heart correlation as the propagators of these approaches have assumed.

(4) *Jung's classification:* He divided all the human beings basically into two distinct types — Introvert and Extrovert — according to their social participation and the interest which they take in social activities. Later on, he further sharpened his two fold division by giving sub types. In this process he took into consideration the four psychological functions —

thinking, feeling, sensation and intuition — in relation to his previous extrovert and introvert types. Diagrammatically, we can represent this division, alongwith main characteristics of each sub-types, as below:

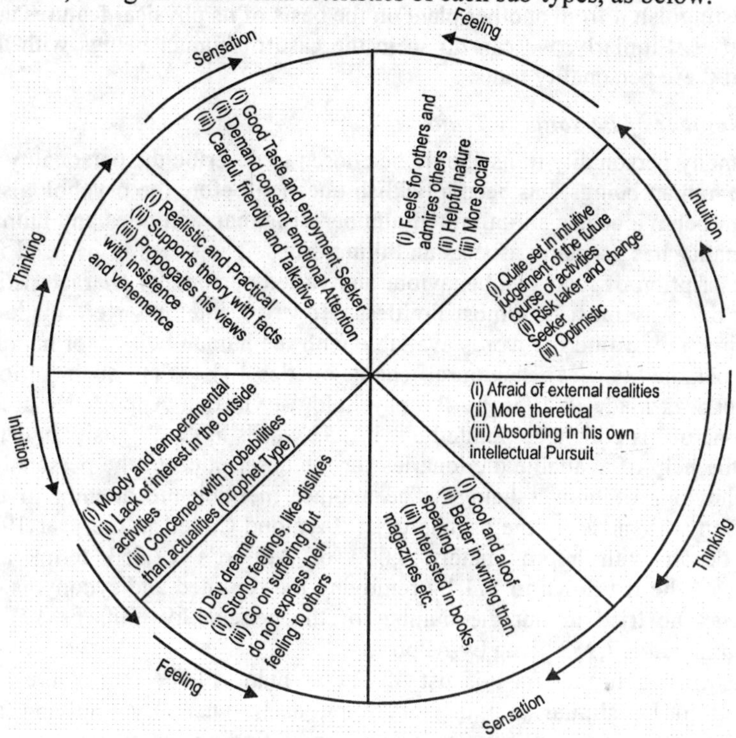

Fig. 17.2: Jung's Description of Personality Types

The classification has been criticised on the ground that in general, such different types of classes as suggested by Jung do not exist. Most of us, on the basis of typical characteristics prescribed for extrovert and introvert, may belong to both of the categories. This brings complication and hence the type approach does not give any clear picture of the classification or description of personality.

(B) Trait Approach

What are Personality traits?

Personality traits are nothing but characteristics of human behaviour that can be used to differentiate one person from another. Among us some are found to be more friendly than others, some are shy and timid and the others are more outgoing, outspoken and brave. These adjectives and characteristics of our behaviour are known as the traits of our personality. These traits are helpful in describing our personality and also distinguish a man's personality from other's personality. Traits in fact, represent attributes and properties of human personality like the colour, height, types of leaves, flowers, stems and roots of the plants. We can describe a plant and distinguish it from another plant on the basis of its physical features and properties. Similarly, we can do so in the case of human beings with the help of these personality traits.

The Number of Personality Traits

How many personality traits should be chosen to describe the personality of all the human beings, has been a ticklish question before the psychologists. Human behaviour has an unlimited number of human activities and human personality has so many aspects and dimensions. The terms to be used for the description of such vast behaviour and varied personality characteristics are in this way must be almost limitless. However, attempts were made in this direction to find the words available with the human beings for naming their personality or behavioural characteristics. The first such serious attempt was made in 1936 by the psychologist Gordon Allport. He along with one of his colleague pointed out 17,953 words in the English language with the help of available dictionaries for the description of the personality or behaviour of human beings. The another mentionable attempt in the direction was made by the psychologist Raymond Cattell in the year 1956 who began with approximately 4,000 of Allport's 17,953 terms and narrowed the list down to 171 by removing the repeated and synonyms. In this way he tried to put the number of the personality traits as 171 in comparison to 17,953 given by Allport.

He worked further on this list of 171 as many of the traits were still seemed to be similar and dependent on each other. By applying the technique of factor analysis (the technique of finding out which types of measurements things and attributes go together) he reduced the list still further for describing human personality and finally concluded that 16 factors given below are sufficient to describe personality. Each of these factors may be seen to carry a set of opposite personality traits *i.e.,* relaxed v/s Tense or practical v/s imaginative, etc.

Table 17.1: The set of opposite traits discovered by Cattell in his sixteen personality factors

Trait		*Opposite Trait*
1. Emotional/easily upset	V/s	Calm/stable
2. Intelligent	V/s	Unintelligent
3. Reserved/unfriendly	V/s	Outgoing/friendly
4. Assertive/dominant	V/s	Not assertive/humble
5. Sober/Serious	V/s	Happy-go-lucky
6. Conscientious	V/s	Expedient
7. Shy/timid	V/s	Venturesome
8. Tender minded	V/s	Tough-minded
9. Suspicious	V/s	Trusting

10. Practical	V/s	Imaginative
11. Shrewd	V/s	Forthright
12. Self-assured/placid	V/s	Apprehensive
13. Conservative	V/s	Experimenting
14. Group oriented	V/s	Self-sufficient
15. Undisciplined	V/s	Self-disciplined
16. Relaxed	V/s	Tense/driven

Further researches in the field of trait conception of the personality have highlighted the repetition and similarity of the terms used by Cattell for describing human behaviour in terms of sixteen dimensions. For example, there stands much similarity and high correlation between the traits represented by factors 1 and 16 and also by factors 3 and 7. The individual who is calm is automatically relaxed and one who is tense can be described as emotional or easily upset. Similarly, who is shy and timid can be described as reserved or unfriendly and an outgoing friendly personality will be found also venturesome. Therefore, the latest researchers have been able to reduce the number of traits as well as the number of dimensions (factors) for describing the human personality (Pediment, Mccral and Costa, 1991) as below:

Table 17.2. Five dimensions of personality and the related traits

Dimension or Factor	*Traits*
1. Extraversion	Traits like talkative, sociable, and adventurous
2. Agreeableness	Traits like good natured, cooperative and likeable.
3. Conscientiousness	Traits like demonstrating responsibility, neatness and task motivation.
4. Emotional stability	Traits like calmness, poise, and composure.
5.Culture	Traits like intelligence and interest in philosophy and art.

Observation of Traits in one's Behaviour or Personality makeup

How can we know the traits of one's personality? The answer is by observing. However, this observation requires that the traits must be demonstrated in one's behaviour for its identification as a part and parcel of one's personality. For this purpose we must be able to understand clearly the relationship between the traits demonstrated by the individual in his behaviour and the situations in which it is being demonstrated.

There exists a perfect relationship between the traits and the situations at the time of their demonstration in one's behaviour which can be understood as below.

1. Traits are more easily expressed in some situations than others. There may be situations where one can express himself without inhibition and also those where one is completely inhibited or constrained.
2. Traits are demonstrated in the situations where they are relevant. For

example, anxiety and fear is only shown up in situations, that are threatening.

3. Traits are situations which are interdependent to each other or in other words they are in a position to influence each other as seen below.
   — *Traits can change situations:* For example if aggressive children enter a play ground, they can change the situation, from peace to fighting within no time.
   — *Situations can change traits:* The traits demonstrated in one's behaviour are changeable. A different setting and environment can make any child self-disciplined or aggressive.

In this way there lies a perfect relationship between the traits of human behaviour and his environmental situation and consequently when we take decision about the traits and personality make up of individuals we must always take it in context with the environmental situations.

Cattell's Theory (Based on Trait approach)

R.B. Cattell adopted trait approach for providing certain specific dimensions to personality so that the human behaviour, related to a particular situation may be predicted. For giving the personality an empirical and scientific base he adopted factor analysis as a technique for this work. How has he done it, let us try to understand it in a non technical way.

(1) Cattell began by attempting to obtain a complete list of all possible human behaviours. He collected a list of 171 words (dictionary words) related with personality and called these Trait elements.

(2) The next step was to find out how they are related. He found that each trait element correlated high with some of others and low with some. In this way he managed to form some specific groups and called them Surface Traits (35 in number).

(3) Again he went on examining these surface traits in terms of their inter-correlations. There was overlapping. The removal of such overlapping gave him his desired basic dimensions which he called Source Traits.

(4) After obtaining source traits (which are 15 in number) he tried to use them to predict behaviour employing what is called a specification equation.

$$\text{Response} = s_1T_1 + s_2T_2 + \ldots s_nT_n$$

In this way the response or behaviour of an individual is predicted from the degree to which he exhibits each score trait (T) modified by the importance of the trait for that response(s).

Let us clear it by an example.

Suppose that academic performance (AP) is predictable from two source traits called intelligence (I) and reading habits (R), then

$$AP = s_1\, 1 + s_2\, R$$

Now also suppose that intelligence is more important for this behaviour than reading habits (in the ratio of 5: 3); then we might have an expression such as

$$AP = 51 + 3R$$

Thus in order to predict Academic performance (A.P.) for an individual we need to know his intelligence and scores on reading habits.

(C) Trait cum Type Approach

H.J. Eysenck, the famous contemporary psychologist has adopted trait cum type approach for explaining the structure of personality.

Eysenck has tried to blend all which he could avail from the previous theories of personality.

While Cattell has tried to give dimensions to personality by giving traits, Eysenck gave it more specification by grouping traits into definite types. Hence, his approach is trait cum type approach.

How the individual behaviour is organised and gets the shape of a definite type can be understood through the Figure 17.4 given below:

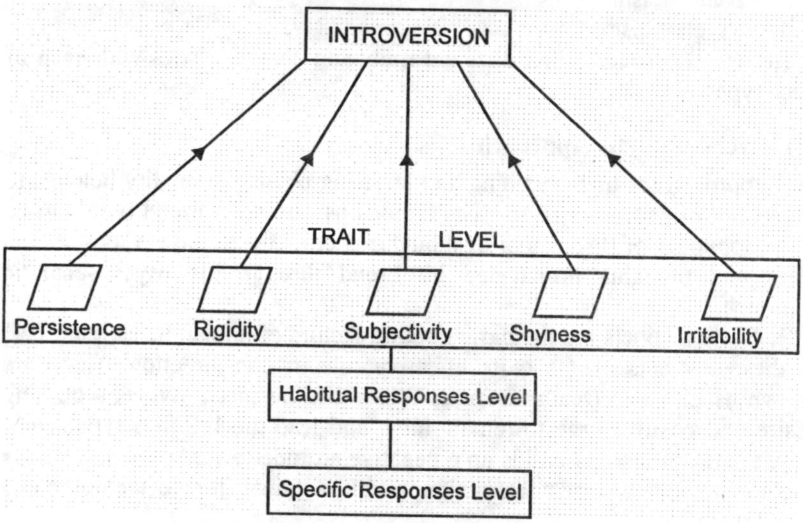

Fig. 17.4: Organisation of Individual Behaviour

We have four levels of behaviour organisation

(i) At the lowest level we have specific responses. They grow out of particular responses to any single act. For example, 'blushing' is a specific response.

(ii) At the second level we have habitual responses. If the individual reacts in the similar fashion when the same situation reoccurs we get habitual responses. For example the responses like

(a) Not easily picking up friendship.

(b) Hesitant to talk to strangers etc. are habitual responses.

(iii) At the third level we have organisation of habitual acts into traits. The behaviour acts which have similarities are said to belong to one group called trait. In the above example the habitual responses no. *(a)* and *(b)* etc. give birth to a group or trait called 'Shyness'.

(iv) At the fourth level we have organisation of these traits into a general types. A type is defined as a group of correlated traits. The traits which are similar in nature give birth to a definite type just as in the fig. 17.4 the traits like persistence, rigidity, shyness, etc. have been grouped into a type which is 'Introversion'.

Now at this final stage, ultimately we obtain a definite type. A person, now can be classified as Introvert if he has traits as described at III level, habits and habit systems as described at level II and responds specifically as described at level I.

Eysenck has given the following distinct types:

1. Introversion.
2. Extraversion.
3. Neuroticism.
4. Psychoticism.

He has also tried to link different traits and characteristics with each of these types.

(D) Psycho-analytic Approach

This approach for understanding and knowing about personality belongs to the school of psycho-analysis. The famous psychologist Freud is said to be the propounder of this school of thoughts. Let us try to have a look on the ideas and thoughts propagated by Freud through his psycho-analytic approach.

1. Basic instincts are the basic guiding factors of human behaviour. Two of these instincts play a quite effective role in this direction. These are known as Life and Death instincts. Where life instinct provides a burning desire and positive urge to remain alive and lead the life in a satisfactory way, the death instinct builds up a negative attitude towards life and guides one's behaviour towards destruction, revolt, aggression or detachment and suicidal tendencies.

2. Human behaviour is by all means centered around the sex needs. The adjustment or maladjustment in one's life mostly depends upon the degree of the gratification of one's sex needs.

3. Mind or psyche play a quite significant role in directing one's behaviour. According to Freud, human mind or psyche can be divided into three compartments in the form of conscious, semi-conscious and unconscious. These three divisions of human mind are responsible for the three types of human behaviour, namely conscious, semi-conscious and unconscious. The unconscious behaviour being 9/10 part of the total

behaviour, always dominates the total behavioural aspects and personality make-up of an individual.

4. Freud put up the idea that the anatomy of our personality is built around the three unified and interrelating systems — Id, Ego and Super Ego, occupying their positions as shown in Fig. 17.5

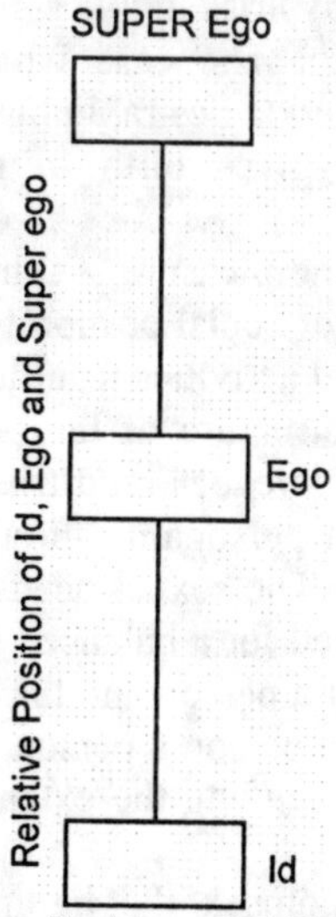

Fig. 17.5: Relative Position of Id, Ego and Super Ego

Id: It is the raw, savage and immoral basic stuff of a man's personality. It consists of such ambitions, desires, tendencies and appetites of an individual as are guided by pleasure seeking principle. It knows no laws, follows no rules and considers only the satisfaction of its needs and appetites.

Ego: If the raw Id were left to its own devices it would bring disastrous effects. Therefore, there is Ego which acts as a policeman to check the unlawful activities of the Id. It is the executive unit with veto powers, It follows the principle of reality and acts with intelligence in controlling selecting and deciding what appetites have to be satisfied and in which way they are to be satisfied.

Super Ego: The super ego is the ethical moral arm of the personality. It is idealistic and does not care for realities. Perfection is its goal rather than pleasure. It is a decision making body which decides what is bad or good, virtue or vice according to the standard of society which it accepts.

All the above personality constituents — Id, Ego and Super ego — are inter-related. Although each has its own function yet it can never exist alone.

Explanation of Personality Characteristics

(1) Freud holds that the individuals who have a strong or powerful ego are said to have strong or balanced personality because in their cases ego is capable of maintaining proper balance between super ego and Id.

(2) But if an individual has weak ego, he will have maladjusted personality. Two situations may arise in this connection:

(*a*) Super ego defeats ego. The case where the super ego is more powerful than ego, it does provide desirable outlet for the repressed wishes and impulses. Therefore, it gives birth to neurotic tendencies in the individual.

(*b*) Id defeats Ego. Here, the pleasure seeking impulses try to dominate the ego and thus do not care for social or moral values. The person engages himself in unlawful or immoral activities resulting in a delinquent character.

In addition to the above structure of the personality, built around the concept of the Id, ego and superego, Freud tried to provide an explanation of the development of human personality through his ideas about sex. He held that sex is a life energy. The sexual needs of the individual are basic needs which have to be satisfied for a balanced growth of the personality. A knowledge of the sex needs of a person and the status of their satisfaction is sufficient to tell us all about a person's personality. He will be an adjusted or maladjusted personality depending the extent to which his sexual needs are satisfied.

So much was his emphasis on sex, that he linked the whole development of the personality with the sex behaviour by putting his theory of psycho-sexual development. In this theory, he outlined the five different psycho-sexual stages for the development of personality namely, oral, anal, phallic, latency and genital.

Let us have a look into these Stages

1. *The oral stage:* According to Freud, the mouth represents the first sex organ for providing pleasure to the child. The beginning is made with the pleasure received from the mother's nipple or the bottle. Thereafter, the child derives pleasure by putting anything, candy, a stick, his own thumb, etc. into his mouth.

2. *The anal stage:* At this stage, the interest of the child shifts from the mouth as the erogenous zone to the organs of elimination, i.e. the anus or the urethra. He derives pleasure by holding back or letting go of the body's waste material through the anus or the urethra. This stage, generally, ranges from two to three years.

3. *The phallic stage:* This phase starts from the age of four years with the shifting of the child's interest from the eliminating organs to the genitals. At this stage children come to note the biological differences between the sexes and derive pleasure by playing with and manipulating the genital organs. This stage, according to Freud, may give rise to a number of complexes like

deprivation and *Electra* complexes in girls and castration and *Oedipus* complexes in boys. The deprivation complex is the result of the feeling generated in the minds of the little girls that they have been deprived of the male organ by their mothers. Castration complex is generated in boys through their fear of being deprived of the male organs certainly as a result of the threat received from elders that the organ would be cut off if they did not give up the habit of playing with it. About the Oedipus and Electra phases, Freud says that they are the result of the sexual attraction or pleasure that children experience in the company of the parent of the opposite sex. In case the parent of the same sex frustrates the desire, expresses his or her resentment and is not friendly to the boy or girl, the child may develop Oedipus or Electra complex by loving the opposite sex parent more and rather hating the like sex parent.

4. *The latency stage:* This period starts from six years in the case of girls and seven to eight years in the case of boys and extends up to the onset of puberty. At this stage, boys and girls prefer to be in the company of their own sex and even neglect or hate members of the opposite sex.

5. *The genital stage:* Puberty is the starting point of the genital stage. The adolescent boy and girl now feels a strange feeling of strong sensation in the genitals and attraction towards the members of the opposite sex. At this stage they may feel pleasure by self-stimulation of the genitals, may fall in love with their own self by taking interest in beautifying and adorning their bodies and may be drawn quite close to members of the opposite sex even to the extent of indulging in sexual intercourse.

Adler's Individual Approach to Personality

Besides Freud, the other psychoanalysis psychologists like Alfred Adler also explained the developmental process of one's personality by putting forward their own views. Mentionable in this connection was the approach of 'individual psychology' put forward by Adler. In fact Adler has an altogether different opinion about the structure and development of personality. While apprising Freudian's structure and development personality, he held that sex is not the life energy or the centre of human activities; the power motive is the central urge and human beings are motivated by the urge to be important or powerful. All of us strive towards superiority but each individual strives in a different way. He called it the style of life. Therefore, the kind of personality one possesses can be understood by studying one's style of life, i.e. the goals of life one has set for one-self and the way one strives to achieve these goals.

He thus initiated the individual approach to the study of personality patterns and maintained that there are no distinct personality types or classes. Each individual is unique in himself because everybody has definite goals and style of his life.

(E) Humanistic Approach

This approach to personality came from a group of psychologists subscribing to the humanistic school of psychology. Humanistic psychology, the so-called third force in psychology (the other two being behavioiurism and psychoanalysis) reflects a humanistic trend in dealing with and understanding human behaviour. In believes in the goodness of man and reposes optimistic confidence in man's positive nature. Contrary to the unconscious of psychoanalytical psychology here, a person's conscious experience (what he or she feels and thinks) forms the basic structure of his or her personality. Consequently, the approach adopted by the humanists does not assume that personality is governed by biological forces from within or that destructive drives are inherent in human beings but instead points out that every one of us has the potential for self-actualization through spontaneity, creativity and personal growth. A number of theories, such as those of Godlstein, Angyal, Rogers and Maslow subscribe to the approach advocated by humanistic psychology. We shall now discuss the viewpoints of the highly influential humanistic thinkers, Abraham Maslow and Carl Rogers.

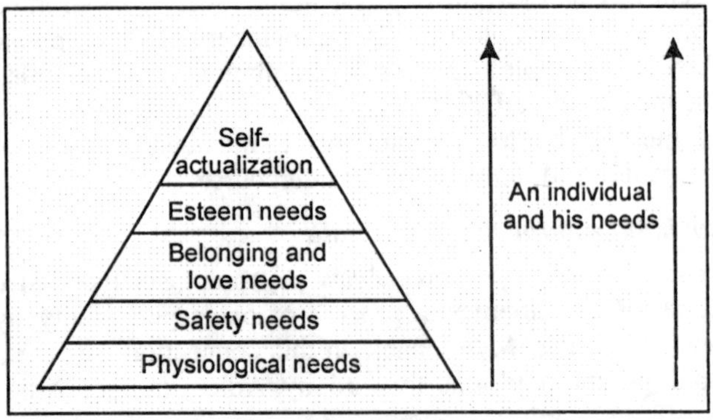

Fig. 17.6: Maslow's Hierarchical Structure of Needs

The self-actualization theory of Abraham Maslow: Abraham H. Maslow, an American psychologist, has been the major theorist adopting the humanistic approach for studying human behaviour and personality. According to his theory, human beings are basically good or neutral rather than evil and there lies in every one an impulse craving towards growth or the fulfilments of one's potentials. The goal is to seek self-actualization, that usually comes from the pursuit of knowledge, the appreciation of beauty, playfulness, self-sufficiency, insight into the truth or other constructive and creative expression. The behaviour or personality of a human being thus depends upon his style of striving towards the ultimate goal of self-realization. However, the path leading towards the ultimate goal may have sub-goals in the form of satisfaction of the lower-order needs. In this way, Maslow's theory of self-actualization suggests a hierarchy of needs (See Fig. 17.6) .

Actually as Maslow suggests pattern of human behaviour is always governed by the satisfaction of our needs from the lower, base level to the upper, top level. We have to satisfy our biological needs for our survival and for our social and psychological needs, we have to strive for the satisfaction in the socio-psychological context. The satisfaction of these need is, however, not the end of man's pursuit for excellence. His craving for the actualization of his inner potential continues till he reaches his ultimate goal of attaining fine humanistic values.

These values or characteristics of a self-actualized person to which one's efforts are directed in terms of the development of his personality have been enumerated by Maslow through sixteen basic characteristics. These characteristics have been arrived at by him through the study of a selected group of thirty-eight persons. This select group had included the well-known personalities past and present, e.g., Albert Einstein, Abraham Lincoln, Roosevelt, etc., and also his own professors and persons who were known for self-actualization in their respective fields. From this study Maslow concluded that the self-actualized people have the following common characteristics which distinguish them from the average person (Source: Maslow, 1962):

1. Ability to perceive reality accurately.
2. Willingness to accept reality readily.
3. Naturalness and spontaneity.
4. Ability to focus on problems rather than on themselves.
5. Need for privacy.
6. Self-sufficiency and independence.
7. Capacity for fresh, spontaneous, non stereo typed appreciation of objects, events and people that they encounter.
8. Ability to attain transcendence.
9. Identification with humankind and shared social bonds with other people.
10. They may have few or many friends but have deep relationships with at least some of these friends.
11. A democratic, egalitarian attitude.
12. Strongly held values and a clear distinction between means and ends.
13. A broad, tolerant sense of humour.
14. Inventiveness and creativity with the ability to see things in new ways.
15. Resistance to confirm or succumb to social pressures.
16. Ability to go beyond dichotomies and bring together opposites.

Thus, the goal for personally development according to Maslow's theory is self-actualization, i.e. realization of one's basic human potential to the maximum extent and as effectively as possible. The theory, thus, presents a very bright picture of human behaviour and personality by setting an ultimate motivating goal of self-actualization. However, it is criticised on account of its not being objective and scientific in its approach, especially in view of its subjective criteria for self-actualization.

Carl Roger's self theory: Carl Ransom Rogers, an American psychologist, in 1947 propounded a new theory of personality called the self theory quite distinct from the earlier theories of personality. He stressed the importance of an individual's self for determining the process of his growth, development, and appropriate adjustment to his environment. There are two basic systems underlying his personality theory — the organism and the self. Rogers considers them as systems operating in one's phenomenological field (a world of subjective experience, the personal and separate reality of each individual). The organism is an individual's entire frame of reference. It represents the totality of his experience — both conscious and unconscious. The second system, the 'self is the accepted, aware part of experience. The self as a system of one's phenomenal field can perhaps be best understood in terms of our concept of I, me or myself.

What we recognize as the personality of an individual is the product of interaction between the above-mentioned systems of one's phenomenological field. The acquisition of the concept of self is a long and continuous process. Human beings have inherited the tendency to develop their self in the process of interpersonal and social experiences which they acquire in the environment. In other words, our inner world (in the form of our natural impulses) interacts with our total range of experience to form the concept of our self. For example, if one is told that one is a handsome person, one tends to include in the concept of one's self, the idea that one is handsome. We are in a continuous process of building the concept of our self in this manner. The concepts of self thus developed may differ from person to person as they are based purely on one's own personal experiences. The concepts of self are sometimes based more on personal needs than on reality, and at other times as Rogers believes, we develop an ideal self, i.e. the kind of person we would like to be.

Rogers does not advance a set of specific stages in the development of personality as proposed by Freud, rather, he advocates continuity of growth in terms of a continuous evolution of the concept of 'self'. Once a concept of self is formed, the individual strives to maintain it by regulating his behaviour. Whatever is consistent with the concept of his self is readily accepted and maintained at the conscious level while that which threatens that image may be totally ignored or buried deep in the unconscious.

The most unfortunate results in the development of personality occur in cases where an individual develops some false self-image. This false image is sometimes so strong that even indisputable reality is vehemently denied. Inconsistency between one's actual image and a false self-image, may then lead to abnormality in one's behaviour. Similarly, the development of an ideal self, too unreasonable and unattainable or too different from one's real self, may result in maladjustment and serious personality disorder.

An individual's adjustment, happiness, growth and development all depend upon the union and harmony between the image of his self and the organism i.e. the experience or situations he meets in his life. Stressing the psychological personality theory, Rogers emphasizes that a person normally possesses considerable capacity for growth and the realization of his individual potential and thus tries to advance continuously towards the development of his self (i.e. self-actualization) to lead to harmony between the concept of his self and his real life experiences resulting in feelings of self-integrity, self-fulfilment and a satisfying sense of psychological growth. The development, however, runs into trouble when the self fails for some reason to incorporate, and learns to live with its own new thoughts, feelings or behaviour. The goal of a therapist as Rogers advocates in his therapy, in such cases lies in bringing the individual in a unified way, from what he or she is not, to what he or she really is.

(F) Learning Approach

The learning theories of personality depict a new developmental approach quite different from psychoanalytic and phenomenological theories of personality in the sense that they emphasize the importance of learning and objectivity to understand personality. The notable psychologists who are known to have developed personality theories are Pavlov, Watson, Guthrie, Thorndike, Skinner, Dollard & Miller; Bandura & Walters, etc. Here for the purpose of illustration, we are briefly describing the learning theory of personality put forward by Bandura and Walters.

Bandura & Walters' social learning theory: Albert Bandura and Richard Walters (1963) came out with an innovative approach to personality in the form of their social learning theory. They advanced the view that what an individual presents to the world at large as his personality, is acquired through a continuous process of structuring and restructuring of experiences, gathered by means of social learning and later imitated in corresponding situations. Social learning may involve real as well as symbolic models. Children, for example, pick up etiquette and attitudes by watching their parents and elders; viewers garner traits and mannerisms from popular actors and models whom they see on television or in films. The imitation of the model's behaviour is further reinforced in the viewer's mind by the recognition or reward the model receives as a result of his actions. An individual thus acquires numerous traits and modes of behaviour from many sources, and all these together contribute to the formation and development of his unique, distinctive personality.

18

Adjustment — Meaning, Nature and Methods

MEANING AND DEFINITIONS OF ADJUSTMENT

"Life presents a continuous chain of struggle for existence and survivals." says Darwin. The observation is very correct as we find in our day-to-day life. Every one of us strives hard for the satisfaction of our needs. While struggling to achieve something if one finds that results are not satisfactory, one either changes one's goal or the procedure. For example, if one aspires to join M.B.B.S. course, one works hard to get good marks in the Pre-Medical class. In case one is not able to get admission due to one's low percentage, one may change one's goal and feel inclined or aspire to join a B.Sc. course for medical representative job.

By restoring to such means, one protects one's self from the possible injury to one ego, failure or frustration. It is a sort of shifting to a more defensive position in order to face the challenge of circumstances after failing in earlier attempt or attempts. This special feature of the living beings is termed as adjustment. Let us now analyse this term by studying some important definitions.

L.S. Shaffer. Adjustment is the process by which living organism maintains a balance between its need and the circumstances that influence the satisfaction of these needs. (1961, p.511)

Gates, Jerslid and others. Adjustment is a continual process by which a person varies his behaviour to produce a more harmonious relationship between himself and environment. (1970, pp. 614-15)

Vonhaller. We can think of adjustment as psychological survival in much the same way as biologist uses the term adaptation to describe physiological survival. (1970, p. 426).

Let us try to analyze these definitions.

Shaffer's definition lays stress on needs and their satisfaction. One feels adjusted to the extent one's needs are gratified or in the way of being gratified. An individual tries to bring changes in his circumstances in order to overcome the difficulties in the realization of his needs. Sometimes he reduces the quantum of his need so that he may feel satisfied within the limited resources of needs and in this way, he tries to keep a balance between his needs and the capacity of realizing these needs. As long as the balance is maintained he remains adjusted. The moment it is disturbed, he drifts to words maladjustment.

The second definition by Gates and Jerslid takes adjustment as a signal of harmonious relationship between a man and his environment. One has to fit oneself in the prevailing circumstances. When we adjust ourselves by this means we are changing in some way to adapt or accommodate ourselves in order to fit as per certain demands of our environment. The conditions in the environment are in a continuous chain of changes. We change our nature in order to fit ourselves in the realm of nature. Thus, the process of adjustment is continuous. We try to change or modify our behaviour for bringing a perfect understanding between ourselves and our environment. For example, if an urban girl is married to a rural boy and made to live a village life, she has to change her behaviour, her habits and her way of life for accommodating herself in the changed circumstances.

The last definition by Vonhaller takes clue from the Darwin's theory of evolution. Darwin maintained that only those organisms most fitted to adapt to the changed circumstances survive. Hence, the individuals who are able to adjust themselves in changed situations in their environment can live in perfect harmony and lead a happy life. In this way, adjustment as a psychological term is a new name for the term adaptation used in biological world. In all sense, adjustment implies a satisfactory adaptation to the demands of day-to-day life.

The above discussion can lead us to summarize in the following way:

— Adjustment is a process that takes us to lead a happy and well-contented life.
— Adjustment helps us in keeping balance between our needs and the capacity to meet these needs.
— Adjustment persuades us to change our way of life according to the demands of the situation.
— Adjustment gives us strength and ability to bring desirable changes in the conditions of our environment.

Besides the demands of one's basic need, society also demands a particular mode of behaviour from its members. In case one thinks only to fulfill one's needs by setting aside the norms, ethics and cultural traditions of one's society, one is not going to be adjusted in one's environment. Here, adjustment also needs one's conformity to the requirement of one's culture and the society. In this way, adjustment does not only cater to one's own needs but also to the demands of the society. Therefore, in defining adjustment in its comprehensive way, we can conclude that *adjustment is a condition or state in which one feels that one's needs have been (or will be) fulfilled and one's behaviour conforms to the requirements of the society and culture.*

NATURE OF ADJUSTMENT—IN THE CONTEXT OF TEACHING AND LEARNING

In the successful running of the teaching acts on the part of teachers and learning activities on the part of learners the process of adjustment plays a quite key role. Teachers and learners have to make a number of adjustments with the teaching-learning situation according to the needs felt by them for doing so. An example we may cite the following:

- A teacher may devise or adopt to new methods of teaching, strategies, devices, techniques and use of one or the other technological means for getting his teaching adjusted to the needs and requirements of the diverse learners present in his class or work situations.
- The teacher may bring desirable modification in the teaching-learning environment, ways of dealing with his students and reinforcing their behaviour and his expectations from the students according to the needs and characteristics as well as learning styles of his learners as well as requirements for doing their well being in all possible manner.
- A learner may try to adapt or adopt himself according to the teaching style, methods and strategies employed by their teacher in their teaching and dealing with students.
- A learner may try to increase his efforts for the realization of the goals set or demands made on him by the existing teaching-learning situation or may bring change in his achievement goals in the light of his own strengths and limitation.
- The learners may learn the use of appropriates devices, aids and equipments and technological means for adopting and adjusting him to the needs and requirements of the existing teaching-learning situations.

ADJUSTMENT AS ACHIEVEMENT OR PROCESS

Adjustment can be interpreted as both, process and the outcome of that process in the form of some attainment or achievement. When a poor child studies under the street light because he has no lighting arrangement at home he is said to be in a process of adjustment. What he attains in terms of success in his examination or the fulfilment of his ambition or pride in his achievement is nothing but the result of his adjustment to his self and his environment. Thus, adjustment as an achievement means how the effectiveness with which an individual can function in changed circumstances and is, as such, related to his adequacy and regarded as an achievement that is accomplished either badly or well (Lazarus, 1976).

Adjustment as a process describes and explains the ways and means of an individual's adaptation to his self and his environment without reference to the quality of such adjustment or its outcome in terms of success or failure. It only shows how individuals or a group or groups of people cope under changing circumstances and what factors influence this adjustment. Let us now consider some salient features of adjustment as an interaction between a person and his environment.

(*i*) *Continuous process:* The process of adjustment is continuous. It starts at one's birth and goes on without stop till one's death. A person as well as his environment are constantly changing as also are his needs in accordance with the demands of the changing external environment. Consequently, the process or terms of an individual's adjustment can be expected to change from situation to situation and according to Arkoff (1968), there is nothing like satisfactory or complete adjustment which can be achieved once and for all time. It is something that is constantly achieved and re-achieved by us.

(*ii*) *Two-way process:* Adjustment is a two-way process and involves not only the process of fitting oneself into available circumstances but also the process of changing the circumstances to fit one's needs. Emphasizing this two-way nature of the adjustment process, Robert W. White (1956) writes:

> The concept of adjustment implies a constant interaction between the person and his environment, each making demands on the other. Sometimes adjustment is accomplished when the person yields and accepts conditions which are beyond his power to change. Sometimes it is achieved when the environment yields to the person's constructive activities. In most cases adjustment is a compromise between these two extremes and maladjustment is a failure to achieve a satisfactory compromise.

AREAS OR SPHERES OF ADJUSTMENT

"For an adequate adjustment one has to make oneself adjusted firstly to ones self and to one's environment. Thus, the spheres, dimensions or aspects of adjustment may be divided mainly in two categories, personal and environmental. For any individual while the adequacy of his own physical and mental health, emotional adjustment and satisfaction of personal needs are vital for the overall adjustment, he needs for making adjustment with the social and occupational world can also not be overlooked. Based on this, we can categorize the overall adjustment of an individual into three spheres, namely personal, social and occupational. Let us try to know more about these three areas or spheres of one's adjustment.

A. Personal Adjustment

Personal adjustment is concerned with an individual's adjustment to himself. Now question arises as to what does the term 'self' mean with regard to personal adjustment. The total individuality incorporating various aspects of his growth and development, personality traits and characteristics and satisfaction of his basic needs may essentially be included in the body of the term 'self'. In this sense the extent to which one remains satisfied with what he owns in terms of his physical and mental development and other personality characteristics and his basic needs remain gratified, he may be called adjusted within the sphere of personal adjustment. Let us now elaborate these components of one's personal adjustment.

1. *Adjustment to Physical Development and Health:* Physical growth and development follow a somewhat definite pattern. A child of a particular age is normally expected to have a certain increase in weight and height, acquire definite somatic structure and physical characteristics and have growth and development with regards to internal organs, body systems and their functioning. In case this growth and development takes place in a normal way and the individual remain satisfied, he remains adjusted otherwise it may lead to frustration and other complexes paving the way for his maladjustment. Similarly, one should keep better physical health free from stressful ailments and diseases so as to enjoy better personal adjustment. In this way, if an individual's physical growth and development as well as his physical strength, abilities and capacities are in conformity with what is expected at his age and he does not feel any difficulty in his physical functioning and general progress due to any kind of defect or inability of his physical organs, he may get along well with his adjustment to his self.

2. *Adjustment with Regard to Mental Development and Health:* The other major aspect of one's personal adjustment is related with his mental development and mental health. Like physical development, an individual of a particular age is expected to function at a certain level of intellectual growth and development. In case one does not acquire even the normal mental capacities and abilities expected at his age, he may feel handicapped in terms of intellectual behaviour and this deficiency (while compared to others) may lead to frustration and complexes. Similarly, one who is not keeping good mental health may turn into a maladjusted personality. Anxiety, distress, situation, pressures, complexes, frustrations all are bitter enemies of one's mental health and these may lead a person to total maladjustment with his self.

3. *Emotional Adjustment:* Emotions play a leading role in controlling and directing one's behaviour and providing a definite shape to his personality make-up. An individual who is capable of expressing his emotions in a proper way at a proper time may be termed as emotionally adjusted. The acquisition of such emotional adjustment may automatically help an individual to act and behave in a desired way, face the life situations properly and feel adjusted in his personal and social life.

4. *Sexual Adjustment:* Sex is also a personal matter like one's physical, mental and emotional adjustments. Moreover, the gratification of sex need is the most important aspect of our life. As long as this need remains in the state of satisfaction, the individual feels comfortable, satisfied and adjusted but as soon as the balance is disturbed, there crops up obstacles in the path of gratification of sex needs and the individual may be drifted towards maladjustment. Studies and researches in this area have established that one's proper sexual development, his proper attitude towards sex and the satisfaction of his sex needs in a desirable and proper way are the essential factors responsible for his adjustment to his self and the environment.

5. *Adjustment with Respect to the Individual Needs:* This sphere of our personal adjustment may also include all such types of adjustments that are concerned with the satisfaction of our personal needs. Among these, we may include the needs like: (i) physiological or organic needs such as hunger, thrust, sleep and rest, etc., (ii) material needs such as need for clothes, shelter and various other material facilities and comforts, (iii) our socio-psychological needs such as need to love and to be loved, need for expression and actualization, need to dominate, get respect and regard, etc. We all, from the very beginning of our life till the end, remain busy in working and struggling for the satisfaction of these needs. In case we get success and feel satisfied, we remain adjusted or else we are compelled to drift towards maladjustment.

B. Social Adjustment

This sphere of adjustment is concerned with one's adjustment to his social surroundings. Such adjustment is as much essential as one's adjustment with his self. In all circumstances, one should feel reasonably satisfied with what he gets in term of his social environment. By doing so, he may get along well with others and keep himself in the category of a socially adjusted person, but if it does not happen he may become a socially maladjusted person. In such circumstances, either he may cut himself off from the society or may turn into an anti-social and criminal personality. In this sense, one's adjustment with his social set up, started from his parents, home and family and extended to the neighbourhood, state, country and encircling whole world, is quite essential for the welfare of his own and the society. Let us try to know in detail about the components of one's social adjustment.

1. *Home and Family Adjustment:* One should feel the comfort and satisfaction in one's home in the spirit of 'Sweet Home'. He must have proper cordial relationships and behavioural adjustment with the members of his family. One who is fed up with his family environment and likes to spend most of the time outside the home so as to avoid the company of the family members is surely a person who is seriously lacking in terms of his home and family adjustment. Contrary to this, when the home and family environment are quite cooperative and congenial, the members of the family get proper opportunity for the satisfaction of their mutual personal needs and social obligations. In such encouraging, mutually sharing, loving and peaceful environment each member works for the progress and welfare of the others besides the development of his own. Such family environment provides a reasonable insurance for the total adjustment and well-being of all the members of the family.

2. *Adjustment with Friends and Relatives*: The social circle of one's friends and relatives is closely linked with the social environment of his home and family. One's behaviour and personality development is very

much influenced, guided and patronized by one's relatives and friends. These are the persons who come to our help in the hour of our need. One may feel secure and satisfied if he has cordial, congenial and harmonious relations with (may be few) his relatives and friends. On the contrary and opposite situations, one is bound to feel lonely, insecure and perturbed at the time of distress and casualties. In this way, the key of one's adjustment lies in getting along well with his friends and relatives.

3. *Adjustment with Neighbours and Other Members of the Community:* Next to our home is the neighbourhood and the community. Most of our physical, psychological and social needs are fulfilled through proper communication, exchange, goodwill and spirit of cooperation maintained with our neighbours and other members of the community. We can't live in harmony and peace with indifferent and spoiled relationships with our immediate neighbours and members of the community. The essential thing is to learn the lesson of togetherness and coexistence with the members of the community inspite of differences of opinions, living standards, language, caste, religion, etc.

It is futile to waste our energy and resources in endless conflicts and tensions created through mutual mistrust, fear, disliking and disrespect, jealousy and envy, false pride and inflated ego. It creates a chain of reaction and ends with the state of dissatisfaction resulting in our maladjustment with our own neighbours and members of the community. Hence, it is always better to try our best to get along well with our neighbours and members of the community. Slowly, this spirit of togetherness, bond of friendship, cooperation, co-existence and peaceful living should be extended to the boundaries of one's nation and even to the world as a close-knit family.

Here the question arises as to what should one do for maintaining proper relationship with the members of his family, friends, relatives, neighbours and members of the community so that he may be well-adjusted in his social set up? The answer lies in one's proper social development and adaptability to the social environment. One should essentially learn the lesson of mutual love and respect, goodwill and trust, cooperation and sharing and other similar qualities and virtues of a social being. One should try to know the norms, modes of living and expectations of the society for adapting himself in the existing pattern of one's community and society. It does not mean that he should blindly lead to conformity, but in all his efforts he must first try to get along with the social set up and then work honestly for the desired changes and needed social progress.

C. Occupational Adjustment

How far we are satisfied with our world of work and means of livelihood decides, to a great extent, our state or adjustment or maladjustment to our self and the environment. From the very beginning, parents aspire for a good occupation or profession for their children. They plan their education accordingly. However, entering into the profession or occupation of one's choice or being in tune with their abilities and capacities depend on a lot of factors. Whatsoever it may be, one's chosen one should learn to adjust and adapt to the needs and requirement of one's profession or occupation. His success in his field of work will depend to a large extent on the sense of satisfaction he feels in performing various duties in his job. He must be reasonably satisfied and should get along well with the men and material resources available in his world of work. Such satisfaction, adaptation and adjustment to one's occupation automatically help in attaining the desired objectives in his personal and social life leading to the overall adjustment to one's self and the environment. Now at this stage, the question may arise as to who should be termed as an adjusted individual in his field of work or occupation. For this, let us think about the possible traits and characteristics generally found in such vocationally or occupationally adjusted persons.

(i) Once entered, they feel no regret about the choice of work or occupation.

(ii) They demonstrate a sense of job satisfaction through the performance of various duties regarding their job or occupation.

(iii) They feel reasonably satisfied with the working conditions and facilities available for carrying out their job duties. They are not in the habit of unnecessarily complaining about limitations and non-availability of resources.

(iv) They get along well with their colleagues and the officials of their world of work. They try to maintain cordial relationship and harmony with them for attaining desired proficiency in their work.

(v) They are committed and have a very positive attitude towards the working and value of their occupation. They do not unnecessarily dream or plan of entering into other occupations. While respecting their own profession, they always strive to achieve a sense of satisfaction by performing their duties honestly and sincerely.

(vi) They are reasonably satisfied with the opportunities provided in their present occupation for promotion and other achievements. They do not get much perturbed despite not getting early opportunities of promotions and other incentives and believe that their work will be 'rewarded' in one way or the other.

(vii) They are usually engaged in bringing necessary improvement and modification in the methods and processes related to their occupation for qualitative improvement. They have creative sparks in them which is often reflected through their styles of functioning.

(viii) They are reasonably satisfied with their occupations in terms of economic returns. They are not found comparing their salaries and financial returns with others and complaining about their chosen occupation.

(ix) They maintain a sense of accountability for the assigned duties and try to maintain the image and respect of their profession by extending desired cooperation to colleagues and administrators.

CHARACTERISTICS OF A WELL ADJUSTED PERSON

A well-adjusted person is supposed to possess the following characteristics:

1. *Physically adjusted:* A well-adjusted individual enjoys wholesome adjustment in terms of his physical health, and physiological well-being. He is physically mature and sound in relation to his age-linked physical and physiological growth and development. What he has in terms of his somatic structure physical development, strength and abilities make him feel secure and satisfied.

2. *Emotionally adjusted:* A well-adjusted individual demonstrates a well-balanced emotional behaviour. He is able to express desirable emotions in a proper amount as per the needs of the situation and his own well-being.

3. *Socially adjusted:* A well-adjusted individual is a socially mature individual. He has the necessary development in terms of social competency and social obligations. He knows his social environment and has a desire and capability to adjust his self to the demands of the social life.

4. *Awareness of his own strengths and limitations:* A well adjusted person knows his own strengths and weaknesses. He tries to make capital out of his assets in some areas by accepting his limitations in others.

5. *Respecting himself and others:* The dislike for oneself is a typical symptom of maladjustment. An adjusted individual has respect for himself as well as for others.

6. *An adequate level of aspiration:* His level of aspiration is neither too low nor too high in terms of his own strengths and abilities. He does not try to reach for the stars and also does not repent over selecting an easier course for his advancement.

7. *Satisfaction of basic needs:* His basic organic, emotional and social needs are fully satisfied or in the process of being satisfied. He does not suffer from emotional cravings and social isolation. He feels reasonably secure and maintains his self-esteem.

8. *Absence of a critical or fault-finding attitude:* He appreciates the goodness in objects, persons or activities. He does not try to look for weaknesses and faults. His observation is scientific rather than critical or punitive. He likes people, admires their good qualities, and wins their affection.

9. *Flexibility in behaviour:* He is not rigid in his attitude or way of life. He can easily accommodate or adapt himself to changed circumstances by making necessary changes in his behaviour.

10. *The capacity to deal with adverse circumstances:* He is not easily overwhelmed by adverse circumstances and has the will and the courage to resist and fight odds. He has an inherent drive to master his environment rather than to passively accept it.

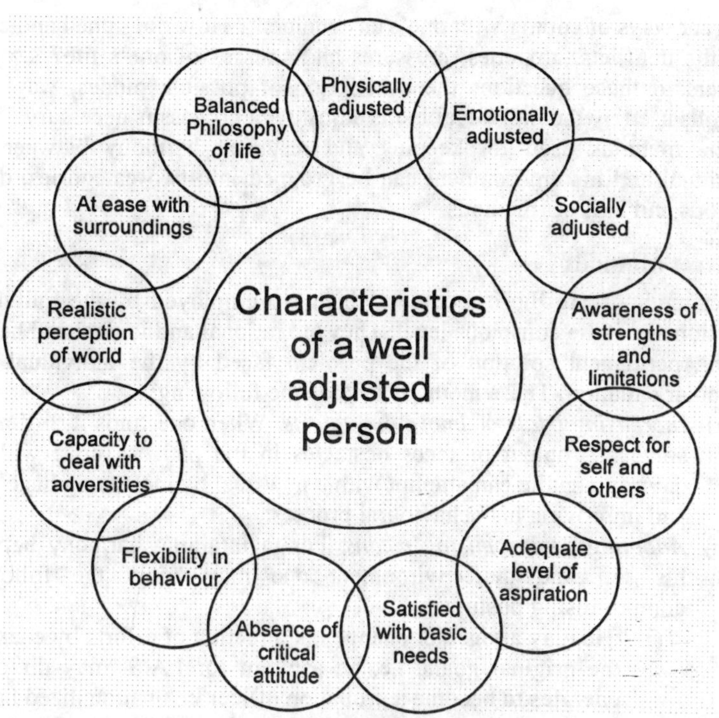

Fig. 18.1: Characteristic of a Well-adjusted Person

11. *A realistic perception of the world:* He holds a realistic vision and is not given to flights of fancy. He always plans, thinks and acts pragmatically.

12. *A feeling of ease with his surroundings:* A well-adjusted individual feels satisfied with his surroundings. He fits in well in his home, family, neighbourhood and other social surroundings. As a student, he likes his school, school-mates, teachers, and feels satisfied with his daily routine. When he enters a profession, he has a love for it and maintains his zeal and enthusiasm despite all odds.

13. *A balanced philosophy of life:* A well-adjusted person has a philosophy which gives direction to his life while keeping in view the demands of changed situations and circumstances. This philosophy is centred around the demands of his society, culture, and his own self so that he does not clash with his environment or with himself.

METHODS OF ADJUSTMENT

In order to lead a healthy, happy and satisfying life one has to learn the various ways of adjustment, i.e. coping with one's environment as effectively as possible. Also he has to safeguard his self against turning into a maladjusted and abnormal personality. How can it be done? What are the different ways of coping with one's environment? How does one handle and face the conflicts, anxieties, pressures and stresses of one's life? To seek answers to these questions the description of possible modes, ways and methods used by the individual in his adjustment process is necessary.

The methods used for keeping and restoring harmony between the individual and his environment can be grouped into two categories, direct methods and indirect methods.

1. Direct Methods

Direct methods are those methods which are employed by the individual intentionally at the conscious level. They are rational and logical and help in getting permanent solution of the problem faced by the individual in a particular situation. These methods include the following:

(a) *Increasing trials or improving efforts.* When one finds it difficult to solve a problem or faces obstacles in the path, to cope with his environment he can attempt with a new zeal by increasing his efforts and improving his behavioural process.

(b) *Adopting compromising means.* For maintaining harmony between his self and the environment one may adopt the following compromising postures:

(i) He may altogether change his direction of efforts by changing the original goals, i.e. an aspirant for I.A.S. may direct his energies to become a probation officer in a nationalized bank.

(ii) He may seek partial substitution of goal like selection for the provincial civil service in place of the I.A.S.

(iii) He may satisfy himself by an apparent substitute for the real thing, e.g., in the case of a child, by a toy car in place of a real car and in the case of a young boy desirous of getting married by a doll in his arms.

(c) *Withdrawal and submissiveness.* One may learn to cope with one's environment by just accepting defeat and surrendering oneself to the powerful forces of environment and circumstances.

(d) *Making proper choices and decisions.* A person adapts himself to, and seeks harmony with, his environment by making use of his intelligence for the proper choices and wise decisions particularly when faced with conflicting situations and stressful moments.

2. Indirect Methods

Indirect methods are those methods by which a person tries to seek temporary adjustment to protect himself for the time being against a psychological danger. These are purely psychic or mental devices — ways of perceiving situations as he wants to see them and imagining that things would happen according to his wishes. That is why these are called defence or mental mechanisms employed in the process of one's adjustment to one's self and the environment. A few important mental mechanisms are:

(a) *Repression:* Repression is a mechanism in which painful experiences, conflicts and unfulfilled desires are pushed down into our unconscious. In this way one unconsciously tries to forget the things that might make him anxious or uncomfortable. One tries to get temporary relief from the tension or anxiety by believing that the tension producing situation does not exist.

(b) *Regression:* Regression means going backward or returning to the past. In this process, an individual tends to regress to his early childhood or infantile responses in order to save himself from mental conflicts and tensions. A man failing in his love affair resorts to regression when he exhibits his love for dolls. Similarly, an elder child may regress and start behaving like an infant when a new sibling is born and he feels neglected.

(c) *Compensation:* This is a mechanism by which an individual tries to balance or cover up his deficiency in one field by exhibiting his strength in another field. For example, an unattractive girl who becomes a bookworm to secure a position in the class is making use of such mechanism in order to attract attention which she is unable to do with her looks.

(d) *Rationalization:* This is a defence mechanism in which a person justifies his otherwise unjustified behaviour by giving socially acceptable reasons for it and thus attempts to defend himself by inventing plausible excuses to explain his conduct. A child makes use of rationalization when he tries to extend lame excuses for his failure. He may blame the teacher or parents or his poor health and thus try to disguise his own weakness and deficiency.

(e) *Projection:* Through projection one tries to see or attribute one's own inferior impulses and traits in other persons or objects. An awkward person sees and criticizes awkwardness in others. Similarly, a student who has been caught in the examination for cheating may satisfy himself by saying that others had also cheated. A person with strong unsatisfied sexual impulses may denounce others for their sexual aims or may try to think in terms of sex for every thing in the world around him. In this way one tries to overlook or defend one's shortcomings and inadequacies by emphasizing that others are worse than he is.

(f) *Identification:* In using this mechanism an individual is found to achieve satisfaction from the success of other people groups or institutions by identifying himself with them. An artist who has not yet achieved success in his field may identify himself with a well-known, well-established artist. One may identify oneself with one's school and feel proud of its fame and reputation. Similarly, hero worship is also a sort of identification where an individual identifies himself with a popular leader or cine actor. He imitates his characteristics, dress and mannerisms and tries to revel in his accomplishments and successes.

(g) *Seclusiveness or Withdrawal:* In using this mechanism an individual tends to withdraw himself from the situation that causes frustration or failure. He makes himself feel safe and secure by running away from the problem. For example, a child, may refuse to participate in games for fear of failure and deceive himself by believing that he could have done well if he had participated. Daydreaming or fantasy also is a sort of withdrawing behaviour in which one withdraws oneself into a world of fantasy or make believe. Thus, instead of feeling threatened by the realities one may become satisfied with unreal, imaginary success in the world of make-believe and imagination.

(h) *Sympathism:* Sympathism is a defence mechanism in which an individual tries to get satisfaction by seeking sympathy and pity for his own failures and inadequacies. Such persons always magnify the difficulties or obstacles in the path of their success and thus convince others to feel sorry for them. For example, a housewife who is not bringing up her children well may try to evoke others, sympathy by telling them how overworked she is because the members of her family do not cooperate with her or how the family is passing through hard times.

All the foregoing defence mechanisms are used unconsciously by a person to protect himself (although only for the time being), against psychological dangers. They are not permanent cures of the trouble as Morgan (1961) observes, *"They merely conceal or disguise the real problem. It is still there, ready to produce anxiety again and again"*. A defence mechanism may thus be regarded as a temporary defence against anxiety and inadequacies. Moreover, the use of such a mechanism may create new difficulties for the individual who uses it. It is a situation similar to the one in which a person tells a lie to save himself from a difficult situation and obtains a temporary respite, but subsequently finds himself in an awkward situation because of his false statement. Therefore, we must keep a close watch on our children to see that they do not make frequent use of such defence mechanisms.

References and Suggested Readings

Adler, A., (1927), *Practice and Theory of Individual Psychology*, New York: Harcourt Brace and World.

Allport, G.W., (1948), *Personality — A Psychological Interpretation*, New York: Henry Holt and Co., Inc.

Allport, G.W., (1961), *Pattern and Growth in Personality*, New York: Holt.

Amidon, Edmund, J. and Hough, J. (1967), *Interaction Analysis Theory: Research and Application*, Reading, Massachusetts California: Addison Wesley.

Anderson, J.R. (2000), *Cognitive Psychology and Its Implication*, New York: Worth Publishers.

Arkoff. Abc (1968), *Adjustment and Mental Health*, New York: McGraw-Hill.

Asian Institute for Teacher Educators (1972), Identification of technical skills of teaching and development of training materials together with suggestions for the development of a model for analysing a classroom.

Atkinson, R.C. and Shiffrin, R.M. (1968), "Human Memory: A proposed system and its control process in K.W. Spence and J.T. Spence (Eds.), *The Psychology of Learning and Motivation: Advances in Research and Theory*, Vol. 2, New York: Academic Press.

Bandura, A. (1977) *Social Learning Theory*, Englewood Chiffs, N.J.: Prentice-Hall.

Bandura, Albert and Walters, R.H., (1963), *Social Learning and Personality Development*, New York: Holt.

Bhatia, H.R., *Elements of Educational Psychology*, Calcutta, Orient Longman, 1968 (3rd edition reprint).

Bigge, M.L. and Hunt, M.P., (1968), *Psychological Foundations of Education*, New York: Harper & Row.

Bigge, Moris, L., (1967), *Learning Theories for Teachers*, Delhi: Universal Book Stall (First Indian reprint).

Boring, E.C., Langfield, H.S. and Weld, H.P. (ed.) (1961), *Foundation of Psychology*, New York: John Wiley.

Brown, A.L. (1987), Metacognition, executive control, self-regulation, and other more mysterious mechanisms, in F.E. Weinert & R.H. Kluwe (eds.), *Metacognition, motivation, and understanding* (pp. 65-116). Hillsdale, New Jersey: Lawrence Erlbaum Associates

Brown, B.B. (1975), *Experimental Mind in Education*, New York: Harper and Row.

Brown, J.S., Collins, A., and Duguid, P. (1989). Situated Cognition and the Culture of Learning, *Educational Researcher*, 18(1), 32-42

Brubacher, J. (1939), *Modern Philosophies of Education*, New York: McGraw Hill.

Cattell, R.B., (1970), quoted by C.S. Hall and G. Lindzey, *Theory of Personality* (2nd ed.), New York: John Wiley.

Clarke, S.C.T. (1970), "General Teaching Theory" in *The Journal of Teacher Education*, Vol. XXI, No. 3. Fall.

Collins English Dictionary: Complete and Abridged 10th edition, (2009), William Collins Harper Collins.

Collins, A. (1991). 'Cognitive apprenticeship and instructional technology', in L. Idol & B.F. Jones (Eds.), *Educational values and cognitive instruction: Implication for reform* (pp. 121-138). Hillsdale, NJ: Lawrence Erlbaum Associates.

Collins, A. Brown, J.S. and Holum, A. (1991). 'Cognitive Apprenticeship: Making thinking visible', *American Educator*, 15(3), 6-11, 38-46.

Collins, A., Brown, J. S., and Newman, S.E. (1989). 'Cognitive apprenticeship: Teaching the craft of reading, writing and mathematics' (Technical Report No. 403). BBN Laboratories, Cambridge, MA. Centre for the Study of Reading, University of Illinois. January, 1987.

Collins, A., Brown, J.S. & Newman, S.E. (1989). Cognitive apprenticeship: Teaching the craft of reading, writing, and mathematics, in L.B. Resnick (Ed.), *Knowing, learning, and instruction: Essays in honor of Robert Glaser* (pp. 453-494). Hillsdale, NJ: Lawrence Erlbaum Associates.

Craik, F.I.M. and Lokhart, R.S. (1972), 'Levels of Processing: A Frame Work for Memory Research', *Journal of Verbal Learning and Verbal Behaviour*, Vol. II, pp. 671-684.

Crow, L.D. and Crow, A., *Adolescent Development and Adjustment*, New York: McGraw-Hill, 1956.

Crow, L.D. and Crow, A., *Child Psychology*, New York: Barney and Noble, 1969 (Reprint)

Crow, L.D. and Crow, A., *Educational Psychology*, New Delhi: Eurasia Publishing House, 1973 (3rd Indian reprint)

Crow, L.D. and Crow, A., *Psychology*, New York: Barnes and Noble, Inc., 1953.

Dictionary.Com (online), 'cognition' retrieved from dictionary.com/browse/cognition on 20th December, 2015.

Douglas, O.B. and Holland, B.F., (1947). *Fundamental of Educational Psychology*, New York: The Macmillan Co.

Erickson, E., *Childhood and Society*, New York: Norton, 1950.

Erickson, E., *Identity, youth and crises*, New York: Norton, 1968.

Eysenck, H.J. etc. al, *Encyclopaedia of Psychology*, New York: Phil. Lib., 1972.

Eysenck, H.J., *Dimensions of Personality*, London: Kegan Paul, 1947.

Eysenck, H.J., *The Structure of Human Personality*, New York: Methuen and Co., 1971 (3rd Ed.).

Flavell, J. H. (1987). Speculations about the nature and development of metacognition. In F. E. Weinert & R.H. Kluwe (Eds.), *Metacognition, Motivation and Understanding* (pp. 21-29). Hillside, New Jersey: Lawrence Erlbaum Associates.

Flavell, J.H. (1979). 'Metacognition and Cognitive Monitoring: A new area of cognitive-developmental inquiry'. *American Psychologist, 34*, 906-911.

Freud, S. (1939), *An Outline of Psychoanalysis*, New York: Norton.

Gage N.S. (1968) 'Theories Teaching' in *Theories of Learning and Instruction*" in E.R. Hlgard, 63rd year book of the National Society for the Study of Education, Chicago University Press.

Gage, N.L., (Ed.) (1963), *Hand Book of Research on Teaching*, Chicago: Rand McNally and Co.

Gagne, R. (1970), *The Conditions of Learning*, 2nd ed., New York: Holt Rinehart and Winston.

Gardner, H. Jerome, S. Bruneir in J.A. Palmer (Ed.), *Fifty Modern Thinkers on Education*, London: Routledge.

Gardner, Howard, *Frames of Mind: The Theory of Multiple Intelligence*, New York: Basic Books, 1983.

Garrett, H.E. (1968), *General Psychology* (Indian edition), New Delhi: Eurasia Publishing House.

Gates, A.I. and others, (1946), *Educational Psychology*, New York. The Macmillan.

Gates, A.I. and Jersild, A.T. (1970), *Educational Psychology*, New York: Macmillan.

Gesell, A., Maturation and Infant Behaviour Pattern, *Psycho. Rev*. 36, 307-319.

Good, Carter, V., *Dictionary of Education*, McGraw-Hill Book Co., 1959.

Green, T.F. (1971), *The Activities of Teaching*, New York: McGraw-Hill.

Griffiths J.H., *The Psychology of Human Behaviour,* George Allen and Unwin, 1935.

Guilford, J.P., *The Nature of Human Intelligence,* New York: McGraw-Hill, 1967.

Guthrie, E.R. and Horton, G.P., *Cats in a Puzzle Box,* New York: Rinehart, 1946.

Guthrie, E.R., Association and the law of effect, *Psychological Review,* 1940, p. 47.

Guthrie, E.R., Association by contiguity, in S. Koch (Ed.), *Psychology: A study of science,* Vol. 2, New York: McGraw-Hill, 1959.

Guthrie, E.R., Conditioning: A theory of learning in terms of stimulus, response and association, in N.B. Henry (Ed.), *The Forty-first Year Book of the National Society for the Study of Education,* Part II. 'The Psychology of Learning', Chicago: University of Chicago Press, 1942, p. 30.

Guthrie, E.R., *The Psychology of Learning,* New York: Harper & Row, 1935.

Guthrie, E.R., *The Psychology of Human Conflict,* New York: Harper & Row, 1938.

Guthrie, E.R., *The Psychology of Learning* (rev. ed.), New York: Harper & Row, 1952.

Hacker, D.J., Metacognition: Definitions and Empirical Foundations. The University of Memphis: http://www.psvc.memphis.edu/trg/meta.htm

Harriman, P.L. (Ed.), *Encyclopaedia of Psychology,* New York: Phil, Lib. 1946.

Havighurst, R. J., *Development Tact and Education,* (3rd ed.), New York: David McKay, 1932.

Havighurst, R.J., *Human Development and Education,* New York: Longmans, 1932.

Hergenhahn, B.R. (1976), *An Introduction to Theories of Learning,* New Jersey: Prentice-Hall.

Hergenhahn, B.R., *An Introduction to Theories of Learning,* New Jersey: Prentice-Hall, 1976.

Hilgard, E. (1958), *Theories of Learning,* London: Methuen.

Hilgard J.R., Learning and Maturation in Pre School Children, *Journal of Genetic Psychology.* 41, 36-56.

Hilgard, R.R. and Bower, G.H., *Theories of Learning,* New Delhi Prentice-Hall of India, 1977.

Hogan, D.M., & Tudge, J.R.H. (1999). Implications of Vygotstky's theory for peer learning, in A. M. O'Donnell & A. King (Eds.), *Cognitive perspectives on peer learning* (pp. 39-65). Mahwah, New Jersey: Lawrence Erlbaum.

Horn, J.L. (1978), The Nature and Development of Intellectual Abilities in R.T. Osborne, C.E. Noble and N. Weyl (Eds.), *Human Variation,* New York: Academic Press.

Hurlock and Schewartz, quoted by Kuppuswamy, B. *Advanced Educational Psychology,* Delhi University Publications, 1964.

Hurlock, E.B. *Child Development* (International ed., 8th printing), New York: McGraw-Hill, 1987.

Hurlock, E.B. *Adolescent Development,* New York: McGraw-Hill, 1959.

Jangira, N.K. and Ajit Singh (1982), *Core Teaching Skills: The Micro teaching Approach,* New Delhi: NCERT.

Jenkins (2000), Constructivism and Evaluation, quoted by Sasi Kumar, P., *Edutrack,* Vol. 9, No. 1, September, 2009.

Jersild, A.T., *et. al., Child Psychology,* New York: Macmillan, 1975.

Joyce Bruce and Weil, Marsha (1972), *Model of Teacher of Englewood Cliffs,* New Jersey: Prentice-Hall.

Kingsley, H.L. and Garry, R, *The Nature and Conditions of Learning.* Prentice Hall, Inc., 1957 (2nd ed.)

Knight, Rex and Knight, Margaret, *A modern introduction to Psychology,* London: University Tutorial Press Ltd., 1952 (3rd ed.)

Kohlberg, L., *Essays on Moral Development,* San Francisco; Harper and Row, 1984.

Kohlberg, L., The Child as a Moral Philosopher, *Psychology Today*, Vol. 2, pp. 25-30, 1968.

Kohlberg, L., The Cognitive Development Approach to Moral Education, *Phi Delta Kappan*, 56. p. 671, 1975.

Kohlberg, L., The development of children's orientation toward moral order: Sequence in the development of moral thought, *Vita Humana*, 6, 11-33, 1963.

Kohlberg, L., 'The Development of Moral Character and Moral Ideology', in M. Hoffman and L. Hoffman (Eds), *Review of Child Development Research*, Vol. I, New York: Russel Sage Foundations, 1964.

Kohlberg, L., 'Moral Stages and Moralization: The Cognitive Development Approach' in T. Lickona (Ed.) *Moral Development and Behaviour*, New York: Holt, Ronechart and Winston, 1976.

Kohler, W. (1929), *Gestalt Psychology*, New York: Leveright.

Kolb, David (1984), *Experiential Learning: Experience as the source of learning and development*, Englewood Cliffs, NJ: Prentice-Hall.

Komisar, N.P. (1966), "Conceptual Analysis of Teaching" *High School Journal*, 50, 14-21.

Kuppuswamy, B., *An introduction to Social Psychology*, Bombay: Publishing House, 1971 (Reprinted)

Lazarus, R.S. (1976), *Patterns of Adjustment*, Tokyo: McGraw-Hill (3rd ed.)

Lazear, David G (1992), *Teaching for multiple intelligences*, Bloomington, Ind.: Phi. Delta Kappa Educational Foundation.

Levin, M.J. (1978), *Psychology–A Biographical Approach*, New York: McGraw-Hill.

Livingston, J. (1997) *Metacognition: An Overview*, State Univ. of New York at Buffalo: http://www.gse.buffalo.edu/fas/shuell/cep564/Metacog.htm

Livingston, J.A. (1996) *Effects of metacognitive instruction on strategy use of college students*. Unpublished manuscript, State University of New York at Buffaloe.

Maslow, A.H. (1962), *Toward a Psychology of Being*, Princeton, N.J.: Van Nostrand.

Mc Dougall William (1949), *An outline of Psychology*, London: Mettuen and Co.

McGeoch, J. A., *The Psychology of Human Learning*, New York: Longmans, 1942.

McGrow, M.B., Growth: *A Study of Johnny and Jimmy*, New York: Appleton-Century-Crofts, 1935.

McIver, R.M. and Page, C.H. (1949), *Society: An Introductory Analysis*, London: Macmillan and Co. Ltd.

McLellan, H. (1994). 'Situated learning: Continuing the conversation'. Educational Technology 34, 7-8.

Metcalfe, J, and Shimamura, A.P. (1994), *Metacognition: Knowing about Knowing*; Cambridge: MA: MIT Press.

Miller, G.A. (1956), "The Magic Number seven plus or minus two, some limits on our capacity for possessing information", *The Psychological Review*, 63, 81-97.

Miller, G.A., Galanter, E. and Pribram K.H., (1960), Plans and Structure of Behaviour, New York: Holt Rinchart and Winston.

Morgan, C.T. (1961), *Introduction to Psychology*, New York: McGraw-Hill.

Morrison, H.C. (1934), *Basic Principles of Education*, Boston: Houghton Mifflin.

Murphy, Gardener, *An Introduction to Psychology*, New Delhi: Oxford and IBH, 1968.

Ormrod, J.E., *Educational Psychology: Developing Learners* (4th ed.), Upper Saddle River, N.J.: Prentice-Hall, 2003.

Pavlov, J.P., (1927), *Conditioned Reflexes*, Oxford, Clarendon Press.

Pasricha, Prem, Educational Psychology, Delhi: University-Publishers, 1963.

Passi, B.K. (ed), (1976) *Becoming Better Teacher; Micro-teaching Approach*, Ahmedabad: Sahitya Mudranalya.

Piaget J., *Equilibration of Cognitive Structures*, New York: Viking Press, 1977.

Piaget, J., *The Moral Judgement of the Child*, New York: Harcourt and Brace, 1932 (and New York: Free Press, 1965).

Piaget, J., *Psychology of Intelligence*, Totowa, N.J.: Little Field Adams, 1966.

Piaget, J., *The Origins of Intelligence in Children*, New York: International University Press, 1952 (and New York: Norton, 1963).

Piedment, Mccral and Costa, Quoted by J.G. Seamen and Douglas T. Kenrick, *Psychology*, New Jersey: Prentice-Hall, 1991.

Pillai, N.P., Pillai, K.S. and Nair, *Psychological Foundations of Education*, Trivandrum: Kala Niketan, 1972.

Pressy Robinson and Horrocks (1967), *Psychology in Education*, (22nd ed.), Delhi: Universal Book Stall.

Prince, Morton, *The Unconscious*, New York: The MacMillan Co., 1972 (2nd ed).

Resnick, L.B. (Ed). (1989). *Knowing, learning, and instruction: Essays in honour of Robert Glaser*. Hillsdale, NJ: Lawrence Erlbaum Associates.

Roberts, M.J., and Erdos, G. (1993). "Strategy, selection and metacognition", *Educational Psychology*, 13, 259-66

Rogers, C.R., (1983), *Freedom to Learn for the 80's*, Columbus, OH: Merrill.

Rogers, C.R. (1980), *A Way of Being*, Boston: Houghton Mifflin.

Rogoff, B. (1990) *Apprenticeship in thinking: cognitive development in social context*. New York: Oxford University Press.

Rose, D. (1995s). 'Apprenticeship and exploration: A new approach to literacy instruction'. Scholastic Literacy Research Paper, 6, 1-8.

Ross, J.S., *Ground Work of Edu. Psychology*, London; George G Harrap & Co., 1951.

Samuel Smiles Quoted by Pathak, P.D. (1973), *Educational Psychology*, Agra: Vinod Pustak Mandir.

Sawrey, J.M. and Telford, C. (1964), *Educational Psychology*, New Delhi: Prentice-Hall of India.

Schun, K.D. (2004), *Learning theories: An educational perspective* (4th edition), Upper Saddle River, NJ,: Pearson.

Shaffer, L.S. (1961) Article in Boring, Long field and Weld (Eds.) *Foundation of Psychology*, New York: Jeva Wiley.

Shaffer, R. (1996), *Social Development*, Oxford: Black Well.

Shunk, D.H. (2000). *Learning theories: An educational perspective* (3rd ed). Upper Saddle River, NJ: Prentice-Hall.

Silverman, R.E. (1966). quoted by R.A. Sharma, *Technology of Teaching*. Meerut: Loyal Book Depot, 1980.

Skinner, B.P., (1974), *About Behaviourism* , New York: Knopt

Skinner, C.E. and Harriman, P.L. (ed.), *Child Psychology*, New York: The Macmillan Company, 1937 (6th print).

Skinner, B.F. (1938), *The Behaviour of Organism*, New York: Appleton Century Crafts.

Skinner, B.F. (1948), *Walden Two*, New York: Macmillan

Skinner, B.F. (1953), *Science and Human Behaviour*, New York, MacMillan.

Skinner, B.F. (1968), *Technology of Teaching*, New York: Appleton Century Crofts.

Skinner, B.F. (1971), *Beyond Freedom and Dignity*, New York: Knopf.

Skinner, CE. (ed.), *Essential of Educational Psychology*, Prentice-Hall, Inc., 1968.

Smith B.O. "A Concept of Teaching", Teacher College Record, LXI, No. 5, 1960.

Smith, B.O., "Toward a theory of Teaching", in Ballack, A.A. (Ed.), *Theory and Research in Teaching*, New York: Teachers College Press, Columbia University. 1963.

Smith, H.P. (1962), *Psychology in Teaching*, Englewood Cliffs, NJ: Prentice-Hall.

Sorenson, Herbert, *Psychology in Education*, New York: McGraw-Hill Company, Inc. 1948.

Sorenson, Herbert, *Psychology in Education*, New York: McGraw-Hill Company, Inc. 1977.

Spitz, Quoted by Hurlock, E.B. (1959), *Child Psychology*, Tokyo: McGraw-Hill.

Stagner, R. and Karwoski, T.F., Quoted by L.D. Crow and Alice Crow, *Educational Psychology*, Eurasia Publishing House, New Delhi, 1973.

Stern, W., *Psychological Methods of Testing Intelligence*, Baltimore, Warwick and York, inc. 1914.

Sternberg, R.J. (1977), *Intelligence, Information Processing and Analytical Reasoning*, Hillsdale, N.J.: Erlbaum.

Sternberg, R.J. (1985) *Beyond IQ: A Triarchic theory of human intelligence*, London: Cambridge University Press.

Sternberg, R.J. (1986b). *Intelligence applied.* New York: Harcourt Brace Jovanovich, Publishers.

Stones, Edgar and Moris, Sidney (1972), *Teaching Practice: Problems and Perspectives*, London: Methuen and Co. Ltd.

Taba, Hilda (1967), *Teachers Handbook for elementary social studies*, Palo Alto, Calif: Addison-Wesley.

Terman. L.M. and Merrill, M.A., *Measuring Intelligence*, Boston: Houghton Miffin, 1937.

Terman, L.M., 'Symposium: Intelligence and its Measurement', *Journal of Edu. Psy.* 12, March, 1921.

Thompson, G.G., *Child Psychology* (First Indian Reprint), New Delhi: Surjeet Publications, 1979.

Thorndike, E.L. (1911), *Animal Intelligence*, New York: Macmillan.

Thorndike, E.L. (1931), *Human Learning*, New York: Cornell University.

Tisdale, Kit (2001). 'Dissertation and distress in a cognitive apprenticeship in reading'. *Reading Research and Instruction*; 41, 51-82.

Tolman, E.C. (1932), *Purpose Behaviour in Animals and Men*, New York: Century Crafts.

Valentine, C.W. (1975), *Psychology and its bearing on Education*, London: The English Language Book Society and Methuen & Co.

Vonhaller, G.B. (1970), *Psychology*, New York: Houghton International.

Vygotsky, L.S., *Mind and Society: The Development of Higher Mental Process*, Cambridge, M.A.: Harvard University Press, 1976.

Vygotsky, L.S., 'The Kind of Speech', in R.W. Rieberd and A.S. Carton (Eds.), *The Collected Works of L.S. Vygotsky*, Volume I: 'Problems of General Psychology' (pp 39, 285), New York: Plenun Press, 1987 (Original Work Published, 1934).

Vygotsky, L.S., *Thought and Language*, Cambridge M.A.: MIT Press, 1962.

Wagnon, M.J. (Ed.), *Readings in Educational Psychology*, New York: Houghton Miffilin Co. 1937.

Watson, J.B. (1913), 'Psychology as a Behavirorist Views it', *Psychological review*. Vol. 20.

Watson, J.B. (1919), *Psychology from the stand point of a Behaviourist*, Philadelphia: J.B. Lipton Otta Co.

Watson, J.B., *Behaviourism*, London: Kegan Paul, 1930.

Webster's Ninth Colligiate Dictionary (1969), Spring Field Massacheusetts, USA: Merriam Weboters Publishers.

Wechsler, D., *The Measurement of Adult Intelligence*, (3rd ed.). New York: Williams and Wilkins Co., 1944.

Woodworth, R.S. and Marquis, D.G, *Psychology*, New York: Henry Holt and Co., 1948 (5th ed.).

Woodworth, R.S., *Psychology*, London: Methuen Co., 1945.

Woolfolk, Anita, *Educational Psychology* (Ninth edition), First Indian Reprint, New York: Pearson, 2004.